On Being and Saying

On Being and Saying

Essays for Richard Cartwright

edited by Judith Jarvis Thomson

The MIT Press
Cambridge, Massachusetts
London, England

© 1987 Massachusetts Institute of Technology

This book was set in Palatino by Datapage Int. Ltd., Dublin, Ireland and printed and bound by Halliday Lithograph in the United States of America.

Library of Congress Cataloging-in-Publication Data

On being and saying.

Includes index.
Contents: The consistency of Frege's Foundations of arithmetic / George Boolos — Russell's "no-classes" theory of classes / Leonard Linsky — Quine's indeterminacy / Charles S. Chihara — [etc.]
1. Philosophy. 2. Cartwright, Richard. I. Cartwright, Richard. II. Thompson, Judith Jarvis.
B29.067   1987   100   87-2934
ISBN 0-262-20063-5

Contents

Preface

Richard L. Cartwright is a philosopher's philosopher. He gives no public lectures, he reviews no books for the popular press, and to the best of my knowledge he has never declared himself on the crises of Modern Man or Modern Science. Like G. E. Moore, he is provoked to philosophize not by the world but by what is said or written by other philosophers. It is to the problems that the world makes for other philosophers and to the problems philosophers make for each other that he has devoted his professional life. He has done so with a love of craftsmanship, with a hatred of the shoddy and shabby, the windy and woolly, and with a passion for the truth—a passion, simply, for *getting things right*—that are unmatched in current philosophy and that have perhaps been matched by no one since Moore himself, whose philosophical manner and attitude Cartwright's so much remind one of.

What have fascinated Cartwright over the years are the central, deepest problems in the philosophy of logic and language and in metaphysics. He has published little: His extraordinarily strict philosophical conscience got in the way of allowing much of his work to be printed. Some of his published essays are well known and indeed are by now classics; others are not as well known but should be. A volume containing those essays, together with some not yet in print, has been brought out by The MIT Press under the title *Philosophical Essays*. It is to mark and in a manner to celebrate that occasion that some of Cartwright's friends and admirers have written the essays collected here—they are concerned with problems or ideas that he himself has worked on.

Because Cartwright has published little, his influence on other philosophers is as much a product of his personal impact on his students and colleagues—at the University of Michigan, at Wayne State University, for twenty years now at MIT—and on those who first met him at conferences and colloquia as it is a product of his written work. He is a devastating critic, and he can become positively enraged by what he thinks a willful failure to be clear or by the intellectual laziness that shows itself in a philosopher who is content with easy victory, that is, in a philosopher who is content to rebut or refute without troubling to look behind the mistake for the confusion (in the case of a great philosopher, the mix of insight and confusion) that generated the mistake. At the same time, he has immense patience for those he thinks serious, and the standard for philosophical discourse that he imposes on himself and sets for others is for all of us who know him *the* standard to be aimed at.

The essays collected here are dedicated to him, with respect and, in equal measure, with affection.

Two notes on the text. Conventions on the use of quotation marks differ from philosopher to philosopher. I have requested the following of all the contributors: that double quotes be used when quoting from others and when referring to words or other linguistic items and that single quotes be reserved for quotes within quotes and for special locutions, such as: the concept 'horse'. Second, I am grateful to George Boolos, who helped me with the editorial tasks involved in preparing the text for publication.

Judith Jarvis Thomson

Contributors

William P. Alston
Department of Philosophy
University of Syracuse
Syracuse, New York

George Boolos
Department of Linguistics and
   Philosophy
Massachusetts Institute of
Technology
Cambridge, Massachusetts

Helen Morris Cartwright
Department of Philosophy
Tufts University
Medford, Massachusetts

Charles E. Caton
Department of Philosophy
University of Illinois
Urbana, Illinois

Charles S. Chihara
Department of Philosophy
University of California
Berkekey, California

Roderick M. Chisholm
Department of Philosophy
Brown University
Providence, Rhode Island

Harold Levin
Department of Philosophy and
   Religion
North Carolina State University
Raleigh, North Carolina

Leonard Linsky
Department of Philosophy
University of Chicago
Chicago, Illinois

Scott Soames
Department of Philosophy
Princeton University
Princeton, New Jersey

Jordan Howard Sobel
Department of Philosophy
University of Toronto
Toronto, Ontario, Canada

Judith Jarvis Thomson
Department of Linguistics and
   Philosophy
Massachusetts Institute of
   Technology
Cambridge, Massachusetts

David Wiggins
University College
Oxford, England

PART ONE

Logic and Language

The Consistency of Frege's *Foundations*
of Arithmetic
George Boolos

Is Frege's *Foundations of Arithmetic* inconsistent? The question may seem to be badly posed. The *Foundations*, which appeared in 1884, contains no formal system like those found in Frege's *Begriffsschrift* (1879) and *Basic Laws of Arithmetic* (vol. 1, 1893, vol. 2, 1903). As is well known, Russell showed the inconsistency of the system of the *Basic Laws* by deriving therein what we now call Russell's paradox. The system of the *Begriffsschrift*, on the other hand, can plausibly be reconstructed as an axiomatic presentation of second-order logic, which is therefore happily subject to the usual consistency proof, consisting in the observation that the universal closures of the axioms and anything derivable from them by the rules of inference are true in any one-element model.[1] Since the *Foundations* contains no formal system at all, our question may be thought to need rewording before an answer to it can be given.

One might nevertheless think that, however reworded and badly posed or not, it must be answered yes. The *Basic Laws*, that is, the system thereof, *is* inconsistent and is widely held to be a formal elaboration of the mathematical program outlined in the earlier *Foundations*, which contains a more thorough development of its program than one is accustomed to find in programmatic works. Thus the inconsistency which Russell found in the later book must have been latent in the earlier one.

Moreover, the characteristic signs of inconsistency can be found in the use Frege makes in the *Foundations* of the central notions of 'object', 'concept', and 'extension'. Objects fall under concepts, but some extensions—numbers, in particular and crucially—contain concepts, and these extensions themselves are objects, according to Frege. Thus, although a division into two types of entity, concepts and objects, can be found in the *Foundations*, it is plain that Frege uses not one but two instantiation relations, 'falling under' (relating some objects to some concepts) and 'being in' (relating some concepts to some objects), and that both relations sometimes obtain reciprocally: The number 1 is an object that falls under 'identical with 1', a concept that is in the number 1. Even more ominously (because of the single negation sign), the number 2 does not fall under 'identical with 0 or 1', which is in 2. Thus the division of the *Foundations*'s entities into two types would appear to offer little protection against Russell's paradox.

It is not only Russell's paradox that threatens. Recall that Frege defines 0 as the number belonging to the concept 'not identical with itself'.[2] If there is such a number, would there not also have to be a number belonging to the concept 'identical with itself', a *greatest* number? Cantor's paradox also threatens.

It is therefore quite plausible to suppose that it is merely through its lack of formality that the *Foundations* escapes outright inconsistency and that, when suitably formalized, the principles employed by Frege in the *Foundations* must be inconsistent.

This plausible and, I suspect, quite common supposition is mistaken, as we shall see. Although Frege freely assumes the existence of needed concepts at every turn, he by no means avails himself of extensions with equal freedom. With one or two insignificant but possibly revealing exceptions, which I discuss later, the *only* extensions whose existence Frege claims in the central sections of the *Foundations* are the extensions of higher-level concepts of the form 'equinumerous with concept F'. (I use the term "equinumerous" as the translation of Frege's *gleichzahlig*.) It turns out that the claim that such extensions exist can be consistently integrated with existence claims for a wide variety of first-level concepts in a way that makes possible the execution of the mathematical program described in sections 68–83 of the *Foundations*. Indeed I shall now present a formal theory, FA ("Frege Arithmetic") that captures the whole content of these central sections and for which a simple consistency proof can be given, one that shows *why* FA is consistent.

FA is a theory whose underlying logic is standard axiomatic second-order logic written in the usual Peano-Russell logical notation. FA could have been presented as an extension of the system of Frege's *Begriffsschrift*. Indeed, there is some evidence that Frege thought of himself as translating *Begriffsschrift* notation into the vernacular when writing the *Foundations*. Not only does the later work abound with allusions and references to the earlier, along with repetitions of claims and arguments for its significance, when Frege defines the ancestral in section 79, he uses the variables x, y, d, and F in exactly the same logical roles they had played in the *Begriffsschrift*.

FA is a system with three sorts of variable: first-order (or object) variables a, b, c, d, m, n, x, y, z, . . . ; unary second-order (or concept) variables F, G, H, . . . ; and binary second-order (or relation) variables φ, ψ, ... The sole nonlogical symbol of the language of FA is η, a two-place predicate letter attaching to a concept variable and an object variable. (η is intended to be reminiscent of $\in$ and may be read "is in the extension." Frege's doctrine that extensions are objects receives expression in the fact that the second argument place of η is to be filled by an object variable.) Thus the atomic formulas of FA are of the forms Fx (F a concept variable), $x\varphi y$, and $F\eta x$. Formulas of FA are constructed from the atomic formulas by means of propositional connectives and quantifiers in the usual manner.

Identity can be taken to have its standard second-order definition: $x = y$ if and only if $\forall F(Fx \leftrightarrow Fy)$. Frege endorses Leibniz's definition (". . . potest substitui . . . salva veritate") in section 65 of the *Foundations* but does not actually do what he might easily have done, viz. state that Leibniz's definition of the identity of x and y can be put: y falls under every concept under which x falls (and vice versa).

The logical axioms and rules of FA are the usual ones for such a second-order system. Among the axioms we may specially mention (i) the universal closures of all formulas of the form

$$\exists F\forall x(Fx \leftrightarrow A(x)),$$

where $A(x)$ is a formula of the language of FA not containing F free; and (ii) the universal closures of all formulas of the form

$$\exists \varphi \forall x\forall y(x\varphi y \leftrightarrow B(x, y)),$$

where $B(x, y)$ is a formula of the language not containing φ free. Throughout sections 68–83 of the *Foundations* Frege assumes, and needs to assume, the existence of various particular concepts and relations. The axioms (i) and (ii) are called comprehension axioms; these will do the work in FA of Frege's concept and relation existence assumptions.

The sole (nonlogical) axiom of the system FA is the single sentence

Numbers: $\forall F\exists! x\forall G(G\eta x \leftrightarrow F \text{ eq } G),$

where F eq G is the obvious formula of the language of FA expressing the equinumerosity of the values of F and G, viz.

$$\exists \varphi[\forall y(Fy \rightarrow \exists! z(y\varphi z \wedge Gz)) \wedge \forall z(Gz \rightarrow \exists! y(y\varphi z \wedge Fy))].$$

Here the sign η is used for the relation that holds between a concept G and the extension of a (higher-level) concept under which G falls; before we used the term "is in" for this relation and "contains" for its converse. In section 68 Frege first asserts that F is equinumerous with G if and only if the extension of 'equinumerous with F' is the same as that of 'equinumerous with G' and then defines the number belonging to the concept F as the extension of the concept 'equinumerous with the concept F'. Since Frege, like Russell, holds that existence and uniqueness are implicit in the use of the definite article, he supposes that for any concept F, there is a unique extension of the concept 'equinumerous with F'. Thus the sentence Numbers expresses this supposition in the language of FA; it is the sole nonlogical assumption[3] utilized by Frege in the course of the mathematical work done in sections 68–83.

How confident may we be that FA is consistent? Recent observations by Harold Hodes and John Burgess bear directly on this question. To explain them, it will be helpful to consider a certain formal sentence, which we shall call Hume's principle:

$$\forall F \forall G(NF = NG \leftrightarrow F \text{ eq } G).$$

Hume's principle is so called because it can be thought of as explicating a remark that Hume makes in the *Treatise* (I, III, I, par. 5), which Frege quotes in the *Foundations*:

> We are possest of a precise standard by which we can judge of the equality and proportion of numbers . . . . When two numbers are so combined, as that the one has always an unite answering to every unite of the other, we pronounce them equal . . . .

The symbol N in Hume's principle is a function sign which when attached to a concept variable makes a term of the same type as object variables; thus $NF = NG$ and $x = NF$ are well-formed. Taking $N. . .$ as abbreviating "the number of . . .s," we may read Hume's principle: The number of F's is the number of G's if and only if the F's can be put into one-one correspondence with the G's. (As Hume said, more or less).

In his article "Logicism and the Ontological Commitments of Arithmetic,"[4] Hodes observes that a certain formula, which he calls "(D)" is satisfiable. He writes:

$$
(D) \quad
\begin{array}{c}
\forall X \exists x \\
\\
\forall Y \exists y
\end{array}
\quad (x = y \leftrightarrow X \text{ eq } Y)
$$

is satisfiable. In fact if we accept standard set theory, it's true.

(I have replaced Hodes's "$(Q_E z)(Xz, Yz)$" by X eq Y." The label "(D)" is missing from the text of his article.) Branching quantifiers, which are notoriously hard to interpret, may always be eliminated in favor of ordinary function quantifiers. Eliminating them from (D) yields the formula $\exists N \exists M \forall X \forall Y(NX = MY \leftrightarrow X \text{ eq } Y)$. Now (D) is satisfiable if and only if Hume's principle is satisfiable. For if (the function quantifier equivalent of) (D) holds in a domain U, then for some functions N, M, $\forall X \forall Y(NX = MY \leftrightarrow X \text{ eq } Y)$ holds in U; $\forall Y(Y \text{ eq } Y)$ holds in U, so does $\forall Y(NY = MY)$, and therefore so does Hume's principle $\forall X \forall Y(NX = NY \leftrightarrow X \text{ eq } Y)$. Conversely, Hume's principle implies (D). Thus a bit of deciphering enables us to see that Hodes' claim is tantamount to the assertion that Hume's principle is satisfiable.

Hodes gives no proof that (D), or Hume's principle, is satisfiable. But Burgess, in a review of Crispin Wright's book *Frege's Conception of Numbers as Objects*,[5] shows that it is. He writes:

> Wright shows why the derivation of Russell's paradox cannot be carried out in $N^=$ [Wright's system, obtained by adjoining a version of Hume's principle to second-order logic], and ought to have pointed out that the system is pro[v]ably consistent. (It has a model whose domain of objects consists of just the cardinals zero, one, two, . . . and aleph-zero.)[6]

It will not be amiss to elaborate this remark. To produce a model M for Hume's principle that also verifies all principles of axiomatic second-order logic, take the domain U of M to be the set $\{0, 1, 2, \ldots, \aleph_0\}$. To ensure that M is a model of axiomatic second-order logic, take the domain of the concept variables to be the set of all subsets of U, and similarly take the domain of the binary (or, more generally, n-ary) relation variables to be the set of all binary (or n-ary) relations of U, that is, the set of sets of ordered pairs (or n-tuples) of members of U.

To complete the definition of M, we must define the function f by which the function sign N is to be interpreted in M. The *cardinality* of a set is the number of members it contains. U has the following important property: *The cardinality of every subset of U is a member of U.* (Notice that the set of natural numbers *lacks* this property.) Thus we may define f as the function whose value for every subset V of U is the cardinality of V. We must now see that Hume's principle is true in M.

Observe that an assignment s of appropriate items to variables satisfies $NF = NG$ in M if and only if the cardinality of $s(F)$ equals the cardinality of $s(G)$ and satisfies F eq G in M if any only if $s(F)$ can be put into one-one correspondence with $s(G)$. Since the cardinality of $s(F)$ is the same as that of $s(G)$ if and only if $s(F)$ can be put into one-one correspondence with $s(G)$, every assignment satisfies $(NF = NG \leftrightarrow F$ eq $G)$ in M, and M is a model for Hume's principle.

A similar argument shows the satisfiability of Numbers: Let the domain of M again be U, and let M specify that η is to apply to a subset V of U and a member u of U if and only if the cardinality of V is u. Then Numbers is true in M. (On receiving the letter from Russell, Frege should have immediately checked into Hilbert's Hotel.)

(It may be of interest to recall the usual proof that the comprehension axioms (i) are true in standard models (like M) for second-order logic: Let $A(x)$ be a formula not containing free F, and let s be an assignment. Let C be the set of objects of which $A(x)$ is true, and let s' be just like s except that $s'(F) = C$. Since $A(x)$ does not contain free F, s' satisfies $\forall x(Fx \leftrightarrow A(x))$

and s satisfies $\exists F \forall x(Fx \leftrightarrow A(x))$. Similarly for the comprehension axioms (ii).).

There is a cluster of worries or objections that might be thought to arise at this point: Does not the appeal to the natural numbers in the consistency proof vitiate Frege's program? How can one invoke the existence of the numbers in order to justify FA? There is a quick answer to this objection: You mean we *shouldn't* give a consistency proof? More fully: We are simply trying to use what we know in order to allay all suspicion that a contradiction is formally derivable in FA, about whose consistency anyone knowing the history of logic might well be quite uncertain. We are not attempting to show that FA is true.

But there is perhaps a more serious worry. At a crucial step of the proof of the consistency (with second-order logic) of the formal sentence called Hume's principle, we made an appeal to an informal principle connecting cardinality and one-one correspondence which can be symbolized as— Hume's principle. (We made this appeal when we said that the cardinality of $s(F)$ is the same as that of $s(G)$ if and only if $s(F)$ can be put into one-one correspondence with $s(G)$.) Should this argument then count as a *proof* of the consistency of Hume's principle? What assurance can any argument give us that a certain sentence is consistent, if the argument appeals to a principle one of whose formalizations is the very sentence we are trying to prove consistent?

The worry is by no means idle. We have attempted to prove the consistency of Hume's principle by arguing that a certain structure M is a model for Hume's principle; in proving that M is a model for Hume's principle we have appealed to an informal version of Hume's principle. A similar service, however, can be performed for the notoriously inconsistent naive comprehension principle $\exists y \forall x(x \in y \leftrightarrow \ldots x \ldots)$ of set theory: By informally invoking the naive comprehension principle, we can argue that all of its instances are true under the interpretation I under which the variables range over all sets that there are and $\in$ applies to a, b if and only if b is a set and a is a member of b. Let $\ldots x \ldots$ be an arbitrary formula not containing free y. (By the naive comprehension principle) let b be the set of just those sets satisfying $\ldots x \ldots$ under I. Then for every a, a and b satisfy $x \in y$ under I if and only if a satisfies $\ldots x \ldots$ under I. Therefore b satisfies $\forall x(x \in y \leftrightarrow \ldots x \ldots)$ under I, and $\exists y \forall x(x \in y \leftrightarrow \ldots x \ldots)$ is true under I. Thus I is a model of all instances of the naive comprehension principle. (Doubtless Frege convinced himself of the truth of the fatal Rule (V) of *Basic Laws* by running through some such argument.) Of course we can *now* see that, *pace* the principle, there is not always a set of just those sets satisfying $\ldots x \ldots$. But how certain can we be that the proof of the consistency of Hume's principle and FA does not contain some similar gross (or subtle) mistake, as does the "proof" just given of the consistency of the naive comprehension principle?

Let us first notice that the argument can be taken to show not merely that FA is consistent, but that *it is provable in standard set theory* that FA is consistent. (Standard set theory is of course ZF, Zermelo-Fraenkel set theory.) The argument can be "carried out" or "replicated" *in* ZF. Thus, if FA is inconsistent, ZF is in error. (Presumably the word "provably" in Burgess' observation refers to an informal, model-theoretic proof, which could be formalized in ZF, or to a formal ZF proof.) Thus anyone who is convinced that nothing false is provable in ZF must regard this argument as a proof that FA is consistent. Moreover, if ZF makes a false claim to the effect that FA, or any other formal theory, is consistent, then ZF is not merely in error but is itself inconsistent, for ZF will then certainly also make the correct claim that there exists a derivation of $\perp$ in FA. (Indeed systems much weaker than ZF, for example, Robinson's arithmetic Q, will then make that correct claim.)

Something even stronger may be said. We shall show that any derivation of an inconsistency in FA can immediately be turned into a derivation of an inconsistency in a well-known theory called "second-order arithmetic" or "analysis," about whose consistency there has never been the slightest doubt. In the language of analysis there are two sorts of variables, one sort ranging over (natural) numbers, the other over sets of and relations on numbers. The axioms of analysis are the usual axioms of arithmetic, a sentence expressing the principle of mathematical induction ("Every set containing 0 and the successor of every member contains every natural number"), and, for each formula of the language, a comprehension axiom expressing the existence of the set or relation defined by the formula.[7] If ZF is consistent, so is analysis; but ZF is stronger than analysis, and the consistency of analysis can be proved in ZF. It is (barely) conceivable that ZF is inconsistent; but unlike ZF, analysis did not arise as a direct response to the set-theoretic antinomies, and the discovery of the inconsistency of analysis would be the most surprising mathematical result ever obtained, precipitating a crisis in the foundations of mathematics compared with which previous "crises" would seem utterly insignificant.

Let us sketch the construction by which proofs of $\perp$ in FA can be turned into proofs of $\perp$ in analysis. The trick is to "code" $\aleph_0$ by 0 and each natural number z by $z + 1$ so that the argument given may be replicated in analysis. It is easy to construct a formula $A(z, F)$ of the language of analysis that expresses the relation "exactly z natural numbers belong to the set F": Simply write down the obvious symbolization of "there exists a one-one correspondence between the natural numbers less than z and the members of *F*." Let Eta(*F, x*) be the formula

$$[\neg \exists z A(z, F) \ \& \ x = 0] \lor [\exists z (A(z, F) \ \& \ x = z + 1)].$$

Then, since $\exists! x \ \text{Eta}(F, x)$ and

$$[\exists x (\text{Eta}(F, x) \land \text{Eta}(G, x)) \leftrightarrow F \ \text{eq} \ G]$$

are theorems of analysis, so is the result

$$\forall F \exists! x \forall G (\text{Eta}(G, x) \leftrightarrow F \ \text{eq} \ G)$$

of substituting Eta(*G, x*) for *G*η*x* in Numbers, as the following argument, which can be formalized in analysis, shows: Let *F* be any set of numbers. Let *x* be such that Eta(*F, x*) holds. Let *G* be any set. Then Eta(*G, x*) holds if and only if *F* eq *G* does. And since *F* eq *F* holds, *x* is unique. Of course each of the comprehension axioms of FA is provable in analysis under these substitutions, since they turn into comprehension axioms of analysis. Thus a proof of $\bot$ in FA immediately yields a proof of $\bot$ in analysis.

It is therefore as certain as anything in mathematics that, if analysis is consistent, so is FA. Later we shall see that the converse holds. (A sketch of a major part of the proof of the converse was given by Frege, in the *Foundations*. Of course.) The connection between FA and Russell's paradox is discussed later. Since the possibility that analysis might be inconsistent at present strikes us as utterly inconceivable, we may relax in the certainty that neither Russell's nor any other contradiction is derivable in FA.

We now want to show that the definitions and theorems of sections 68–83 of the *Foundations* can be stated and proved in FA, *in the manner indicated by Frege*. I am not sure that it is possible to appreciate the magnitude and character of Frege's accomplishment without going through at least some of the hard details of the derivation of arithmetic from Numbers, in particular those of the proof that every natural number has a successor, but readers who wish take it on faith that the derivation can be carried out in FA along a path *very* close to Frege's may skim over some of the next seventeen paragraphs. Do not forget that it is Frege himself who has made formalization of his work routine.

In the course of replicating in FA Frege's treatment of arithmetic, we shall of course make definitional extensions of FA. For example, as Frege defined the number belonging to the concept *F* as the extension of the concept 'equinumerous to *F*', so we introduce a function symbol *N*, taking a concept variable and making a term of the type of object variables, and then define *NF* = *x* to mean $\forall G (G \eta x \leftrightarrow F \ \text{eq} \ G)$; the introduction of the symbol *N* together with this definition is of course licensed by Numbers. It will also prove convenient to introduce terms [*x*: *A*(*x*)] for concepts: [*x*: *A*(*x*)]*t* is to mean *A*(*t*); *F* = [*x*: *A*(*x*)] is to mean $\forall x (Fx \leftrightarrow A(x))$; [*x*: *A*(*x*)]η*y* is to mean $\exists F (F = [x: A(x)] \land F \eta y)$; [*x*: *A*(*x*)] = [*x*: *B*(*x*)] is to mean

$\forall x(A(x) \leftrightarrow B(x))$, etc. The introduction of such terms is of course licensed by the comprehension axioms (i).

Sections 70–73 provide the familiar definition of equinumerosity. In 73, Frege proves Hume's principle. Note that the comprehension axioms (ii) provide the facts concerning equinumerosity needed for this theorem to be provable. Once Hume's principle is proved, *Frege makes no further use of extensions.*[8,9]

In 72 Frege defines "number": "*n* is a number" is to mean "there exists a concept such that *n* is the number which belongs to it." In parallel, we make the definition in FA: $Zx \leftrightarrow \exists F(NF = x)$. In 74 Frege defines 0 as the number belonging to the concept 'not identical with itself'; we define in FA: $0 = N[x: x \neq x]$. The content of 75 is given in the easy theorem of FA:

$$\forall F \forall G([\forall x \neg Fx \rightarrow ((\forall x \neg Gx \leftrightarrow F \text{ eq } G) \wedge NF = 0)]$$
$$\wedge [NF = 0 \rightarrow \forall x \neg Fx]).$$

In 76 Frege defines "the relation in which every two adjacent members of the series of natural numbers stand to each other."[10] Correspondingly, we define nSm (read "*n* succeeds *m*"):

$$\exists F \exists x \exists G(Fx \wedge NF = n \wedge \forall y(Gy \leftrightarrow Fy \wedge y \neq x) \wedge NG = m).$$

$\neg 0Sa$ immediately follows in FA from this definition: Zero succeeds nothing. In 77 Frege defines the number 1. We make the corresponding definition: $1 = N[x: x = 0]$. $1S0$ is easily derived in FA.

The theorems corresponding to those of 78 are proved without difficulty:

(1) $aS0 \rightarrow a = 1$,

(2) $NF = 1 \rightarrow \exists xFx$,

(3) $NF = 1 \rightarrow (Fx \wedge Fy \rightarrow x = y)$,

(4) $\exists xFx \wedge \forall x \forall y(Fx \wedge Fy \rightarrow x = y) \rightarrow NF = 1$,

(5) $\forall a \forall b \forall c \forall d(aSc \wedge bSd \rightarrow (a = b \leftrightarrow c = d))$,

(6) $\forall n(Zn \wedge n \neq 0 \rightarrow \exists m(Zm \wedge nSm))$.

Although Frege and we have now defined "number," defined 0 and 1, proved that they are different numbers, proved that "succeeds" is one-one, and proved that every non-zero number is a successor, "finite number," that is, "natural number," has not yet been defined; nor has it been shown that every natural number has a successor.

In 79 Frege defines the ancestral of φ, "*y* follows *x* in the φ-series," as in the *Begriffsschrift*. Thus in FA we define $x\varphi * y$:

$$\forall F(\forall a(x\varphi a \rightarrow Fa) \wedge \forall d \forall a(Fd \wedge d\varphi a \rightarrow Fa) \rightarrow Fy).$$

80 is a commentary on 79. At the beginning of 81 Frege introduces the terminology "y is a member of the φ-series beginning with x" and "x is a member of the φ-series ending with y" to mean: either y follows x in the φ-series or y is identical with x. Frege uses the phrase "in the series of natural numbers" instead of "in the φ-series" when φ is the converse of the succeeds relation. In FA we define mPn to mean nSm, $m < n$ to mean $mP * n$, and $m \leqslant n$ to mean $m < n \lor m = n$. Frege defines "n is a finite number" only at the end of section 83. In FA we define Fin n to mean $0 \leqslant n$.

In 82 and 83 Frege outlines a proof that every finite number has a successor. He adds that, in proving that a successor of n always exists (if n is finite), it will have been proved that "there is no last member of this series." (He obviously means the sequence of finite numbers). This will certainly have been shown if it is also shown that no finite number follows itself in the series of natural numbers; in 83 Frege indicates that this proposition is necessary and how to prove it.

Frege's ingenious idea is that we can prove that every finite number has a successor by proving that if n is finite, the number of numbers less than or equal to n—in Frege's terminology "the number which belongs to the concept 'member of the series of natural numbers ending the n''"—succeeds n. Frege's outline can be expanded into a proof in FA of: Fin $n \to N[x: x \leqslant n]Sn$. Since $ZN[x: x \leqslant n]$ is provable in FA, so is (Fin $n \to \exists x(Zx \land xSn)$).

In 82 Frege claims that certain propositions are provable; the translations of these into FA are aSd & $N[x: x \leqslant d]Sd \to N[x: x \leqslant a]Sa$ and $N[x: x \leqslant 0]S0$. Frege adds that the statement that for finite n the number of numbers less than or equal to n succeeds n then follows from these by applying the definition of "follows in the series of natural numbers."

$N[x: x \leqslant 0]S0$ is easily derived in FA: $xP * y \to \exists aaPy$ follows from the definition of the ancestral; consider $[z: \exists aaPz]$. Since $\neg 0Sa$ and $1S0$ are theorems, so are $\neg aP0$, $\neg aP * 0$, $x \leqslant 0 \leftrightarrow x = 0$, and $N[x: x \leqslant 0] = N[x: x = 0]$, from which, together with the definition of 1, $N[x: x \leqslant 0]S0$ follows.

But the derivation of aSd & $N[x: x \leqslant d]Sd \to N[x: x \leqslant a]Sa$ is not so easy. Frege says that, to prove it, we must prove that $a = N[x: x \leqslant a$ & $x \neq a]$; for which we must prove that $x \leqslant a$ & $x \neq a$ if and only if $x \leqslant d$, for which in turn we need Fin $a \to \neg a < a$. This last proposition is again to be proved, says Frege, by appeal to the definition of the ancestral; it is the fact that we need the statement that no finite number follows itself, he writes, that obliges us to attach to $N[x: x \leqslant n]Sn$ the antecedent Fin n.

An interpretive difficulty now arises: It is uncertain whether or not Frege is assuming the finiteness of a and d in section 82. Although he does not say so, it would appear that he must be assuming that d, at least, is finite, for he wants to show $(aSd$ & $N[x: x \leqslant d]Sd \rightarrow N[x: x \leqslant a]Sa)$ by showing $aSd \rightarrow (x \leqslant a$ & $x \neq a \leftrightarrow x \leqslant d)$. Without assuming the finiteness of a and d, he can certainly show $aSd \rightarrow \forall x(x < a \leftrightarrow x \leqslant d)$. However, $\neg a < a$, or something like it, is needed to pass from $x < a$ to $(x \leqslant a$ & $x \neq a)$, and Frege would therefore appear to need Fin a. But since Fin 0 is trivially provable and $\forall d \forall e(dPa$ & Fin $d \rightarrow$ Fin $a)$ easily follows from propositions 91 and 98, $(xPy \rightarrow xP * y)$ and $(xP * y$ & $yP * z \rightarrow xP * z)$, of the *Begriffs-schrift*, Frege's argument can be made to work in FA, provided that we take him as assuming that d (and therefore a) is finite. Let us see how.

From 91 and 98, $dPa \rightarrow (xP * d \vee x = d \rightarrow xP * a)$ easily follows. We also want to prove $dPa \rightarrow (xP * a \rightarrow xP * d \vee x = d)$, for which it suffices to take $F = [z: \exists ddPz$ & $\forall d(dPz \rightarrow xP * d \vee x = d)]$, and show $(xP * a \rightarrow Fa)$ by showing, as usual, $(xPb \rightarrow Fb)$ and $(Fa$ & $aPb \rightarrow Fb)$.

$(xPb \rightarrow Fb)$: Suppose xPb. Then the first half of Fb is trivial; and if dPb, then by 78(5) of the *Foundations*, $x = d$, whence $xP * d \vee x = d$. As for $(Fa$ & $aPb \rightarrow Fb)$, suppose Fa and aPb. The first half of Fb is again trivial; now suppose dPb. By 78(5), $d = a$. Since Fa, for some c, cPa, and then $xP * c \vee x = c$. Since cPa and $d = a$, cPd. But then by 91 and 98, $xP * d$, whence $xP * d \vee x = d$. Thus $(xP * a \rightarrow Fa)$, whence $dPa \rightarrow (xP * a \rightarrow xP * d \vee x = d)$ and $dPa \rightarrow (xP * a \leftrightarrow xP * d \vee x = d)$ follow.

We must now prove

(**)   Fin $a \rightarrow \neg aP * a$.

Since $\neg 0P * 0$, it suffices to show $0P * a \rightarrow \neg aP * a$. We readily prove $(0Pb \rightarrow \neg bP * b)$ and $(\neg aP * a$ & $aPb \rightarrow \neg bP * b)$: If $0Pb$ and $bP * b$, then by (*), $bP * 0 \vee b = 0$, whence by 91 and 98, $0P * 0$, impossible; if $\neg aP * a$, aPb, and $bP * b$, then by (*), $bP * a \vee b = a$, whence by 91 and 98, $aP * a$, contradiction.

Combining (*) and (**) yields

$$dPa \text{ & Fin } a \rightarrow ((xP * a \vee x = a) \text{ & } x \neq a \leftrightarrow xP * d \vee x = d).$$

Abbreviating, we have

$$dPa \text{ & Fin } a \rightarrow (x \leqslant a \text{ & } x \neq a \leftrightarrow x \leqslant d])$$

and then by Hume's principle

$$dPa \text{ & Fin } a \rightarrow N[x: x \leqslant a \text{ & } x \neq a] = N[x: x \leqslant d].$$

Thus, if Fin d, $N[x: x \leqslant d]Sd$, and dPa, then Fin a and aSd; since $a \leqslant a$,

$$N[x: x \leqslant a]SN[x: x \leqslant a \text{ & } x \neq a] = N[x: x \leqslant d];$$

since aSd, by 78(5), $N[x: x \leqslant d] = a$, and therefore $N[x: x \leqslant a]Sa$. Since Fin 0 and $N[x: x \leqslant 0]S0$, we conclude

Fin $n \rightarrow$ (Fin n & $N[x: x \leqslant n]Sn$),

whence Fin $n \rightarrow N[x: x \leqslant n]Sn$.

O.K., stop skimming now. One noteworthy aspect of Frege's derivation of what are in effect the Peano postulates is that so much can be derived from what appears to be so little. Whether or not Numbers is a purely logical principle is a question that we shall consider at length in what follows. I now want to consider the status of the other principles employed by Frege, which, having argued the matter elsewhere, I shall assume are properly regarded as logical. Frege shows these principles capable of yielding conditionals whose antecedent is the apparently trivial and in any event trivially consistent Numbers and whose consequents are propositions like $\forall m(\text{Fin } m \rightarrow \exists n(Zn \wedge nSm))$. The consequents would "not in any wise appear to have been thought in " Numbers; thus these conditionals at least look synthetic, and Frege himself would appear to have shown the principles and rules of logic that generate such weighty conditionals to be synthetic. But if the principles of Frege's logic count as synthetic, then a reduction of arithmetic to logic gives us no reason to think arithmetic analytic. There is a criticism of Kant to which Frege is nevertheless entitled: Kant had no conception of this sort of analysis and no idea that content could be thus created by deduction.

The hard deductions found in the *Begriffsschrift* and the *Foundations* would make evident, if it were not already so, the utter vagueness of the notions of *containment* and of *analyticity*: Even though *containment* appears to be closed under obvious consequence, it is certainly not closed under consequence; there is often no saying just when conclusions stop being contained in their premises.

In particular, the argument Frege uses to prove the existence of successors—show by induction on finite numbers n that the number belonging to the concept $[x: x \leqslant n]$ succeeds n—is a fine example of the way in which content is created. "Through the present example" wrote Frege in the *Begriffsschrift*

> we see how pure thought . . . can, solely from the content that results from its own constitution, bring forth judgments that at first sight appear to be possible only on the basis of some intuition. This can be compared with condensation, through which it is possible to transform the air that to a child's consciousness appears as nothing into a visible fluid that forms drops.

That successors appear to have been condensed by Frege out of less than thin air may well have heightened some of its readers' suspicions that the principles employed in the *Foundations* are inconsistent.

On the other hand, Frege's construction of the natural numbers foreshadows von Neumann's well-known construction of them, the consistency of which was never in doubt. Frege defines 0 as the number of things that are non-self-identical; von Neumann defines 0 as the set of things that are non-self-identical. Frege shows that n is succeeded by the number of numbers less than or equal to n; von Neumann defines the successor of n as the set of numbers less than or equal to n. Peano arithmetic based on the von Neumann definition of the natural numbers can be carried out (interpreted) in a surprisingly weak theory of sets sometimes called General Set Theory, the axioms of which are:

Extensionality: $\forall x \forall y (\forall z (z \in x \leftrightarrow z \in y) \rightarrow x = y)$,

Adjunction: $\forall w \forall z \exists y \forall x (x \in y \leftrightarrow x \in z \vee x = w)$, and all

Separation axioms: $\forall z \exists y \forall x (x \in y \leftrightarrow x \in z \wedge A(x))$.

There is a familiar model for general set theory in the natural numbers: $x \in y$ if and only if starting at zero and counting from right to left, one finds a 1 at the xth place of the binary numeral for y. It is obvious that extensionality, adjunction, and separation hold in this model. Thus it has been clear all along that something *rather* like what Frege was doing in the *Foundations* could consistently be done.

The results of the *Foundations* that the series of finite numbers has no last member and that the "less than" relation on the finite numbers is irreflexive complement those of the *Begriffsschrift*, whose main theorems, when applied to the finite numbers, are that "less than" is transitive (98) and connected (133). Much more of mathematics can be developed in FA than Frege carried out in his three logic books. (It would be interesting to know how much of the *Basic Laws* can be salvaged in FA.) Since addition and multiplication can be defined in any of several familiar ways and their basic properties proved from the definitions, the whole of analysis can be proved (more precisely, interpreted) in FA. (The equiconsistency of analysis and FA can be proved in Primitive Recursive Arithmetic.) Thus it is a vast amount of mathematics that can be carried out in FA.

Instead of discussing this rather familiar material, I want instead to take a look at certain strange features of FA, one of which was alluded to earlier. Frege defined 0 as the number belonging to the concept 'not identical with itself'. What is the number belonging to the concept 'identical with itself'? What is the number belonging to the concept 'finite number'? Frege introduces the symbol ∞_1 to denote the latter number, shows that ∞_1 succeeds itself, and concludes that it is not finite. But, although Frege does not consider the former number and hence does not deal with the question of whether the two are identical, it is clear that he must admit the existence of such a number. The statement that there is a number that is the number of all the things there are (among them itself) is antithetical to Zermelo-Fraenkelian doctrine, but as a view of infinity it is not altogether uncommonsensical. The thought that there is only one infinite number, *infinity*, which is the number of all the things there are (and at the same time the number of *all* the finite numbers), is not much more unreasonable than the view that there is no such thing as infinity or infinite numbers. In any event the view is certainly easier to believe than the claim that there are so many infinite numbers that there is no set or number, finite or infinite, of them all.

But can we decide the question of whether these numbers are the same? Not in FA. $N[x: x = x] = N[x: \text{Fin } x]$ is true in some models of FA, for example, the one given, and false in others, as we can readily see. Let U' be the set of all ordinals $\leqslant \aleph_1$, and let η be true of V, u ($V \subseteq U'$, $u \in U'$) if and only if the (finite or infinite) cardinality of V is u. Numbers is then true in this structure, Fin x is satisfied by the natural numbers, $N[x: \text{Fin } x]$ denotes $\aleph_0$, but $N[x: x = x]$ denotes $\aleph_1$. $N[x: x = x] = N[x: \text{Fin } x]$ is thus an undecidable sentence of FA. Of course, so is $\exists x \neg Zx$, but $N[x: x = x] = N[x: \text{Fin } x]$ is an undecidable sentence about numbers. From Frege's somewhat sketchy remarks on Cantor, one can conjecture that Frege would have probably regarded $N[x: x = x] = N[x: \text{Fin } x]$ as false.

I now turn to the way Russell's paradox bears on the philosophical aims of the *Foundations*. My view is a more or less common one: As a result of the discovery of Russell's paradox our idea of logical truth has changed drastically, and we now see arithmetic's commitment to the existence of infinitely many objects as a greater difficulty for logicism than Russell's paradox itself.

But is not Frege committed to views that generate Russell's paradox? Does he not suppose that every predicate determines a concept and every concept has a unique extension? In section 83 he says:

> And for this, again, it is necessary to prove that this concept has an extension identical with that of the concept 'member of the series of natural numbers ending with d'.

In section 68 he mentions the extension of the concept 'line parallel to line a'. And the number belonging to the concept F is defined as the extension of the concept 'equinumerous with the concept F'. How, in view of his avowed opinions on the existence of extensions, can he be thought to escape Russell's paradox?

The first quotation can be dealt with quickly, as a turn of phrase. Had Frege written ". . . to prove that an object falls under this concept if and only if it is a member of the series of . . .," it would have made no difference to the argument. The extension of the concept 'line parallel to the line a' is used merely to enable the reader to understand the point of the definition of number. (These are the insignificant but possibly revealing exceptions mentioned to the claim that the only extensions to whose existence Frege explicitly commits himself in 68–83 are those of concepts of the form 'equinumerous to the concept F'.) Thus, if there is a serious objection to Frege's introduction of extensions of concepts, it must concern the definition of numbers as extensions of concepts of the form 'equinumerous with the concept F'.

And of course there is one. According to Frege, for every concept F there is a unique object x, an 'extension', such that for every concept G, G bears a certain relation, 'being in', designated by η, to x if and only if the objects that fall under F are correlated one-one with those that fall under G; that is, Numbers holds. And although the language of FA, in which Numbers is expressed, is not one in which the most familiar version of Russell's contradiction $\exists x \forall y(y\eta x \leftrightarrow \neg y\eta y)$ is a well-formed sentence, it is not true that Frege is now safe from all versions of Russell's paradox.

For consider Rule (V) of Frege's *Basic Laws*:

$$\forall F \exists! x \forall G(G\eta x \leftrightarrow \forall y(Fy \leftrightarrow Gy)),$$

which yields an inconsistency in the familiar way.

Suppose Rule (V) true. By comprehension, let $F = [y : \exists G(G\eta y \wedge \neg Gy)]$. Then for some x,

$$(*) \quad \forall G(G\eta x \leftrightarrow \forall y(Fy \leftrightarrow Gy)).$$

Since $\forall y(Fy \leftrightarrow Fy)$, by $(*)$ $F\eta x$. If $\neg Fx$, then $\forall G(G\eta x \rightarrow Gx)$, whence Fx; but if Fx, then for some G, $G\eta x$ and $\neg Gx$, whence by $(*)$, $\neg Fx$, contradiction.

Or consider the simpler

SuperRussell: $\exists x \forall G(G\eta x \leftrightarrow \exists y(Gy \wedge \neg G\eta y)).$

Suppose SuperRussell true. Let x be such that for every G, $G\eta x$ if and only if $\exists y(Gy \wedge \neg G\eta y)$. By comprehension, let $F = [y : y = x]$. Then, $F\eta x$ iff $\exists y(Fy \wedge \neg F\eta y)$, iff $\exists y(y = x \wedge \neg F\eta y)$, iff $\neg F\eta x$, contradiction.

SuperRussell and Rule (V) are sentences of the language of FA about the existence of extensions every bit as much as Numbers is. Just as Numbers asserts the existence (and uniqueness) of an extension containing just those concepts that are equinumerous with any given concept, so SuperRussell asserts the existence of an extension containing just those concepts that fail to be in some object falling under them and Rule (V) asserts the existence (and uniqueness) of an extension containing just those concepts under which fall the same objects as fall under any given concept. Frege must deny that SuperRussell and Rule (V) are principles of logic—if he maintains that the comprehension axioms are principles of logic. Principles of logic cannot imply falsity. But then Frege cannot maintain both that every predicate of concepts determines a higher-level concept and that every higher-level concept determines an extension and would thus appear to be deprived of any way at all to distinguish Numbers from SuperRussell and Rule (V) as a principle of logic.

Too bad. The principles Frege *employs* in the *Foundations* are consistent. Arithmetic can be developed on their basis in the elegant manner sketched there. And although Frege couldn't and we can't supply a reason for regarding Numbers (but nothing bad) as a logical truth, Frege was better off than he has been thought to be. After all, the major part of what he was trying to do—develop arithmetic on the basis of consistent, fundamental, and simple principles concerning objects, concepts, and extensions—can be done, in the way he indicated. The threat to the *Foundations* posed by Russell's paradox is to the philosophical significance of the mathematics therein and not at all to the mathematics itself.

It is unsurprising that we cannot regard Numbers as a purely logical principle. Consistent though it is, FA implies the existence of infinitely many objects, in a strong sense: Not only does FA imply $\exists x \exists y (x \neq y)$, $\exists x \exists y \exists z (x \neq y \land x \neq z \land y \neq z)$, etc., it implies $\exists F (\text{DedInf } F)$, where DedInf F is a formula expressing that F is Dedekind infinite, for example, $\exists x \exists G (\neg Gx \land \forall y (Fy \leftrightarrow Gy \lor y = x) \land F \text{ eq } G)$. In logic we ban the empty domain as a concession to technical convenience but draw the line there: We firmly believe that the existence of even two objects, let alone infinitely many, cannot be guaranteed by logic alone. After all, logical truth is just *truth no matter what things we may be talking about and no matter what our (nonlogical) words mean.* Since there might be fewer than two items that we happen to be talking about, we cannot take even $\exists x \exists y x \neq y$ to be valid.

How then, we might now think, *could* logicism ever have been thought to be a mildly plausible philosophy of mathematics? Is it not obviously demonstrably inadequate? How, for example, could the theorem

$$\forall x \neg x < x \land \forall x \forall y \forall z (x < y \land y < z \rightarrow x < z) \land \forall x \exists y x < y,$$

of (one standard formulation of) arithmetic, a statement that holds in no finite domain but which expresses a basic fact about the standard ordering of the natural numbers, be even a "disguised" truth of logic?[11] The axiom of infinity was soon enough recognized by Russell as both indispensable to his program and as damaging to the claims that could be made on behalf of the program; and it is hard to imagine anyone now taking up even a small cudgel for $\exists x \exists y x \neq y$.

I have been arguing for these claims: (1) Numbers is no logical truth; and therefore (2) Frege did not demonstrate the truth of logicism in the *Foundations of Arithmetic*. (3) Logic is synthetic if mathematics is, because (4) there are many interesting, logically true conditionals with antecedent Numbers whose mathematical content is not appreciably less than that of their consequents. To these I want to add: (5) Since we have no under-standing of the role of logic or mathematics in cognition, the failure of logicism is at present quite without significance for our understanding of mentality. Had Frege succeeded in eliminating the nonlogical residue from his *Foundations*, the question would remain what the information that arith-metic is *logic* tells us about the cognitive status of arithmetic. But Frege's work is not to be disparaged as a (failed) attempt to inform us about the role of mathematics in thought. It is a powerful mathematical[12] analysis of the notion of natural number, by means of which we can see how a vast body of mathematics can be deduced from one simple and obviously consistent principle, an analysis no less philosophical for its rigor, profundity, and surprise.

A fantasy: After the *Begriffsschrift* Frege writes, not *The Foundations of Arithmetic*, but another book with the same title whose main claim is that, since arithmetic is deducible by logic alone from the triviality "the number of F's is the same as the number of G's if and only if the F's can be correlated one-one with the G's," arithmetic is analytic, not synthetic, as Kant supposed. Frege then argues for the analyticity of $NF = NG \leftrightarrow F$ eq G on the ground that both halves of the biconditional have the same content, express the same thought. He considers an attempted defense of Kant: Since the existence of an object can be inferred from $NF = NF$, $NF = NF$ must be regarded as synthetic, and therefore so must $NF = NG \leftrightarrow F$ eq G. Frege replies that $7 + 5 = 7 + 5$ is analytic.

If Frege had abandoned one of his major goals—the quest for an under-standing of numbers not as objects but as 'logical' objects—taken as a starting point the self-evident and consistent $\forall F \forall G(NF = NG \leftrightarrow F$ eq $G)$, and worked out the consequences of this one axiom in the *Begriffsschrift*, he would have been wholly justified in claiming to have discovered *a* founda-tion for arithmetic. To do so would have been to trade a vain philosophical hope for a thoroughgoing mathematical success. Not a bad deal. He could also have plausibly claimed to demonstrate the analyticity of arithmetic. (Of course his own work completely undermines the interest of such a claim.)

Perhaps the saddest effect of Russell's paradox was to obscure from Frege and us the value of Frege's most important work. Frege stands to us as Kant stood to Frege's contemporaries. *The Basic Laws of Arithmetic* was his *magnum opus*. Are you sure there's nothing of interest in those parts of the *Basic Laws* that aren't in prose?

Notes

The papers by Paul Benacerraf, Harold Hodes, and Charles Parsons cited have been major influences on this one. I would like to thank Paul Benacerraf, Sylvain Bromberger, John

Burgess, W. D. Hart, James Higginbotham, Harold Hodes, Paul Horwich, Hilary Putnam, Elisha Sacks, Thomas Scanlon, and Judith Jarvis Thomson for helpful comments. Research for this paper was carried out under grant SES-8607415 from the National Science Foundation.

1. I. S. Russinoff, "Frege's Problem about Concepts," Ph.D. dissertation, MIT, Department of Linguistics and Philosophy, 1983.

2. Plurals find happy employment here, as elsewhere in the discussion of concepts: For example, instead of "the number belonging to the concept 'horse'," one can say "the number of horses." 0 is thus *defined* by Frege to be the number of things that are not self-identical. And Frege was right!

3. It is nonlogical by my lights, though not, of course, by Frege's.

4. *Journal of Philosophy* (1984), 81(3): 138.

5. Aberdeen University Press (Aberdeen, 1983).

6. *The Philosophical Review* (1984), 93(4): 638–640. The text of the review has "probably consistent," which is an obvious misprint.

7. A standard reference concerning analysis is section 8.5 of J. R. Shoenfield's *Mathematical Logic* (Reading, Mass.: Addison-Wesley, 1967).

8. See Charles Parsons, "Frege's Theory of Number," in his *Mathematics in Philosophy: Selected Essays* (Ithaca, N.Y.: Cornell University Press, 1983), 164. Parsons writes, "the proof of Peano's axioms can be carried out on the basis of this axiom not only in Frege's own formal system but also in Russell's theory of types and in the other systems of set theory constructed to remedy the paradoxes, which of course showed Frege's system inconsistent." He does not consider the effect of adjoining the axiom to the system of the *Begriffsschrift*.

9. In his estimable *Frege's Conception of Numbers as Objects* (Aberdeen: Aberdeen University Press, 1983), Wright sketches a derivation of the Peano axioms in a system of higher-order logic to which a version of Hume's principle is adjoined as an axiom. Wright discusses the question of whether such a system would be consistent, attempts to reproduce various well-known paradoxes in such a system, is unsuccessful, and concludes on page 156 that "there are grounds, if not for optimism, at least for a cautious confidence that a system of the requisite sort is capable of consistent formulation." Wright's instincts are correct, as Hodes and Burgess have seen. It may be of interest to note that FA supplies the answer to a question raised by Wright on page 156 of his book. It is a theorem of FA that the number of numbers that fall under none of the concepts of which they are the numbers is *one*. (Zero is the only such number.)

10. Note that, although Frege here introduces the expression "folgt in der naturlichen Zahlenreihe unmittelbar auf" for the *succeeds* relation, he will define "finite" number only at the end of section 83.

11. See Paul Benacerraf, "Logicism: Some Considerations," Ph.D. dissertation, Princeton University, Department of Philosophy, 1960.

12. See Paul Benacerraf, "The Last Logicist," in *Midwest Studies in Philosophy VI*, P. French, T. Uehling, and H. Wettstein, eds. (Minneapolis: University of Minnesota Press, 1981), 17–35.

Russell's "No-Classes" Theory of Classes
Leonard Linsky

Russell found classes to be creatures of darkness beginning with his earliest discussions of them in 1903 in *The Principles of Mathematics* (second edition, 1937). The *Principles* antedates any conception of philosophy as linguistic analysis, so Russell does not express his misgivings about classes as an inability to fix a clear meaning of the word "class." He expresses his qualms as a failure to "see" a kind of object clearly. He takes the notion of class to be "indefinable." This means that the concept cannot be broken down into a number of constituent concepts of which it is composed. The concept is a "simple" one—like Moore's yellow. We can come to know it only through a kind of direct acquaintance and not through analysis or definition. Russell says: "The discussion of indefinables—which forms the chief part of philosophical logic—is the endeavor to see clearly, and to make others see clearly, the entities concerned, in order that the mind may have that kind of acquaintance with them which it has with redness or the taste of a pineapple" (1937, p. xv). Such passages are reminiscent of things Plato says about seeing the Forms with "the eye of the soul." Indeed the epistemological Platonism here expressed by Russell seems to be an almost inevitable accompaniment to the ontological Platonism (realism) that is a central feature of both Plato's dialogues and Russell's *Principles of Mathematics*. Russell goes on to say: "In the case of classes, I must confess, I have failed to perceive any concept fulfilling the conditions requisite for the notion of *class*" (1937, p. xvi). In a letter to Frege dated 8 August 1902, Russell writes: "I still lack a direct intuition, a direct insight into what you call a range of values: logically it is necessary, but it remains for me a justified hypothesis" (Frege 1980, pp. 144–145).

Of course, a principal reason for Russell's qualms about classes is his discovery of the antinomy about the class of all classes that are not members of themselves. So long as he saw no resolution for this, he could not believe himself to have an adequate conception of the nature of classes. But this is not the whole explanation. Russell also discovered an analogous antinomy about properties (or propositional functions). Yet this did not cause him to be skeptical about attributes and propositional functions. He never expressed an inability to "see" these things clearly—to doubt that he knew them in the way he did the taste of pineapple.

How can we account for this asymmetry in Russell's attitude toward classes on the one hand and properties (attributes, concepts, propositional functions) on the other? For one thing there is what Russell refers to as "the ancient problem of the One and the Many" (Whitehead and Russell 1910, p. 72).

> Is a class which has many terms to be regarded as itself one or many? Taking the class as equivalent simply to the numerical conjunction '*A* and *B* and *C* and etc.', it seems plain that it is many; yet it is quite necessary that we should be able to count classes as one each, and we do habitually speak of *a* class. Thus classes would seem to be one in one sense and many in another. (1937, p. 76)

What we see here is not a passing aberration or early confusion that Russell will soon see through. The same reason for skepticism about the existence of classes is expressed in Russell's most mature writing about classes in *Principia Mathematica*. "If there is such an object as a class, it must be in some sense *one* object, yet it is only of classes that *many* can be predicated. Hence, if we admit classes as objects, we must suppose that the same object can be both one and many, which seems impossible" (Whitehead and Russell 1910, p. 72n). In *Our Knowledge of the External World* (1914), Russell gives yet another version of the "ancient problem." "In the third or fourth century B.C. there lived a Chinese philosopher named Hui Tzu, who maintained that 'a bay horse and a dun cow are three; because taken separately they are two, and taken together they are one: two and one make three' " (p. 224). Russell concludes that what is shown here is that "collections of things" are not things. "It is only because the bay horse and the dun cow taken together are not a new thing that we can escape the conclusion that there are three things wherever there are two" (Russell 1929, p. 224). Hence classes are not things; they are a *façon de parler*.

The quotations from *Our Knowledge of the External World* reflect the "no-classes" theory of *Principia*: "collections of things," (classes) are not things. In *Principles* Russell resolves the difficulty by distinguishing the class *as one* from the class *as many*. For example, "*class of all rational animals* which denotes the human race as one term, is different from *men*, which denotes men, i.e. the human race as many" (1937, p. 76). Russell's conclusion is that the class as one is different from the class as many. We are not dealing with two different ways of viewing the *same* thing. "But it is more correct, I think, to infer an ultimate distinction between a class as many and a class as one, to hold that the many are only many, and not also one. The class as one may be identified with the whole composed of the terms of the class i.e., in the case of men, the class as one will be the human race" (1937, p. 76).

This solution leads only to another difficulty. In his account of the constituents of propositions, Russell has committed himself to the view, opposed to Frege, that every constituent of a proposition can play the role of logical subject. It is in this way that he avoids Frege's paradox about the concept 'horse'. But now, if we hold "that the many are only many and not also one," the following problem arises: "But can we now avoid the contradiction always to be feared, where there is something that cannot be made a logical subject?" (Russell 1937, p. 76). Russell resolves *this* difficulty by deciding that assertions need not be about single subjects; they may be about many subjects. He concludes: "[T]his removes the contradiction which arose, in the case of concepts, from the impossibility of making assertions about them unless they were turned into subjects. This impossibility being here absent, the contradiction which was to be feared does not arise" (1937, p. 77). What Russell is saying here is that there is no difficulty in making assertions about classes as many so long as we recognize that an assertion need not be about a single logical subject. "In such a proposition as '*A* and *B* are two', there is no logical subject: the assertion is not about *A*, nor about *B*, nor about the whole composed of both, but strictly and only about *A* and *B*" (1937, pp. 76–77).

If the class as one is always to be distinguished from the class as many, another perplexity arises in the case of the null class and unit classes. The null class has no members, so there can be no such thing as the null class as many; and a unit class has only one member so there is no distinction between a unit class as one and as many. Russell concludes: "The first consequence is that there is no such thing as the null-class, though there are null class-concepts. The second is, that a class having only one term is to be identified, contrary to Peano's usage, with that one term" (1937, p. 68).

The rejection of the null class and of unit classes (as distinct from their members) in turn creates a problem in the theory of cardinal numbers. Russell holds that "numbers are . . . applicable essentially to classes" (1937, p. 112). More specifically, he says: "Mathematically, a number is nothing but a class of similar classes" (1937, p. 116). The rejection of the null class brings with it, accordingly, the rejection of the cardinal number 0. If unit classes are to be identified with their unit members, the cardinal number 1 (the class of all unit classes) becomes wrongly identified with the universal class—the class of everything.

Besides these difficulties about the One and the Many and about "the contradiction," there is another argument for skepticism about classes in *Principles of Mathematics*. Russell gives the argument briefly in *My Philosophical Development*. Like "the contradiction," it is closely associated with Cantor's theorem: "[A] class of n terms has 2^n sub-classes. This proposition is still true when *n* is infinite. What Cantor proved was that, even in this case, 2^n is greater that *n*. Applying this, as I did, to all the things in the universe, one arrives at the conclusion that there are more classes of things than there are things. It follows that classes are not 'things' " (Russell 1959, pp. 80–81). At the time of *Principles* then, Russell was already well on the way to his later no-classes theory. "The conclusion to which I was led was that classes are merely a convenience in discourse" (Russell 1959, p. 81). "A class is . . . only an expression. It is only a convenient way of talking about the values of the variable for which the function is true" (1959, p. 82).

II

The difficulties here are not peculiar to Russell. Cantor's 1895 definition of class leads to its own perplexities. Cantor's celebrated definition runs as follows: "Unter einer 'Menge' verstehen wir jede Zusammenfassung *M* von bestimmten wholunterschiedenen Objekten *m* unserer Anschauung oder unseres Denkens (welche die 'Elemente' von *M* gennant werden) zu einem Ganzen" [By an aggregate we are to understand any collection into a whole *M* of definite and separate objects *m* of our intuition or our thought] (Cantor 1895–1897, p. 282). The use of the words "intuition" and "thought" gives the whole definition a psychological cast, and leaves the implication that the "collection" is itself a mental act. The suggestion of psychologism is soon reenforced, and it becomes explicit in Cantor's account of the cardinal numbers. "We will call by the name 'power' or 'cardinal number' of *M* the general concept which by means of our active faculty of thought, arises from the aggregate *M* when we make abstraction of the nature of its various elements *m* and the order in which they are given" (Cantor 1915, p. 86). The results of this double act of abstraction are the cardinal numbers or powers associated with each set. But the double act of abstraction will never produce zero. No act of our intuition or our thought can collect "definite and separate" objects into the null class. In the case of the null class, there is no element to be the target even of the first act of abstraction. This, perhaps, explains why, when Cantor turns to his account of "the finite cardinal numbers," he begins his construction with the cardinal number 1 and not with 0 (Cantor 1895–1897, section 5).

Cantor now provides us with a more detailed account of the double act of abstraction that gives us the cardinal numbers.

> We denote the result of this double act of abstraction, the cardinal number or power of *M*, by $\bar{\bar{M}}$. Since every single element *m*, if we abstract from its nature, becomes a 'unit', the cardinal number $\bar{\bar{M}}$ is a definite aggregate composed of units, and this number has existence

in our mind as an intellectual image or projection of the given aggregate *M*. (Cantor 1915, p. 86).

If we abstract from the nature of the units, how, Frege asks, do they remain distinguishable? What distinguishes one from another? In whose mind does the number exist? Is my number 2 the same as yours? This line of criticism is, of course, inspired by Frege's attack on abstraction, the idea of the unit, and psychologism in section III of *Die Grundlagen der Arithmetik*. Abstraction, Frege remarks, is a powerful lye. Is it really necessary, he asks, to first "collect" together all the citizens of Germany before we can assign them a cardinal number?

None of these perplexities attend Russell's conception of classes. Psychologism in logic was never a temptation for him. For Russell the concept of class is indefinable. It can be correctly characterized only with the use of terms synonymous with it. For the Russell of *Principia*, what is logically prior is the class concept (propositional function). A class is the extension of a class concept. In this he agrees with Frege. With Cantor, on the one hand, and the Russell of *Principia* and Frege on the other, we have two quite different conceptions of the nature of classes. Here I follow Charles Parsons's discussion in his paper "Some Remarks on Frege's Conception of Extension" (Parsons 1976). Parsons describes the differences as follows:

> One appeals to intuitions associated with ordinary notions such as 'collection' or 'aggregate'. According to it, a set is 'formed' or 'constituted' from its *elements*. The axioms of set theory can then be motivated by ideas such as that sets can be formed from given elements in a quite arbitrary way, and that *any* set can be obtained by iterated application of such set formation, beginning either with nothing or with individuals that are not sets. According to the other, the paradigm of a set is the extension of a *predicate*. Terms denoting sets are nominalized predicates and sets are distinguished (e.g., from attributes), by the fact that predicates true of the same objects have the same set as their extension. Generally, the axioms of set theory are viewed as assumptions as to what predicates have extensions. (Parsons 1976, p. 265)

It is Cantor who is the founder of the iterative conception according to which a class (set) is formed or constituted from its elements. It is this conception that is formulated in his celebrated 1895 definition. Whatever the perplexities about abstraction, psychologism, the cardinal number 0, associated with Cantor's account, it does not lead to antinomy. The class of all classes that are not members of themselves cannot be constituted from its elements. On this conception the elements are logically prior; a class arises by collecting them "into a whole," and self-membership is excluded. Frege and the Russell of the *Principia* are the founders of the other, logical conception that makes the class concept logically prior. A class is the extension of a concept. This conception presents no difficulties about the null class, the unit class as distinct from its unit member, 0 and 1, and the ancient problem of the One and the Many. But in its naive form, it leads swiftly and directly to Russell's antinomy. It is no accident that Russell, not Cantor, discovered it; it is remarkable that Frege did not also discover it independently, especially as he expressed some uncertainty about the consistency of his fifth axiom, which embodies his theory of extensions.

Following Wang and Gödel we may speak of Cantor's iterative concept as the mathematical concept of sets and of Frege's concept of extensions as the logical concept (Wang 1983, p. 537). We have, in the last paragraphs associated Russell with Frege as cofounder of the logical concept. This is true for the Russell of the no-classes theory of *Principia*, but the Russell of *Principles* is uneasily divided between the two conceptions. When, in *Prin-ciples*, he writes about the class as one and the class as many, of classes as "plural objects," and the problem of the One and the Many, he shows the influence of Cantor, including the use of Cantor's own Platonic terminology. In 1883 Cantor defined a set as follows: "Unter einer 'Mannig-faltigkeit' oder 'Menge' verstehe ich nämlich allgemein jedes Viele, welches sich als Eines denken lässt, d. h. jeden Inbegriff bestimmter Elemente, welcher durch ein Gesetz zu einem Ganzen verbunden werden kann" [every Many, which can be thought of as One, i.e. every totality of definite elements that can be united into a whole by a law] (Cantor 1932, p. 204n).

Russell, however, also writes about "the genesis of classes from an intensional standpoint" (1937, p. 67). According to this standpoint, "every predicate (provided it can be sometimes truly predicated) gives rise to a class" (1937, p. 67). He contrasts this with the mathematical concept that, he says, has an "extensional genesis" (1937, p. 67). Here he clearly has in mind the class as constituted by its members. "Here it is not predicates and denoting that are relevant, but terms connected by the word *and*, in the sense in which this word stands for a *numerical* conjunction. Thus Brown and Jones are a class, and Brown singly is a class. This is the extensional genesis of classes" (1937, p. 67). It is this conception that leads Russell to the problem of the One and the Many, while the intensional conception, according to which "every predicate . . . gives rise to a class" leads Russell to "the contradiction." The fact that Russell attempts, in *Principles*, to maintain both standpoints explains, in part, I believe, his inability "to perceive any concept fulfilling the conditions requisite for the notion of *class*" (1937, pp. xv–xvi). In a celebrated letter to Dedekind, dated "Halle, 28 July 1899" (not published until 1932), Cantor formulated the earliest attempt to resolve the antinomies of the theory of sets. His language recalls the 1883 definition and his solution anticipates future developments. Cantor's discussion turns entirely on the interplay between the class as one and the class as many. (This connection between Russell and Cantor was suggested to me by William Tait.)

> If we start from the notion of a definite multiplicity [*Vielheit*] (a system, a totality) of things, it is necessary, as I discovered, to distinguish two kinds of multiplicities (by this I always mean definite multiplicities). For a multiplicity can be such that the assumption that *all* of its elements 'are together' leads to a contradiction, so that it is impossible to conceive of the multiplicity as a unity, as 'one finished thing'. Such multiplicities I call *absolutely infinite* or *inconsistent* multiplicities. . . . If, on the other hand, the totality of the elements of a multiplicity can be thought of without contradiction as 'being together', so that they can be gathered together into *one* thing', I call it a *consistent multiplicity* or a 'set'. (In French and in Italian this notion is aptly expressed by the words 'ensemble' and 'insieme'.) (Van Heijenoort 1967, p. 114)

Cantor's "multiplicities" are, intuitively, the same as Russell's classes as many. Cantor's "consistent multiplicities" are those that can be gathered together as *one* thing. These are, intuitively, the same as Russell's "classes as one." Inconsistent multiplicities are those that cannot be gathered together as one on pain of contradiction. Cantor does not consider the Russell antinomy in his letter, although he does discuss the antimony first published by Cesare Burali-Forti in 1897 and since known by his name. He concludes his discussion of the contradiction as follows: "The system Ω of all [ordinal] numbers is an inconsistent, absolutely infinite multiplicity" (Van Heijenoort 1967, p. 115). Although Cantor does not consider Russell's contradiction, his resolution is near to hand. The class of all classes that are not members of themselves is an inconsistent multiplicity that cannot be gathered together as one finished thing. Cantor's criterion as to when a multiplicity can be considered as one thing is not given with precision. The idea becomes sharply defined in subsequent developments when it is specified that a multiplicity is a set ("one thing") whenever it is an element of another multiplicity. The class of all classes that are not members of themselves is not an element. In contemporary terms, it is not a set.

It is remarkable that Russell had the same idea as Cantor, quite independently. In a letter to Frege dated 10 July 1902 Russell writes:

> Concerning the contradiction, I did not express myself clearly enough. I believe that classes cannot always be admitted as proper names. A class consisting of more than one object is in the first place

not *one* object but many. Now an ordinary class does form *one* whole; thus soldiers for example form an army. But this does not seem to me to be a necessity of thought, though it is essential if we want to use a class as a proper name. I believe I can therefore say without contradiction that certain classes . . . are mere manifolds [*nur Vielheiten*] and do not form wholes at all. This is why there arise false propositions and even contradictions if they are regarded as units. (Frege 1980, p. 137)

The class of all classes that are not members of themselves is one such "manifold" that does not form a "whole," it must not be regarded as a "unit." In his first letter to Frege of 16 June 1902, in which Russell informs him of his discovery of the contradiction, Russell also proposes this resolution of it. "[T]here is no class (as a whole) of those classes which, as wholes, are not members of themselves. From this I conclude that under certain circumstances a definable set does not form a whole" (Frege 1980, p. 131).

Russell is led to this line of thought when considering classes in their "extensional genesis," which leads to the mathematical or iterative concept of sets and which he explicitly opposes to Frege's logical conception. In a letter to Frege dated 24 July 1902, he writes:

And in general, if one connects ranges of values closely with concepts, as you do, it seems doubtful whether two concepts with the same extension have the same range of values or only equivalent ranges of values. I find it hard to see what a class really is if it does not consist of objects but is nevertheless supposed to be the same for two concepts with the same extension. Yet I admit that the reason you adduce against the extensional view . . . seems to be irrefutable. (Frege 1980, p. 139)

What is striking about this passage is Russell's claim that the most basic characteristic of classes, their extensionality, follows immediately from the concept according to which classes "consist of objects"—Cantor's conception. At the same time, he is unable to see how the extensionality of classes follows from Frege's logical conception "which connects ranges of values closely with concepts." Russell's ultimate resolution of his antinomy, however, abandons this direction in favor of the logical conception of classes in the form of his no-classes theory.

It would be wrong to suppose that either intuitive conception, the mathematical or the logical, was held in its pure form and totally to the exclusion of the other conception by either Cantor or Russell. Rather what is found is a mixture of the two with one conception tending to dominate. In Russell's case it is different conceptions that dominate the mixture at the time of *Principles* and at the time of *Principia*. In Cantor's case the presence of the logical conception is indicated by his reference to laws ("every totality of elements that can be united into a whole by a law") in his 1883 definition. The only purist is Frege who does seem to hold exclusively to the logical conception in a pure undiluted form.

III

For Russell the concept of class was beset with difficulties, and most of these difficulties seemed to him not to afflict class concepts (attributes, propositional functions). The class concept 'even prime number' is readily distinguished from the number 2, which is the only object falling under that concept, and the class concept 'present king of France' is an unobjectionable as any other even though nothing falls under it. Also, each class concept is a single logical subject, however many objects fall under it. Hence Russell's asymmetry of skepticism. The one remaining difficulty is, of course, "the contradiction."

Russell formulates "the contradiction" both in terms of predicates and in terms of classes (1937, p. 102). Thus from the start he held the view that there is a single contradiction capable of appearing in various forms. Given his general skepticism about classes, which rests on considerations apart from those connected with the contradiction, it was natural for Russell to assume that the most fundamental form of the antinomy was the intensional form concerning predicates. In Russell's celebrated letter of 16 June 1902, in which he informs Frege of the existence of the antinomy, he gives both formulations (Frege 1980, pp. 130–131). For Frege, of course, it is the extensional formulation in terms of classes that is most important, because it brings with it the downfall of his system. Predicates (concepts, functions) for Frege are arranged in a simple type hierarchy, but classes are all "objects" without distinction of type. This leads directly to the inconsistency of his set theory.

Russell writes in his intellectual autobiography, *My Philosophical Development*, that his discovery of the theory of descriptions was his first real insight into the solution of the antinomy about classes. "Throughout 1903 and 1904, my work was almost wholly devoted to this matter [the contradiction], but without any vestige of success. My first success was the theory of descriptions, in the spring of 1905" (1959, p. 79). Now, nothing in Russell's "On Denoting" of 1905 directly concerns the antinomies or the theory of logical types, so just what in the theory of descriptions did Russell find to lead to his final resolution of the antinomies? The answer must be that the key to Russell's solution to his problem about denoting lies in his use of the idea of an incomplete symbol. An incomplete symbol, such as a definite description, is one that has the superficial grammar of a singular term but functions logically as a syncategorematic expression that contributes to the sense of the whole proposition containing it while having no independent meaning of its own. Class abstracts on this view have no independent meaning and they refer to nothing. In particular, they do not stand for classes. If such a theory of classes can be carried through, it will treat classes as logical constructions whose real existence need not be assumed. This is what Russell accomplishes in his no-classes theory. It does not rest on an explicit denial of the reality of classes, but it proceeds without having ever to explicitly commit itself to their reality. The no-classes theory that Russell finally adopts implements his initial skepticism about classes. It treats them as a mere *façon de parler*.

The logical construction of classes out of propositional functions is effected by definition *20.01.

$$\text{*20.01} \quad f\{\hat{z}(\psi z)\}. = :(\exists \varphi):\varphi!x. \equiv_x .\psi x: f\{\varphi!\hat{z}\} \quad \text{Df.}$$

This provides a contextual definition of the class abstract $\hat{z}(\psi z)$ in the propositional context $f\{\hat{z}(\psi z)\}$; hence it provides for the elimination of class abstracts from any atomic propositional context containing them. Classes differ from propositional functions solely on the ground of extensionality. Classes are extensions, whereas propositional functions are intensions. This means that coextensive propositional functions need not be identical, but classes whose members are the same are themselves the same. In order to justify definition *20.01 therefore, we see that, it is necessary that it should secure the extensionality of classes. Extensionality is expressed as

$$\vdash:.\hat{z}(\varphi z) = \hat{z}(\psi z). \equiv :\varphi x. \equiv_x .\psi x.$$

The proof is as follows: $\hat{z}(\varphi z) = \hat{z}(\psi z)$ expands, by definition *20.01 (and Russell's convention, which accords to the first occurring incomplete symbol the largest scope), to

$$(\exists \chi):\varphi x. \equiv_x .\chi!x:\chi!\hat{z} = \hat{z}(\psi z).$$

Another application of definition *20.01 effects the elimination of the remaining class abstract:

$$(\exists \chi):.\varphi x. \equiv_x .\chi!x:.(\exists \theta): \psi x. \equiv_x .\theta!x:\chi!\hat{z} = \theta!\hat{z}.$$

This is equivalent to

$$(\exists \chi, \theta): \varphi x. \equiv_x .\chi!x:\psi x. \equiv_x .\theta!x:\chi!\hat{z} = \theta!\hat{z}.$$

This, by laws of identity is equivalent to

$$(\exists \chi):\varphi x. \equiv_x .\chi!x:\psi x. \equiv_x .\chi!x.$$

$(\exists \chi):\varphi x. \equiv_x .\chi!x$ is an axiom of reducibility; hence the last displayed formula is equivalent to

$$\psi x. \equiv_x .\varphi x \qquad \text{Q.E.D.}$$

(All of this proof is taken from Whitehead and Russell (1910, p. 78).

A second definition, *20.02, introduces $\in$ contextually as a relation between an individual and a propositional function:

$$*20.02 \quad x \in (\varphi!\hat{z}). = .\varphi!x \quad \text{Df.}$$

The only role for this definition is to enable Russell to introduce $\in$ in its usual meaning as the relation of class membership—$x \in \hat{z}(\varphi z)$. Definition *20.02 does this together with definition *20.01 by securing the law of class comprehension.

$$*20.3 \quad \vdash : x \in \hat{z}(\psi z). \equiv .\psi x.$$

It is of interest to examine the proof of this theorem in order to see how crucial the axiom of reducability is to Russell's entire construction. (We have already seen one example of this in the proof of the extensionality of classes.)

The proof for theorem *20.3 is as follows:

$$x \in \hat{z}(\psi z). \equiv :.(\exists \varphi):.\psi y. \equiv_y .\varphi!y : x \in (\varphi!\hat{z})$$

is a theorem by definition *20.01. This, by definition *20.02, is equivalent to

$$x \in \hat{z}(\psi z). \equiv :.(\exists \varphi):.\psi y. \equiv_y .\varphi!y : \varphi!x,$$

which, by second-order logic, is equivalent to

$$x \in \hat{z}(\psi z). \equiv :.(\exists \varphi):.\psi y. \equiv_y .\varphi!y : \psi x.$$

Again, by quantifier laws, this is equivalent to

$$x \in \hat{z}(\psi z). \equiv :.(\exists \varphi):\psi y. \equiv_y .\varphi!y :.\psi x.$$

The left conjunct of the right-hand side of this biconditional is an axiom of reducibility. Hence the biconditional itself is equivalent to

$$x \in \hat{z}(\psi z). \equiv .\psi x, \qquad \text{Q.E.D.}$$

We can now return to our discussion of Russell's resolution of his antinomy about classes in *Principia Mathematica*. The antinomy arises from consideration of the class of all classes that are not members of themselves:

$$\hat{\alpha} \, (\alpha \notin \alpha).$$

Suppose first that this class is a member of itself:

$$\hat{\alpha} \, (\alpha \notin \alpha) \in \hat{\alpha} \, (\alpha \notin \alpha).$$

Then, by the appropriate form of the law of class comprehension proven in what follows,

$$\hat{\alpha}\,(\alpha \notin \alpha) \notin \alpha\,(\alpha \notin \alpha).$$

Conversely, if $\hat{\alpha}\,(\alpha \notin \alpha)$ is not a member of itself, then by the same law it does not satisfy its own defining condition, that is,

$$\hat{\alpha}\,(\alpha \notin \alpha) \in \hat{\alpha}\,(\alpha \notin \alpha).$$

Hence "the contradiction."

To see how Russell resolves the antinomy, we must first reformulate it within his no-classes theory of classes. Because the existence of classes is not assumed in the *Principia*, the antinomy must make its appearance in its predicative form if it is to be dealt with at all. First, an explanation is required of the use of the lowercase Greek letters α and β in the formulation of the antinomy. These are explained as schematic letters that hold places for class abstracts. "The representation of a class by a single letter α can now be understood. For the denotation of α is ambiguous, in so far as it is undecided as to which of the symbols $\hat{z}(\varphi z)$, $\hat{z}(\psi z)$, $\hat{z}(\chi z)$, etc. it is to stand for, where $\varphi\hat{z}$, $\psi\hat{z}$, $\chi\hat{z}$, etc. are the various determining functions of the class" (Whitehead and Russell 1910, p. 80). Accordingly, Russell introduces the expression $\hat{\alpha}(f\alpha)$ for the class of classes that satisfies the condition $f\alpha$, and he provides a contextual definition for it with definition *20.08, which is an analogue of *20.01:

$$*20.08. \quad f\{\hat{\alpha}(\psi\alpha)\}. = :(\exists\varphi):\psi\alpha. \equiv_{\alpha} .\varphi!\alpha : f(\varphi!\hat{\alpha}) \quad \text{Df.}$$

(see also Whitehead and Russell 1910, p. 79). Similarly, he introduces an analogue of definition *20.02:

$$*20.081. \quad \alpha \in \psi!\alpha. = .\psi!\alpha \quad \text{Df.}$$

(see also Whitehead and Russell 1910, p. 79). This, in turn, enables Russell to prove the required form of the law of class comprehension:

$$\gamma \in \hat{\alpha}(f\alpha). \equiv .f\gamma.$$

We can now turn our attention to the class of all classes that are not members of themselves, $\hat{\alpha}(\alpha \notin \alpha)$. To formulate the antinomy we must consider the purported proposition

$$\hat{\alpha}\,(\alpha \notin \alpha) \in \hat{\alpha}\,(\alpha \notin \alpha).$$

But, if this collection of symbols were to have a meaning, it would mean, by double application of definition *20.08,

$$(\exists g): \alpha \notin \alpha. \equiv_{\alpha} .g!\alpha : g!\hat{\gamma} \notin g!\hat{\gamma}.$$

This, in turn, by definition *20.081 expands to

$$(\exists g): \sim (\alpha \in \alpha). \equiv_\alpha .g!\alpha: \sim \{g!(g!\hat{\gamma})\}.$$

Here the expression $g!(g!\hat{\gamma})$ occurs, and it assigns a propositional function as argument to itself. This is prohibited by the theory of logical types, and this is Russell's resolution of his antinomy about classes.

The definition *20.08 uses the letter α as a subscript to express universal quantification, and indeed Russell feels free to use lowercase Greek letters as apparent (bound) variables. This will perhaps puzzle contemporary readers familiar with Quine's dictum: *to be is to be a value of a bound variable*. The use of lowercase Greek letters as bound variables ranging over classes, is prima facie incompatible with Russell's explicit program of treating classes as logical fictions. Two more definitions set the matter straight:

*20.07 $(\alpha).f(\alpha). = .(\varphi)f\{\hat{z}(\varphi!z)\}$ Df.

*20.071 $(\exists\alpha).f(\alpha). = .(\exists\varphi).f\{\hat{z}(\varphi!z)\}$ Df.

By eliminating the class abstract, we see that *20.07 becomes

$$(\alpha).f(\alpha). = .(\varphi):(\exists\psi).\varphi!x \equiv_x \psi!x.f\{\psi\hat{z}\}   \text{Df.}$$

In similar fashion, definition *20.08 effects the elimination of the class abstract from *20.071. Thus there is no real quantification over classes. It also is a mere *façon de parler* (Whitehead and Russell 1910, p. 81). Russell concludes, "Accordingly, in mathematical reasoning, we can dismiss the whole apparatus of functions and think only of classes as 'quasi-things', capable of immediate representation by a single name" (Whitehead and Russell 1910, p. 81). Classes are quasi-things and quantification over them is quasi-quantification. The schematic letters α, β do not really play the role of bound variables. Definitions *20.07 and *20.071 expose the fiction.

Definitions *20.07 and *20.071 introduce lowercase Greek letters as bound (apparent) variables that range over classes, but the classes are all determined by predicative functions. Nevertheless, there is no real loss of generality here in view of the theorem.

*20.151 $\vdash.(\exists\varphi).\hat{z}(\psi z) = \hat{z}(\varphi!z).$

Russell remarks: "In virtue of this proposition, all classes can be obtained from predicative functions. This fact is especially important when classes are used as apparent variables" (Whitehead and Russell 1910, p. 192). He notes that definitions *20.07 and *20.071 make reference only to classes determined by predicative functions, but then he observes, "In virtue of *20.151 this places no limitations upon the classes concerned" (Whitehead and Russell 1910, p. 192).

IV

Russell's resolution of his antinomy about classes turns on the rejection of the expression $g!(g!ŷ)$ as not well formed. The justification for this is that a function cannot take itself as argument according to the theory of types. This is also Russell's resolution of the antinomy in its predicative form; thus Russell has vindicated his original conviction that we are dealing essentially with just one antinomy. The rejection of $g!(g!ŷ)$ does not turn on any specific consideration about the internal structure of the propositional function. *No* function whatever can take itself as argument. In particular, this prohibition does not depend on the range of values of the quantifiers occurring in the propositional function. Considerations of quantifiers do not enter into the resolution of this antinomy. The resolution invokes only the simple type hierarchy that consists of a ground level of "individuals," propositional functions from individuals to propositions, functions of *these* functions to propositions, and so on up to any finite iteration. Transfinite types are disallowed.

According to the ramified theory of types a propositional function that contains quantifications over propositional functions of order n or that contains free variables whose values are propositional functions of order n is itself at least of order $n + 1$. The range of significance of a propositional function must always be restricted to a given order, and the range of any bound variable must be confined to functions of a given order. Consequently, no function can fall within the range of one of its own bound variables. A function that falls within the range of one of its own quantifiers is said to be *impredicative,* and the ramified theory of types excludes this kind of impredicativity. It is clear that this kind of impredicativity is not, on Russell's analysis, the source of the antinomy about classes. Consequently, his resolution of the antinomy does not depend on the exclusion of this kind of impredicativity by the ramified theory of types.

Impredicative propositional functions are excluded by what Russell calls the "vicious-circle" principle. Russell's analysis of the antinomies finds them as arising, in one way or another, from violations of the vicious-circle principle and as thus committing a kind of fallacy of circularity. Gödel claims that there are actually three forms of the principle involved in Russell's analysis. "This led to the formulation of a principle which says that no totality can contain members definable only in terms of this totality, or members involving or presupposing this totality" (Gödel 1983, p. 454). What is prohibited by these forms of the principle is the definition or specification of any object with the use of a quantifier within whose range there falls the very object being defined or specified. Gödel notes that none of these forms of the vicious-circle principle inhibits the predicative form of Russell's antinomy. "In order to make this principle applicable to the intensional paradoxes, still another principle had to be assumed, namely that 'every propositional function presupposes the totality of its values' and evidently also the totality of its possible arguments" (Gödel 1983, p. 454). Gödel adds, in explanation, "Otherwise the concept of 'not applying to itself', would presuppose no totality (since it involves no quantifications), and the vicious circle principle would not prevent its application to itself" (Gödel 1983, p. 454). If every propositional function presupposes the totality of its arguments, it evidently cannot itself be one of its arguments, for such a propositional function would circularly presuppose itself. We have seen that on Russell's theory of classes the extensional form of the antinomy (about classes) reduces to the intensional form involving self-predication. Hence it is this last form of the vicious-circle principle, which prohibits a propositional function from being among its own arguments, that is the only form involved in the resolution of the antinomy about classes.

The importance of the vicious-circle principle, for Russell, is that it constitutes his analysis of the fallacy that lies at the root of the logical and set-theoretic antinomies. Therefore it is Russell's philosophical justification for the ramified theory of types. But what justifies the vicious-circle principle in its turn? We ask our question in the present context, specifically, about that form of the principle, as distinguished by Gödel, that prohibits any propositional function from taking itself as argument. It is granted, of course, that any well-determined function must have both a well-determined domain and a well-determined range. But why can't a function belong to its own domain? The obvious answer is that this threatens antinomy. But this was not Russell's answer, for, because the vicious-circle principle is his justification for the theory of types, he cannot in turn call on the theory of types to justify the vicious-circle principle. Russell believed that this form of the vicious-circle principle followed from the very nature of propositional functions.

"It would seem," Russell says, "that the essential characteristic of a function is *ambiguity*" (Whitehead and Russell 1910, p. 39). When we assert a propositional function, Russell holds that there is no one thing that is the object of our assertion. "When we speak of 'φx', where x is not specified, we mean one value of the function, but not a definite one. We may express this by saying that 'φx' *ambiguously denotes* φa, φb, φc, etc., where φa, φb, φc, etc. are the various values of 'φx' " (Whitehead and Russell 1910, p. 39). The use of the expression "ambiguously denotes" here indicates that what Russell is referring to is a *concept* and not an open sentence, in spite of the quotation marks, 'φx'. "When we say that 'φx' ambiguously denotes φa, φb, φc, etc., we mean that 'φx' means one of the objects φa, φb, φc, etc. though not a definite one, but an undetermined one" (Whitehead and Russell 1910, p. 39). Russell then observes that the function φx is well defined only if the objects φa, φb, φc, etc. are well defined. "It follows from this that no function can have among its values anything which presupposes the function, for if it had, we could not regard the objects ambiguously denoted by the function as definite until the function was definite, while conversely, as we have just seen, the function cannot be definite until its values are definite" (Whitehead and Russell 1910, p. 39).

Let us briefly summarize the argument of the last few paragraphs. Russell analyzes the antinomy about classes as arising from a vicious-circle fallacy. In particular, no function can apply to itself as argument. In order for this to be a genuine explanation, there must be an argument for it that is independent of the consideration that allowing functions to apply to themselves leads directly to the intensional form of the antinomy. Russell provides that argument in the considerations that lead him to conclude that the relevant prohibition arises from the very nature of propositional functions. "A function is what ambiguously denotes some one of a certain totality, namely the values of the function; hence this totality cannot contain any members which involve the function, since, if it did, it would contain members involving the totality, which by the vicious-circle principle, no totality can do" (Whitehead and Russell 1910, p. 39).

For Russell, then, a function is an object whose essence is to be ambiguous. It is this that explains, perhaps, why the "ancient problem of the One and the Many," which so puzzled Russell about classes, does not produce in him a corresponding skepticism about propositional functions. One can hardly raise the question of whether an ambiguity is one or many. In particular, classes, if they exist, are supposed to be full-fledged objects with a clear ontological status. A propositional function, by contrast, seems to be somewhere between being and nonbeing. It was in just such considerations of the attenuated and unsubstantial character of propositional functions that Russell, early on, sought a solution for his antinomy. In section 85 of *Principles*, written shortly after his discovery of the antinomy in early 1901, he writes: "It is to be observed that, according to the theory of propositional functions here advocated, the φ in φx is not a separate and distinguishable entity: it lives in propositions of the form φx and cannot survive analysis. . . . If φ were a distinguishable entity, there would be a proposition asserting φ of itself, which we denote by $\varphi(\varphi)$; there would also be a proposition not-$\varphi(\varphi)$, denying $\varphi(\varphi)$" (Russell 1937, p. 88). Russell then goes on to derive the intensional (predicative) form of his antinomy. He resolves the antinomy as follows: "The contradiction is avoided by the recognition that the functional part of a propositional function is not an independent entity" (Russell 1937, p. 88). From this it follows that propositional functions cannot be logical subjects. Russell expresses a doubt as to whether this view is itself consistent (1937, p. 88).

He does not tell us what contradiction it is to which he fears this view of propositional functions may lead, but he had earlier discovered Frege's paradox of the concept 'horse' (Russell 1937, p. 46). He concludes from this that "this results from the previous argument that every constituent of every proposition must, on pain of self-contradiction, be capable of being made a logical subject" (1937, p. 48).

Russell's view, at the time of *Principles*, is much like Frege's idea of functions as "incomplete" and "unsaturated" entities that cannot play the role of logical subjects. But Russell is, unlike Frege, unwilling to embrace the paradox to which it leads, and in *Principia* he finds another reason to deny that functions can take themselves as arguments. Russell retains his view of the attenuated and unsubstantial nature of propositional functions, but it leaves the actual logic of *Principia Mathematica* unaffected. So far as that logic is concerned, propositional functions are as solid as rocks. They fall within the range of values of *Principia*'s higher-order quantifiers, and expressions for them have uninhibited access to the identity predicate. To be a value of a bound variable is to be, to reverse Quine's dictum. No identity without an entity, to reverse another. Identity is, after all, *idem-entity*, to invoke yet a third.

Propositional functions cannot take themselves as arguments because, on Russell's *Principia* view, their arguments and values are logically prior to them. Given a collection of objects and one of propositions, we can make sense of functions whose domain is the collection of objects and whose range is the collection of propositions. This gives us a new collection to be the domain of a new collection of functions. What we have is an iterative concept of functions, which is formally similar to Cantor's original iterative concept of sets. Just as Cantor's concept excludes self-membership, Russell's concept excludes self-predication.

V

In his introduction to the first edition of *Principia Mathematica*, Russell explicitly rejects the extensional interpretation of propositional functions:

> [T]wo functions may well be formally equivalent without being identical; for example
>
> $x =$ Scott. $\equiv_x .x =$ the author of Waverley
>
> but the function '$\hat{z} =$ the author of Waverley' has the property that George IV wished to know whether its value with the argument 'Scott' was true, whereas the function '$\hat{z} =$ Scott' has no such property, and therefore the two functions are not identical. (Whitehead and Russell 1910, pp. 83–84)

It is evident from this quotation that Russell requires propositional functions to be intensional in order to enable him to provide a solution to the problem of informative statements of identity. In *Principles* he asks, "Why is it ever worthwhile to affirm identity?" (1937, p. 64), and it is clear that his problem is the same as Frege's. If it is true that $a = b$, how can this tell us anything other than just that $a = a$? How can $\hat{x}(\varphi x) = \hat{x}(\psi x)$ ever differ in "cognitive value," to use Frege's expression, from $\hat{x}(\varphi x) = \hat{x}(\varphi x)$, provided that the former is true? "Creatures with a heart are creatures with a kidney" is informative, whereas "Creatures with a heart are creatures with a heart" is not.

The Russellian solution to this form of Frege's puzzle is exactly the same as his solution to the form of the puzzle involving definite descriptions. Classes are regarded as logical constructions and their names—class abstracts—are incomplete symbols, just as are definite descriptions. Classes are not part of the ultimate logical furniture of the world. The basic definition is given in definition *20.01. The informative identity $\hat{x}(\theta x) = \hat{x}(\psi x)$ is, in accordance with this definition, an abbreviation for

(1) $(\exists \varphi){:}.\varphi! x. \equiv_x .\psi x{:}.(\exists \pi){:} \pi! x. \equiv_x .\theta x{:} \pi! \hat{x} = \varphi! \hat{x}.$

The trivial identity $\hat{x}(\theta x) = \hat{x}(\theta x)$, on the other hand, is an abbreviation of

(2) $(\exists \varphi){:}.\varphi! x. \equiv_x .\theta x{:}.(\exists \pi){:}\pi! x. \equiv_x .\theta x{:} \pi! \hat{x} = \varphi! \hat{x}.$

If Russell is to have a solution to Frege's puzzle on his no-classes theory, formulas (1) and (2) must differ in cognitive value. But formulas (1) and (2) differ only in that formula (1) contains a reference to the propositional function $\psi \hat{x}$, whereas (2) contains a reference to the propositional function $\theta \hat{x}$. On the extensional interpretation $\psi \hat{x}$ and $\theta \hat{x}$ are the *same* propositional function, because by formula (1) they are coextensive with propositional functions identical with each other. On the extensional interpretation, coextensiveness is the principle of individuation for propositional functions. On Russell's denotational theory of meaning, formulas (1) and (2) cannot differ in meaning on this extensional interpretation of propositional functions. The conclusion is that propositional functions must be intensions on pain of depriving Russell of his solution to this form of Frege's paradox about identity. The no-classes theory constructs extensions out of intensions.

Our discussion of Russell's no-classes theory applies only to the first edition of *Principia Mathematica*. In the second edition (1925), Russell adopts Wittgenstein's thesis of extensionality.

> There is another course recommended by Wittgenstein for philosophical reasons. This is to assume that functions of propositions are always truth-functions, and that a function can only occur in a

proposition through its values. . . . It involves the consequence that all functions of functions are extensional. . . . We are not prepared to assert that this theory is certainly right, but it has seemed worthwhile to work out its consequences in the following pages. (Whitehead and Russell 1925, p. xiv)

One consequence, not noted by Russell, is that the no-classes theory is abandoned in the second edition of *Principia*. If all functions are extensional, there ceases to be any difference between classes and propositional functions. Classes then, are assumed outright in the second edition. They are not logical constructions.[1]

Note

1. This section is an elaboration of pages 27–28 of Linsky (1983).

Bibliography

Cantor, Georg. 1895–1897. "Beiträge zur Begündung der transfiniten Mengenlehre," in his *Gesammelte Abhandlungen Mathematischen und Philosophischen Inhalts*, 282–356.

Cantor, Georg. 1932. *Gesammelte Abhandlungen Mathematischen und Philosophischen Inhalts*, Ernst Zermelo, ed. Hidesheim: Georg Olms Verlagsbuchhandlung.

Cantor, Georg. 1915. *Contributions to the Founding of the Theory of Transfinite Numbers*, P. E. B. Jourdain, trans. New York: Dover.

Frege, Gottlob. 1980. *Philosophical and Mathematical Correspondence of Gottlob Frege*, Brian McGuinness, ed., Hans Kaal, trans. Chicago: University of Chicago Press.

Frege, Gottlob. 1885. *Die Grundlagen der Arithmetik*. Breslau: Verlag von Wilhelm Koebner.

Gödel, Kurt. 1983. "Russell's mathematical logic," in *Philosophy of Mathematics*, Paul Benacerraf and Hilary Putnam, eds. Cambridge: Cambridge University Press, 447–469.

Linsky, Leonard. 1983. *Oblique Contexts*. Chicago: University of Chicago Press.

Parsons, Charles. 1976. "Some remarks on Frege's conception of extension," in *Studien zu Frege*, Matthias Schirn, ed. Stuttgart-Bad Cannstadt: Frommann Verlag, vol. 1, 265–277.

Russell, Bertrand. 1929. *Our Knowledge of the External World*. Chicago: Open Court. First edition, 1914.

Russell, Bertrand. 1937. *Principles of Mathematics*, Second edition. New York: Norton. First edition, 1903. Cambridge: The University Press.

Russell, Bertrand. 1959. *My Philosophical Development*. New York: Simon and Schuster.

Van Heijenoort, Jean. 1967. *From Frege to Gödel*. Cambridge, Mass.: Harvard University Press.

Wang, Hao. 1983. "The concept of set," in *Philosophy of Mathematics*, Paul Benacerraf and Hilary Putnam, eds. Cambridge: Cambridge University Press, 530–570.

Whitehead, A. N., and Russell, Bertrand. 1910. *Principia Mathematica*. Cambridge: The University Press. Second edition, 1925.

Quine's Indeterminacy
Charles S. Chihara

I

In a recent article George Bealer sets out to refute what he considers to be the central thesis of functionalism—a thesis that he describes with the words "the standard mental relations have direct functional definitions based on the principles of psychology" (1984, p. 283). The refutation he envisages would show that there exists "a demonstrably different system of deviant relations that make the principles of psychology come out true when we hold constant the interpretation of the physical and logical constants contained in these principles" (p. 283). Bealer constructs his refutation by making use of Willard Quine's famous thesis of the indeterminacy of translation, which is described as the thesis that "there exists more than one fully adequate translation manual for each radically foreign language" (p. 289).

Whether or not Bealer has accurately described Quine's indeterminacy thesis, how he applies the thesis is striking. He postulates a radically alien language L for which there are two fully adequate translation manuals. He then assumes, without so much as a word of justification, that these two translation manuals generate two functions f and h that map sentences of L onto their English translations. Why he thinks that a fully adequate manual of translation must always give a unique translation for every foreign sentence is not clear to me. It is surely not obvious. Thus, insofar as it can be imagined that we have a single manual for translating French into English, there does not seem to be any one English sentence that is given as the translation of "Donnez moi cette boite": "Give me that box," "Give me that can," "Give me that carton," etc. all seem equally acceptable. Even more surprising is the assumption Bealer makes that for every English sentence S there is a unique sentence of L that is $f^{-1}(S)$, that is, he assumes that f (and presumably h) must be one-to-one functions. Furthermore, he goes on to claim (also without any attempt at justification) that, when the pair f and h are suitably chosen and the function g is defined by composition by

$$g(x) = h(f^{-1}(x)),$$

then for all English sentences S, $g(g(S)) = S$. Why Bealer thinks he is justified in assuming that f and h can be so chosen as to have such special properties is a mystery to me. Can all these special features be attributed to the manuals of translation mentioned in Quine's indeterminacy thesis? As a first step in answering this question, let us examine some of Quine's writings on this topic.

II

The following passage is frequently taken to express the thesis in question:

> [M]anuals for translating one language into another can be set up in divergent ways, all compatible with the totality of speech dispositions, yet incompatible with one another. (Quine 1960, p. 78)

The phrase "can be set up" cannot be taken to mean "can in fact be set up," because no one has been able to produce such a pair of manuals. It must mean something similar to "can in principle be set up." Now what does the phrase "compatible with the totality of speech dispositions" mean? In particular, what are speech dispositions? How are they to be characterized? And how would one specify the *totality* of such dispositions? (Can we even assume that there is such a thing?) Furthermore, what would it even mean to say that some manual of translation is compatible with a speech disposition? Isn't compatibility a relation that obtains between propositions, statements, or sentences? We obtain some clarification in Quine (1969d), where it is claimed that "the totality of possible observations of verbal behavior, made and unmade, is compatible with systems of analytic hypotheses of translation that are incompatible with one another" (pp. 302–303). Gilbert Harman, on the other hand, has described the thesis in the following way:

> Quine's thesis of the indeterminacy of radical translation claims that translation from one natural language into another resembles translation of number theory into set theory in that various equally good alternative but non-equivalent schemes of translation are always possible. (1969, pp. 14–15)

Notice that, where Quine spoke of alternative manuals of translation compatible with the totality of possible observations of verbal behavior. Harman spoke of equally good ones. Suppose that manuals of translation M_1 and M_2 are compatible with the totality of possible observations of the verbal behavior of some speaker of a foreign language. Does it follow that they are equally good? If so, why? After all, "equally good" must mean something similar to "equally supported by all the evidence"; so, does "compatibility with all observations of verbal behavior" imply "equally supported by all the evidence"? Suppose that H and G are theories logically compatible with some finite set S of observation sentences. Does it follow that H and G are equally supported by S? It would seem not. Thus imagine that H is the conjunction of the elements of S and that G is the conjunction of H with some large cardinality axiom of set theory. Then H is conclusively supported by S, whereas G is not. Indeed, G may receive only small support from S. It should be mentioned that in his discussion of Harman's paper Quine praises Harman's defense of his indeterminacy thesis and does not express any qualms about the way in which the thesis is described.

Another question that comes to mind is this: Just how good are the equally good ones supposed to be? Can we regard "equally good" as being equivalent to "equally bad"? An answer to this last question is suggested in Quine (1974a), where it is said (by Saul Kripke) that, according to Quine's indeterminacy thesis, "there are supposed to be two hypotheses that give a perfect fit" (p. 480). Quine agrees with Kripke and later says: "[E]ven where there was perfect fit, one should still expect multiple choice. This is where indeterminacy of translation comes in" (p. 482).

But what is a perfect fit? Or to put it another way, what are the manuals of translation supposed to fit perfectly? Evidently they are to fit all the evidence perfectly; that is, they must be equally supported by all the evidence in such a way that it is not possible to construct any other manual of translation that is a better fit, that is, one better supported by the evidence (the idea being that, if a manual is a perfect fit, then there cannot be a manual that is a better fit). Furthermore, the evidence being talked about here is not just the evidence that has been gathered thus far but *all the evidence that could be gathered throughout time.*

The italicized phrase needs clarification. Clearly there is a sense of "could" in which all the evidence that could be gathered would include contradictory and completely bizarre statements. No manual of translation would even roughly fit such a totality of evidence. So the phrase must be taken more narrowly. Reconsider Quine's statement that the manuals would be compatible with all possible observations of verbal behavior. We can understand Quine's use of the term "possible" here by comparing this statement with the earlier one in which the manuals were said to be compatible with the totality of speech dispositions. The speech dispositions issue in verbal behavior, but not all the behavior is observed. Quine wanted to include in the evidence to be considered not just the observation of verbal behavior actually made but even observations that could have been made had an attentive observer been present. Furthermore, it is clear that Quine would also want to include evidence that could have been gathered had anyone taken the trouble to perform the appropriate experiments or run the appropriate tests: so, for example, there is to be included observations of verbal behavior that could have been made had the speakers been asked such and such in such and such situations. No time limit is placed on when the evidence is obtained, for we do not want to rule out the possibility that relevant evidence may be gathered even long after there are no more speakers of the foreign language in question.

We can now distinguish three different statements of the thesis that Quine has either given or endorsed:

(A) It is possible to construct two or more manuals for translating one language into another that are incompatible with one another and yet are compatible with the totality of all possible observations of verbal behavior.

(B) It is possible to construct two or more manuals for translating one language into another that are incompatible with one another and yet are equally supported by all the evidence that could be obtained throughout time.

(C) It is possible to construct two or more manuals for translating one language into another that are incompatible with one another and yet are perfect fits; that is, they are equally supported by all the evidence that could be gathered throughout time and it is not possible to construct a manual of translation that is incompatible with these and that is also better supported by all the evidence.

It can be seen that Bealer's statement of the thesis comes close to (C), especially when "fully adequate" is taken to mean "perfectly fitting."

III

Many philosophers have thought that Quine's reasons for espousing the indeterminacy thesis are to be found in his discussions of the "Gavagai" example. But Quine tells us that the "real ground of the doctrine is very different, broader and deeper" (1970, p. 178). The real ground, evidently, is to be found in the fact (if it is a fact) that one can have two physical theories P and P^* that are incompatible with each other and yet compatible with all possible data. The argument then is given in these words:

Insofar as the truth of a physical theory is underdetermined by observables, the translation of the foreigner's physical theory is underdetermined by translation of his observation sentence. . . . Our translation of his observation sentences no more fixes our translation of his physical theory than our own possible observations fix our own physical theory. (Quine 1970, pp. 179–180)

But who would have thought otherwise? Let us grant, for the sake of argument, that translation of the foreigner's observation sentences does not 'fix' the translation of the sentences of his physical theory. Why does the thesis of the indeterminacy of translation follow? Does Quine believe that unless translation of the observation sentences 'fixes' the translation of the rest of the language, indeterminacy must inevitably follow? And what grounds does Quine give for such a belief?

Quine's reasoning is remarkably loose here. The indeterminacy thesis asserts the possibility of constructing two or more manuals of translation that are perfect fits. The reasoning does not imply the possibility of constructing even one perfect fit, so how can it show the possibility of two or more such? Perhaps it is being assumed that it is always possible to construct at least one perfect fit. Then Quine would need to show only that there would have to be more than one. This Quine may think he has done in arguing that our translation of his observation sentences does not fix the translation of the foreigner's physical theory. But there is still an enormous gap in his reasoning. And it is hard to see why Quine thought he had a convincing argument.

Perhaps we can obtain some idea of how Quine was reasoning by exploring his use of the term "observation sentence." Quine tells us (1969a) that "an observation sentence is one on which all speakers of the language give the same verdict when given the same concurrent stimulation" (pp. 86–87). And later he claims that "observation sentences are precisely the ones we can correlate with observable circumstances of the occasion of utterance or assent ... [and they] afford the only entry to a language" (p. 89). Thus Quine's idea may be that, if translation of the observation sentences does not fix translation of the rest of the language, nothing else will. And this may be connected with his claim that "observation sentences are the repository of evidence for scientific hypotheses" (Quine 1969a, p. 88). He may have thought at this time that the only kind of evidential statement that could support a claim of the adequacy of a manual of translation would be statements of correlations between observable circumstances and utterances of, or assent to, observation sentences.[1] That something similar to this may be what is going on in his argument is suggested by the interesting *Synthese* discussion, in which, under much pressure from Michael Dummett and Harman, Quine says:

> [W]hat I've been really concerned with or motivated by in this stuff about translation and indeterminacy hasn't been primarily translation but cognitive meaning and analyticity and the like, and for that sort of purpose what would be fundamental for me ... is the matter of assent and dissent in connection with stimulus-meaning. The further sort of information we would get by going after what's natural or suitable to say would be important for genuine, serious, practical translation. (1974a, p. 493)

Soon after, Harman remarks: "What bothers me, then, about the indeterminacy thesis is that it begins to sound like the thesis that inasmuch as you restrict the data, more theories will be compatible with it" (Quine 1974a, p. 494). Quine's response to Harman's charge is striking: "I'm not trying to push a paradox," he says. But he does not rebut Harman's characterization of his thesis either!

Consider an analogy. A valid sentence of first-order logic is one that is true under all interpretations of the language. By restricting what counts as an interpretation, one can, in effect, enlarge the class of valid sentences. Analogously it is reasonable to suppose that, as one restricts what counts as evidence, one enlarges the class of 'perfect fits', that is, the manuals of translation that perfectly fit all the evidence.

Well, why can't one reply that Quine is free to choose what he means or intends by "evidence" in stating his thesis? After all, it is Quine's thesis; isn't it up to him to decide what the thesis is to be? A reply of this sort fails to take account of the uses to which the indeterminacy thesis is put by Quine, for Quine believes that his indeterminacy thesis shows that there is no such thing as "the right manual of translation." Why? Because he thinks it is in principle possible to produce two or more manuals that are perfect fits. Then it would be reasonable to argue as follows: If there exist two nonequivalent manuals for translating the foreigner's language into English, say M_1 and M_2, and these are both perfect fits, how can one say that M_1, as opposed to M_2, is the right one? What would "right" mean? But suppose, as is being suggested, that Quine's thesis turns out to be not what we have taken it to be but instead the much weaker thesis, "It is possible to construct two or more . . . that fit all the evidence of such and such a sort." One cannot then go on to conclude from indeterminacy, as Quine does, that "where indeterminacy of translation applies, there is no real question of right choice" (Quine 1969d, p. 303)—unless, of course, one can also prove that all the evidence of such and such kind is all the evidence that is relevant.

But what other kind of evidence could there be? In order to explore this question, let us examine briefly the evidence Quine cites in support of his belief in the existence of sets.

IV

Sets, for Quine, are unchanging abstract objects whose existence one can reasonably postulate, for we have the same sort of reasons for postulating the existence of sets, he believes, that we have for postulating the existence of molecules: Basically, we have a kind of scientific evidence for the existence of sets. To understand Quine's views on this matter, it is useful to review the principal points in his "Posits and Reality" (1966a). In this article Quine considers the question of what evidence the scientist can muster for belief in the existence of molecules, given that molecules are too small to be directly observed. The answer generally given is that there is a large fund of "indirect evidence" obtained by experimentation and theory testing involving a variety of different phenomena from such diverse areas of study as biology, chemistry, and atomic physics.

> The point is that these miscellaneous phenomena can, if we assume the molecular theory, be marshalled under the familiar laws of motion. The fancifulness of thus assuming a substructure of moving particles of imperceptible size is offset by a gain in naturalness and scope on the part of the aggregate laws of physics. (Quine 1966a, pp. 233–234)

Thus the 'indirect evidence' mentioned turns out to consist of certain 'benefits' engendered by the acceptance of the doctrine of molecules. These "benefits" turn out to be simplicity of theory, familiarity with the principles used, increase in the scope of testable consequences, extension of theory, and agreement with experimentation. But these are benefits that give the physicist reasons for using the molecular theory. Do they also afford any real evidence of the truth of the molecular theory? "Might the molecular doctrine," Quine asks, "not be ever so useful in organizing and extending our knowledge of the behavior of observable things, and yet be factually false?" (1966a, p. 235). He does not attempt to answer this question straight off but instead investigates the reasons we have for believing in common sense bodies, such as tables and automobiles. After all, he suggests, what we are directly aware of are such things as visual patches, tactile feels, sounds, tastes, and smells. So, if we have any evidence for the existence of common sense objects, "we have it only in the way in which we may be said to have evidence for the existence of molecules. . . . The positing of either sort of body is good science insofar merely as it helps us formulate our laws" (1966a, p. 237).

Quine then reconsiders the question of whether such benefits as simplicity of theory and familiarity of principles that are garnered through the postulation of molecules provide us with any real evidence of the truth of the molecular theory. He concludes that, if we take the position in the molecular case that no evidence is provided, then we would be stuck with holding that we have no evidence for the existence of common sense bodies either. We should have to say that tables and automobiles are unreal. But this, according to Quine, would be absurd:

> We cannot significantly question the reality of the external world, or deny that there is evidence of external objects in the testimony of our senses; for to do so is simply to dissociate the terms 'reality' and

'evidence' from the very applications which originally did most to invest those terms with whatever intelligibility they may have for us. (Quine 1966b, p. 216)

In "Posits and Reality" (1966a) an additional reason is given for rejecting the hypothesis that physical objects are unreal: "The positing of physical objects must be seen not as an *ex post facto* systematization of data, but as a move prior to which no appreciable data would be available to systematize" (p. 216). So we must conclude, according to Quine, both that *the benefits we mentioned do count as evidence*, indeed "the best evidence of reality we can ask," and that "we can hope for no surer touchstone of reality."

Such being what evidence is, according to Quine's lights, we can understand his response to the logical positivist's position that one cannot have empirical evidence for such statements as "sets exist":

> I think the positivists were mistaken when they despaired of evidence in such cases and accordingly tried to draw up boundaries that would exclude such sentences as meaningless. Existence statements in this philosophical vein do admit of evidence, in the sense that we can have reasons, and essentially scientific reasons, for including numbers or classes or the like in the range of values of our variables. (Quine 1969b, p. 97)

What are these "scientific reasons"? They turn out to involve general considerations of the sort described in Quine's discussion of physical bodies and molecules. Indeed, at one point Quine suggests comparing the benefits of postulating attributes with those resulting from the postulation of classes (1969e, p. 23). Thus problems with individuation of attributes might require a certain disruption of the logic of the overall conceptual scheme, and this might require a more complicated logical theory than would be required if only classes were postulated. In this way simplicity considerations would indicate that classes should be postulated instead of attributes. What is clear is that the weighing of the kind of evidence talked about in this context is a rather nebulous and vaguely specified matter that involves comparisons of the overall theories that result from adopting competing hypotheses.

Still, if it is reasonable to use this kind of evidence to justify one's belief in classes and material bodies, as Quine has claimed, then surely it should also be taken into account in assessing competing manuals of translation. And notice that when it comes to the question of whether sets exist, Quine does not say that there is no right answer, for not only does he think that the affirmative answer is right but he also thinks that there is evidence to support his answer.

V

The weakness of Quine's justification of the indeterminacy thesis should now be evident. When evidence includes the sorts of benefits that Quine cites in support of his belief in sets, then one cannot without justification limit the evidence to be considered in evaluating the adequacy of manuals of translation to just such things as correlations between observable circumstances and occasions of utterances or assent: Practically everything becomes relevant, including theoretical considerations bearing on psychology, sociology, anthropology, linguistics, biology, chemistry, and physics. Taking into account the more theoretical and global kind of evidence requires taking into account the whole of science: It is the effect of incorporating the competing theories of translation into the whole of science that must be judged. Now how would one show that it is in principle always possible to construct two or more manuals of translation that are incompatible with each other and that fit perfectly all the evidence that could be gathered throughout all time when evidence is taken in this more inclusive sense? It is not at all obvious. Certainly we should not be satisfied with the sort of "quick and dirty" justifications that are all too often given in conversations.

How might Quine try to fill the gap in his argument? We have seen that Quine seems to take (A), (B), and (C) as coming to the same thing; all three are taken to express his indeterminacy thesis. This suggest a line of reasoning: If one could show that (A) is equivalent to (C) relative to some defensible theory, it would take Quine a long way toward providing the missing justification, for (A) is stated in terms of compatibility with a certain kind of evidence (viz. observations of verbal behavior), whereas (C) is stated in terms of equal support by all evidence. Now Harman has noted (1979, p. 10) that Quine does not seem to distinguish the following:

(1) *T* and *U* are empirically equivalent if and only if they are *compatible with* the same observational evidence.

(2) *T* and *U* are empirically equivalent if and only if they are *supported equally by* the same observational evidence.

Harman puts forward some suggestions as to why Quine may regard statements (1) and (2) as coming to the same thing, all of these reasons having to do with beliefs Quine may have about empirical support. Thus, although (1) and (2) are not logically equivalent, they may be equivalent *relative to some theory of confirmation or evidence that Quine accepts*. Then, by defending such a theory, Quine could provide a justification for taking (1) and (2) as coming to the same thing. By this route he could also provide a justification for taking (C) as coming to the same thing as:

> (C*) It is possible to construct two or more manuals of translation that are incompatible with each other and yet are compatible with all the evidence that could be gathered throughout all time.

The difference between (C*) and (A) comes down to the kind of evidence with which the two manuals are to be compatible. But because we are concerned only with logical compatibility, one can make a strong case for taking (C*) to come to the same thing as (A). The reason is that the global, systematic sort of evidence that Quine discusses in connection with ontological justification would not seem to be significant when it is logical compatibility with the evidence that is at issue. Thus, if M_1 and M_2 are rival manuals of translation, both compatible with a set E of sentences giving correlations between observable circumstances and occasions of utterances or assent, then it is plausible to maintain that they will also be compatible with an enlarged set of sentences containing E as a subset but also containing sentences expressing such facts as increase in scope and simplicity of overall theory, which are regarded by Quine as evidence when he discusses ontological justifications.

All this suggests that we should investigate Quine's views about empirical support to see if he can in fact justify taking (C) and (C*) to be equivalent relative to his theory of support. Certainly there are articles in which Quine adheres to a view of empirical support that at least suggests the sort of background theory that is needed. For example, Quine (1974b) sympathetically discusses Karl Popper's doctrine that evidence can never support a hypothesis but may serve only to refute it. The idea is put forward that the only kind of support a categorical universal hypothesis is ever given by any evidence is negative support, that is, "the mere absence of refutation" (p. 218). Another idea Quine advances in that article, which is relevant to our concerns here, is to be found in his closing statements that "a scientific theory consists of laws in conjunction, not alternation; and its evidence lies in the singular consequences. . . . Failure of such a consequence refutes the theory" (p. 220). Here Quine seems to have completely forgotten the views about evidence that he puts forward in discussing ontological justification.

The view of empirical support expressed (1974b) is similar to that put forward by Quine in *The Web of Belief* (Quine and Ullian 1970):

> What confirms a hypothesis, insofar as it gets confirmed, is the verification of its predictions. When more particularly, the hypothesis is a generalization arrived at by induction, those predictions are simply instances of the generalization. Thus, what confirms an induction are its instances. (p. 66)

As is well known, such a view seems to give rise to a number of notorious paradoxes. For example, as Quine sees it, a nonblack nonraven is an instance of the generalization that *all nonblack things are nonravens*. Hence it would seem that observing a white shoe (a nonblack nonraven) would confirm the generalization and hence the logically equivalent generalization "All ravens are black." To avoid this apparent absurdity, Quine stipulates that any instance of ⌜All S are P⌝ confirms the generalization so long as S and P are projectible. The reason why observing a white shoe does not confirm "All ravens are black" according to this view is because "only a black raven can confirm 'All ravens are black', the complements not being projectible" (Quine 1969c, p. 115). For Quine, nonprojectible traits are not suited to induction and do not count toward confirmation of generalizations (Quine and Ullian 1970, p. 57). How to determine what traits are projectible is left to our intuitions of natural kinds: The totality of black things is a natural kind; the totality of nonblack things is not. In this way Quine has a way of resolving the grue paradox: The predicate "is grue" is not projectible, because the totality of grue things is not a natural kind (for details, see Chihara (1981), p. 427).

One reason why I am doubtful that Quine's views on confirmation and evidence could be brought in to produce a compelling argument that statements (C) and (C*) come to the same thing is that I find these views defective and unworkable. A detailed critique of Quine's ideas on empirical support would be out of place here—especially because I have done that elsewhere (in Chihara 1981)—but the following provides some small indication of my dissatisfaction with these views.

The basic elements of Quine's analyses of confirmation are to be found in the views of most of the positivists he was so instrumental in undermining: There is a rule of simple induction; statements and hypotheses are taken to be either believed or not believed (an all-or-nothing view, in contrast with the Bayesian view of confirmation according to which an agent is pictured as having degrees of confidence in the various statements and theories considered); evidence supporting a hypothesis is given as a set of observation sentences that are consistent (or compatible) with the hypothesis; and there is no mechanism in the analyses for determining the degree or amount of support an evidential statement gives some hypothesis. Given this framework, it is not terribly surprising that Quine would tend not to distinguish "equally supported by all the evidence" from "compatible with all the evidence." But I see these factors as pointing to the poverty of Quine's views on empirical support. A more adequate view will take into account not only gradations of belief, as is done in the Bayesian theory of confirmation, but also the more theoretical, global factors that Quine mentions in his discussions of ontological justifications. (The Bayesian takes account of such theoretical factors in determining the agent's subjective prior probability distribution; see in this regard Chihara (1981), p. 433).

Quine's analyses of the confirmational paradoxes, using the mentioned elements, illustrate some of the weaknesses of the view. Why don't I conclude from an unbroken string of instances of "Every moment of my life is a moment followed by one in which I am alive" that the generalization is true? Quine suggests (Quine and Ullian 1970, p. 57) that it is because the predicate "is a moment followed by one in which I am alive" is not projectible. But this doctrine of projectibility is riddled with problems. Take the generalization "All the students taking Dance 151 are nonmale." Suppose that we have obtained by some appropriate sampling technique a large amount of data that tells us that of the fifty students in the sample who are in Dance 151, each is nonmale. In other words, we have fifty instances of the generalization in question and no counterinstances. Intuitively we would have some confirmation of the generalization. But nonmale is not projectible; for the totality of nonmales is not a natural kind. Hence, according to Quine's account, we do not have any confirmation.[2] Surely the consequences of Quine's views here are as counterintuitive as the paradoxes they were developed to solve. Do we really need to appeal to the nonprojectibility of certain predicates in order to avoid these confirmational paradoxes? I think not. For example, consider the puzzle that Quine attempts to resolve by affirming the nonprojectibility of "is a moment followed by one in which I am alive." Surely we do not need to appeal to a doctrine of projectibility to see why we do not infer our own immortality from the data mentioned. Quine seems to have overlooked the enormous fund of background theories that we accept as relevant to such a possible inference—theories having to do with the biological processes of living and dying, which are sufficient to account for our reluctance to draw the inference in question.[3] (I cannot help wondering here if Quine was not similarly caught in the grip of his positivistic view of confirmation when he analyzed the empirical support that manuals of translation could have, thus overlooking the significance of background theories and the global kind of evidence mentioned earlier.)

Quine's principal response to my criticisms of his views on confirmation (Quine 1981) is to charge that he does not have a theory of confirmation "worthy of the name," thus suggesting that I was criticizing a straw man. Presumably Quine wants to hold that the many views about confirmation and empirical support that he has put forward over the years do not add up to any kind of theory ("worthy of the name"). I find it ironic that he puts so much weight on the word "theory" here, for in another place he has written:

In *Word and Object* and related writings my use of the term 'theory' is not technical. For these purposes a man's theory on a given subject may be conceived, nearly enough, as the class of all those sentences, within some limited vocabulary appropriate to the desired subject matter, that he believes. (1969d, p. 309)

Surely, given this explication of the term "theory," Quine *does* have a theory of confirmation. But more important, nothing of importance in my criticism hangs on whether or not Quine has a *theory* of confirmation, in some technical sense of "theory." Quine would not deny that he has *views* on confirmation; and all my points could be made in terms of these views. For example, I ended the paper by predicting a reassessment of many of Quine's doctrines based on critical evaluations of his use of an inadequate theory of confirmation and empirical support. Nothing of philosophical importance is changed when one replaces the word "theory" in that sentence by the word "view."

VI

Bealer's refutation of functionalism begins by assuming not only the truth of Quine's indeterminacy thesis but also the premise that the manuals of translation in question would have certain specific features. Bealer does not attempt to justify either the indeterminacy thesis or the assumption of the specific features; he relies on Quine. Quine's own argument for the thesis, I have argued, is not convincing. Nor does it justify Bealer's postulation of the special features. What is remarkable is that Bealer presents his argument against functionalism as a *refutation*; that is, he treats the indeterminacy thesis not as a controversial thesis but as an established fact. It is a mark of Quine's enormous prestige and reputation that the theses he espouses are taken in this way, even when the arguments with which he supports them are quite weak.

Notes

This paper was written while I was on sabbatical from the University of California, with the support of a Fellowship for Independent Study and Research from the National Endowment for the Humanities. A version of this paper was read in Paris on 6 June 1986 at the Seminaire "Philosophie de l'esprit," CNRS, Action de Recherche Integrée sur les Sciences de la Communication.

1. In the two paragraphs that follow the passage quoted, Quine tries to show that, if theories A and B are both compatible with all possible data, it might be possible for us to adopt A for ourselves and still remain free to translate the foreigner either as believing A or as believing B. But even if that were so, what reason would we have for thinking that no matter what new evidence was obtained, we would always be in the position of having no more reason for attributing belief in A to the foreigner than belief in B? Quine goes on

to say: "In this event no basis for a choice can be gained by exposing the foreigner to new physical data and noting his verbal response, since the theories A and B fit all observations equally well" (1970, p. 180). Here again Quine seems to take too narrow a view of what evidence is relevant to making translations. Why restrict ourselves to just what would prompt the foreigner to accept or reject the theories in question in response to physical data? After all, the foreigner states and explains his theory using words and mathematical symbols that occur in countless other sentences of the language, and these words and symbols are in turn explained in terms of other words and symbols, etc. And all these words may be used in an infinite variety of circumstances. Aren't we back in the situation of providing a manual for translating the foreigner's language into English, where practically anything could be relevant to deciding whether one manual of translation is better supported than another?

2. It should be noted that we do not obtain confirmation here, according to Quine's doctrine, because just one of the relevant predicates is not projectible. To obtain confirmation, according to Quine, both predicates involved must be projectible. Thus, in the case of the grue paradox, "All emeralds are grue" is not confirmed by observing grue emeralds because "grue" is not projectible. There is no suggestion that "emeralds" is not projectible.

3. To see how one might deal with the other confirmational paradoxes Quine discusses, without making use of a doctrine of projectible predicates, see Chihara (1981).

Bibliography

Bealer, George. 1984. "Mind and anti-mind: Why thinking has no functional definitions." *Midwest Studies in Philosophy* 9: 283–328.

Chihara, Charles. 1981. "Quine and the confirmational paradoxes." *Midwest Studies in Philosophy* 6: 425–452.

Harman, Gilbert. 1969. "An introduction to 'Translation and Meaning,' Chapter Two of *Word and Object*," in *Words and Objections*, Donald Davidson and Jaakko Hintikka, eds. Dordrecht: Reidel, 14–26.

Harman, Gilbert. 1979. "Meaning and theory," in *Essays on the Philosophy of W. V. Quine*, Robert Shahan and Chris Swoyer, eds. Norman: University of Oklahoma Press, 9–20.

Quine, Willard. 1960. *Word and Object*. Cambridge, Mass.: MIT Press.

Quine, Willard. 1966a. "Posits and reality," in his *The Ways of Paradox and Other Essays*. New York: Random House, 233–241.

Quine, Willard. 1966b. "The scope and language of science," in his *The Ways of Paradox and Other Essays*. New York: Random House, 215–232.

Quine, Willard. 1969a. "Epistemology naturalized," in his *Ontological Relativity and Other Essays*. New York: Columbia University Press, 69–90.

Quine, Willard. 1969b. "Existence and quantification," in his *Ontological Relativity and Other Essays*. New York: Columbia University Press, 91–113.

Quine, Willard. 1969c. "Natural kinds," in his *Ontological Relativity and Other Essays*. New York: Columbia University Press, 114–138.

Quine, Willard. 1969d. "Reply to Chomsky," in *Words and Objections*, Donald Davidson and Jaakko Hintikka, eds. Dordrecht: Reidel, 302–311.

Quine, Willard. 1969e. "Speaking of objects," in his *Ontological Relativity and Other Essays*. New York: Columbia University Press.

Quine, Willard. 1970. "On the reasons for indeterminacy of translation." *Journal of Philosophy* 67: 178–183.

Quine, Willard. 1974a. "First general discussion session." *Synthese* 27: 481–508.

Quine, Willard. 1974b. "On Popper's negative methodology," in *The Philosophy of Karl Popper*, P. A. Schilpp. ed. La Salle, Ill.: Open Court, 218–220.

Quine, Willard. 1981. "Reply to Chihara." *Midwest Studies in Philosophy* 6: 453–454.

Quine, Willard, and J. S. Ullian. 1970. *The Web of Belief*. New York: Random House.

Justifying Symbolizations

Harold Levin

Logic, I tell my students, is the study of reasoning. To offer this approximation of the truth causes me no pang of conscience (perhaps, because scores of repetitions have elevated my threshold of pang). Logic, I continue, is also distinguished in containing the oldest, best-developed, most stable, and most widely accepted philosophical theory. Glib introductions of possible situations, which I represent at one moment as total universes and at other moments as spatiotemporally compact portions of our own histories, and of statements, which I represent as sentences having truth values in all possible situations, bring no blush to my cheeks. Presentation of the definition of entailment as preservation of truth across all possible situations, followed by disclosure of the resulting validity of all arguments with inconsistent premise sets or with necessary conclusions, still provides me the puckish glee of a conjurer materializing coins from an incredulous subject's ear. In short, I am content to explain what I am about in my introductory logic classes along familiar lines, simplifying and suppressing details and disputes as is pedagogically appropriate in that setting. For the most part, regarding the ideology of elementary logic, I share the grace of the philistine, enjoy dreamless sleep and robust digestion.

But early in each journey through my logic course there is a place of dread in which my voice is a bit too loud, my self-confidence shades into bluster, and my pace quickens with anxiety. So I hold my head erect, whistle a happy tune, and tell one of a variety of unsatisfying stories about why we symbolize "if-then" sentences as material conditionals. I have come to believe that detailing the sources of my unease in this matter will be more than a supererogatory act of autobiography. I think that we ought to be more troubled than we are by the difficulty of giving a coherent and plausible account of symbolization that accords with our practice both in and out of logic class and also supports the claim that logic is (inter alia) the study of reasoning. I have chosen modest aims in the hope of substantial success rather than pursue more substantial aims with modest success. Accordingly, in this paper I explain what obstacles lie in the way of a satisfying account of our common symbolization practice and what wider

significance these obstacles have for the philosophy of language; I then
suggest some paths through the tangled undergrowth.

I

The standard view of our symbolization practice in elementary logic is this:
What we call symbolization is description—description by means of a
simple, computationally convenient notation for logically significant structural features of sentences. We devote our attention to the sentential logic
(SL) of truth functions. Within SL, symbolization is description of the
truth-functional structure of the symbolized sentence by means of an SL
statement form. More precisely:

> An SL symbolization of a sentence S is a sequence of pairs, (S, s),
> $(S_1, p_1), \ldots, (S_n, p_n)$, where s is an SL statement form, the p_i are distinct
> atomic SL statement forms (SL statement letters) for $1 \leqslant i \leqslant n$, the
> atoms of s are included within the set of p_i, and $S_1, \ldots, S_n$ are sen-
> tences.

Given a symbolization of a sentence S, we say that

> the statement form s paired with S notates S (or is a notation for S).

We also call the association of statement letters with sentences, the (S_i, p_i),
the *key to the symbolization*.

> A symbolization is *accurate* if the relationship in truth value between
> the sentences $S_1, \ldots, S_n$ and S in all possible situations is the truth
> function determined by $p_1, \ldots, p_n$ and s in the obvious way.

There will be many accurate symbolizations of any sentence, including the
uninformative

$(S, p), (S, p),$

for any sentence letter p. Also among the accurate symbolizations are
irrelevantly complex symbolizations, such as

$(S, s \wedge (t \vee \neg t)), (S_1, p_1), \ldots, (S_n, p_n),$

where

$(S, s), (S_1, p_1), \ldots, (S_n, p_n)$

is an accurate symbolization of S and t is any SL statement form with atoms
included in the p_i. We write

$\mathrm{acc}(S, s)$

to indicate that there is an accurate symbolization of S by s.

If acc(S, s) and acc(T, t) and if S entails T, we say that the *symbolizations capture the entailment* if s SL-entails t. In other words, symbolizations of T and S capture the entailment of T by S if every assignment of truth value to the sentence letters in the symbolization of S, s that makes s true also makes the symbolization of T, t true. Symbolizations may be accurate and fail to capture all but the most trivial entailments; symbolizations may capture all entailments and be grossly inaccurate. We call a symbolization that captures enough entailments to serve the purpose to which it is put an *informative symbolization* (for the intended purpose). For the purposes to which we put symbolization in applications of logic, such as the detection and verification of inconsistency and validity, we aim for symbolizations that are both accurate and suitably informative. Accuracy and informativeness play a role with respect to symbolization similar to the role played by soundness and completeness with respect to inference rules. Either one alone is no guarantee of usefulness, but the combination of the two properties makes for an interesting and useful result. By the way, the property of relevance of a symbolization alluded to earlier (absence of irrelevant complexity, not to be confused with "Pittsburgh" relevance), is easy to enforce, although not important for the usefulness of symbolizations. Use of a suitably chosen normal form, such as perfect disjunctive normal form, can lead to symbolizations that lack major irrelevance.

The discussion so far has concerned the products of symbolization but not the process. On the standard view, accurate, informative, relevant symbolization can be obtained for the most part by analyzing the structure of the sentences to be symbolized. In many cases there are syntactically real constituents combined by compound-sentence-forming constructions in ways that directly mimic the formation of a compound SL statement form from atoms and truth functions. For instance, the sentence

Jack went up the hill, but Jill didn't

can be formed from the constituents "Jack went up the hill" and "Jill went up the hill" by a negation construction applied to the latter constituent followed by a conjunction construction applied to a pair of sentences. This structural analysis is reflected in the natural symbolization

(Jack went up the hill, but Jill didn't, $p \land \neg q$),

(Jack went up the hill, p), (Jill went up the hill, q).

There are other, equally accurate, equally informative symbolizations, such as the one that notates the sentence as $\neg(q \lor \neg p)$, that are not structurally derived. We use the abbreviation struct(S, s) for the subrelation of acc(S, s) that relates sentences to accurate, structurally derived notations.

The use to which symbolization is put in applying SL to the analysis of reasoning in English requires only that the relation acc hold between a sentence and its notation. Nonetheless, we usually restrict our symbolization practice so that the relation struct holds when possible. There are thus two ways of construing statement forms, such as $p \wedge \neg q$, as descriptions of sentences—a looser way corresponding to the practice of acc-symbolization and a tighter way corresponding to the practice of struct-symbolization. By the standards of acc-symbolization, $p \wedge \neg q$ describes any sentence with truth value suitably related to the truth values of two suitable "components." By the standards of struct-symbolization, $p \wedge \neg q$ describes a sentence formed by a conjunction construction from two constituents, the second of which is formed by a negation construction. A (binary) *conjunction construction* is any sentence-forming construction combining two component sentences so that the truth values of compound and components are related by the conjunction truth function in all possible situations. Part of the lore of struct-symbolization of English is the cataloguing of English conjunction constructions. In general, sentence-forming constructions manipulate their component sentences by addition, deletion, and rearrangement of phrases, words, and morphemes. The most frequently encountered constructions among logic symbolization exercises are either stilted but easy to describe or colloquial but difficult to define precisely. An easy-to-describe English negation construction fills in the blank of "It is not the case that————" with a sentence. A colloquial negation construction combines a contracted form of "not" with the main verb of a component sentence in ways that are much easier to speak than to speak about.

Another element of the lore of struct-symbolization of English is the cataloguing of grouping devices, which in English play the role played by parentheses within the notation of SL statement forms. "Jack went up the hill and Jill went up the hill" and "Jack and Jill went up the hill" are formed by two versions of the conjunction construction. The second version groups its components in such a fashion that no ambiguity of grouping arises when the sentence is embedded as a clause in a larger sentence, such as "Jack and Jill went up the hill unless Jill got ill." In this respect the second construction acts as if parentheses surround the resulting compound, whereas the first construction does not act this way. "Jack went up the hill and Jill went up the hill unless Jill got ill" is ambiguous as a result of indeterminate grouping.

Much of our symbolization practice can be explained in terms of acc-symbolization alone, without mention of struct-symbolization. We can explain the purpose of symbolization and conditions for success of symbolization in terms of acc-symbolization. But struct-symbolization is important when we wish to understand how we symbolize and how we can know (or have grounds for the belief) that we have produced an acc-symbolization.

Struct-symbolization is important in the epistemological investigation of our symbolization practice.

Struct-symbolization will not suffice, even for logic exercise examples. There are other more diffuse relationships that also underlie our symbolization practice. Explicit description of these paraphrastic devices for symbolization is no easy matter. Many of the manifold skills involved in understanding connected discourse are implicated. When I notate the sentences

> Either the president was asleep or his handler miscued him.
> Reagan wasn't asleep.
> So he was miscued

as

$p \lor q$,
$\neg p$,
q,

I am making use of knowledge of factual reference, anaphoric reference and ellipsis. What general strategies underly my symbolization of

> $S_1 =$ Either a hammer or a wrench will do the job

as

> $(S_1, p \land q)$, (A hammer will do the job, p), (A wrench will do the job, q)

and of

> $S_2 =$ Either Hammer or Wrench will do the job

as

> $(S_2, p \lor q)$, (Hammer will do the job, p), (Wrench will do the job, q)

or of

> $S_3 =$ McGonigal isn't drinking unless he got paid

as

> $(S_3, \neg p \lor q)$, (McGonigal is drinking, p), (McGonigal got paid, q)

and of

> $S_4 =$ McGonigal isn't drinking unless he is alone or with company

as

> (S_4, p), (McGonigal is drinking, p)

I do not know. I understand better what mechanisms underlie my symbolization of

S_5 = At least two of the three men developed rashes

as

$(S_5, (p \wedge q) \vee (p \wedge r) \vee (q \wedge r))$,
(The first man developed a rash, p),
(The second man developed a rash, q),
(The third man developed a rash, r),

but it seems that quite general "problem solving strategies" are involved rather than more narrowly linguistic facts. So even on the standard view of symbolization being described here, there is much that is mysterious about our symbolization practice when we depart, as we often do, from the domain of struct-symbolization.

Nonetheless the standard view of symbolization permits a simple and convincing account of the purpose and value of symbolization to be stated. The fundamental fact for explaining the point of symbolization is that accurate, informative (entailment capturing) symbolization is possible, indeed common. We extend the notion of (accurate) symbolization to sequences of sentences and SL statement forms as follows:

$(\langle S_1, \ldots, S_k \rangle, \langle s_1, \ldots, s_k \rangle)K$ is an (accurate) symbolization if K is a symbolization key and the sequence of symbolizations $(S_1, s_1)K, \ldots, (S_k, s_k)K$ are all (accurate) symbolizations.

Then, if $(\langle S_1, S_2 \rangle, \langle s_1, s_2 \rangle)K$ is an accurate symbolization of $\langle S_1, S_2 \rangle$ and if s_1 SL-entails s_2, then S_1 entails S_2. Of course, there are easy computations to determine SL-entailment (and to verify more demanding species of formal entailment). Accurate symbolization is the means by which we bring a well-developed, precise, and objective theory of formal entailment, such as SL-entailment, to bear on specific examples of reasoning formulated in English. The reliability of the results obtained by applying logical theory through symbolization depends critically on the ability to ensure or verify the accuracy of a proposed symbolization. From the perspective of a desire to mechanize the evaluation of reasoning, the step of symbolization is the hardest and the least well understood. Struct-symbolization presents the promise of a symbolization algorithm, but even within the domain of sentences that have accurate, informative SL symbolizations, we have only limited success in formulating symbolization algorithms. Thus application of SL is a handicraft rather than a science at present. In spite of the unsatisfactory state of the theory of symbolization of English within SL, the aim and justification of the practice are clear and cogent.

Accurate symbolization preserves nonentailment, not entailment. So if the statement forms *s* and *t* that notate the sentences *S* and *T*, respectively, lack the relation of nonentailment (that is, if *s* SL-entails *t*), then *S* entails *T*. Lack of SL-entailment between *s* and *t* is not diagnostic of lack of entailment between *S* and *T*. Our usual symbolization practice yields a partial (positive) test for entailment. A negative result, however, is not wholly without significance. Suppose that $p \vee q$ and q are notations for two sentences S_1 and S_2. $p \vee q$ does not SL-entail q. But we do know that the only counterexample to the entailment is the case in which p is true and q is not. The existence of a possible situation in which the sentence associated with p is true and the sentence associated with q is false may be more evident than the nonentailment of S_2 by S_1. For the current example the detailed information about counterexample-producing truth value assignments is not likely to improve on our intuitions of nonentailment. But in more complex cases, we may sometimes discover nonentailment in this way through our symbolization practice.

To summarize the standard view of symbolization: We symbolize as part of a technique to investigate the logical properties of particular statements, sets of statements and arguments—properties such as logical truth, inconsistency and validity. If a symbolization is accurate, the formal methods of logic can be used algorithmically to verify (in the case of SL, to decide) the presence of the logical properties of interest. There is an extensive class of sentences that can be accurately symbolized by straightforward techniques of structural symbolization. Structural symbolization is the principal symbolization technique and, when applied within its range of reliability, it produces accurate symbolization.

II

That is the standard view of our symbolization practice. It is not a bad view. It coherently and plausibly describes why we symbolize (the point of the practice), defines standards of correctness for symbolization ("accuracy"), and even attempts an account of how we are able to engage in the practice and meet the standards of correctness ("struct-symbolization"). In fact, if English were a better-behaved language, the standard view would be substantially correct (although not wholly complete). If we were even less ambitious in our applications of logic to verify the validity of arguments in English than we are, the standard view would suffice. For instance, if we were to limit ourselves to sentences involving as the only sentence-forming connective phrases, "It is not the case that," "and," and "or," then the standard view would be quite satisfactory. But, judging by the practice of logic textbook writers and of most of us who use symbolization as a step in proving or discovering the validity of a piece of reasoning, we also want to symbolize sentences containing "unless," "if-then," and "only if." Indeed, an informal survey of the exercises presented in logic texts concerning the application of SL to arguments in English shows that the vast majority of cases involve one or more instances of the connective phrases "unless," "if-then," and "only if." Although it is too strong to claim that barring these phrases from the realm of what can be accurately symbolized would make logic useless, nonetheless to so limit symbolization would be a radical departure from common, almost universal practice.

We commonly symbolize sentences of the form "if p, then q" as $p \rightarrow q$. In other words we treat "if-then" as an expression of the material-conditional truth functor, yielding False only when the first component is True and the second False and yielding True in all other cases. There is a substantial body of opinion and supporting argument in the literature favoring the view that "if-then" does not always (or ever) express a material conditional or any other truth functor. There is also, it should be mentioned, a body of opinion and supporting argument in the literature that favors the view that "if-then" usually (or at least often) expresses the material-conditional truth functor. It would be an interesting sociological study to survey the body of professional philosophers to determine how these views are distributed, and to see whether the view held in any way materially affects the teaching of elementary logic. Here I do not attack or defend either side in this controversy. Instead, my interest in this section is in mapping the connections among the standard view of our symbolization practice, that practice itself, views about the "if-then" construction, and the kinds of evidence and argument used to support these views. In the third and final section I consider what the state of the argument concerning the nature of "if-then" reveals about our understanding of fundamental issues in the theory of meaning for natural language.

The blank or puzzled looks on our students' faces are clear indications of the uncertain status of "if-then." It is easy to elicit the truth tables for "not" and "and" from a class, even from a class with no prior exposure to logic. But a truth table for "if-then" comes only with leading questions and carefully chosen explanations. Even then, the False-True case and the False-False case require extra sleight of hand. For example, I sometimes explain truth functors as "logical operations that make claims about the truth values of one or more of the component sentences of a compound sentence." Conjunctions are two-place truth functors that claim that both components are True, disjunctions are two-place truth functors that claim at least one component is True, and negations are one-place truth functors that claim that the sole component is False. Conditionals are two-place truth functors that make a sort of prediction about the truth values of the two components; namely, if the first component is True, then so is the second. To illustrate, I perform a simple demonstration, such as reaching into my pocket and removing a coin in my closed hand. I then make a prediction such as this: If this coin is a quarter, then it is heads up. With a little prodding I can get the class to agree that revealing a quarter that is heads up verifies my prediction; in that case my prediction came true. We also can agree that, when I reveal a quarter tails up, I have falsified my prediction; the prediction did not come true, or was false. When I retry the demonstration, revealing a penny in my hand, I can get most to admit that my prediction did not come out false. With a wave of the hand and a promise of useful consequences to follow, we agree to say that the prediction came true in this case also.

The verbal characterizations of conjunction, disjunction, and negation provide ways to remember the truth table for those constructions without tying them to the English phrases "and," "or," and "not." This is useful to encourage understanding conjunction, for instance, as an abstract, language-independent notion. On the other hand, the verbal formula offered to explain the conditional construction serves expressly to connect the conditional with "if-then." We would have been more honest, as well as more uniform, if we had used the formulation "it is not the case that my first component is True but my second component is not." But, using this honest characterization of the material conditional would have left the connection of conditional with "if-then" unilluminated. Defects in my favorite ways of explaining the material-conditional truth functor so that it is not entirely unmotivated to claim that "if-then" sentences express material conditionals constitute no serious argument against that claim. At best, noting the defects is ad hominem self-criticism. Nonetheless it is a fact transcending mere autobiography that there is substantially more difficulty in explaining the connection between the material conditional and our ordinary symbolization practice (which treats "if-then" as expressing material conditionals) in a way that fits in with a systematic account of the aims and standards of symbolization. Even the most unabashed proponents of the view that "if-then" is a material-conditional expression in English feel the need to present substantially more of a defense of that view than of similar views about "and," "or," and "not."

There are, of course, less peculiarly idiosyncratic difficulties for the treatment of "if-then" as a form of material conditional. It is difficult to see how to complete the following truth table:

	p	q	if p then q
1	T	T	
2	T	F	F
3	F	T	
4	F	F	

Let us take the case at line 2 for granted. Even the most unabashed proponent of a non-truth-functional "if-then" grants that much. Most text-book attempts to justify putting T in the remaining rows consider case 1 to be a relatively easy matter and lavish greater attention on cases 3 and 4, which are treated alike. In this respect my own account is exemplary. But none of the three cases—1, 3, or 4—is immune from what appear, at least superficially, to be clear counterexamples. To cite just one (my favorite): Consider the case in which p is "I am in Raleigh, North Carolina" and q is "I am in North Carolina" and in which (as is the case while I write these words) both p and q are true. It is natural to assert or assent to "If I am in Raleigh, North Carolina, then I am in North Carolina" and unusual, or even bizarre, to deny it. When both p and q are True, the material conditional $p \to q$ is True and so is the material conditional $q \to p$. Yet it is natural to deny or dissent from "If I am in North Carolina, then I am in Raleigh, North Carolina." I talk of asserting, denying, assenting, and dissenting here to avoid outright begging the question of truth value; after all, I promised no partisanship with respect to the truth functionality of "if-then." I must go a little out on a limb, though. I intend you to imagine hearing the two (converse) sentences with no knowledge of my whereabouts (or ignoring that knowledge). Whatever special features you may find present in the two sentences, whatever theory you may have exempting sentences with just such features from the class of "if-then" sentences to be treated as material conditionals, everyday use of English prepares us to assent to one and deny the other of the pair, despite knowledge that I am in Raleigh. Similar examples give rise to similar difficulties with case 4. And, in the same spirit, taking p first as "I am in Lizard Lick, North Carolina" and then as "I am in Cambridge, Massachusetts" and taking q as "I am in North Carolina" we cast doubt on the truth functionality of "if-then" in case 3 as well.

Although I will put off until later a general discussion of attempts to dispose of purported counterexamples to the truth functionality of "if-then," I want to forestall some complaints about my possible counterexample above. It was chosen with some care. First, the component sentences are meant to be fully specific and to have a determinate truth value. If you are tempted to hear generality with respect to time where none is intended (or expressed), use instead the variant "I am now in North Carolina" and make similar changes in the other sentences involved. Second, although I have encouraged you to dissociate your assessment of the truth value of the "if-then" sentences from your assessment of the truth values of the various components, this is not because I have an entailment view of "if-then" in mind. I identify Raleigh as Raleigh, North Carolina, because there are other cities with the same name. But the mention of the state in both antecedent and consequent is not at all necessary to the example. Any description of the cities will do just as well. Furthermore, although I do not intend to defend this view here, as an independent metaphysical thesis I believe that the statement expressed by "If I am in Raleigh, then I am in North Carolina" is a contingent truth; that is, I see no reason why the way in which state boundaries are drawn figures in the identity conditions for cities.

I have surely failed to establish that the standard account of our symbolization practice is mistaken. Nor have I established that "if-then" is always or usually non-truth-functional. What I have done so far in this section is establish a presumptive case against the view that "if-then" is truth functional. This presumption in turn casts some doubt on the standard account of our symbolization practice (or on the legitimacy of many cases of symbolization). We symbolize numerous "if-then" sentences. Furthermore, we symbolize them in a way that strongly suggests struct-symbolization. We identify an "if-then" sentence by obvious, superficial aspects of its structure and, for the most part, we symbolize uniformly all such sentences. But, according to the standard account of symbolization presented in section I, this requires that "if-then" express a truth function, namely, the material conditional. Yet that would appear not to be the case. If we are called on, for instance, to explain why the argument

> If I am in Raleigh, then I am in North Carolina
> I am not in North Carolina
> _____
> I am not in Raleigh

is valid, we would without hesitation appeal to the SL validity of the argument form

$$p \rightarrow q$$
$$\neg q$$
$$\overline{\neg p}$$

But the legitimacy of this appeal, when symbolization is justified by the standard account, is cast into doubt by a presumption against the truth functionality of "if-then." Logic as the abstract theory of validity or the abstract theory of truth-functional structure makes no empirical claims about sentences or phrases of English. But our usual practice in applying logic presupposes (or some such thing) that "if-then" is a truth function or that some story can be told that allows us to act as if it were. Anyone who writes a logic book or teaches a logic course is aware of this situation. There are several main styles of storytelling employed to try to rationalize what we teach our students to do when we teach them to symbolize. I now survey some of those stories.

The first story is this: The standard view of symbolization is correct. We can apply SL to arguments with "if-then" sentences nonetheless. How can this be? The troublesome observations cited (the presumptive counterexamples) serve to establish at most that there is a significant class of cases of "if-then" sentence that is not suited to our symbolization practice. But there is also a significant class of cases that is suited to our practice; it is only those statements that we can legitimately symbolize according to the standard view. The class of compliant "if-then" sentences can be variously picked out in several distinct variations of the story. On one view, subjunctive, modalized, and generalized "if-then" sentences are ruled unsuitable, whereas simple indicative "if-then" sentences are, for the most part, material conditionals. Unfortunately, as I trust the earlier discussion shows, presumptive counterexamples can be readily found in such simple, syntactically defined sets of "if-then" sentences.

Another variation of the first story claims that (some at least) "if-then" sentences have several "senses," one of which is a material-conditional "sense." The bare claim that there are several senses of "if-then" is a hollow one without details. It could be true in an uninteresting way if all that was claimed was the existence of a manufactured material-conditional use of "if-then" peculiar to logicians. However, there are several more convincing ways of supporting the claim that a material-conditional sense of "if-then" exists. Here is one of the better ones: There is a material-conditional sense of "if-then" that I call the mathematical sense. I take it for granted that mathematicians commonly use "if-then" as a two-place sentence construction, that "if-then" sentences are commonly used to formulate statements in the course of expressing mathematical propositions and in presenting proofs and definitions. For instance:

If T (a specific triangle) is equilateral, then T is equiangular.

I also take it for granted that the common mathematical uses of "if-then" are intended to and, indeed, generally believed to support the style of inference commonly called conditional proof. That is, whenever an argument of the form

p_1
$\vdots$
p_n
$$\frac{p}{q}$$

is valid, so is the argument of the form

p_1
$\vdots$
p_n

if p, then q.

This single fact about the behavior of "if-then" as used by mathematicians has the consequence that "if p, then q" has the truth table of the material conditional, for

$$p \rightarrow q$$
$$\underline{p}$$
$$q$$

is certainly valid. Thus, by the conditional proof principle cited:

$$\frac{p \rightarrow q}{\text{if } p, \text{ then } q}$$

is also valid. Because it is universally held that

$$\frac{\text{if } p, \text{ then } q}{p \rightarrow q}$$

is valid, we have the result that the mathematical sense of "if p, then q" and of "$p \rightarrow q$" are logically equivalent. A similar, although interestingly different, account establishes a nontrivial computational sense of "if-then" that also has the truth table of the material conditional.

Now we can wrap up a coherent account of a significant portion of our symbolization practice and application of SL based on the standard view. SL is a tool well suited to formalizing (some of) the logical structure of mathematical discourse and reasoning. Our account explains the success of our practice with respect to the aims of that practice. The only fault of this account of how logic can be applied to sentences containing "if-then" is the narrowness of the range of applications certified by the account. Indeed, if logic textbook authors took this account seriously, they would need to alter their books seriously or include strong disclaimers. I know of no introductory logic text that limits its symbolization examples or exercises involving "if-then" to mathematical English. So either the examples and exercises would need to be redone or some excusing or justifying remarks would need to be made. For instance, the exercises might be described as exercises in discovering and describing structure that (unrealistically) ignore the possibility of several senses of "if-then" by treating all cases as expressing the material conditional. It might be further explained that this treatment is justified for mathematical discourse but questionable for ordinary discourse with obvious consequences for the reliability of the results obtained. Although this modest approach is defensible, it has two adverse side effects. First, it leaves us without a rationale for applying SL to arguments in ordinary or even philosophical language unless we can establish that the uses of "if-then" involved are material-conditional-expressing ones. Second, the (plausible) background of the account involves claims about senses of "if-then" and mathematical senses distinct from ordinary senses. Although it is natural to talk this way, there are serious difficulties with the conceptual scheme underlying such talk and with its application to the case of "if-then." More of this in part III.

The third variation of the story under consideration—that only some "if-then" statements cannot be accurately symbolized in SL—is the most radical. It attacks the presumptive counterexamples head on; they are not true counterexamples. The basic strategy is to explain our admittedly strong urges to assent and dissent from the statements involved in the putative counterexamples to the truth functionality of "if-then" as something other than a response to the truth values of the statements. A notion of acceptability or assertion condition is formulated, and it is argued that, although the "if-then" statements in question have the same truth value as the corresponding material conditionals, the various "if-then" statements differ in acceptability or assertability. Such accounts bear a heavy burden of theory and evidence. I postpone further discussion until part III.

The three variations of a story to justify our symbolization practice considered so far have all accepted the standard view of that practice, namely, that in symbolization we aim to describe accurately the logically significant structure of statements. Another line of justification for our symbolization practice considers modifications to the standard view. One modification is that we can apply techniques of a theory of logical form by symbolizing not the statements of interest themselves but other statements bearing suitable logical relations to the originals: For instance, one aspect of paraphrase, which plays an important role in supplementing struct-symbolization, is finding logically equivalent statements with more regular structure than the statement originally presented. In many cases, however, logical equivalence is not necessary, and a weaker connection, such as entailment, will suffice to explain the reliability of our practice. For instance, whenever p entails q and q is one premise of a valid argument, then the argument obtained by replacing (the premise occurrence of)q by p is also valid. So we can apply SL to determine the validity of

> If I am in Raleigh, then I am in North Carolina
> I am not in North Carolina
> _____
> I am not in Raleigh

by using SL to determine the validity of

> I am in Raleigh $\rightarrow$ I am in North Carolina
> I am not in North Carolina
> _____
> I am not in Raleigh

because by all accounts "If I am in Raleigh, then I am in North Carolina" entails "I am in Raleigh $\rightarrow$ I am in North Carolina." We have applied the general strategy with p as an "if-then" statement and q as the corresponding " $\rightarrow$ " statement.

This justification of our symbolization practice—call it the entailment view—shares with the earlier-mentioned three accounts the consequence of limiting the class of cases to which it is justifiable to apply SL. However, the boundaries of the class are drawn in a different way. In the current instance there is the following limitation: "If-then" statements having positive occurrence in one of the premises or negative occurrence in the conclusion of an argument may be symbolized as a material conditional. So, for example, arguments corresponding to the following SL forms are within the range of SL:

$$
\begin{array}{cccc}
p \rightarrow q & p & p \rightarrow q & p \rightarrow q \\
\neg q & \neg q & q \rightarrow r & p \rightarrow \neg q \\
\hline
\neg p & \neg(p \rightarrow q) & p & \neg p \\
& & \hline
& & r &
\end{array}
$$

whereas argument corresponding to the following SL forms are not within the range of SL:

$$
\begin{array}{cccc}
p \rightarrow q & p \rightarrow q & p \rightarrow q & \neg(p \rightarrow q) \\
\hline
\neg q \rightarrow \neg p & q \rightarrow r & q \rightarrow r & q \\
& \hline & \hline & \\
& p \rightarrow r & (p \vee q) \rightarrow r &
\end{array}
$$

The class of justifiable applications of SL, according to the current account, is too narrow to explain our actual symbolization practice. It excludes argument forms that are clearly acceptable in mathematical contexts. The class of acceptable arguments is a lower limit that must be agreeable to anyone who does not deny that "if-then" entails a material conditional. A hybrid view that says that all mathematical "if-thens" can be symbolized as material conditionals and follows the current policy in nonmathematical cases gives reasonably broad coverage that can be justified in a straightforward way. A theory of logical form applicable to such a combined class of cases would be worthy of study. But our symbolization practice, both in and out of logic classrooms, exceeds these bounds. We set problems for our students and have no hesitation ourselves in applying SL to problems such as

> If Molly is happy, then Leopold is happy
> If Leopold is happy, then Stephen is happy
> _____
> If Molly is happy, then Stephen is happy.

This argument is not "mathematical," and the conclusion has a positive occurrence of "if-then." So the argument is not a suitable candidate for analysis by SL under even the broad, hybrid interpretation of the entailment line of justification.

Let us now consider briefly another line of justification of our symbolization practice that shares with the entailment line the general feature of questioning the standard view of our practice. More particularly, the line of justification to be discussed now rejects some of the underlying linguistic theory presupposed in the standard view. In brief, the presupposed linguistic theory of the standard view is (1) that logical properties such as validity of arguments are to be accounted for by facts about the distribution of truth values of statements across possible situations, (2) that the sentences involved in an argument express statements, and (3) that each statement has a truth value in each possible situation. The apparent non-truth-functional behavior of "if-then" sentences can be attributed to their failure to express (assert) statements in the way required by the presupposed linguistic theory of the standard view. For instance, "if-then" sentences might perform conditional assertions rather than assertions of conditional statements. There are other variations on the theme that "if-then" sentences do not express statements—for instance, that "if-then" sentences supply warrants for inference. These views have two major difficulties. The first difficulty is in providing an alternative to the standard view as part of a justification of our symbolization practice. The second difficulty is in accounting for the substantial portion of our practice that lies beyond the scope of theories of the kind in question. For example, on conditional assertion views of "if-then" sentences, it is difficult to explain the possibility of iterated "if-thens" such as

If the glass breaks if I drop it, then it is fragile.

or

If Molly is happy, then Leopold is content if Stephen is miserable.

Negated "if-thens" also present difficulties for nonassertional accounts.

The alternatives to the standard view just considered (that symbolization of "if-then" by material conditional is often acceptable because the material conditional is entailed by the "if-then," or that "if-then" sentences do not assert conditionals at all but provide information suitable for use as premises of arguments in other ways) are neutral with respect to the issues of whether our customary symbolization practice is unjustifiable or even flat out mistaken, and if mistaken, how radically we must limit our application of SL in order to be on safe ground. The most radical (and final) story about the justification of our symbolization practice to be considered here is that, except for isolated havens such as mathematical reasoning, our ordinary use of "if-then" sentences is not generally subject to justified logical analysis in the manner of our usual practice. We exceed the bounds of systematic justification when we symbolize "if-then" as a material conditional. Sometimes the results of symbolization will yield correct answers, sometimes incorrect answers, but the answers will be (outside the special cases such as mathematics) unjustifiable by any version of the standard view, although there may well be theories of logical form other than SL that can contribute to a justification along the lines of the standard view. Such a radical view not only deals a crippling blow to our habitual symbolization practice but also leaves us without an account of how we tell the good arguments from the bad ones. We may also wonder why SL seems to work as well as it does or why logicians pretend that SL works in spite of appearances to the contrary.

Consider a popular radical theory of "if-then," that "if p, then q" asserts something along these lines: In the world closest to the actual world in which p is true, q is also true. This theory provides an alternative account of the semantics of "if-then" sentences that agrees with many of the presumptive counterexamples cited earlier. Proponents of this sort of theory explain that our usual symbolization practice is often acceptable when properly construed. Strictly, the inferences cited are not valid but, in most cases to which we apply the inferences, there are additional, uncited premises that are both true and sufficient to produce valid inferences even on the preferred semantics for "if-then." For example, the story goes:

if p, then q
if q, then r
———————
if p, then r

is not, strictly, a valid form of argument. But in most cases in which the premises are true, so is an additional premise:

if p and q, then r,

which, when added to the original premises, produces a valid argument to the conclusion.

There are two sorts of difficulty with the account just sketched that are worth noting here. First, our original data concerning "if-then" sentences includes presumptive counterexamples to this particular non-truth-functional semantics for "if-then" as well as to the material-conditional semantics and other views discussed. In particular, the present view agrees with the material-conditional view in both the cases in which the antecedent is true. That is, on the current view, whenever the first component of an "if-then" statement is true, the whole statement has the same truth value as its second component. Thus the sentences

> If I am in Raleigh, then I am in North Carolina
> If I am in North Carolina, then I am in Raleigh

provide as much of a counterexample to the current non-truth-functional view as they do to the previously discussed material-conditional view. So we must either explain away the presumptive counterexamples or specify a limited range of applicability for the view by defining subclasses of the "if-then" sentences. Second, we must make plausible the claim that our customary practice of counting as valid certain arguments that appear to be invalid on the current view is due to suppressed or unnoticed additional premises. This can be a delicate matter. For instance, I might agree that for some specific argument of the form

> if p, then q
> if q, then r
> ───────────
> if p, then r,

which I consider valid, the statement

> if p and q, then r

can be added as an additional premise. My reason may be not that I think that the additional premise just happens to be true but rather that I think the additional premise is entailed by the two original premises. I might even go on to claim that (in this case at least) the "if-thens" involved are material conditionals, citing the validity of the argument as my evidence.

It is time to take stock. We have considered a variety of stories for reconciling the standard view of our symbolization practice (or modifications of the standard view) with some of the uncooperative facts about that practice. Some of the stories say that things are not as our linguistic intuitions seem to tell us. Some of the stories say that we must sort out the compliant "if-thens" from the uncompliant ones and that the standard view can be used only to justify symbolization of compliant "if-thens." In order for these stories to be more than stories, to be supported by evidence, we need to be much more precise about the structure of linguistic theory, the relation between linguistic and logical theories, and the ways in which theory-laden claims about linguistic and logical properties of sentences can be supported by linguistic and logical data. These matters are discussed in the next section.

The questions of how and to what extent we can justify our actual symbolization practice within the standard view of that practice have been left unresolved here. My current inclination, as far as teaching elementary logic is concerned, is to find a position that (1) can be simply and briefly stated, (2) maximizes the justified scope of symbolization practice, and (3) minimizes the number of false or counterintuitive claims made in defending or applying the view. I favor a hybrid of the material-conditional mathematical "if-then," the entailment strategy for nonmathematical "if-thens," and warnings about possible incorrect results in all other cases. This will do for a standard logic class. However, it is not the whole truth of the matter and certainly is inadequate as a principled justification of the "if-then" portion of our symbolization practice.

III

In this section I discuss some of the ways in which explaining and justifying our symbolization practice involves substantive, complex, and unresolved issues of linguistic theory and the relationship between linguistic theory and logical theory. In the previous two sections I presented the standard view of the justification of our symbolization practice within SL and enumerated difficulties for the standard view involving apparent flaws in the practice of symbolizing "if-then" sentences as material conditionals. As a result of concentrating on the acutely troublesome "if-then" construction, it may seem that difficulties with the standard view of symbolization are limited to that construction, which is important but not strictly essential to reasoning. However, justifying our treatment of "if-then" is only the most acutely troublesome aspect of justifying our symbolization practice. Other aspects, usually taken for granted or dealt with perfunctorily, also involve substantive issues of linguistic theory.

    Molly is not happy

is certainly a negation of

    Molly is happy.

Yet

    Someone is not happy

is not a negation of

    Someone is happy.

Why do we call the former use of "not" a case of negation and the latter not a case of negation? In the former case the two statements have opposite truth values, whereas in the latter case the two statements may both be true. Why don't we take this data as evidence for the view that "not" at least sometimes expresses a non-truth-functional sentence operator? No one publishes notes in *Analysis* citing such examples as counterexamples to the double negation inference pattern.

Someone is happy
_____
It is not the case that someone is not happy

is surely an invalid argument. Why is that fact not worrisome? Fundamental beliefs about linguistic theory and logical theory seem to underly our interpretation of the data. We believe that sentences have structure, that sentence meaning depends on sentence structure, that truth conditions depend on sentence meaning, and that logical properties, such as entailment, are to be explained in terms of truth conditions. Now it is certainly possible to claim that an argument is valid or invalid and that sentences have certain truth conditions without claiming anything about the meaning or the structure of the sentences. But an account of how we know about an entailment or about truth conditions (*how* we know, not *what* we know) and of why we interpret data in certain ways will incorporate claims about meaning and sentence structure.

There are two notions of sentence structure that ought not be conflated. Concrete structure ("concatenation structure") analyzes a phrase into consecutive constituent phrases. We can represent such structure by use of parentheses. For example:

(Molly ((is not) happy)).

If desired, we can also label the bracketing by phrase categories, such as S, NP, and VP. Abstract structure also analyzes phrases into subphrases but does not require that the subphrases combine only by concatenation to form the phrase. Details of word order and spelling (word formation) are left unspecified. When we describe formal languages, we usually give concrete structures. Most structural descriptions of natural language involve abstract structures. There are two motives for abstraction in describing sentence structure for natural languages. One motive is the syntactic complexity of natural language and the search for generalizations across all human languages or within language families. It is an open question exactly how much abstraction is required for a purely syntactic description of English, for instance; it appears that substantial abstraction is needed to meet reasonable goals of syntactic description. A second, quite distinct motive for abstraction in description of sentence structure is the desire to provide the basis for an account of sentence and phrase meaning in terms of word meaning and phrase structure. An abstract structure (description) for one of the sentences given might be

NEG(Molly is happy).

The symbol NEG can have a syntactic and a semantic interpretation. When interpreted as an element of syntactic structure, NEG is an operation that places the word "not" in the proper place (and makes other adjustments to the main verb). When interpreted as an element of semantic structure, NEG is the familiar negation truth functor. In this case syntactic and semantic structure are straightforwardly related and compatible.

We may easily imagine that the syntactic interpretation of NEG mentioned is such that

NEG(Someone is happy)

is an abstract syntactic structure for

Someone is not happy.

At any rate, it is a nontrivial, nonobvious claim that such a syntactic NEG operation is impossible or mistaken in some way. It is not even true that such a syntactic NEG is incompatible with a semantic interpretation of NEG. What is true is that a semantic interpretation of NEG cannot be a truth function in the current instance ("Someone is not happy"). Semantics does countenance non-truth-functional operators, but it is hard to imagine what the operator could be in this case. Of course, there is a familiar alternative account of the structure of the last sentence (SOMEQ is an existential quantifier):

SOMEQ(NEG(is happy)),

in which syntactic and semantic versions of the familiar operations of existential quantification and negation occur.

I have just sketched two accounts of the form (syntactic and semantic) of "Someone is not happy." Regardless of these or any other accounts of the linguistic form of that sentence,

(Someone is not happy, $\neg p$), (Someone is happy, p)

is not an accurate symbolization. We know that the symbolization is not accurate because we know that the truth values of the two sentences are not suitably related. For the purposes of these investigations, our knowledge about the relationship of the truth values of the two sentences is taken as a datum. I do not imagine (in this instance) that any investigation of syntax or semantics will change our beliefs in this regard. We do not (consciously) use a theory of structure to aid us in symbolization of the two example sentences. However, if we inquire how we know that in one instance $\neg p$ is (the notation of) an accurate symbolization whereas in the other instance it is not, theories of structure will figure prominently in the answer. There are at least two construals of the question, How do we know that S is an accurate symbolization? The first construal takes the question to be a request for justification, for reasons or evidence that support the knowledge claim. There are epistemological views that hold that some knowledge claims need or are capable of no justification in this sense. It seems wildly implausible that knowledge of an accurate SL symbolization for a statement should be either self-justificatory or incapable of justification. If justification is to be sought, claims about the syntactic and semantic structure of the sentences expressing the statement are good candidates. A second construal takes the question to be a request for a method (algorithm or procedure) for symbolizing, either the method used by a particular symbolizer or a method that produces accurate symbolization. Again, claims about linguistic structure will likely be elements of a satisfactory answer.

A successful representation of the logical form of a statement is a summary of a class of entailment relations in which the statement figures. There are many schemes of representation of logical form, including such notations as Venn diagrams, which encode logical information in ways that reflect nothing of the syntactic structure and little of the semantic structure of the original statement. Although Venn diagrams do not represent syntactic and semantic structure directly, knowledge of syntactic and semantic structure seems to be the only candidate to explain systematically how we determine which Venn diagram to use to represent the logical form of a particular statement. So, even if we acknowledge that notations for logical form are not (necessarily) notations for syntactic or semantic structure (even if we correctly characterize acc-symbolization), we do not thereby commit ourselves to the claim that there is no connection between theories of logical form and theories of syntactic and semantic structure. Nonetheless, the connection between logical form and linguistic form can be indirect and subtle.

Let us take for granted the traditional view of the logical form of such sentences as

Molly is not happy

and

Someone is not happy

as represented earlier, namely

NEG(Molly is happy)

and

SOMEQ(NEG(is happy)).

These representations of logical form (informally presented) correctly capture some of the entailment relations of their respective statements. On the face of it, NEG appears to be a logical operation that operates on a statement to produce a statement and also to be a logical operation that operates on a one-place predicate to produce a statement. According to the traditional view of the connection between logical form and linguistic structure, the dual role of the logical operation NEG corresponds to a dual meaning for the negation-expressing word "not." That is, on the traditional view, "not" is ambiguous (although the meanings are systematically related, to be sure). I do not undertake reconstructing the line of reasoning that I have been calling "the traditional view" because it is complex and because I do not endorse its conclusion that "not" is ambiguous. There are several strategies for avoiding the conclusion that "not" is ambiguous. One, due in modern form to Montague, treats proper names (and singular terms generally) on a par with quantifiers. Thus

Molly is not happy

has the logical structure (MOLLYQ is a singular quantifier)

MOLLYQ(NEG(is happy)).

NEG can then be taken as an operator on one-place predicates in both cases. However, when we consider the statements

Everyone is not happy

and

Not everyone is happy

the appearance of ambiguity of "not" resurfaces, because in the latter sentence NEG applies to a sentence rather than to a one-place predicate. However, it is possible to salvage a univocal "not" by allowing the logical operator expressed (the negation truth functor) to combine with a truth value in one way and with a predicate in a second way. Negation combines with a truth value as a function applied to an argument. Negation combines with a predicate as a function composed with a second function. There are persuasive reasons to support the use of multiple modes of semantic combination far exceeding the present ad hoc treatment of negation. For the purposes of this paper, the upshot of these remarks is that the traditional view of the logical form of sentences involving "not" is only loosely connected with a detailed semantics for "not." In particular, the standard account of the logical form of sentences involving "not" neither requires nor excludes sentence negation distinct from predicate negation. The traditional view of the logical form of sentences involving "not" constrains the syntax and semantics, but the constraints are indirect. The whole system of structures must cohere. However, neither the logical form, the syntactic structure, nor the semantic structure by itself dictates the details of the other two aspects of structure.

To reinforce the claim of looseness in the coupling of logical form to syntactic structure, consider again the case of negation using "not." In the account sketched we suggested that in logical structure the negation operator, NEG, could be univocally a sentence operator. Does our general view about the connections between syntactic structure, semantic structure, and logical structure then require that "not" also be syntactically a sentence operator? If logical form and syntactic structure are not required to be identical, then it is not clear exactly what it means to say that "not" is syntactically a sentence operator. A related and more well-defined question concerns the constituent membership of "not" in sentences. In particular, we can ask whether "not" is a member only of the sentence constituent of

> Someone is not happy

or of a smaller constituent, such as the verb phrase constituent. That is, we can ask whether the syntactic structure of the sentence looks like

> (not(someone is happy))

or

> (someone(not(is happy)))

or some other alternative.

The view about the logical form of the sentence "Someone is not happy" does not demand one or the other of the given syntactic structures, not even supposing (as I do) that the syntactic structure is the basis for semantic interpretation, which determines the logical form. The two sample syntactic structures given are obviously not concrete structures because they get the word order wrong. If we take

> (not(someone is happy))

as an abstract structure in which "not" is a sentence constituent but not a verb phrase constituent, it is still open whether or not the concrete word order corresponding to that structure has "not" occurring between "is" and "happy." Although such a proposal may seem outlandish in this case, it seems quite natural in the case of

> (not(Molly is happy)).

The reason why proposing "not" to be syntactically a sentential constituent in "someone is not happy" seems outlandish is that we then have the scopes of "someone" and "not" in reverse order from the scopes of the corresponding elements of logical form, SOMEQ and NEG. That is, the outlandish proposal seems outlandish because the scope appears to reverse in passing from syntactic to logical structures. On our schematic account of the relation between syntactic, semantic, and logical structure, it would seem that scope relations among operations appearing in logical form are the result of scope relations present in semantic structure. It is certainly natural to suppose that scope relations among operator meanings in semantic structure are a reflection of congruent scope relations among operator expressions within syntactic structure. So we would expect a syntactic structure in which "not" contains within its scope "some" to correspond to a logical form with the scope of negation surrounding the scope of existential quantification. That is, we would expect that the syntactic structure

not(someone(is happy))

to correspond to the logical form

NEG(SOMEQ(is happy))

but not to the form

SOMEQ(NEG(is happy))

under discussion.

Our expectation in this regard may be natural but need not be met. Syntactic scope—constituent membership—need not correspond directly to semantic scope. For instance, in the sentence

Everyone here knows someone here

the "scope" relations of the quantifier-expressing phrases "everyone here" and "someone here" are either nonoverlapping, as in

((everyone here)(knows(someone here))),

or, possibly, nested so that "someone" is within the scope of everyone" (if subject noun phrases are quantifierlike operators that operate on predicates expressed by verb phrases). Many people consider the sentence to be ambiguous in a way that depends on variant semantic scoping of two quantifier operators. It is not obvious that such variation in scope must be inherited from congruent variation in syntactic structure. It is at least possible that the step from syntax to semantic interpretation involves adding operator scope information, which is not present in the syntactic structure. Of course, in the original sentence,

Someone is not happy

we do not find such ambiguity. So we expect the syntactic and semantic scope relations to agree. This is natural enough, but even if we never consider it necessary to defend the view, it is a substantive constraint on the relation between syntactic and semantic structure.

So far the moral to be drawn from the present example is cautionary. There are at least several distinct notions of sentence structure that are related in ill-understood ways. There is no easy inference from properties of one sort of structure to properties of another sort of structure, even assuming that semantics interprets syntax and determines logical form. To the extent that the data of our experience with sentences, sentence meanings, and sentence entailment relations provide information about structure, it is a subtle matter to determine the relevant notion of structure. Several positions about the relation between the data (our intuitions about structure, truth conditions, and entailment relations) and claims about logical form suggest themselves:

1. Logical form is directly evident in the data—it is itself the subject of intuition.

2. Logical form is implied by the directly evident data about sentence structure.

3. The semantics of "not," for instance, as the sentential negation truth functor is directly present to intuition.

4. The traditional view of the logical form of a sentence is (indirectly) supported by general systematic considerations, but is not directly present in the data.

A serious account of the sources of our knowledge of logical form will need to investigate such views. Remember that I have let myself off the hook by announcing the "modest aim" of setting out reasons to be dissatisfied with our usual glib account of the justification for our symbolization practice.

Determining structure in some appropriate sense is not the only problem we face when we symbolize; nor is accounting for our knowledge of structure the only problem we face when we justify our symbolization practice. We must know the effect on logical form of the sentence connective "and" and distinguish it from the sentence connective "or." That is, we must attend to word meaning as well as to sentence structure. There is less agreement about meaning than there is about structure. But, when we restrict our attention to that aspect of the meaning of sentence connectives that determines entailment relations and further restrict our attention to truth functors such as conjunction and disjunction, we give the impression (at least in discussions of the elementary logic of truth functions) of having matters well in hand. I do not propose a radical critique of our customary symbolization practice, but I will again suggest that the justification we give for our practice is inadequate and that a satisfactory account is likely to be quite complicated.

Let us take it for granted that "or" and its variant "either/or" is a truth functor in English. It is generally accepted that "or" expresses disjunction. I limit my remarks at present to disjunction-expressing uses of "or," leaving open the issue of whether there are other uses as well. Let us also take for granted that, with respect to specifying the meaning of truth functors, our purposes require only that the truth table be given. What could be simpler?

Surely we need only write down the truth table for disjunction and be done. But which truth table should we write down? It is commonplace to describe two sorts of disjunction (often called "inclusive" and "exclusive") and commonplace to claim that "or" is ambiguous, having among its interpretations both sorts of disjunction. These observations suggest a small problem to be faced in symbolizing statements involving "or," namely, the choice of an interpretation for "or. This problem is neither theoretically deep nor practically difficult. Ambiguity is a fact of life to be accepted in dealing with natural languages. Symbolizing statements containing ambiguous words or phrases is, in most cases, a matter of ascertaining the intentions of the author of the statement when possible, interpreting the statements in such a way as to produce entailment or nonentailment as required by the conditions of an exercise, or, failing resolution of the ambiguity, noting the ambiguity and the results of the various univocal interpretations of the ambiguous material. So the commonplace view finds no great difficulty in the symbolization of "or," merely a minor complication.

What reason is there to support the claim that "or" is ambiguous? Reasons are seldom given for the claim. When reasons are given, they fall into one of three sorts. First, there clearly is a pair of related truth functions called inclusive disjunction and exclusive disjunction. Second, in some languages, such as Latin and Polish, there are univocal phrases expressing inclusive disjunction and exclusive disjunction that are commonly translated into English as "or." Third, when we encounter statements of the sort p or q, we often ask the author, "Do you mean p or q or both, or do you mean p or q but not both?" So there are two meanings we could mean by "or" sentences: We sometimes mean one and sometimes mean the other, and we can attribute the difference in sentence meaning to a difference in meaning of the sentence connective "or." The argument from the set of three observations to the conclusion that "or" is ambiguous is, of course, not a case of entailment. Rather, the conclusion is indirectly supported by the set of three observations. The ambiguity of "or" is compatible with the data and is part of a plausible account that explains or predicts the data by attributing the observed difference in sentence meaning to a difference in the meaning of "or."

Such an argument should make us confident in the ambiguity of "or" only to the extent that we are confident that there are no substantially different but at least as plausible alternative accounts of the data. To be sure, there are alternative accounts of the data. For instance, because any sentence containing "or" will also contain other words, ambiguity in the interpretation of the sentence could be attributed to ambiguity in one or more of those other words. This alternative to the ambiguity of "or" is not an attractive alternative; it is quite implausible. Even if we were considering merely one specific sentence involving "or," such as "Jack went up the hill or Jill went up the hill," attributing the multiplicity of meaning to a multiplicity of meaning for "Jack," "went," "up," "the," "hill," or "Jill" is unpromising, to say the least. Of course, we have accepted as data the wholesale ambiguity of sentences involving (in the proper way) "or," so that we would be required to attribute a simple, systematic pairing of sentence meanings to a pairing of meanings for some-word-or-other in all the "or" sentences. Thus, if we must attribute the ambiguity of "or" sentences to an ambiguity in one of the constituent words, the only and hence the most plausible candidate is "or" itself.

Ambiguous constituent words are not the only source of ambiguity in a phrase. A sentence may be ambiguous even though no word of it has more than one meaning. Multiple phrase structure is a source of multiple phrase meaning. There are sentences containing "or" that are ambiguous as a result of, multiple structure, for example, "Jack went up the hill and Jill went up the hill or Jill was ill." But this is a special example. Many "or" sentences cannot plausibly be taken to have structural ambiguity. In addition, the structural ambiguity of the present example does not explain the specific differences in meaning associated with inclusive and exclusive disjunction. In fact, on each of the two structurally disambiguated interpretations of the example sentence,

Either Jack and Jill went up the hill or Jill was ill

and

Jack went up the hill and either Jill went up the hill or was ill

there is an additional dimension of ambiguity that can be attributed to interpreting "or" first as an inclusive disjunction and then as an exclusive disjunction. Structural ambiguity does not explain the possibility of multiple interpretations of all sentences containing "or." Furthermore, multiplicity of structure produces ambiguity in the example by means of the familiar mechanism of variation in scope of logical operators, in this case conjunction and disjunction. But in sentences containing only "or" as a connective, there is no possible variation of scope. So the presumed ambiguity of sentences containing "or" is not plausibly of structural origin.

We have just considered two explanations of the ambiguity of "or" sentences alternative to the lexical ambiguity of "or" itself. Each alternative was substantially less plausible than the commonplace claim that "or" is ambiguous—which common claim will account for the data in question. Some such elimination of less plausible alternatives lies behind the common view, although the reasoning is not usually made so painfully explicit. After all, what else could explain the data in question? Up to this point we have been able to proceed with the workable but imprecise terminology of everyday nontechnical talk about meaning. Now we must be just a little bit more discriminating. I do not deny the original data on which this discussion of the ambiguity of "or" has been based, namely, that we are often in doubt whether someone who says

p or q

means

p or q or both

or

p or q but not both.

We have so far assumed that ambiguity and multiple meanings are the same phenomenon, that structural and lexical ambiguity are the only mechanisms producing sentences with multiple meanings. But this is not the case. Many linguistic devices other than lexical ambiguity and structural ambiguity produce sentences with multiple meanings: indexical and demonstrative elements, ellipsis, vagueness, and generality, for example.

The sentence

John did it

might mean that John ate the last bagel, or it might mean that John refused a MacArthur grant, although "did it" is not, strictly ambiguous and certainly does not number "ate the last bagel" or "refused a MacArthur grant" among its synonyms. Similar remarks apply to "John did" and "did." In order to talk a bit more precisely about these and related cases, let us use the term "meaning" for the context-independent, explicitly represented, intersubjective interpretation of a word or phrase. We reserve the term "information conveyed" for the context-dependent message that a speaker or writer intends to be represented by an instance of a word or phrase. Information conveyed may be highly idiosyncratic and may even include private codes. Meaning is what is expressed by a phrase to someone with textbook knowledge of grammar and vocabulary isolated from any influence of context. This distinction is crude but will serve the purpose to which it is put here. The data we have so far uncritically accepted concerning multiple interpretations for "or" sentences do not come with a clear and unmistakable label as data about meaning. They might just as well be data about information conveyed or about some intermediate aspect of interpretation. In the case of the sentence "John did it," "John ate the last bagel" does not have the same meaning but may in appropriate circumstances convey the same information.

Suppose that

Scylla ate the men or Charybdis drowned the men

is elliptical for one or the other of the following:

Scylla ate the men or Charybdis drowned the men or both.
Scylla ate the men or Charybdis drowned the men but not both.

This account explains the data of multiple interpretations of "or" sentences as a case of multiple interpretations conveyed but does so without attributing lexical ambiguity to "or." The ellipsis account is actually neutral about the meaning of "or"; it is compatible with both inclusive and exclusive disjunction.

Generality is another means by which multiple items of information can be conveyed by sentences having a single meaning if I am told

Someone said that you drink on the job.

I may inquire

Do you mean that goody-two-shoes Prudence or that rat fink Elmo?

If I am told

A varmint upended your garbage can.

I may inquire

Do you mean a raccoon or a possum or something else?

Of course, "someone" does not mean Prudence or Elmo, and "varmint" does not mean raccoon or possum. But sometimes, when a person makes a general claim, they also are in a position to make a more specific claim, and sometimes they even use the more general statement to convey the information expressed by the more specific statement. So I may say "someone" when I intend to convey information about a specific person. Asking for the specifics behind a general statement is similar to asking for the disambiguation of an ambiguous statement, although the range of answers in the former case is greater than in the latter case and the range of answers in the former case is not determined solely by linguistic considerations as it is in the latter case.

The same informal talk that supports the notion of two senses of "or" supports the notion of two sorts of disjunction and hence of a generic notion of disjunction that has as species inclusive and exclusive disjunction. That being the case, it is not absurd to consider that "or" has the generic sense of disjunction as its meaning. How do the accounts that explain the data of multiple interpretations of "or" sentences as cases of multiplicity of information conveyed differ with respect to logical theory from the original account that explained the data as a case of ambiguity? We consider here just the general disjunction account. First, on the general disjunction account there is no sense (meaning) of "or" on which

p or q

turns out false when both p and q are true. There is no sense of "animal" on which

My dog, Ingrid, is an animal

is false, even though cats and elephants are animals. Second, there is no sense of "or" on which an argument

p. Therefore p or q

is invalid nor on which

p or q. p. Therefore not q

is valid. So the alternative account of the data makes a substantial difference when it comes to attributing logical properties to arguments. Nonetheless, it would be misleading to suggest that adopting one rather than another of the accounts would make a noticeable difference in our symbolization practice. For example, we would likely notate the argument

Either that footprint was made by a raccoon or a possum
A possum made that footprint
_____

No raccoon made that footprint

as

p exclusive-disjunction q
q
_____

not p.

Our symbolization practice might not vary, but the explanation and justification of that practice would vary. On the ambiguity of "or" account, the symbolization would be a case of struct-symbolization. On the generality of "or" account, the symbolization would not be a case of struct-symbolization at all. Rather, it would be a case of symbolizing more than is present in the meaning of the original argument, strictly construed; the information conveyed is symbolized. In retrospect, struct-symbolization may play a much smaller role in our symbolization practice than the standard account given in part I suggested. There are many cases of sentences involving "and," "or," and "not" as well as "if-then," "only if," and "unless," which ought not be considered cases of struct-symbolization just because we lack alternative accounts. Justifying our symbolization practice is not an easy matter and will involve difficult and substantive issues of linguistic theory. The time has come to reexamine the symbolization of conditionals expressed using "if." The first problem we face is identifying instances of the "if" conditional kind. It is generally believed that there are various uses of "if," only some of which express conditionals. There also may be various kinds of conditionals. Distinguishing conditional from nonconditional "ifs" in a principled way is no trivial matter; difficult issues of structure and meaning confront us. For example, among the intuitively clearest cases of nonconditional "ifs" is the following:

I wonder if Alma is happy.

Setting aside for the moment epistemological scruples of the kind I have been expressing (concerning the difficulty of justifying intuitively evident claims about structure and meaning), I find that it is easy to sketch an approximate account of the use of "if" involved here in a way that clearly distinguishes that use from the conditional-expressing sentence connective use. The natural and intended interpretation of the sentence has "wonder" in the role of a transitive verb and "if Alma is happy" in the role of a complement of that verb. The complement clause can also be introduced by "whether," as in

I wonder whether Alma is happy.

without altering the meaning. So there is a structural and a lexical distinction between "if" in "I wonder if Alma is happy" and in standard conditional uses. I do not press this naive analysis of one use of "if." It is offered only to be suggestive of two points. First, an analysis of logical form, whatever it may say about conditionals in general, will not treat all "if" sentences as expressing conditionals. Thus the class of data against which a theory of the logical behavior and semantics of conditionals is to be tested can and should be limited in such a way that some "if" sentences are excluded. Second, the exclusion of "if" sentences from the data to be accounted for by a theory of conditionals must be based on a standard that does not trivialize the theory of conditionals. A standard that simply ruled out any "if" sentences that differed in entailments from the "genuine" conditionals as characterized by the theory would beg the question of the correctness of the theory in selecting the data by which to judge the theory. A non-question-begging standard for excluding some "if" sentences from the class of genuine conditionals might involve structural and lexical observations such as those already sketched. The observations concerning structure and lexical attributes are laden with linguistic theory. Regardless of the degree of obviousness of the claim that a specific "if" does not express a genuine conditional, the justification of such a claim will involve elaborate chains of evidence and theory.

The taxonomy of "ifs" encountered in discussions of the logic of conditionals is neither universal nor well justified. The commonly cited exceptional "ifs" fall into a number of kinds, which I enumerate and then discuss:

Coffee-table "ifs,"
Monkey's uncle "ifs,"
Generalized "ifs,"
Subjunctive "ifs."

Coffee-table "ifs" are those such as

There's coffee on the table, if you want some.

On most accounts coffee-table "ifs" are excluded from the class of genuine conditionals. What grounds are there for such a classification? Coffee-table sentences seem to have the same structure as genuine conditionals. The "if" joins clauses that are complete sentences. The clauses can be inverted:

If you want some, there's coffee on the table.

Some speakers, however, balk at inserting "then" between the clauses and judge

If you want some, then there's coffee on the table

to be odd or altered in meaning.

But the chief grounds for segregating coffee-table sentences are not syntactic or structural. Rather, coffee-table "ifs" are treated specially because they are supposed to bear entailment relations to sentences that do not bear those relations to genuine conditionals. If "there's coffee on the table, if you want some" entails a sentence that is not entailed by a genuine conditional with antecedent "you want some coffee" and consequent "there's coffee on the table," then it would certainly seem that "There's coffee on the table, if you want some" is not a genuine conditional. Let us take it for granted that "There's coffee on the table, if you want some" entails and is entailed by "There's coffee on the table." No genuine conditional entails its consequent, and some candidate genuine conditionals (the non-truth-functional ones) are not entailed by their consequents, or so the story goes. More precisely:

$$\frac{\text{if } p, \text{then } q}{q}$$

is invalid for the various accounts of conditionals considered in section II; however, this reasoning is deficient. It may be that conditionals as a class do not entail their consequents, but it does not follow that no particular conditional entails its consequent. A conditional with a logically true antecedent entails its consequent.

Consider for a moment another sort of "if" sentence, monkey's-uncle sentences, such as

If he's a brain surgeon, I'm a monkey's uncle.

When understood as intended, such sentences are taken to imply the negation of the antecedent. Of course,

$$\frac{\text{if } p, \text{ then } q}{\text{not } p}$$

not a valid form of argument for genuine conditionals. We leave it open whether the implication of "He's no brain surgeon" is an entailment in the strict sense; the data are not uncompromising. Similarly, the data about the coffee-table sentences include the fact that coffee-table sentences imply their consequents. There is no reason to say that there is entailment in one case and mere implication of some weaker kind in the other case. If we allow mere implication in both cases (coffee-table and monkey's-uncle "ifs"), then general facts about the behavior of conditionals and plausible hypotheses about shared but implicit additional premises explain both cases of implication. "I'm a monkey's uncle" is absurd; so by modus tollens we conclude, "He's not a brain surgeon." Because your desires are irrelevant to the current contents of the coffee table, there is coffee on the table whether you want some or not, and so there is coffee on the table. The irrelevance of your desires can be considered to be an additional premise of the form

if (q if p), then (q if not p).

Note that, as long as we are willing to add additional (plausibly intended and understood) premises when we symbolize, we may treat coffee-table and monkey's-uncle "ifs" as expressing genuine conditionals. Such a practice is of no real use for genuinely nonconditional "ifs," such as "I wonder if Alma is happy." The facts usually cited about what follows or does not follow from various "if" sentences are not sufficient to support a taxonomy of genuine and spurious conditionals.

Generalized conditionals are sentences such as

If a number is divisible by 4, then it is divisible by 2.

which are typically notated in quantifier logic as universally quantified conditionals:

Every number x is such that (if 4 divides x, then 2 divides x).

The notation reflects an analysis of structure in which a universal quantifier is the main logical operator of the sentence; within the scope of the quantifier is a (material-) conditional operator. The components of the conditional are one-place predicate expressions. Generalized conditionals are supposed to have a structure that is reflected in its essentials by the quantifier logic notation; they are not genuine conditionals, although they contain genuine conditionals as components. The component clauses of generalized conditionals are syntactically sentences (they consist of the same sequence of words as some sentences), although they express predicates. This is clear in the consequent of the example; "it" plays the role of a variable rather than of a referring expression. But even in the case of the antecedent of the example, "a number is divisible by 4," which appears to have a quantifier expression as its grammatical subject, it is helpful in giving a semantic analysis if we can also take this clause to express a predicate (which is within the scope of both a conditional and a quantifier). That is, it is helpful to treat "a number" as a variable with a role similar to the role of "it" in the consequent clause. On this analysis there is no syntactically explicit universal quantifier in the sentence. Rather, the sentence expresses a conditional predicate such as

If 4 divides x and x is a number, then 2 divides x.

The view is not without complications. For instance, we must be careful about the scope relations of the supposed implicit universal quantifier and the explicit negation in

It is not the case that if a number is even, it is divisible by 4.

In any event, generalized conditionals have either a universal quantifier with scope including the whole conditional or are conditionals with predicate rather than sentence components.

It is tempting to explain away some especially troublesome apparent conditionals as generalized conditionals. Remember that, on two of the more popular views about conditionals, a conditional is true whenever both components are true. Remember also that we are (strongly) tempted to assent to

If I am in Raleigh, then I am in North Carolina

and to dissent from

If I am in North Carolina, then I am in Raleigh

even in those cases in which I happen to be in Raleigh and hence also in North Carolina. Now there are many possible responses to this situation. One response is to accept the assent and dissent as genuine indications of truth and falsity, respectively, but to reject the claim that either sentence is a genuine conditional. This is a tempting response because my assent and dissent are emphatically and unmistakably sincere, because there are no relevant geographical facts about which I am ignorant or mistaken, and because I become testy when my competence as a native speaker is questioned concerning such simple matters. Instead of saying that the sentences are genuine conditionals, we might say that the sentences are disguised generalized conditionals and that they behave just as we should expect generalized conditionals to behave. For instance:

If a number is divisible by 4, then it is even

is true. But,

If it is even, then a number is divisible by 4

is false. So switching the components of a generalized conditional can alter the truth value. In the case of "If I am in Raleigh, then I am in North Carolina," the two component clauses appear to be sentences having truth values. But, so the story goes, the appearance is misleading.

If I am in Raleigh at a time, then I am in North Carolina at that time

supposedly makes explicit the predicates involved. But consider the related sentences

If I am now in Raleigh, I am now in North Carolina.

If I am in North Carolina, I am now in Raleigh.

These sentences cannot be said to be even implicitly general in the way the earlier examples were. Yet these two sentences are just as strongly and for the same reasons considered to differ in truth value. So appeal to generalized conditionals does not seem to dispose of this troublesome sort of case.

It is still possible to have the semantic benefits of universal quantification without making a predicate out of what is manifestly a sentence. The trick requires complicating the semantic value assigned to sentences; it is the familiar trick Kripke taught us in his semantic analysis of modal logic. "It is necessary that" operates on sentences having truth values, but the operator does not operate on truth values. Sentences have truth values, but they also have propositions—distributions of truth values across possible worlds. The necessity operator is in essence a universal quantifier with respect to the collection of possible worlds. So our troublesome sentences might be taken to mean (roughly), respectively,

Every world (of the appropriate sort) is such that, if I am now in Raleigh in that world, then I am now in North Carolina in that world.

Every world (of the appropriate sort) is such that, if I am now in North Carolina in that world, then I am now in Raleigh in that world.

There is a subtle but important difference between this proposal and the preceding one. In the current proposal we suggest complicating the semantic value of a sentence in a familiar and independently motivated way without a change in either the structural analysis of the sentence or in the relation between structure and interpretation. In the preceding proposal we suggest an implausible structural analysis. Even though generalized conditionals are not genuine conditionals, some sort of universal quantifier could play a role in the semantics of genuine conditionals.

The fourth sort of "if" sentence often set aside preliminary to discussions of symbolization is the subjunctive "if." Advocates of a material-conditional "if" favor segregating "ifs" with clauses in the subjunctive mood. The reason is that among subjunctive "ifs" are the counterfactual conditionals, and it is extremely counterintuitive to claim that all counterfactuals are true. A counterfactual "if" has a false antecedent and, so the story goes, in asserting a counterfactual conditional, one asserts or implies the falsehood of the antecedent. For example:

> If Mondale had defeated Reagan in '84, a Democrat would be in the White House

and

> If Mondale had defeated Reagan in '84, a La Rouchian would be in the White House

are both counterfactuals, but only the first is likely to be considered true. Furthermore, the grounds for asserting the truth of the first and the falsehood of the second have nothing to do with the actual outcome of the '84 election; the grounds are simply that Mondale is a Democrat. Of course, one can have exactly the same sort of grounds supporting indicative "ifs," such as

> If Cuomo wins the '88 election, then a Democrat will be in the White House.

I have so far resisted the temptation to argue directly for one or another semantic treatment of conditionals and will continue to do so. Instead let us consider the systematic effect on views about the semantics of conditionals of two alternative accounts of how mood (subjunctive and indicative) enters into the structure of conditionals.

One view of the matter is that subjunctive mood belongs to the clauses of an "if" sentence. There is but a single sentence connective, "if-then," that appears in both indicative and subjunctive conditionals. Just as the component clauses of some "ifs" are negated whereas the components of others are unnegated, the components of some are present tense whereas others are future tense, and the components of some "ifs" are indicative whereas other are subjunctive. There is a respect in which polarity (positive or negative), tense, and mood are similar. All can be expressed by a prefix attached to a bare sentence. For instance:

It is not the case that Jack is home.
It will be the case that Jack is home.
It were the case that Jack is home.

However, the subjunctive clause does not stand on its own as a sentence; it requires a larger context, such as

If it were the case that Jack is home, then Jill would be home.

Notice also that the subjunctive antecedent (in this case) is expressed with "were" and that the subjunctive consequent is expressed with "would be." From the standpoint of explaining symbolization practice, this view of subjunctive mood together with the failure of subjunctive clauses to stand alone as sentences gives rise to a vexing problem. The problem is the identity of the entities symbolized by sentence letters, such as p and q. The account of symbolization given in section I allowed manipulation of the sentence constituents in forming a compound statement. But the current view of "if" is that mood is not supplied or altered by the construction. The constituent sentences fill in the blanks of the pattern

if————, then————.

So in the statement form

if p, then q

p and q stand for the component sentences unaltered. How then are we to symbolize this argument?

If Jack were home, then Jill would be home
Jill is not home
_____
Jack is not home.

The naive symbolization

if p, then q
not q
_____
not p

has much to recommend it. But does p stand for "Jack is home" or "Jack were home" or some third, more abstract thing common to both? Of course, if mood were irrelevant from the standpoint of semantics and logic, then beggers might ride.

A second view of mood and conditionals is that there really are two distinct sorts of "ifs," indicative and subjunctive. We can emphasize this supposed difference by proposing two connective phrases:

If it is the case that————, then it is the case that————.
If it were the case that————, then it would be the case that————.

Exactly the same sentences can replace the blanks in the two cases to produce indicative and subjunctive conditionals, respectively. Of course, nothing in this proposal requires that there be any logically significant semantic distinction between indicative and subjunctive conditionals. Appealing as this view may be from the standpoint of a simple account of symbolization, it is not without difficulties. Subjunctive mood is intimately related to conditional statement. Indeed, mood alone will form a conditional sentence from two clauses without the aid of "if":

Were Jack home, Jill would be home.

This conditional seems to differ little in its entailment relations from

If Jack is home, then Jill is home.

So it seems that subjunctive mood and "if" are equally effective, independent means of forming conditionals. Combination of subjunctive mood and "if" in a single sentence is of stylistic interest but not of logical interest. Two morals: Far from being beyond the pale of analyses of conditionals, subjunctive mood conditionals are "redundantly genuine" conditionals. Also, sentence letters such as p must stand for something more abstract than an actual sequence of words in order to accommodate shifts in mood (and possibly even tense) such as we encounter in arguments with subjunctive conditional premises.

Remember now my original "modest aim": to present some evidence that justifying our ordinary symbolization practice is no easy matter and that a proper justification will involve many difficult claims about structure and meaning. If you find yourself now thinking that I have made many unsupported accusations about "not," "or," and "if" and if you think that the many things claimed in the literature of logical form are no better supported by evidence or argument than are my several hypotheses, then I have accomplished my aim. If you are at all like me, you will, all my excuses notwithstanding, want some "bottom line" concerning the treatment of "if" statements within elementary logic. Accordingly I now sketch a semantics (unoriginal) for a broad class of "if" statements, discuss how three of the troublesome cases from section II might be accommodated within the semantic framework, and offer advice (disappointing, I'm afraid) on teaching symbolization.

The semantic account I offer really consists of three families of accounts. All three families are versions of the familiar Ramsey-Stalnaker-Thomason semantics. They are based on a system of possible worlds and an alternative relation among worlds with a measure of "closeness" of related worlds. I speak of families of interpretations because there is no single alternative relation or measure of closeness of alternatives; they vary from context to context in ways we do not attempt to specify. Let us call the alternatives to a given world that are within a certain (unspecified) distance of that world and are worlds in which a given proposition p is true the p-neighborhood of the given world. With respect to a given world w and a given conditional, if p, then q, the three truth conditions are:

1. Within the p-neighborhood of w, q is true in at least one world.
2. Within the p-neighborhood of w, q is true in the closest world to w.
3. Within the p-neighborhood of w, q is true in all worlds.

Call these possible, actual, and necessary conditionals, respectively. I do not claim that "if" is ambiguous; I have no more reason to do so than I have to call "or" ambiguous. There may simply be a generic conditional of which these three are species. The possible conditional does not seem to be readily expressed by simple "if" sentences without an explicit modal element in the consequent, as in

If I take a coin from my pocket, it might be a penny.

But the actual and necessary conditionals seem to be expressed by simple conditionals—so it seems to me, at least.

Indeed my treatment of the Raleigh–North Carolina conditionals takes them to express necessary conditionals even though no modal word appears in the clauses. Some slender evidence for multiple interpretations of a single conditional corresponding to two of the given species comes from telling a suitable story in which I have a rigid itinerary with my only stop in North Carolina being Raleigh. I may then claim (in the actual conditional sense):

If I am in North Carolina, then I am in Raleigh.

Some may prefer to let the whole burden of the truth-value shift for this sentence fall on a shift in the alternative relation or on the closeness measure: I prefer the current explanation.

Let us call a conditional, if q, then r, stable with respect to p whenever the truth of the conditional

if q and p, then r

is guaranteed by the truth of

if q, then r

Failing stability we say that the effect of q is not independent of p. We get counterexamples to transitivity of conditionals when stability fails. For example, suppose that Stephen is morose, that Molly is happy if either her lover or her husband is happy, and that Leopold is happy because Molly is happy while Stephen is morose, but Leopold would be despondent if Molly and her lover were both happy. This state of affairs seems to be one in which

>   If Stephen is happy, then Molly is happy

and

>   If Molly is happy, then Leopold is happy

are both true while

>   If Stephen is happy, then Leopold is happy

is false. The second conditional is not stable; the effect of Molly's happiness is not independent of Stephen's happiness. This is the stuff out of which non-truth-functional conditionals are made. But if we assume, as we do barring special background information, that the effect of the antecedent of the second conditional is independent of the antecedent of the first conditional, then the third conditional follows. Conditionals do not require special auxiliary assumptions to be non-truth-functional. However, in logic textbook exercises, the rules of the game are that any dependencies not explicitly stated or evident are to be ignored. So, in this case at least, our ordinary symbolization practice is understandable and can be explained by a relatively simple and natural assumption about the intentions of exercise writers.

With so much uncritical acceptance of non-truth-functional "ifs," I may seem to have abandoned my defense of the material conditional as the conditional of mathematics or else to be driven to yet another sense of "if." But on the assumption that mathematical statements are either true in all the worlds of the alternative relation or false in all, the semantics presented yield the material conditional as a bonus. Consider any purely mathematical conditional in which the antecedent and consequent have constant truth value in all worlds. Then what happens in any one world happens in all worlds, and the three truth conditions reduce to the material conditional. This is pleasant because a plausible feature of the class of sentences in question together with the general semantics of conditionals yields the seemingly special behavior of mathematical conditionals in a natural way.

As for a story to tell in logic class, I have little to add to my original recommendation of a hybrid: material conditionals for mathematics and other eternal subject matter, and material conditionals that are entailed by genuine conditionals for contingent subject matters encountered outside of logic exercises. You may also wish to explain how most logic exercises are intended to be solved under the assumption of independence of all relevant situations and thus allow further use of material conditionals. Then again, you may not. If you should happen to have a student ask you how your recommended symbolization practice bears on the project of getting a computer to understand English, smile and say "A very good question. That's a long and complicated story."

Substitutivity

Scott Soames

I

In his 1962 article "Propositions," Richard Cartwright identified propositions with what is said or asserted by assertive utterances of sentences. He distinguished the proposition asserted by an utterance from various things with which it might be confused, including the sentence uttered, its meaning, the act of uttering it, and the sentence token produced. In distinguishing the proposition asserted from the meaning of the sentence used to assert it, Cartwright relied heavily on observations about indexical and context-sensitive sentences.

For example, he pointed out that the meaning of sentence (1) or (2) in what follows cannot be the proposition it is used to assert, for the simple reason that there is no such single proposition.[1]

(1) It is raining.

(2) Botvinnik uses it.

Rather, he noted, the meanings of these sentences allow distinct utterances of them to express different propositions. Although Cartwright did not attempt to provide a systematic characterization of the propositions expressed by these sentences in different contexts of utterance, he did note the importance of contextually determined reference for this task. Thus, in speaking of (1), he says that the fact about its meaning that allows different utterances of it to express different propositions is that one who utters it "speaks correctly only if he refers to the weather at the time of his utterance and in his (more or less) immediate vicinity" (Cartwright 1962, p. 93).

In recent years a conception of semantics has grown up under the influence of David Kaplan and others that preserves Cartwright's central observations.[2] According to this conception the meaning of a sentence is a function from contexts of utterance to propositions expressed in those contexts. Sentences containing indexicals and other context-sensitive elements express different propositions in different contexts. Propositions determine functions from circumstances of evaluation to truth values.

These functions give the truth conditions of propositions. The truth conditions of a sentence, as used in a particular context, are the truth conditions of the proposition it expresses in that context.

These points are illustrated by

(3)   I am American.

This sentence, as used in a context C, is true with respect to an arbitrary circumstance of evaluation E if and only if the referent of "I" in C is in the extension of "American" in E. Since the referent of "I" in a context is just the designated agent (speaker) in the context, this means that (3) is true with respect to C and E if and only if the agent (speaker) in C is an American in E. Thus an utterance of (3) by Reagan expresses a proposition that is true in a circumstance E if and only if Reagan is an American in E (whether or not he ever speaks in E).

Undoubtedly Reagan thinks of himself as the fortieth president of the United States. This may even be his favorite, most privileged description of himself. Still, the proposition expressed by his utterance of (3) is not the proposition that the fortieth president of the United States is American. Since there are circumstances in which the latter proposition is true but the former proposition is not, they cannot be identical. This result, together with an elementary principle of compositionality, establishes that the contribution made by "I" to the proposition expressed by (3) in the context is not the sense of the description "the fortieth president of the United States."

This reasoning can be extended to all descriptions that denote someone other than Reagan, with respect to some circumstance of evaluation. If, following David Kaplan and Nathan Salmon, we account for the truth conditions of examples such as

(4)   In the future I will be dead, but my policies will live on

by taking Reagan's (present) utterance of "I" to denote him even in circumstances in which he does not exist, we can extend the result to descriptions such as "the x: x = Reagan" and "the x: actually x is the fortieth president of the United States" (which denote Reagan in all circumstances in which he exists but denote nothing in circumstances in which he does not).[3] These points are not, of course, restricted to "I" but apply to proper names and other indexicals that designate contingently existing objects. Finally, as David Kaplan (1977), Saul Kripke (1980), and John Perry (1977) have emphasized, the semantic mechanism determining reference with respect to a circumstance for a name or indexical (as used in a context) is not the satisfaction in the circumstance of an associated description. In short, names and indexicals are *nondescriptional* as well as *rigid*.

A singular term is rigid if and only if it refers to the same object in all circumstances with respect to a fixed context of utterance. It is descriptional if and only if its referent with respect to an arbitrary circumstance E (and fixed context C) is, by definition, the unique satisfier of a condition Sx, with respect to E (and C). There are, of course, rigid descriptions, for example, "the even prime." However, even if a description is rigid and so picks out the same object in every circumstance, its referent is determined in each circumstance by means of satisfaction of an associated condition. By contrast, the referent of a name or indexical is determined just once, in the context. In presenting a semantics, one standardly does define the referent of such a term t with respect to a context C and arbitrary circumstance E. However, given the referent of t in C, there is no further process one invokes to determine reference at alternative circumstances. Rather, one simply *stipulates* that the referent of t with respect to C and an arbitrary circumstance E is its referent in C.

What bearing does this difference in reference determination have on theses about the propositional contents of names and indexicals (relative to contexts) and the propositions expressed by sentences containing them? It is easy to proceed incautiously here. Given that propositional content determines reference and that reference of names and indexicals is not determined descriptively, one is tempted to conclude both that the content of a name or indexical (relative to a context) is never the same as the content of a description and that the proposition expressed by $\ulcorner S(n) \urcorner$ (in a context) is never the same as the proposition expressed by $\ulcorner S(d) \urcorner$, where d is a description and n is a name or indexical. However, these inferences are fallacious.

The reason they are is that we have not yet said enough about what propositions and propositional contents are. We have taken propositions to be objects of the attitudes of saying and asserting, as well as bearers of truth values in circumstances of evaluation. Suppose, however, that one were to add that circumstances of evaluation are possible worlds and that the proposition expressed by a sentence (in a context C) is the set of worlds in which it is true (as used in C).[4] On this conception the propositional content of a singular term (relative to C) is the function from worlds W to referents of the term with respect to W (and C). Thus "2" and "the even prime" are assigned the same 'propositional content', and the following (a) and (b) sentences are assigned the same 'proposition'—even though the (b) sentences arise from the (a) sentences by substituting a singular term with one propositional content for a singular term with a different content.[5]

(5a)   Reagan is American.
(5b)   The actual fortieth president of the United States is American.

(6a)   Three squared is less than 10.
(6b)   Five is less than 10.

In attempting to distinguish these propositions, one cannot simply stip-ulate that they are different because they are complexes constructed out of different component parts (the propositional contents of constituent ex-pressions). Although such a view of propositions is, I think, correct, it cannot be established by semantic fiat. Rather, one must appeal to pre-theoretic facts that support it over and against alternative conceptions. This appeal cannot, of course, be restricted to facts about the truth values of propositions in different circumstances of evaluation, for the (a) and (b) propositions do not differ in this respect. What we need are some common-place observations about propositional attitudes. It is possible to say, assert, or express (believe, consider, or prove) one of the (a) propositions without saying, asserting, or expressing (believing, considering, or prov-ing) the corresponding (b) proposition. Thus the propositions are different.

By appealing to observations of this kind, one can make a plausible case for two negative theses: First, the propositional content of a name or indexical (relative to a context) is never the same as that of a description; second, the proposition expressed by a sentence containing such a term is never the same as the proposition expressed by a sentence that results from substituting a description for the name or indexical. However, these nega-tive conclusions, together with the claim that names and indexicals are rigid, do not add up to a positive specification of their propositional contents (relative to contexts) or of the propositions expressed by sen-tences containing them.

We may take it that the propositional contents of terms (relative to contexts) determine their referents with respect to circumstances of evalu-ation (in the sense that two terms with the same content must agree in reference in all circumstances). Still, our conclusions about names and in-dexicals are compatible with a variety of hypotheses about their contents. For all that has been said so far, the content of such a term (relative to a context) could be its referent: it could be a pair consisting of its referent plus a descriptive condition associated with it by the speaker; it could be a triple consisting of this pair plus the character or linguistic meaning of the term; it could be a quadruple containing all this plus the term itself; or it could be any number of other things.

At issue are the conditions under which substitution of one name or indexical for another in a simple sentence preserves the proposition it expresses. The idea behind the more baroque alternatives is to restrict such substitution by encoding into propositions many of the linguistic and contextual peculiarities of utterances expressing them. This idea is not entirely without foundation in our pretheoretic linguistic practice. For ex-ample, when we report in indirect discourse what proposition someone has asserted or expressed, we typically try to keep as close to the person's own words as is feasible, relative to the conversational purposes and standards of accuracy prevailing in the reporting discourse.

However, there are definite limits to this presumption of linguistic fidelity. If someone speaking German utters a sentence containing the name "Deutschland," we can typically report in English the proposition he expressed using the name "Germany." Thus sentences containing different names may express the same proposition. Similarly, two people who utter

(7)   Reagan is persistent

may assert the same thing even if they have contrasting views of Reagan and associate radically different descriptive content with his name. Thus utterances of a sentence by speakers who associate different descriptive content with one of its names may express the same proposition.

Finally, utterances of the sentences in (8) may express the same proposition in their respective contexts, provided that the indexicals they contain refer to the same individual in those contexts:

(8a)   I am persistent.
(8b)   You are persistent.
(8c)   He is persistent.

Thus utterances of sentences with different meanings (characters) may express the same proposition. This should not be surprising, since one of the primary functions of indexicals is to allow the expression of the same proposition from different points of view.

In all these cases observations about propositional attitudes (saying, asserting, expressing) are used to identify or distinguish various propositions. These observations provide substantial support for two well-known semantic theses:[6]

Thesis 1
Names and indexicals are *directly referential*; that is, the propositional content of such a term, relative to a context, is its referent in the context.

Thesis 2
Simple sentences containing directly referential terms express *singular propositions* (relative to contexts), that is, propositions containing individuals as constituents.

II

What consequences do these theses have for the substitutivity of coreferential names and indexicals? By themselves they have none. However, in conjunction with other plausible principles—some of which were instrumental in establishing them—they have consequences that are profound and wide ranging.

The most obvious of these have to do with simple sentences, free of nonextensional operators. A plausible principle governing such sentences is that substitution of expressions with the same propositional content preserves the proposition expressed.

> *Random Compositionality*
> Let *S* be a simple, extensional sentence containing one or more occurrences of an expression *e*. Let *S'* arise from *S* by substituting an occurrence of *e'* for any (single) occurrence of *e* in *S*. If the propositional content of *e* in context *C* is identical with the propositional content of *e'* in context *C*, then the proposition expressed by *S* in *C* is identical with the proposition expressed by *S'* in *C*.[7]

The conjunction of this principle with the thesis that names and indexicals are directly referential entails that substitution of coreferential names or indexicals for one another in a simple, extensional sentence preserves the proposition expressed.

This conclusion has a number of consequences, some welcome and some not. Among the former is the intuitively correct result that the sentences in (7) and (8) express the same proposition in contexts in which their names and indexicals are coreferential. Among the latter is the problematic result that the sentence pairs in (9) and (10) also do.

> (9a)   I am Scott Soames.
> (9b)   Scott Soames is Scott Soames.

> (10a)   Tully shaved Cicero.
> (10b)   Cicero shaved Cicero.

It is important to be clear about what is and what is not problematic about this result. The result does *not* entail that utterances of the sentences in each example convey the same information. In the case of sentence (9a), its meaning guarantees that it is true in the context of utterance if and only if the speaker of the utterance is Scott Soames. Since this is not so for (9b), competent hearers can be expected to find utterances of (9a) informative in a way that utterances of (9b) are not—even if they express the same (trivial) proposition.

The case of (10) is a little more complicated but still analogous. The proposition expressed by sentence (10b) (and, by hypothesis, (10a)) is nontrivial. Thus utterances of both sentences are informative. However, the (total) information conveyed by an utterance of one may differ from that conveyed by an utterance of the other. For example, suppose that *x* associates one set of descriptive criteria, *D*, with the name "Tully" and another set, D', with the name "Cicero." It is not important whether D and D' represent information about the referent that is complete or incomplete, accurate or inaccurate. We may suppose that these descriptive criteria are not *semantically* associated with the names at all. Still, if x takes an utterance of (10a) to be true, he will be in a position to conclude that $\ulcorner D$ shaved $D'\urcorner$ is true and hence to acquire a belief in the proposition it expresses. Since this belief would not arise from an utterance of (10b), the utterances convey different information. Similarly, if x takes an utterance of (10b) to be true, he will be in a position to conclude that someone was a self-shaver. Since this belief would not arise from an utterance of (10a),[8] the two do not convey the same information—even if they do express the same proposition.

Therefore, what is problematic about the conclusion that the (a) and (b) sentences in (9) and (10) express the same propositions (in their respective contexts) is not a matter of differences in the informativeness of utterances of these sentences. What is problematic about the result arises from the assumption that propositions are the objects of attitudes such as saying, asserting, and expressing (denying, believing, and considering). The conjunction of this assumption with the direct reference thesis and random compositionality entails that it is impossible to assert (deny, etc.) the proposition expressed by one of the sentences in the pair without asserting (denying, etc.) the proposition expressed (in the relevant context) by the other. This is counterintuitive. Ordinarily we are inclined to think that one can deny that I am Scott Soames without denying that Scott Soames is Scott Soames or assert that Cicero shaved Cicero without asserting that Tully did.

So far the only substitutivity results explicitly considered have involved simple, extensional sentences. However, these results have natural corollaries involving complex, nonextensional examples. There is, of course, no reason why substitution of expressions with the same propositional content should always preserve truth value, let alone the proposition expressed. It is easy to specify quotation, or quotationlike, operators that block such substitution. However, substitutivity in sentences containing familiar modal or propositional attitude constructions seems well-nigh irresistible.

In the case of the attitudes the argument leading to this result may be summarized as follows:

Truth-Preserving Substitution in Attitude Constructions
A. Propositions are objects of the attitudes saying, asserting, and expressing (denying, believing, considering, etc.); that is, these attitudes are relations to propositions.

B. The verbs "assert," "deny," "believe," etc. are two-place predicates relating individuals and propositions. An individual i satisfies ⌜x asserts (denies, etc.) NP⌝ in a context C if and only if i asserts (denies, etc.) the proposition denoted by NP in C.[9]

C. An individual i satisfies ⌜x asserts (denies, etc.) the proposition that S⌝ in a context C if and only if i asserts (denies, etc.) the denotation of ⌜the proposition that S⌝ in C, that is, the proposition expressed by S in C.

D. An individual i satisfies ⌜x asserts (denies, etc.) that S⌝ in C if and only if i asserts (denies, etc.) the proposition expressed by S in C.

E. It follows that, if S is a sentence for which random compositionality holds, if S' arises from S by substituting an expression e' for an occurrence of an expression e in S, and if the propositional content of e in a context C is identical with the propositional content of e' in C, then i satisfies ⌜x asserts (denies, etc.) that S⌝ in C if and only if i satisfies ⌜x asserts (denies, etc.) that S'⌝ in C.

F. When Thesis 1, about direct reference, is added, it follows that substitution of coreferential names and indexicals in attitude constructions preserves truth value.

Some of the consequences of F are counterintuitive. However, they are not easily avoided. In particular, direct reference theorists cannot divorce themselves from these consequences by professing agnosticism regarding the supplementary assumptions A through D, used to derive F.[10] It is true that the direct reference thesis does not itself make any claims about attitudes or attitude sentences. However, it is also true that without assumptions about the attitudes the thesis could not have been given its original motivation. To refuse to endorse these assumptions is to jeopardize crucial arguments for the thesis.

But this only makes the problem more acute, for to endorse the assumptions, together with direct reference, is to be committed to some notably counterintuitive conclusions. Thus direct reference theorists seem to be left in an uncomfortable position. The very assumptions that made the direct reference thesis initially compelling lead to substitutivity results that seem to undermine it.

III

Nevertheless, the correct response to these results is not, I think, to give up direct reference. One reason it is not is that essentially the same problems arise in cases in which there is little doubt that the expressions undergoing substitution do have the same content, for example, cases involving garden variety synonymies.[11] Let us assume, for the sake of argument, the following:

(11)   "Doctor" and "physician," as well as "fortnight" and "period of fourteen days," are synonymous and hence have the same propositional contents.

The combination of this plus random compositionality yields the conclusion that the (a) and (b) sentences of (12) and (13) express the same proposition.

(12a)   Doctors are doctors.
(12b)   Physicians are doctors.

(13a)   The meeting lasted a period of fourteen days if and only if it lasted a period of fourteen days.
(13b)   The meeting lasted a period of fourteen days if and only if it lasted a fortnight.

Many, I think, would find these results counterintuitive—on the grounds that ordinarily we think it possible to assert (deny, believe, etc.) one of the propositions in the pair without asserting (denying, believing, etc.) the other.

Following Benson Mates (1950), we can give the problem a further twist. Consider examples (14a) and (14b):

(14a)   Whoever believes (asserts, etc.) that the meeting lasted less than a period of fourteen days believes (asserts, etc.) that the meeting lasted less than a period of fourteen days.
(14b)   Whoever believes (asserts, etc.) that the meeting lasted less than a period of fourteen days believes (asserts, etc.) that the meeting lasted less than a fortnight.

Sentence (14a) is clearly true. The combination of (11), assumptions A through D, and random compositionality yields the result that (14b) is also true. However, the two examples seem to differ markedly in status. It is hard to imagine anyone doubting proposition (14a); but it seems easy to imagine someone doubting proposition (14b). Thus, if doubt is an attitude toward a proposition, it would seem the (a) and (b) sentences must express different propositions. But how can they, for they differ only in the substitution of one synonym for another?

The force of the question derives from a plausible extension of random compositionality to sentences containing attitude verbs. The conjunction of this extension with (11) entails that sentences (14a) and (14b) express the same proposition. We also get the conclusion that the examples in (15) have the same truth value.

(15a)   Nobody doubts that (14a).
(15b)   Nobody doubts that (14b).[12]

But these results are counterintuitive.

There are two points to notice about this problem. First, the way to deal with it is not to deny (11). From denials of this sort we would quickly reach the conclusion that no two expressions can have the same content, a conclusion that would wreak havoc with our intuitions about meaning in general and attitude reports in particular. Second, the problem confronting us here is analogous to the one in section II involving direct reference—so much so that it seems advisable to look for a single solution to both. If there is such a solution, it will not turn on denying that the expressions undergoing substitution have the same content.

IV

In 1954 Alonzo Church and Hilary Putnam offered different, but potentially generalizable, solutions to the Mates puzzle. According the Church, (14a) and (14b) express the same proposition, and (15a) and (15b) have the same truth value. The argument for this rested on elementary claims about translation. First, if S' is a proper German translation of a sentence S of English, then S and S' have the same truth values in their respective languages. Second, since "fortnight" has no single-word German translation, its translation is the same as that of "period of fourteen days." Because of this, sentences (15a) and (15b) have the same German translation and hence the same truth value.

According to Church, what makes this result initially counterintuitive is that it is confused with other, metalinguistic, claims that are false. For example, the claim that the sentences in (15) have the same truth value may be confused with the claim that those in (16) or (17) do:

(16a)   Nobody doubts that whoever satisfies (in English) the sentential matrix "x believes that the meeting lasted less than a period of fourteen days" satisfies (in English) the sentential matrix "x believes that the meeting lasted less than a period of fourteen days."

(16b)   Nobody doubts that whoever satisfies (in English) the sentential matrix "x believes that the meeting lasted less than a period of fourteen days" satisfies (in English) the sentential matrix "x believes that the meeting lasted less than a fortnight."

(17a)   Nobody doubts that whoever sincerely assents (in English) to "the meeting lasted less than a period of fourteen days" sincerely assents (in English) to "the meeting lasted less than a period of fourteen days."

(17b)   Nobody doubts that whoever sincerely assents (in English) to "the meeting lasted less than a period of fourteen days" sincerely assents (in English) to "the meeting lasted less than a fortnight."

The (a) and (b) sentences in these examples do have different truth values. Thus, if one does not properly distinguish them from their counterparts in (15), one will be led to conclude, incorrectly, that (15a) and (15b) also differ in truth value.

Unlike Church, Putnam did not take the intuition that (15a) and (15b) have different truth values to be based on linguistic confusion; rather, he regarded it as accurate. According to Putnam, (14a) and (14b) have different contents, and (15a) and (15b) have different truth values. Similarly, he held that sentences such as (12a) and (12b) differ in content and that propositional attitude ascriptions in which one of them is substituted for the other may differ in truth value. These conclusions conflict with the combination of claim (11), which Putnam accepted, plus random compositionality, and assumptions A through D about the attitudes. For largely historical reasons, these latter assumptions were not under consideration in Putnam's discussion. However, the discussion can be recast in a way that takes them for granted without affecting the essential dispute over sentences (12) through (15).[13] When this is done, the point at issue becomes random compositionality. In effect, what Putnam noticed was that there might be a good reason to reject this principle.

Random compositionality gains much of its plausibility from the observation that the content of a sentence (in a context) is determined by the contents of its constituent parts (in the context). However, this observation is incomplete. For example, sentences (18a) and (18b) are made up of parts with the same semantic content:

(18a)   John loves Mary.
(18b)   Mary loves John.

However, the sentences have different contents because those parts are put together in different ways. We might express this by saying that the content of a sentence is determined by the contents of its parts plus the way the parts are structured.

It should follow that sentences with the same structure and semantically equivalent parts have the same content. But what counts as sameness of structure? Do the following (a) and (b) sentences have the same or different structures?

(19a)   *Rab.*
(19b)   *Raa.*

(20a)   All *F*'s are *G*'s.
(20b)   All *F*'s are *F*'s.

The answer depends on one's notion of structure. In one sense the pairs have the same structures—in each case they would be assigned the same constituent structure tree by a standard syntax. In another sense, however, they do not. Thus, when doing logic, we say that the sentences have different *logical structures* in virtue of the fact that the (b) sentences contain two occurrences of the same constituent, whereas the (a) sentences contain one occurrence each of different constituents.

Suppose now that this notion of structure is used to determine the content of a sentence from its structure plus the contents of its parts. Under this analysis the (a) and (b) sentences in (19) and (20) may have different contents, even if the contents of their constituents, *"a"* and *"b," "F"* and *"G,"* are the same. According to Putnam, random compositionality fails because substitution in these cases changes structure and, thereby, content. The same may be said for the sentence pairs (12) through (15).

V

We need not at this point try to evaluate the relative merits of the Church and Putnam proposals. However, one initial advantage of Putnam's approach is worth noting. Ordinary speakers do, I think, have pre-theoretic intuitions that the examples in (15) may have different truth values and that those in (12) through (14) may represent different beliefs. Putnam's proposal respects these intuitions in a way that Church's does not.

The semantic intuitions of ordinary competent speakers are not, of course, infallible. Thus Putnam's advantage on this score is not in itself a refutation of Church's position. However, the intuitions of such speakers are, in general, the best evidence we have in semantics and so cannot be taken lightly. If there is a way of respecting them in this case that does not run into trouble elsewhere, then it should be preferred.

Another desirable feature of Putnam's suggestion is the way it general-izes. The results involving belief sentences are easily extended to other attitude ascriptions (saying, asserting, expressing, etc.). Putnam's approach also applies to cases involving substitution of directly referential singular terms.

If names and indexicals are directly referential, then the content of "Cicero" is the same as the content of "Tully," and the content of "I" is the same as the content of "Scott Soames" in a context in which I am the agent (speaker). However, substitution of one for the other in (9) and (10) changes logical structure and so, on the Putnam account, changes the proposition expressed. Thus one can preserve the intuition that it is possible to deny that I am Scott Soames without denying that Scott Soames is Scott Soames and to assert that Cicero shaved Cicero without asserting that Tully did. By contrast, substitution of coreferential names and indexicals in (7) and (8) preserves both logical structure and proposition expressed. In this way one retains the positive results about substitutivity that helped motivate the direct reference thesis while avoiding some of the most notorious substitution problems that seemed to undermine it.

This application to direct reference was not, of course, envisioned in 1954.[14] In recent years, however, the idea behind Putnam's proposal has been rediscovered and used in connection with direct reference theory by Mark Richard (1983; forthcoming) and by David Kaplan (1985). The details of their respective proposals differ in several respects that need not concern us here.[15] What is important is whether the apparent difficulties for the direct reference thesis posed by problematic substitutions can be overcome using Putnam's basic idea.

In investigating this question, I adopt assumptions A through D about the attitudes given in section II plus versions of Theses 1 and 2 that extend the direct reference analysis to variables.

Thesis 1*
Names, indexicals, and variables are *directly referential*—the propositional content of such a term, relative to a context C and assignment f of objects as referents to variables, is its referent relative to C and f.

Thesis 2*
Sentences containing names and indexicals, as well as formulas containing free occurrences of variables, express *singular propositions* relative to contexts and assignments.[16]

I further assume that propositions are complexes that reflect the structure of the sentences that express them. In the case of simple sentences the propositions are made up of properties corresponding to predicates and individuals corresponding to directly referential terms. In more complex cases operators such as "and," "or," and "not," definite and indefinite descriptions, and quantifiers contribute higher-order elements to structurally complex propositions whose constituents are (or encode) the semantic contents of the constituents of sentences that express them.[17]

Finally, we need a way of representing in propositions the kinds of distinctions in the logical structures of sentences that are crucial to

Putnam's proposal. For example, we must distinguish the propositions expressed by the (a) and (b) sentences in (21) and (22), where t and t' are distinct directly referential terms that refer to the same thing:

(21a) Rt, t'.
(21b) Rt, t.

(22a) $Ft \wedge Gt'$.
(22b) $Ft \wedge Gt$.

The propositions expressed by the (a) sentences can be represented as follows:[18]

(21a′) $\langle\langle o, o \rangle, R^* \rangle$,
(22a′) $\langle \text{Conj}, \langle\langle\langle o \rangle, F^* \rangle, \langle\langle o \rangle, G^* \rangle\rangle\rangle$.

To get the propositions expressed by the (b) sentences, we need to add something that reflects the repeated occurrences of the same term in these examples. There are, of course, many ways to do this. For the sake of vividness let us think of the (b) propositions as arising from the (a) propositions by adding 'wires' connecting the different occurrences of o in the propositions:[19]

(21b′) $\langle\langle \overline{o, o} \rangle, R^* \rangle$,
(22b′) $\langle \text{Conj}, \langle\langle\langle \overline{o} \rangle, F^* \rangle, \langle\langle o \rangle, G^* \rangle\rangle\rangle$.

Multiple occurrences of the same predicates, or other constants, can be similarly represented.

The question at issue, then, is this: Does propositional encoding of repeated occurrences of the same expression successfully resolve the puzzles involving substitution of expressions with the same content? In particular, does it resolve puzzles involving substitution of names, indexicals, and variables with the same referent? I argue that it does not.

VI

The first point to notice is that the extra-structure idea fails to block some of the most problematic substitutions. For example, since the structure of sentence (23a) is the same as that of (23b), the propositions they express are identified, and the ascriptions (24a) and (24b) are treated as equivalent:[20]

(23a) Superman is stronger than Clark Kent.
(23b) Clark Kent is stronger than Superman.

(24a) Lois Lane said (believed, etc.) that Superman is stronger than Clark Kent.

(24b)   Lois Lane said (believed, ect.) that Clark Kent is stronger than Superman.

But these results are no less counterintuitive than those the extra-structure idea is designed to block. In general, interchanging t and t' in (21a) and (22a) is as problematic as substituting one of these terms for the other. It would seem, therefore, that the cases ought to be treated similarly. Making the attitudes sensitive to extra structure does not do this.

A similar point holds for examples involving conjunction:

(25a)   The ancients said (believed, etc.) that Phosphorus was visible only in the morning and Hesperus was visible only in the evening.

(25b)   The ancients said (believed, etc.) that Phosphorus was visible only in the morning and Phosphorus was visible only in the evening.

We may take it that (25a) is true and that the introduction of extra structure into propositions blocks the inference to (25b). However, nothing blocks the move from (25a) to

(25c)   The ancients said (believed, etc.) that Phosphorus was visible only in the morning and the ancients said (believed, etc.) that Hesperus was visible only in the evening

and from there to

(25d)   The ancients said (believed, etc.) that Phosphorus was visible only in the morning and the ancients said (believed, etc.) that Phosphorus was visible only in the evening

and

(25e)   The ancients said (believed, etc.) that Phosphorus was visible only in the morning and that Phosphorus was visible only in the evening.[21]

If the goal is to preserve pretheoretic intuition, there is little to be gained by holding that (25b) is false whereas (25d) and (25e) are true. But this is what the extra-structure approach is committed to. In general, when substitution in a conjunction within the scope of an attitude verb is blocked, substitution in the separate conjuncts is allowed, counterintuitive or not.

Another problem similar to this illustrates the overreliance of the extra-structure approach on accidental matters of syntax. We assume that the semantic content of the directly referential proper name "Phosphorus" is not the same as that of the description "the x: x = Phosphorus." The former is just the planet Venus, whereas the latter is a complex consisting of an operation corresponding to the definite article plus that property of being identical with Venus. Nevertheless, a competent speaker who sincerely assents to sentence (26a) typically will assent to (26b):

    (26a)   Hesperus is distinct from Phosphorus.
    (26b)   Hesperus is distinct from the x: $x =$ Phosphorus.

Suppose now that we introduce a new syntactically simple term, "Vesperus," which we stipulate to have the same semantic content as the description.[22] Next we substitute "Vesperus" for the description in

    (27a) A says (believes, etc.) that Hesperus is distinct from the x: $x =$ Phosphorus

to get

    (27b) A says (believes, etc.) that Hesperus is distinct from Vesperus.

Having derived (27b), we can now substitute "Phosphorus" for "Hesperus" without changing structure to get

    (27c) A says (believes, etc.) that Phosphorus is distinct from Vesperus.

But this is problematic. Although (27c) comes out true on the extra-structure proposal, intuitively it seems to be on a par with

    (27d) A says (believes, etc.) that Phosphorus is distinct from the x: $x =$ Phosphorus

which the proposal is designed to block.

So far I have argued that the extra-structure proposal does not carve semantic reality at the joints. For every problematic substitution that it blocks, there are others, intuitively no different, that it allows. Although this does not show that the proposal is false, it does suggest that there is less to be said for it than might first have been imagined.[23]

In addition to this, there is another, more powerful criticism to be made. The proposal was motivated by the idea that the examples in (28) may differ in truth value even when expressions e and e' have the same semantic content:

    (28a) A says (believes, etc.) that . . .e. . .e. . . .
    (28b) A says (believes, etc.) that . . .e'. . .e. . . .

The proposal implements this idea by introducing a mechanism that makes such sameness of content an insufficient basis for deriving one from the other. However, it does not preclude the possibility that other factors might bring it about that (28a) and (28b) have the same truth value. Of course, if such factors could always be found, then the proposal would lose its motivation. Given the background assumptions in section V together with some pretheoretic attitude ascriptions, we can show that this is the case.

Consider again the familiar example of Hesperus and Phosphorus. By encoding extra structure into propositions, one can distinguish the proposition expressed by (29a) from the propositions expressed by (29b) and (29c):

(29a)   Phosphorus is Phosphorus.
(29b)   That (pointing in the morning at Venus) is Phosphorus.
(29c)   Hesperus is Phosphorus.

Note, however, that the proposition expressed by (29b) is still identified with the one expressed by (29c).

We may assume that the ancients sincerely and reflectively assented to (translations of) (29a) and dissented from (translations of) (29c). Surely, however, they also produced sincere, reflective utterances of the sort illustrated by (29b). Moreover, the following attitude ascription seems clearly correct:

(30)   The ancients said (believed, etc.) that that (pointing in the morning at Venus) was Phosphorus.

But then, even the extra-structure proposal predicts that ascriptions (31a) and (31b) are true:

(31a)   The ancients said (believed, etc.) that Hesperus was Phosphorus.
(31b)   The ancients said (believed, etc.) that that (pointing in the morning at Venus) was Hesperus.

The point is a general one. Let e and e' be expressions with the same content. Suppose that (28a) is true and that (28b) appears, pretheoretically, to be false. Typically one can find or introduce another expression e^* with the same content as e, such that

(28b*) A says (believes, etc.) that . . . e^* . . . e . . .

is unproblematically true (because, for example, the agent realizes that e and e^* have the same content). But given the truth of (28b*), the extra-structure proposal is committed to the truth of (28b). Thus, no real progress has been made on examples such as this. Although the proposal makes the move from (28a) to (28b) depend on more than content alone, the ease with which intermediaries of the sort (28b*) can be produced robs the proposal of its intended significance.[24]

A similar moral can be drawn from ascriptions involving quantifying-in. Let us suppose that Lois Lane sees Clark Kent shaving in his office at the

Daily Planet and on the basis of this sincerely and assertively utters "Clark Kent shaves Clark Kent." Surely, there is someone—Clark Kent—of whom Lois Lane says and believes that he shaves Clark Kent. Thus both sentences (32a) and (32b) are true:

> (32a) Lois Lane says (believes) that Clark Kent shaves Clark Kent.
> (32b) $\exists x[x = $ Clark Kent $\wedge$ Lois Lane says (believes) that x shaves Clark Kent].

According to the extra-structure proposal, (32a) ascribes to Lois the property of standing in a relation to a 'wired proposition', the structure of which incorporates the double occurrence of the name in the complement clause. However, (32b) does not. Instead, it requires that Lois stand in the appropriate attitude relation to the proposition expressed by "x shaves Clark Kent" under an assignment of Clark Kent as value of "x." Since "x," "Clark Kent," and "Superman" are different terms with the same content (with respect to the assignment of Clark Kent to "x"), it follows that this proposition is the same as that expressed by "Superman shaves Clark Kent." Thus the truth of (32b) guarantees the truth of

> (32c) Lois Lane says (believes) that Superman shaves Clark Kent.

As before, the problem is general. According to the extra-structure approach, (33a) can be true when (33c) is false only when (33b) is also false:

> (33a) A says (believes, etc.)$. . .t. . .t. . . .$
> (33b) $\exists x[x = t \wedge A$ says (believes, etc.)$. . .x. . .t. . .].$
> (33c) A says (believes, etc.)$. . .t'. . .t.$

However, in a great many cases in which (33a) is true, it seems obvious that (33b) is also. Thus proponents of extra structure face a dilemma. If they grant the truth of (33b), they must countenance ascriptions that their theory was designed to avoid. However, if they reject (33b), they miss an obvious truth.[25]

Similar reasoning applies to the inference from (33c) to (33a). Although the extra-structure proposal does not license it simply on the basis of identical content on the part of t and t', arguments appealing to pre-theoretic intuitions can often be found to sanction it. For example, Professor McX, looking through the open back door of the faculty lounge, sees Y walking down the hall and says to a visitor, "He (pointing to Y) is a professor in the department." A few seconds later Y passes by the front door, and McX says, "He (pointing to Y again) is a graduate student in the department." Although McX does not realize that he has pointed twice to the same individual, Y, who has overheard the remarks, can correctly report, "McX said both that I am a professor in the department and that I am a graduate student in the department." A third party may report, "There is someone such that McX said both that he is a professor in the department and that he is a graduate student in the department."

Developing the example further, we can have McX conjoin his remarks:

(34)   Who is in the department? Let me see. He (pointing to Y as he passes the back door) is a professor in the department and (turning) he (pointing to Y as he passes the front door) is a graduate student in the department.

On the basis of this, the following ascriptions seem clearly true:

(35a)   McX says that he (pointing to Y as he passes the back door) is a professor in the department and he (pointing to Y as he passes the front door) is a graduate student in the department.

(35b)   McX says that I am a professor in the department and I am a graduate student in the department. [Uttered by Y]

(35c)   ∃z[McX says that z is a professor in the department and z is a graduate student in the department.]

(35d)   McX says that Y is a professor in the department and Y is a graduate student in the department [where "Y" is a proper name of Y].

Following Kaplan, I take (35a) to contain two different demonstratives: "he" plus the first demonstration and "he" plus the second demonstration. Thus it has the same form as (33c). Sentence (35b), on the other hand, has the form (33a). Since (35b) is clearly true, the extra-structure proposal is again faced with a dilemma. If it fails to countenance the move from (35a) to (35b), it misses an obvious truth. However, if it allows the move, it predicts that

(35e)   McX says that t^* is a professor in the department and t^* is a graduate student in the department

will be true for any directly referential term t^* that refers to Y—and thereby countenances the ascriptions it was designed to falsify.[26]

VII

For all these reasons it seems to me that the extra-structure proposal fails. However, its failure is instructive. The examples involving indexicals and variables point to something important about attitude ascriptions. Typically, when we report someone's attitudes in indirect discourse, we are expected to keep as close to the words he or she used, or would use, as is feasible. However, this expectation of linguistic fidelity is not an absolute semantic requirement but a pragmatic desideratum that can be outweighed by other factors. This is evident in reports of assertions or beliefs expressed in other languages. It is also evident in cases in which indexicals are used.

For example, when one talks about oneself, one is expected to do so in the first, rather than the third, person. This applies even when reporting someone else's beliefs or assertions about oneself. Thus, if I were to report Richard Cartwright's remark, "Scott Soames is one of my former students," in most contexts I would be expected to use sentence (36a) rather than (36b):

(36a)   Richard Cartwright said that I was one of his former students.
(36b)   Richard Cartwright said that Scott Soames was one of his former students.

Here, deviation from the exact words of the agent of the attitude is not only acceptable but preferred.

The McX and Y example given in section VI exploits this fact. When Y reports McX's remark about him, he has little choice but to use occurrences of "I" in place of the demonstratives used by McX. However, the result of this substitution is striking. Although the sentence used by McX indicates that he took himself to be talking about two individuals,[27] Y's sentence indicates that the assertion concerns a single individual. In short, the logical structures and cognitive perspectives associated with the two sentences are different. Nevertheless, the second is a truthful report of the assertion made by the first. This shows that reports of propositions asserted are not semantically required to preserve the logical structures or cognitive perspectives of the sentences used to assert them.

This result is not limited to cases in which the sentence assertively uttered contains indexicals or in which the subject of the assertion actually reports it. Imagine The Ancient Babylonian looking up in the sky in the morning and uttering (37a) and looking up in the sky in the evening and uttering (37b):

(37a)   Phosphorus is a beautiful star visible only in the morning.
(37b)   Hesperus is a beautiful star visible only in the evening.

Although Venus cannot report these ramarks, this does not stop us from semantically evaluating (38a) and (38b) as true in a context in which Venus is the designated agent:

(38a)   The Ancient Babylonian said that I was a beautiful star visible only in the morning.
(38b)   The Ancient Babylonian said that I was a beautiful star visible only in the evening.

If The Ancient Babylonian conjoined sentences (37a) and (37b), (38c) would be true in a context with Venus as agent:

(38c)   The Ancient Babylonian said that I was a beautiful star visible only in the morning and I was a beautiful star visible only in the evening.

What about (39) and (40)?

(39a)   The Ancient Babylonian said that Venus was a beautiful star visible only in the morning.

(39b)   The Ancient Babylonian said that Venus was a beautiful star visible only in the evening.

(39c)   The Ancient Babylonian said that Venus was a beautiful star visible only in the morning and Venus was a beautiful star visible only in the evening.

(40a)   The Ancient Babylonian said that Hesperus was a beautiful star visible only in the morning.

(40b)   The Ancient Babylonian said that Phosphorus was a beautiful star visible only in the evening.

(40c)   The Ancient Babylonian said that Hesperus was a beautiful star visible only in the morning and Phosphorus was a beautiful star visible only in the evening.

If names are directly referential, then these reports should be true. Why, then, do they seem objectionable?

The answer, I believe, lies in the pragmatic desideratum of being maximally faithful to the words of the agent. When reporting the assertions from the perspective of Venus, the ability to use the first person pronoun allows us to deviate from the agent's words; and the reports sound fine. When reporting from the perspective of a third party, we need some excuse for not using the agent's own words (or strict translations of them). In the case of (39) there may be one—the name "Venus" may be familiar to the speaker and to the speaker's audience, whereas the names "Hesperus" and "Phosphorus" may not be. In such a situation utterances of the sentences in (39) are not only true but pragmatically appropriate.

The examples in (40) seem much worse. Here, the reports contain the names used by the agent. However, the way they are used in the reports conflicts with the way they were used by the agent. Since it is hard to imagine any conversational justification for this, they are naturally heard as incorrect. And they are. However, the principle they violate—remain faithful to the words of the agent unless there is reason to deviate—is pragmatic. Thus, the reports may be true after all. (The same analysis applies to sentences (24) and (32).)

VIII

If this is right, then the intuitions motivating the extra-structure proposal conflate pragmatic inappropriateness with semantic incorrectness. However, there is more motivating the proposal than this—at least in its extension to direct reference theory. An important insight behind it is the observation that a sincere, reflective speaker who assertively uttered a sentence

(41b) Rt, t

would standardly assert (and believe) a proposition that someone who assertively uttered the sentence

(41a) Rt, t'

would not (where t and t' are different, but coreferential, directly referential terms). This observation is correct. However, it does not show that (41a) and (41b) express different propositions.

Someone who assertively utters a sentence standardly asserts the proposition semantically expressed by the sentence in the context. However, the speaker often asserts other propositions as well. For example, someone assertively uttering a conjunction asserts not only the conjunctive proposition but also the propositions expressed by the conjuncts. Similarly, someone who asserts that Hesperus is a planet visible in the evening (standardly) asserts that there is a planet visible in the evening.

Competent conversational participants who recognize the two occurrences of t in sentence (41b) to be occurrences of the same term can be expected to accept (41b) if and only if they accept

(41c) $[\lambda x Rx, x]t$

(that is, 't self-R's'). Since conversational participants typically do recognize this, someone who sincerely and assertively utters (41b) can usually be taken to believe, and to have asserted, the proposition expressed by (41c). Moreover, the pragmatic requirement that the reporter be faithful to the words of the agent is responsible for the fact that utterances of

(42) A said (believes) that Rt, t

often give rise to the suggestion that

(43) A said (believes) that $[\lambda x Rx, x]t$

is true. All this combines to create the impression that the proposition expressed by (41b) is the same as the proposition expressed by (41c). However, this is an illusion.

Let us first distinguish (41a) from (41c). The former contains a two-place predicate plus occurrences of a pair of terms. The latter contains a compound one-place predicate plus a single occurrence of a term. Corresponding to this difference in structure, the proposition expressed by (41a) attributes the relation R to a pair consisting of an object and itself; the proposition expressed by (41c) attributes the one-place relational property of bearing-R-to-oneself to a single object. Not only are these propositions different, an individual may assert or believe one without asserting or believing the other. For example, one may assert or believe the proposition that Hesperus is not Phosphorus without asserting or believing the proposition that Hesperus is non-self-identical.

What about (41b)? Does it express the same proposition as (41a) or as (41c)? The extra-structure proposal, in effect, equates the proposition expressed by (41b) with the proposition expressed by (41c). I believe this to be a mistake.

First there is the matter of structure. Like (41a), (41b) consists of a two-place predicate plùs a pair of occurrences of singular terms. Unlike (41c), (41b) does not contain a one-place predicate expressing the relational property of bearing-R-to-oneself. These differences are significant if, as I have suggested, propositions encode the structure of the sentences that express them. According to this independently plausible conception, (41b) and (41c) express different propositions. If, as I have assumed, the propositions are Russellian, and thus contain the objects designated by occurrences of directly referential terms, then (41b) expresses the same proposition as (41a).

The lambda operator used in (41c) is, of course, not part of standard English. However, English does contain a number of devices that may be used to the same end, for example, reflexive pronouns, the formation of adjectives such as, "self-shaver" from two-place predicates, and the use of conjunctions to connect subsentential constituents. The first two of these are illustrated in (44):

(44a)   Reagan shaves himself, and Bush does too.
(44b)   Reagan is a self-shaver, and Bush is too.
(44c)   Reagan shaves Reagan, and Bush does too.

In each case the proposition expressed by the second conjunct is the same as that expressed by the first, save for the different contributions of the subjects of the two clauses. In (44a) and (44b) the proposition expressed by the second conjunct attributes to Bush the property of shaving oneself. In (44c) that proposition attributes to Bush the property of shaving Reagan. Since these properties are different, the propositions expressed by the respective conjuncts are different. Since these differences are inherited from the first conjuncts, the proposition expressed by the initial conjuncts in (44a) and (44b) differs from that expressed by the initial conjunct of (44c).

Next there is the matter of the attitudes. If truth-preserving inferences from (45a) to (45b) are as common as I have indicated, then similar inferences from (45b) to (45c) must often be blocked—for it seems undeniable that (45a) may be true when (45c) is not:

(45a)   *A* says (believes, etc.). . .*t*. . .*t′*. . . .

(45b)   *A* says (believes, etc.). . .*t*. . .*t*. . . .

(45c)   *A* says (believes, etc.) $[\lambda x(. . .x. . .x. . .)]t$.

This is borne out by previous examples.

In the case of McX and Y, McX's utterance of (34) attributed to Y both the property of being a professor in the department and the property of being a graduate student in the department. Thus the ascriptions (35b) through (35d) are true. Similarly, The Ancient Babylonian's utterance of the conjunction of sentences (37a) and (37b) attributed to Venus the property of being a beautiful star visible only in the morning and the property of being a beautiful star visible only in the evening. Thus the ascriptions (38c) and (39c) are true. However, McX did not attribute the uninstantiated property of being a graduate-student-professor-in-the-department to anyone; and The Ancient Babylonian did not attribute the contradictory property of being a beautiful-star-visible-only-in-the-morning-and-only-in-the-evening to anything.

There ought to be a way of reflecting these facts in attitude ascriptions. And there is. The ascriptions that report joint attributions of properties (to Y and to Venus) are of the form (45b)—with occurrences of the same term in different (sentential) conjuncts. These are true. Ascriptions that report attributions of compound properties are represented by (45c). These are false.

The latter are most naturally expressed in English by combining a single occurrence of a directly referential term with a compound subsentential consitituent, as in the following examples:

(35*)   McX said that Y was (both) a professor and a graduate student in the department—or, McX said that Y was a graduate student professor in the department.

(38*)   The Ancient Babylonian said that I was a beautiful star visible in the morning and evening.[28] [Said by Venus]

There is, I think, a significant contrast between these ascriptions and those in (35), (38) and (39). Although the intuitions are delicate and subject to potential pragmatic interference, the ascriptions in (35), (38), and (39) seem, intuitively, to be true, whereas (35*) and (38*) do not. These intuitions support my critique of the extra-structure proposal and provide evidence for the accompanying alternative analysis.[29]

IX

This analysis is, in effect, an extension of Church's treatment of the Mates puzzle to examples involving directly referential singular terms. Like Church, I hold that attitudes are relations to propositions, that ascriptions such as

(46)   *A* says (believes) that *S*

report relations to the proposition expressed by *S* (relative to contexts and assignments to variables) and that (random) substitution of expressions with the same (propositional) content in such constructions preserves both truth value and proposition expressed. I differ from Church in taking coreferential names, indexicals, and variables to have the same (propositional) content.

The decision to treat these terms as directly referential leads, in certain cases, to the derivation of problematic attitude ascriptions from unproblematic ones. However, this occurs even without direct reference, as is illustrated by the parallel between (47) and (48):

(47a)   *A* says (believes) that doctors are doctors.
(47b)   *A* says (believes) that physicians are doctors.

(48a)   *A* says (believes) that Phosphorus is Phosphorus.
(48b)   *A* says (believes) that Hesperus is Phosphorus.

Although the (a) sentences may appear to differ in truth value from the (b) sentences, this appearance is due to pragmatic considerations, most notably, the requirement that the reporter be maximally faithful to the words of the agent unless there is reason to deviate. Since in cases like this there often is no such reason, utterances of these sentences will suggest to the hearer that the reporter has been maximally faithful to the agent's own words. In these particular examples this suggestion takes on added significance because of the triviality of the propositions semantically expressed by the complement clauses. Thus it is natural to regard utterances of (47b) and (48b) as incorrect when the suggestions are false. Such utterances are incorrect, but that does not mean that the propositions semantically expressed by these sentences are false.

One potential difference between Church's synonyms and my coreferential, directly referential terms is worth noting. There is some plausibility in holding that anyone who understands both "doctor" and "physician" knows that they are synonymous.[30] If one does hold this, one may characterize anyone who rejects sentence (49) as someone who fails to understand one of its terms:

(49)   Physicians are doctors.

But, if one fails to understand a term, then one's dispositions to accept or reject sentences containing it will not be reliable indications of whether or not one believes the propositions they express. The same may be true of the relation between one's assertive utterances and one's assertions. Thus a person's dissent from sentence (49) or assertive utterance of its negation might well be taken as proof of linguistic confusion rather than as evidence for the truth of

(50a)   A believed (asserted) that physicians are not doctors

and

(50b)   A believed (asserted) that doctors are not doctors.

Indeed, there is some plausibility in holding that these examples cannot be true.

The situation is different with directly referential singular terms. There is no plausibility in holding that anyone who understands both "Hesperus" and "Phosphorus" knows that they refer to the same thing. Thus dissent from sentence (51), or assertive utterance of its negation, cannot be taken as showing linguistic confusion but rather must be seen as evidence for the truth of (52a) and (52b):

(51)   Hesperus is Phosphorus.

(52a)   A believed (asserted) that Hesperus is not Phosphorus.
(52b)   A believed (asserted) that Hesperus is not Hesperus.

The counterintuitiveness of utterances of (52b) are, I maintain, due both to violations of the pragmatic principle of fidelity to the words of the agent and to confusion of (52b) with

(52c)   A believed (asserted) that Hesperus is non-self-identical.

Despite this possible difference between (50) and (52), the contrast does not represent a general difference between Church-type cases and those involving directly referential terms. The point can be made using Church's example.

(14a)   Whoever believes (asserts, etc.) that the meeting lasted less than a period of fourteen days believes (asserts, etc.) that the meeting lasted less than a period of fourteen days.
(14b)   Whoever believes (asserts, etc.) that the meeting lasted less than a period of fourteen days believes (asserts, etc.) that the meeting lasted less than a fortnight.

(15a)   Nobody doubts that (14a).
(15b)   Nobody doubts that (14b).

According to Church—and me—the (a) sentences in these examples express the same propositions as the corresponding (b) sentences. However, not everyone who assents to (a) will assent to (b). We know this is true in the case of (15), since Putnam assented to (15a) while dissenting from (15b).[31] Now Putnam is, and was, a sincere, reflective, competent speaker. Certainly, his different treatment of sentences (15a) and (15b) was not evidence that he misunderstood "fortnight" or "period of fourteen days." Nor was it evidence that he did not understand the words "doubt" and "believe"—or the sentences themselves. He may have had the wrong semantic theory about these examples—I think he did—but he understood them in the sense relevant to linguistic competence as well as anyone.

Because of this, his dissent from sentence (15b) and acceptance of its negation cannot be dismissed as unreliable indicators of his attitude toward the propositions they express. Had he assertively uttered both (15a) and the negation of (15b), he would have asserted both propositions. Furthermore, his assertions would have been accurate reflections of his beliefs. Because sentences (15a) and (15b) express the same proposition, this means that Putnam would have asserted and believed both a proposition and its negation—without having made any straightforward logical error. This is just the sort of thing that we find in cases involving direct reference.[32]

If these conclusions are correct, then a widespread picture of our relationship to what we assert and believe is faulty. We are apt to think of this relationship as direct, unmediated, and fully transparent to introspection and observation. It is not. Propositions are contents of various intermediaries with which we are intimately related—sentences, belief states, and other modes of presentation. To assert or believe a proposition P is to stand in the right relation to an appropriate intermediary with P as content.[33] In cases involving language, our ordinary linguistic competence ensures that we have a reasonable pretheoretic grasp of when two people have said the same thing or expressed the same belief. However, since linguistic competence does not guarantee the possession of a correct semantic theory, theoretical investigation is capable of yielding some surprising conclusions about our beliefs and assertions.

In undertaking such an investigation, I believe it is crucial to take seriously the notion of a proposition as the information expressed by a sentence. In this respect Richard Cartwright's 1962 article, "Propositions," is a classic. At a time when many philosophers either dismissed or misidentified propositions, Cartwright clarified the strong intuitive case for countenancing them and exposed the misidentifications. With characteristic modesty he concluded the article by indicating that, although he had said what propositions are not, he had not said what they are. "To distinguish them from other things is not by itself to provide either means for their detection or rules for distinguishing one of them from another" (Cartwright 1962,

p. 103). There is today a resurgence of interest in propositions and no dirth of attempts to provide rules for distinguishing among them. It would be nice to think that these attempts will be as successful in this part of the task as Cartwright's paper was in its.

Notes

I would like to thank the Philosophy Department at the University of Washington for use of their facilities during the summer of 1986, when this paper was written. I would also like to thank Ali Akhtar Kazmi for his useful comments on the initial draft.

1. Following Cartwright, I have spoken of the proposition asserted by an utterance. This is a convenient simplification. Although an unambiguous sentence expresses a single proposition in a context, a speaker who utters it often asserts a number of propositions in addition to the one semantically expressed by the sentence uttered. (See section VIII.) Cartwright's point regarding sentences (1) and (2) is not this one but rather the more fundamental observation that these sentences express different propositions in different contexts.

2. See, in particular, Kaplan (1977), Salmon (1986a), and Soames (1987).

3. A description, $\ulcorner$the x: $Fx\urcorner$, refers with respect to a circumstance E (and context C) to the unique object *in the domain of E* that satisfies $\ulcorner Fx\urcorner$ with respect to E (and C). When $\ulcorner Fx\urcorner$ is $\ulcorner$actually $Gx\urcorner$, the description refers with respect to E (and C), if at all, to the unique object existing in E that satisfies $\ulcorner Gx\urcorner$ in the circumstance of the context C. See Salmon (1981), chapter 1, for a discussion of these issues plus arguments for the claim that names and indexicals are *nondescriptional* (Salmon's terminology).

4. For the sake of simplicity, I assume that a proposition is always either true or false with respect to a world.

5. I assume that only those who exist (at a given time) in a world are Americans (at that time) in the world.

6. The term "directly referential" has been used in the literature in two main ways: as it is in Thesis 1 and as a synonym for "nondescriptional." The two conceptions are different and should not be confused. I always use the term in the sense of Thesis 1.

In Soames (1985; 1987), Thesis 1 is used to show that propositions must encode much of the structure of the sentences that express them. A natural way of looking at this is to take propositions to be structured complexes whose constituents are the propositional contents of subsentential expressions, relative to contexts.

7. Substitution of e' for multiple occurrences of e are handled by repeated applications of the principle. The terminology "random compositionality" is due to Kaplan (1985). Note that, if the content of e in C is the same as that of e' in C', then the proposition expressed by S in C will be the same as that expressed by S' in C', provided that S does not contain other expressions whose contents vary between C and C'.

8. Note that this holds even if x associates the same (incomplete) descriptive material—for example, "a famous Roman"—with both names, or associates no descriptive material at all with them. See section VIII, and note 12 of Soames (1985) for further discussion.

9. Some verbs, such as "believe," take NP arguments other than those denoting propositions, as in "John believes Mary." I put aside such uses for present purposes. Other verbs, such as "say" and "think," do not take full NP arguments at all. For these one moves directly from statement A to statement D.

10. This agnostic position seems to be taken by Almog (1985) and Wettstein (1986).

11. Other cases, noted in Church (1982), Kripke (1979), Salmon (1986), and Soames (1987), involve substitution of coreferential variables (with respect to an assignment) and substitution of a name for its translation ("London"/"Londres," "Peking"/"Beijing").

12. In these examples, "(14a)" and "(14b)" are abbreviations of the previous examples, rather than terms referring to them. The conclusion that (15a) and (15b) have the same truth value can be gotten either from an extension of random compositionality to sentences containing multiple embeddings of propositional attitude ascriptions or from assumptions A through D together with an extension of random compositionality to sentences with a single level of embedding.

13. Mates, Putnam, and Church were all responding to Carnap's proposal (1947) that S and S' are synonymous, and express the same belief, if and only if they are intensionally isomorphic. Carnap proposed that an individual i satisfies $\ulcorner x$ believes that $S\urcorner$ in English if and only if there is a language L and sentence S' such that S in English is intensionally isomorphic to S' in L, and i is disposed to assent to S' as a sentence of L. In the subsequent debate three objections were brought against this proposal.

Church (1950) argued that the analysis wrongly characterized the content of ordinary beliefs, such as the belief that the earth is round, as being about sentences. Instead of relating individuals to sentences, belief ascriptions should, Church thought, be analyzed as relating individuals to propositions. Church (1954) argued that, in any case, intensional isomorphism was too weak for Carnap's purposes because it allowed substitution of nonsynonymous constants with the same intension. Mates (1950) argued that, no matter how closely two simple sentences were related, one could always embed them in structures such as (15) in such a way that speakers would assent to one but not the other (and indeed would assent to one and the negation of the other).

Putnam's article (1954) was a defense of Carnap against Church (1950) and Mates (1950). Regarding Mates (1950), Putnam's proposal was that the definition of "intensionally isomorphic" should require S and S' to have the same *logical* structure in the sense discussed at the end of section IV (as well as being made up of constituents with the same intensions). In reconstructing Putnam's proposal, I follow Church in analyzing "believe" as relating individuals to structured propositions and Carnap in taking that relation to hold in virtue of a relation between the individual and a mode of representation that expresses the proposition. In this framework Putnam's proposal requires sentences expressing the same proposition to have the same logical structure.

14. However, Putnam did apply his analysis to certain sentences containing singular terms. For example, although he took '5' and 'V' to be synonymous, he distinguished the contents of '5 is identical with 5' and '5 is identical with V' on the basis of the different logical structures of the two sentences.

15. Kaplan (1985) accepts assumptions A through D, restricts himself to ascriptions in which the only directly referential terms are names (no indexicals and no quantifying-in), and argues against random compositionality. Richard (1983) holds that beliefs are relations to propositions but maintains that a belief ascription $\ulcorner x$ believes that $S\urcorner$ not only reports the proposition believed but also provides information about the sentence, or representation, acceptance of which is responsible for the agent's belief. This is illustrated by the relationship between the following ascriptions (i) and (ii), in which the terms are variables or indexicals that refer to the same thing (relative to their respective contexts and assignments):

(i) x believes that . . .t. . .t. . . .

(ii) x believes that . . .t. . .t'. . . .

Although the complements of ascriptions (i) and (ii) express the same proposition P, the ascriptions are assigned different truth conditions. In order for ascription (i) to be true, the agent must believe P in virtue of accepting a sentence containing occurrences of directly referential terms (indexicals) with the same character. The truth conditions assigned to ascription (ii) are the same except that the sentence accepted by the agent may contain either occurrences of directly referential terms with the same character or occurrences with different characters. Thus Richard (1983) characterizes the truth of ascription (i) as guaranteeing the truth of ascription (ii), but not vice versa.

The system in Richard (1983) does not cover cases involving names. (Since distinct names t and t' with the same referent have the same character, a simple extension of that system to include them would treat an agent's acceptance of $\ulcorner S(t, t')\urcorner$ as equivalent to the acceptance of $\ulcorner S(t, t)\urcorner$—which Richard does not want.) However, Richard (forthcoming) considers a modification of his 1983 system that accommodates names. On this account ascription (i) is true provided that the sentence accepted by the agent contains two occurrences of a single name; ascription (ii) is true provided that the accepted sentence contains occurrences of different names. Thus, in his forthcoming article neither (i) nor (ii) implies the other (where t and t' in (i) and (ii) are either names or variables).

The arguments given in the text bear in slightly different ways on all these proposals. For an argument directed specifically against Richard's claim that the truth of belief ascriptions requires more than a correct report of the proposition believed, see Soames (1987), note 24.

16. I use

    (i) $\exists x$ A believes that Fx

to represent the English sentences

    (ii)   Someone is such that A believes that he is F

    (iii) A believes of someone that he is F.

Note that in sentence (i) the occurrence of "x" in the complement does not contribute an object to the proposition expressed. However, the assumption that variables are directly referential plays a crucial role in evaluating its truth value. Sentence (i) is true if and only if there is an object o such that the following is true with respect to an assignment of o to "x":

    (iv) A believes that Fx.

Sentence (iv) is true with respect to such an assignment if and only if the referent of "A" believes the proposition expressed by $\ulcorner Fx\urcorner$ with respect to the assignment. Theses 1* and 2* characterize this as a singular proposition.

17. See Soames (1987) for details.

18. R^* is the relation expressed by the predicate in (21); F^* and G^* are properties expressed by the predicates in (22); and o is the referent of the directly referential terms.

19. This picture is due to Kaplan (1985). Another way of encoding the syntax would be to assimilate sentences (21b) and (22b) to

    (i) $[\lambda x Rx, x]t$

and

    (ii) $[\lambda x(Fx \wedge Gx)]t$.

The predicates formed by lambda abstraction express one-place properties. If we choose to represent these as functions from objects to singular propositions, the propositions expressed would then be (iii) and (iv), where f maps an arbitrary object y onto $\langle\langle y, y\rangle, R^*\rangle$ and h maps y onto $\langle \text{Conj}, \langle\langle\langle y\rangle, F^*\rangle, \langle\langle y\rangle, G^*\rangle\rangle\rangle$:

(iii) $\langle\langle o\rangle, f\rangle$,

(iv) $\langle\langle o\rangle, h\rangle$.

20. This point was made by David Lewis at the Princeton version of Kaplan (1985).

21. I assume that, if $\ulcorner A$ said (believed, etc.) that P and $Q\urcorner$ is true, then so are $\ulcorner A$ said (believed, etc.) that $P\urcorner$ and $\ulcorner A$ said (believed, etc.) that $Q\urcorner$. However, the basic point of the argument could be reconstructed without assuming this. (I also take (25e) to be equivalent to (25d).)

22. The argument here parallels one given by Church (1954) against Carnap. Church says:

> Again by the Principle of Tolerance it is possible to introduce a predicator constant which shall be synonymous with a specified abstraction expression of the form $(\lambda x)[. \ x. \ .]$; or to introduce an individual constant synonymous with a specified individual description of the form $(\iota x)[. \ x. \ .]$. And (unlike the case of synonymous primitive constants) it may be held that something like this actually occurs in formalized languages commonly constructed—namely those in which definitions are treated as introducing new notations into the object language, rather than as metatheoretic abbreviations. But whether or not the process is called definition, it is clear by the Principle of Tolerance that nothing prevents us from introducing (say) a predicator constant R as synonymous with the abstraction expression $(\lambda x)[. \ x. \ .]$, and taking $R \equiv (\lambda x)[. \ x. \ .]$ as an axiom. And if this is done, then R must be interchangeable with $(\lambda x)[. \ x. \ .]$ in all contexts, including belief contexts, being synonymous with $(\lambda x)[. \ x. \ .]$ by the very construction of the language—by definition, if we choose to call it that. (Church 1954, p. 67)

23. Richard (1983) deals with examples such as those in (25) by positing a dichotomy between (25b), on the one hand, and sentences (25d) and (25e), on the other. Sentence (25b) is said to be false, whereas sentences (25d) and (25e) are claimed to be true but pragmatically inappropriate or misleading.

Kaplan rejects this dichotomy, hoping for a way to treat all three sentences as false. Although Kaplan (1985) did not contain an explicit semantic mechanism for doing this, he suggested that perhaps a semantics that relativized the truth conditions of attitude ascriptions to a discourse might solve the problem. Roughly put, the idea is that the truth of (25d) would require the existence of a pair of sentences, S and S', accepted or assertively uttered by the agent, expressing the reported propositions, and anchored by a one-one (order-preserving) mapping from names in S and S' to names in the complements of the reports.

It might even be thought that the interchange problem illustrated by (24) could be handled in this way. Suppose that the speaker associates descriptions D and D' with the names h and p. One might maintain that sentence (i) can be true only if it is true relative to the discourse (ii):

(i) x believes Rh, p.

(ii) x believes h is D, x believes p is D', x believes Rh, p.

If the agent associated D and D' with h and p, respectively, then this proposal could assign different truth values to (i) and (iii):

(iii) x believes Rp, h.

One problem with the attempt to relativize the semantics of belief ascriptions to discourses is that it seems to give up the independently motivated assumptions A through D analyzing "believe" as a two-place predicate of individuals and propositions. However, even if we put this aside, the proposal for treating the interchange problem gives the wrong results when the descriptive information associated with names by the speaker conflicts with that associated with the names by the agent. For example, if the speaker associates "the first star seen in the evening" with p and "the first star seen in the morning" with h and the agent reverses those associations, the proposal will incorrectly characterize (i) as true and (iii) as false when the agent rejects the complement of (i) and accepts the complement of (iii).

The point here is that, when the names used by the agent appear in the belief report, they should be used as the agent used them. In my opinion this is a pragmatic rather than a semantic fact. In section VII I apply it uniformly to the sentences in (24) and (25).

24. Examples involving only names, or general terms, can easily be produced. Imagine speakers that have three names for Venus—"Hesperus" and "Venus," which are applied freely and interchangeably to Venus when seen in the evening, and "Phosphorus," which is applied to Venus when seen in the morning. These speakers readily assent to (translations of) "Venus is Hesperus" and dissent from "Hesperus is Phosphorus" and "Venus is Phosphorus." Nevertheless, the extra-structure proposal characterizes them as believing that Hesperus is Phosphorus and that Venus is Phosphorus.

A similar example using general terms can be constructed in a language in which "surgeon," "physician," and "doctor" are synonyms.

25. In Richard (1983) the truth of (33a) guarantees the truth of (33c); however, the move from (33c) to (33a) is blocked. This is unattractive. It does not help to be told that the ancients did not believe that Hesperus was not Hesperus, if it is granted that they did believe that Hesperus was not Phosphorus and that Phosphorus was Hesperus. The system in Richard (forthcoming) blocks the move from (33a) to (33c) at the cost of blocking the move to (33b)—which is also unattractive. Quantification is not treated by Kaplan (1985).

26. The system in Richard (1983) would use terms with different characters to represent the two demonstratives in (34) and (35a). An extension of the system treating assertion on the model of belief would incorrectly characterize sentences (35b) through (35d) as false. The same is true of Richard (forthcoming).

27. I take the different demonstrations to be parts of McX's sentence.

28. In order to facilitate the conjoining of subsentential constituents, I have simplified the example by eliminating occurrences of "only." This does not affect the main issue.

29. A thorough and illuminating investigation of the distinction between the simple sentences (41a) through (41c) as well as the ascriptions (42) and (43) is given in Salmon (1986b). These issues are also briefly discussed in Soames (1985), note 12.

30. I do not hold this myself. However, for purposes of the present argument, it is not necessary to challenge the view here.

31. In point of fact, Putnam's examples involved "Greeks" and "Hellenes" rather than "fortnight" and "period of fourteen days"; but this makes no difference.

32. The argument can be given at one less level of embedding if we grant, as I believe we should, that a fully competent speaker who understands sentences (14a) and (14b) may sincerely and reflectively assent both to the former and to the negation of the latter. In my view such a speaker asserts and believes the proposition expressed by the negation of (14b). Moreover, he has made no straightforward logical error even though this proposition is also expressed by the negation of a logical truth, namely (14a).

This view apparently conflicts with that of Church, who concludes (1954) by saying that Mates does not really doubt the proposition expressed by (14b)—no matter what he himself may say. If to doubt P is to consider P and take up a skeptical attitude toward it (such as believing its negation), then I think that Church's conclusion is false. However, on this conception of the attitude of doubting, doubting P does not involve not believing P. Although Mates did doubt the proposition expressed by sentence (14b), he also believed it—by virtue of his attitude toward (14a).

33. This conception is developed in Salmon (1986a) and Soames (1987).

References

Almog, Joseph. 1985. "Form and content." *Noûs* 19: 603–616.

Carnap, Rudolf. 1947. *Meaning and Necessity*. Chicago: University of Chicago Press.

Cartwright, Richard. 1962. "Propositions," in *Analytical Philosophy*, R. J. Butler, ed. Oxford: Basil Blackwell, 81–103.

Church, Alonzo. 1950. "Carnap's analysis of statements of assertion and belief," *Analysis* 10: 98–99.

Church, Alonzo. 1954. "Intensional isomorphism and identity of belief." *Philosophical Studies* 5: 65–73. To be reprinted in *Propositions and Attitudes*, N. Salmon and S. Soames, eds. (forthcoming).

Church, Alonzo. 1982. "A remark concerning Quine's paradox about modality." *Analisis Filosofico* 2: 25–34 (in Spanish). English version to appear in *Propositions and Attitudes*, N. Salmon and S. Soames, eds. (forthcoming).

Kaplan, David. 1977. "Demonstratives." UCLA Department of Philosophy (unpublished). To appear in *Themes from David Kaplan*, J. Almog, J. Perry, and H. Wettstein, eds. (forthcoming).

Kaplan, David. 1985. "Word, object, and belief." Unpublished talks given in May at Princeton University, and in July at the meetings of the Association for Symbolic Logic, Stanford University.

Kripke, Saul. 1980. *Naming and Necessity*. Cambridge, Mass.: Harvard University Press and Basil Blackwell. Originally printed in *Semantics of Natural Language*, D. Davidson and G. Harman, eds. (Dordrecht: Reidel, 1972), 253–355, 763–769.

Kripke, Saul. 1979. "A puzzle about belief," in *Meaning and Use*, A. Margalit, ed. Dordrecht: Reidel, 239–275. To be reprinted in *Propositions and Attitudes*, N. Salmon and S. Soames, eds. (forthcoming).

Mates, Benson. 1950. "Synonymity." *University of California Publications in Philosophy* 25: 210–226. Reprinted in *Semantics and the Philosophy of Language*, L. Linsky, ed. (Champaign: University of Illinois Press, 1952), 111–136.

Perry, John. 1977. "Frege on demonstratives." *The Philosophical Review* 86: 474–497.

Putnam, Hilary. 1954. "Synonymity, and the analysis of belief sentences." *Analysis* 14: 114–122.

Richard, Mark. 1983. "Direct reference and ascriptions of belief." *Journal of Philosophical Logic* 12: 425–452. To be reprinted in *Propositions and Attitudes*, N. Salmon and S. Soames, eds. (forthcoming).

Richard, Mark. Forthcoming. "Quantification and Leibniz's law." *The Philosophical Review*.

Salmon, Nathan. 1981. *Reference and Essence*. Princeton, N.J.: Princeton University Press.

Salmon, Nathan. 1986a. *Frege's Puzzle*. Cambridge, Mass.: The MIT Press. A Bradford Book.

Salmon, Nathan. 1986b. "Reflexivity." *Notre Dame Journal of Formal Logic* 27: 401–429. To be reprinted in *Propositions and Attitudes*, N. Salmon and S. Soames, eds. (forthcoming).

Soames, Scott. 1985. "Lost innocence." *Linguistics and Philosophy* 8: 59–71. To be reprinted in *The Philosopher's Annual*, Vol. 8, P. Grim, C. J. Martin, and P. Athay, eds. (Atascadero, Calif.: Ridgeview Press, forthcoming).

Soames, Scott. (1987). "Direct reference, propositional attitudes, and semantic content." *Philosophical Topics* 15. To be reprinted in *Propositions and Attitudes*, N. Salmon and S. Soames, eds. (forthcoming).

Wettstein, Howard. 1986. "Has semantics rested on a mistake?" *Journal of Philosophy* 83: 185–209.

Moore's Paradox, Sincerity Conditions, and Epistemic Qualification
Charles E. Caton

1

This is not a scholarly paper on Moore's paradox. Many of the points I make have been made by others (long ago in some cases), and I hope they will acquiesce in my putting them in the present context without further acknowledgment. I want to suggest in this paper that a Moore paradox of the statemental type has to do with epistemic force rather than merely with sincerity conditions of illocutionary acts (if with them at all). Although something like a sufficient condition for an utterance to be odd in the Moore-paradoxical way will emerge, I do not try to say what conditions it is *necessary* to have to have a paradox of this type. The main reason for this is that the original paradigms primarily dealt with in connection with Moore's paradox have involved two forms of sentence that are (supposedly) suited for making statements, viz.

(A)   *p*, but I don't believe that *p*

and

(B)   Not-*p*, but I believe that *p*

although it is a feature of the account of Moore's paradox to be given here that the utterance of many other forms of sentence can involve what is apparently the same sort of oddity, that of sentences whose use is somehow impossible or ruled out although they do not involve self-contradiction.

In fact, I have no evidence, other than that of linguistic intuition and the plausibility of my descriptions of them, that the original paradigms of Moore's paradox and the other examples of odd utterances I deal with exhibit one and the same sort of oddity. But because it appears that a unified account of all of them can be given, I conduct my discussion under the assumption that just one kind of oddity is in question. (For further remarks on the larger picture, see section V.)

When statemental utterances are in question, the present account falls under the type of account of Moore's paradox sometimes called the "saying and disbelieving" line. Although popular, it is not particularly well named, because even paradoxes using sentences of form (A) have to do not with disbelieving things but with saying that one does; nor does this name mention implying (or indicating, etc.) what one believes, reference to which is essential. According to this account, the statemental conjunctive utterances that are Moore paradoxical are so because what is said in uttering one of the conjuncts (its propositional content) is logically incompatible with what is merely implied by uttering the other conjunct. Actually, it is a matter here of what *would* be the case if these utterances were made in the normal assertive way, because in fact they are in a sense impossible utterances (or things that one cannot say) and probably never actually get uttered in this way. Interchanging assertion and denial, as in cases of form (B), gives rise to an analogous type of utterance that we might call the "denying and believing" form of Moore's paradox and make similar comments about.

Thus, as examples of the original paradigms of Moore's paradox, we have such utterances as

(1)   It is raining, but I don't believe that it is

and

(2)   It is not raining, but I believe that it is.

Actually, completeness requires dealing with a third form, as a result of an ambiguity in (A), as a result of a phenomenon known to linguists as "raising" and resulting in a difference in the scope of the negation with respect to "believe." Let "(A1)" stand for the sentence form (A) interpreted as involving narrow scope of the negation (with respect to "believe"), and let "(A2)" stand for (A) with the wider scope. (The "not" in (A), understood this way, was said to have been "raised" (transformationally) from the complement clause; the one in sentence (A2) was not raised.) (A) on interpretation (A1) thus means

(A1) p, but I believe that it is not the case that p

whereas on interpretation (A2) it means

(A2) p, but it is not the case that I believe that p.

The "saying and disbelieving" line on Moore paradoxes of this form can still be construed as holding that what uttering the first conjunct implies (in the sense in question) is explicitly denied by the second conjunct, because the second conjunct (like that of an utterance of the same form disambiguated the other way) is still logically contrary to the implicatum of uttering the first conjunct.

A "denying and believing" line would be the analogue of those just mentioned, holding instead that uttering the first conjunct of a Moore-paradoxical utterance of form (B) implied (in the sense in question) that the speaker did not believe what the second conjunct explicitly says the speaker believes.

The account of Moore's paradox that I try to develop in what follows belongs, broadly, to the saying-and-disbelieving, denying-and-believing type of account, but I try to pursue systematically the suggestion (implicit in some of the earlier literature) that the conflict involved is one involving epistemic force or what I have elsewhere (Caton 1966, 1981) called epistemic qualifiers.

II

In this section I explain what I take to be the broad outlines of the system of epistemic qualification, starting with some discussion of the kind of pragmatic relations that I believe define these broad outlines, and then try to locate belief (important in connection with Moore's paradox) within it.

Discourse Relations

As I use the term, a *remark* is any illocutionary act in the most complete sense, including content, of Austin (1962), Alston (1964), or Searle (1969). Where convenient, I talk about the *content* of a remark, its *illocutionary force* (= what type of illocutionary act was performed in issuing it), the *sentence* used or that could be used to make it, a *clause* that could be used to express it, etc.

By a *discourse* (or *d-*) *relation*, I mean a relation between remarks in a discourse. One example of a discourse relation is *d-commitment*: if making a certain remark in a discourse commits one to making another remark in that discourse, there is a certain relation between the two remarks involved; it is sometimes even ordinarily called commitment (although of course other things are also) and may be called d-commitment. A special case of d-commitment is the relation deriving from the fact that the propositional content of a certain remark one makes logically entails that of a certain other remark. Another example of a d-relation is the relation holding between two remarks as a result of the fact that making one of them in a certain discourse *excludes* making the other, on pain of incoherence (uninterpretability) of that discourse; this relation between remarks may be called *d-exclusion* or *d-incompatibility*.

These two d-relations may be related definitionally, because if one is d-committed to making a certain remark R_2 by what one has already said R_1, surely R_1 is d-incompatible with agreeing with the negation of R_2. This must be the case at least when statemental remarks are in question.

Epistemic Qualification

Three further concepts are useful in expounding the nature of our system of epistemic qualification. The fundamental one is that of an epistemic state, and deriving from it are those of an epistemic qualifier and of an epistemic qualifying expression.

By an *epistemic state* here I refer to knowledge (in the propositional sense of knowing that *p*, for some proposition *p*), its various species or types, such as remembering and realizing, and the various states that are contrary to it, in the sense that it cannot be at one and the same time that one is in one of those states and also knows that *p*. For example, if one just thinks that *p* (and does not know that *p*), then obviously one cannot also know that *p*. (I think here of responding to the question of whether one *knows* that *p* or (just) *thinks* that *p*.) But also, if one suspects that *p*, then equally, I think, one cannot also then know that *p*.

Just referring to knowledge, its types, and its competitors might not, I think, delimit a complete natural class of epistemic states, for it might be that there are states functioning in the same sort of linguistic and conceptual way that are compatible with knowledge without being types of it. In particular, belief may be of this sort; yet the epistemic qualifier 'I believe'[1] correlated with it is plainly in the same business as those related to the epistemic states mentioned: By itself, it is a qualifier of middling strength, competing on the one hand, for example, with those related to knowing and being certain and on the other with, for example, those related to inclination to believe, suspicion, and thinking it possible that *p*. So I must confess that up to this point I do not have a satisfactory definition of epistemic states nor therefore of epistemic qualifiers or epistemic qualifying expressions.

By an *epistemic qualifier* I mean a qualification or modification of a proposition occurring in one's discourse so as to indicate what one takes one's epistemic state to be with regard to that proposition at the time it occurs, so qualified, in the discourse.

By an *epistemic qualifying expression* I mean a linguistic expression (or other linguistic device) that is used to express an epistemic qualifier, that is, to indicate what epistemic state the speaker takes her/himself to be in with respect to an indicated proposition. Examples of epistemic qualifying expressions are "I know," "I think," "I believe," "I'm certain," "I feel certain," "It seems to me," "I incline to think." Those in this group may be called *personal epistemic qualifiers* because they explicitly mention the speaker. Ones that may be called *impersonal*, because they do not explicitly mention the speaker, include "It is certain," "It is virtually certain," "It is definite," "It must be" (or the auxiliary ". . .must. . ."), "It is overwhelmingly probable," "It is likely," "There is a good chance," "It is possible," and "It may be" (or the auxiliary ". . .may. . ."). I also call the epistemic qualifier expressed by a certain epistemic qualifying expression a personal or impersonal epistemic qualifier, according as the epistemic qualifying expression is personal or impersonal.

Because epistemic qualifying expressions usually have other uses besides their use to express a certain epistemic qualification of an indicated proposition, where necessary I speak of an epistemic qualifying expression "functioning to express an epistemic qualifier." For example, in the conditional statement

(3)   When it is certain that she has left, the desk clerk will use his pass key to let the officers in

the epistemic qualifying expression "it is certain" is not being used to indicate what epistemic state the speaker takes her/himself to be in at the time of utterance with respect to some proposition (notably not with respect to the proposition that the person referred to has left); that is, the epistemic qualifying expression is not there functioning to express an epistemic qualifier, as it would be (for example) in the statement that

(4)   It is certain that she has left

given, say, in answer to the question of whether it is certain that the person referred to has left.

Personal epistemic qualifying expressions containing one of the verbs that denote epistemic states seem to tend to function to express epistemic qualifiers when in what one might call the Austinian position in their conjugation, viz. the first-person singular present indicative active. This is, of course, the position in which performative (or illocutionary act) verbs have their striking performative force. If there is some reason why there should be this coincidence, it is not known to me. (It may be noted that Austin included as (possible) performative verbs some that might, perhaps, have been better regarded as epistemic qualifying expressions; these were "doubt," "believe," and "know" (Austin 1962, p. 161). Note, though, that not even all personal epistemic qualifying expressions function to express epistemic qualifiers only in the Austinian position, at least not if "It seems to me that p" counts as a personal one.)

One epistemic qualifying device important in connection with Moore paradoxes (and illocutionary acts) is not in English and other familiar languages a word or phrase but rather a device linguists might call a *zero-form*, that is, the absence of any other indication of the speaker's epistemic state. Because a person who uses this device can often be said to have made a "flat statement," I appropriate this term and call the epistemic qualifier thus expressed the *flat-statement epistemic qualifier*, denoting it by Q_{fs}. (I see no reason to suppose that there is more than one.) Epistemic qualifying expressions do not appear to be ambiguous as to what epistemic state they denote, although what they convey in a particular application may well be what Toulmin (1958, ch. 1) calls "field-dependent." It thus seems legitimate to refer to a mapping from epistemic qualifying devices into epistemic states and of a one-to-one correlation between sets of equivalent epistemic qualifying devices and epistemic states.

Epistemic states, epistemic qualifiers, and epistemic qualifying expressions exhibit what may be termed *epistemic strength*: epistemic states, in that some of them are preferable to others if one wants to be in as evidentially good a state with respect to some matter as one can; epistemic qualifiers, in that they are associated with this epistemic preferability through being correlated with epistemic states; and epistemic qualifying devices, in that they express these so correlated epistemic qualifiers. A number of conversational moves reflect this ordering of epistemic qualifiers, for example, those involving remarks of the form "It's not just that $Q_1(p)$; (but also/ rather) $Q_2(p)$," as in "I don't just believe that p; I know that p."

Three broad strength groups of epistemic qualifiers can be distinguished, using the relation of d-incompatibility, as follows: a *strong* epistemic qualifier Q_s may be defined as one such that saying that $Q_s(p)$ is d-incompatible with saying that it may be that not-p; for example, "I know," "I'm certain," "It is certain." The flat-statement qualifier is among these. A *moderate* epistemic qualifier Q_m may be defined as one such that saying that $Q_m(p)$ is d-compatible with saying that it may be that not-p, but is d-incompatible with saying that $Q_m(\text{not-}p)$; for example, "I am almost certain," "I believe," "It is likely." And a *weak* epistemic qualifier Q_w may be defined as one such that saying that $Q_w(p)$ is d-compatible with saying that $Q_w(\text{not-}p)$; for example, "There is some evidence," "It is possible," "...may...".

Two epistemic qualifiers Q_1 and Q_2 can be incompatible in the sense that for no proposition p is any discourse coherent that contains both the remark that $Q_1(p)$ and the remark that $Q_2(p)$, neither having been withdrawn. (I refer to serious literal remarks here.) For example, the epistemic qualifiers 'I know' and 'I guess' are, I believe, incompatible in this sense.

I have reference throughout to the system expressible in English, which is I believe similar to that expressed in other familiar languages. This overall system of epistemic qualification seems to be largely constituted by relations of the various sorts that have so far been mentioned, together with further ones, some of which are mentioned later.

My epistemic qualification line on Moore's paradox is that these paradoxical utterances arise from epistemically qualifying propositional factors in an utterance in ways that are not consistent with the system of epistemic qualification.

Belief and Epistemic Qualification

"I think" and "I believe" do not allow all the same completions and constructions, but in the part of their use that I am concerned with here they seem to be synonymous, and I refer to them interchangeably. In particular, either can be used to formulate the original examples of Moore's paradox. Because they can also be so used for many of the additional examples dealt with here, it is important to clarify how the epistemic qualifier 'I believe' functions in the system of epistemic qualification.

But the epistemic qualifying expression "I believe" is problematical in that it appears to correlate both with a less and also with a more comprehensive epistemic state. (By "more comprehensive" I mean that a given subject will almost always be in the more comprehensive state with respect to more propositions than he or she will be with respect to the other.) For example, it seems to have a broad sense in a question such as

(5)   Did Aristotle believe that the earth was round?

where the fact that Aristotle regarded the matter as quite certain does not mean that sentence (5) should be answered in the negative; on the contrary, it would mean that it should be answered in the affirmative. Yet with respect to the question

(6)   Did Aristotle *know* that the earth was round or just *believe* that it was?

that Aristotle knew or was certain that the earth was round would mean that the second alternative was a factually incorrect answer.

Thus, in the epistemic qualifier–epistemic state correlation, the narrow use of "I believe" seems not to correlate with the epistemic state referred to in historical belief reports but rather (if it correlates with any at all) with a narrower epistemic state. Yet we do not, I think, feel that "believe" has changed its meaning from the one case to the other or that we must ask for disambiguation of a sentence such as

(7)   Aristotle believed that the earth was round.

I do not say that the string (7) is not, in context, associated with two different meanings (or propositional types), I think it is: one related to question (5), expressing an affirmative answer to it, and the other to a question such as question (6), giving the second alternative in answer. But I do not think these derive from two different lexical meanings of "believe."

We seem, then, to confront a puzzle about "I believe": How can it exhibit linguistic behavior of kinds associated with an ambiguous expression but apparently without being ambiguous?

Since Grice (1975), good method dictates that in analyzing conversational phenomena we try to explain as many effects as we can in terms of his maxims of conversation, rather than postulating a multiplicity of meanings of the expressions involved; this is vulgarly called "gricing" the use of the expression in question.

Let me try to do that here. Suppose that the actual lexical meaning of the verb "to believe" is that associated with the broader use. Then its curious behavior in Austinian position may be griced using the maxim of quality (or quantity), as follows. This epistemic qualifying expression functions to express an epistemic qualifier in situations in which it would be appropriate (according to this maxim) to say that $Q'(p)$, with a stronger epistemic qualifier Q', if one candidly could (that is, if one was in a position to do so); because one does not, the inference is that one can not. So the force of "I believe that p" is (unless explicitly canceled) that of "I merely/just believe that p." The "merely/just" fits the case because the unused alternative is "I know" or "I'm certain," which involves stronger epistemic qualifiers. Because this sort of situation is often faced, what Grice calls a *generalized conversational implicature* would develop, so that the phrase would be regularly understood in the way inferred here, unless explicitly canceled. For the implicature to be a conversational (or generalized conversational) one, it does need to be cancelable; and it apparently can be canceled, as in "Aristotle not only *believed* that the earth was round; he was absolutely *certain* that it was."

(It is hard to know which of Grice's maxims is involved because he does not relate evidence and information to the epistemic qualification of the remarks involved. If epistemic qualification is included—and how can it not be?—then the maxim of quantity is presumably the maxim involved: "I believe that p" would convey less (purported) information than "I know that p," for example. If, somehow, the epistemic qualification is not included, then the maxim of quality would presumably be the one involved: The quality of "I believe that p," in the sense of the evidential basis for conveying that p (epistemic qualified that way) would not be as high as that of "I know that p." If the maxims were revised so as to deal explicitly with epistemic qualification, this problem would, I imagine, solve itself.)

If "I believe" can be griced in this way (or some other), it remains an open question whether or not knowledge entails belief. For simplicity, let us suppose that it does. Then personal epistemic qualifiers, at least, can be divided into those that entail belief (the *doxastic epistemic qualifiers*, as they may be called) and those that do not (although they are, perhaps, not incompatible with belief, for example, thinking it possible that p). There would be a broad epistemic state denoted by "believe," which, when its correlated epistemic qualifying expression occurred in Austinian position, would by the Gricean implicature (unless canceled) narrow down to the epistemic state correlated with just/merely believing, that is, to believing without (putatively) knowing. "I believe" would be correlated with the epistemic state of being in some doxastic epistemic state or other, which would be compatible (we are supposing) with knowing and also with not knowing but would be incompatible with not believing, whether in the sense of (A1) or in that of (A2).

III

John Searle's account of Moore's paradox is that, in a Moore-paradoxical utterance, such as

(1)   It is raining, but I don't believe that it is

in the assertive utterance of the first conjunct, one does not *say* but rather *expresses* the putative fact that a certain "sincerity condition" holds, which the second conjunct explicitly denies. In the case of utterance (1), the sincerity condition is that the speaker believes that it is raining, and the denial of this condition is that the speaker does not believe it is raining. Thus Searle's account of Moore's paradox is explicitly tied to a speech act, the illocutionary act that would be performed in a normal assertive utterance of "It is raining" (and to the saying-and-disbelieving form of Moore's paradox).

Searle's account as he gives it cannot be correct, because his statement of sincerity conditions for assertive utterances is not correct. That it is not is not made especially salient by examples such as utterance (1), because "I don't believe that it is raining" expresses either disbelief (in the sense of believing that it is not the case that it is raining) or a denial of belief (its not being the case that one believes that it is raining), the utterance of either of which is d-incompatible with "it is raining." What one expresses by saying that it is raining is, however, not, as Searle says, that one believes that it is raining, if "believes" is taken in the narrow way, but rather the flat-statement epistemic qualifier, something similar to one's (not just thinking but) *knowing* that it is raining.

Others have said that what is implied or expressed by a speaker who says that *p* is either that the speaker believes or that the speaker knows that *p*, but I think this is pretty clearly wrong, because a Moore paradox of the given form (1) is forthcoming in any case. That something with this epistemic force is what is expressed is clear from the fact that, if what the speaker would express as

(8)   I believe that it is raining

were what was expressed, that is, was the epistemically strongest thing expressed (as opposed to said, in a strict sense), then one could follow the utterance of "It is raining" with that of

(9)   It may not be raining

without withdrawing or qualifying remark (8), just as one can follow an utterance of sentence (8) with an utterance of sentence (9) (linked with "but," say). But one cannot, just as one cannot follow an utterance of

(10)   I know that it is raining

with an utterance of sentence (9), without withdrawing or qualifying remark (10).

If, on the other hand, it is the broader use of "believe" that Searle has in mind in connection with his sincerity condition, one that would cover claims to know that p, unadorned flat statements that p, saying that one believes that p, etc., then there is a problem about the sincerity condition of epistemically qualified statements. In the case of a statement such as (10), the sincerity condition would be (what the speaker could express as)

(11)   I believe that I know that it is raining.

Similarly, for a statement such as

(12)   I am certain that it is raining

the sincerity condition would be

(13)   I believe that I am certain that it is raining.

That is, the epistemic qualifying expression of whatever qualifier was explicit in the original statement would turn up within the scope of "I believe" in the statement of the sincerity condition of the original statement. Now, although statements such as (11) and (13) have interpretations, they are not the right things to be sincerity conditions; rather, they are, as far as I can see, either metalinguistic statements (in the context equivalent to "I believe the right word to describe the situation is that I *know* that it is raining") or statements expressing uncertainty about the state one is in ("Yes, on further consideration it *is certainty* that I feel"), neither of which is necessarily present in sincere utterances of sentences (10) and (12) and certainly not as their sincerity conditions.

The correct sincerity condition in the case of utterance (12), surely, is just that the speaker *is* certain that it is raining. In the case of (10), where truth of the proposition said to be known is (presumably) logically entailed, the sincerity condition (which of course can be satisfied without entailing it) may be described as being that the speaker *takes* it that (or perhaps that the speaker *assumes* that) he or she knows that it is raining. In neither the case of statement (10) nor statement (12) is belief involved in the way Searle describes. Perhaps knowing and being certain that p are doxastic epistemic qualifiers. If so, then denying that one believes that p would be as Moore paradoxical as if believing that p were the sincerity condition of saying that it is raining. But "believe" taken broadly cannot, apparently, be used to state accurately an overall pattern of sincerity conditions of the kind Searle gives (1983, p. 9) for statemental utterances. The uniformity he finds in their sincerity conditions does not exist. These conditions are more specific and are relative to the epistemic qualifiers involved.

IV

According to the account of Moore's paradox that I wish to present here, Moore paradoxes are one kind of epistemic qualifier conflict, in the sense (already described) of d-incompatibility of epistemically qualified utterances. That is, Moore paradoxes are, on this account, cases in which epistemic qualifiers are so applied to propositional contents that d-incompatible (but not contradictory) illocutionary acts result. I now try to spell out what the conflict is in the case of Moore's original paradigms of the paradox. Their particular case is complicated by their involving the problematical concept of belief.

The system of epistemic qualification is constituted by various d-relations among epistemically qualified utterances; it is these relations that define the several roles of the epistemic qualifiers in the system. In some cases these relationships can be encapsulated in general principles or rules. I state several of these and use them in the explanations of Moore paradoxicality.

It appears to be the case that one of the general principles of the sort just mentioned is, briefly, that an epistemic qualifier d-incompatible with a given epistemic qualifier is d-incompatible with any stronger epistemic qualifier. More precisely stated:

(I)   If saying that $Q_1(p)$ is d-incompatible with saying that $Q_2(q)$ and if Q_3 is stronger than Q_1, then saying that $Q_3(p)$ is also d-incompatible with saying that $Q_2(q)$.

Suppose that this is, in fact, a principle constitutive of or derivative from the system of epistemic qualifiers. Then one particular instance of principle (I) is that involved in a Moore paradox of form (A1), that is, the kind of case in which $q = \text{not-}p$, $Q_1 = Q_2 = \text{'I believe'}$, and $Q_3 = Q_{fs}$. 'I believe' is a moderately strong epistemic qualifier, so that (by definition of that strength) saying that $Q_1(p)$ is d-incompatible with saying that $Q_1(\text{not-}p)$, that is (in this case), with saying that $Q_2(q)$. Thus the first condition in the antecedent of (I) is satisfied for these choices of epistemic qualifiers and contents. Because Q_{fs} is plainly stronger than 'I believe', the second condition is also satisfied, so that by (I) it follows that saying that $Q_{fs}(p)$ is d-incompatible with saying that one believes that not-p, which in form (A1) is what "I don't believe that p" means. Thus the two conjuncts in an instance of form (A1) are d-incompatible, and a fluent speaker is able to see right off that the utterance as a whole is something that in the relevant sense one cannot say. Furthermore, an instance of form (A1) satisfies the defining condition on Moore paradoxes that the utterance is not self-contradictory. As usual, we verify that such an instance is not self-contradictory by putting it into a non-Austinian position in its conjugation and finding that what it then expresses might well have been true; for example, it might well have been true that it was raining but I did not believe that it was.

Principle (I) may also be invoked to explain the paradoxicality of Moore paradoxes of the form (B). Because d-incompatibility is (presumably) a symmetric relation, the same choice of epistemic qualifiers, rewriting p as not-p and q as p, suffices.

Moore paradoxes of form (A2) require a more complicated treatment, because the scope of the negation in the second conjunct is here to be understood as wider than that of the epistemic qualifier 'I believe'. However, a minimal assumption from epistemic qualification-enriched speech-act theory seems to suffice, for there seems to be some such principle as

(II)   Saying that $Q_{fs}(p)$ is d-incompatible with denying that $Q_m(p)$.

To take the case at hand, saying that it is raining (with flat-statement epistemic qualification) seems clearly d-incompatible with denying that one believes it is raining; thus the following conversation becomes odd at the point where such a denial would occur:

(C1)   X: It is raining.
        Y: You think it is raining?
        X: No, it is not true that I think it is raining.

I mean, of course, ordinary or regular denying rather than metalinguistic denying, as in "It is not true that I *think* it is raining; I *know* it is." The almost overwhelming temptation to take X's second remark in dialogue (C1) to involve withdrawal of X's first remark would be explained by (C1)'s otherwise being counter to principle (I). And a Moore paradox of form (A2) is an instance of principle (II), its two conjuncts being the incompatible utterances in question.

There is a problem inherent in trying to make plausible the postulation of principles such as (I) and (II), viz. that they must be (i) simple, familiar, and obvious, so as to make it plausible to impute knowledge of and obedience to them to speakers generally, and yet that (ii) they must fit the examples in question fairly simply, so that it may plausibly be supposed that their quick application is automatically made by a fluent speaker.

Conditions (i) and (ii) operating together tend to make the principles look ad hoc. A methodological antidote is to show that there are many cases that can be explained by the principles, not just the ones one is working on. I do believe that their postulation will be borne out by such further consideration, although I cannot undertake it here.

As we saw and as Searle points out, his account of Moore's paradox would generalize to any illocutionary act with a sincerity condition, that is (if Searle is right (1969, p. 65, under 2)), to almost any illocutionary act whatever. But, unfortunately, his account is defective in at least the way indicated. However, some Moore-paradoxical-looking utterances do seem to be explicable in terms of his account but not mine, for example, his "I promise that p but I do not intend that p" (1979, p. 5). It may be that the propositional contents of these nonstatemental utterances are not epistemically qualified. If so, a different sort of explanation of their oddity than the present one is required. But even this sort of utterance can be odd in the way the present account claims that statemental Moore paradoxes are, for the present account of Moore's paradox generalizes not just to other sorts of illocutionary act (and not to them just because of their sincerity conditions, where, however, epistemic qualification may figure), but to utterances involving epistemic qualifier conflicts generally, which can manifest themselves in a variety of ways that are independent of illocutionary force, as I try to illustrate in a moment.

The question is, What exactly is necessary in order to have a paradoxical utterance resembling a Moore paradox (besides its being noncontradictory as a whole)? Because weak epistemic strength is not defined in terms of a d-incompatibility (but rather a d-compatibility), it might be thought that Moore-paradoxical utterances (in this perhaps extended sense) have to involve a pair of epistemically qualified propositions, at least one of which is at least moderately epistemically qualified. However, the following seems to be a counterinstance:

(14)   It may be that his sister has gone, but it may be that he does not have a sister

where the first conjunct may (perfectly ordinarily and indeed as usual) be taken in a sense that accepts the presupposition (the denial of which is the proposition epistemically qualified in the second conjunct) that he has a sister, in which case the two conjuncts are d-incompatible.

I am not, in fact, at all sure what, in general, is necessary in order to have a Moore paradox. As we have seen and in the list to be given, a variety of features involved in or suggested by the original paradigms or by Searle's (or others') account of Moore's paradox are *not*, apparently, required in order to have what seems similar paradoxicality.

But let me say first what it is that on the present line is characteristic of these utterances: a conflict between two epistemically qualified propositions somehow or other involved in them. (The problem is to see *how* they must be involved in them.) Three things seem to figure in this, viz. (1) the unqualified content of the propositions, (2) their epistemic qualification (that is, how they are epistemically qualified, what epistemic force they are propounded with), and (3) the logical form, in a broad sense, of the utterance overall.

The following general remarks may be made concerning these factors: As to point 1, the contents may be contrary to one another in the familiar content-logical sense, that is, the truth-value-possibilities sense in which propositions not epistemically qualified may stand. This contrariety might, when these contents are epistemically qualified, make the overall utterance self-contradictory (in an utterance-logical sense, that is, in a sense appropriate to utterances involving epistemic qualification, rather than simply content-logical relationships), in which case it would (by definition) not be a Moore paradox. But the particular epistemic qualifiers involved might be personal epistemic qualifiers, in which case Moore's paradox could result, as in the original paradigms of forms (A) and (B). The statement "It is raining, but it is not raining" is just self-contradictory (content- and utterance-wise); but "It is raining, but I don't believe that it is" is a Moore paradox. "It is raining, but it may not be raining," with the impersonal epistemic qualifier '. . .may. . .' (= 'it may be') is perhaps problematic (because of its peculiar indirect-discourse properties), although maybe either a contradiction or a Moore paradox.

However, as to point 2, their epistemic qualification, the contents of two epistemically qualified propositions, may be consistent in the content-logical sense and yet produce a paradoxical utterance because of the relationship between the epistemic qualifiers (this being one constituent part of the system of epistemic qualifiers). The example in item (iii) on the following list, viz.

(15)   It is raining, and/but it may be raining

involves one and the same self-consistent proposition as the contents involved, for example. The problem is with the epistemic qualifiers, the strong flat-statement qualifier and a weak epistemic qualifier, there being (to encapsulate this little part of the system) some principle, constitutive of these respective epistemic qualifiers, to the effect that

(III)   One cannot say that $Q_{fs}(p)$ and $Q_w(p)$.

So another sort of conflict between epistemically qualified propositions derives not from a conflict between their contents but rather from the ways those contents are there epistemically qualified.

But, to bring in point 3, the epistemically qualified propositions involved in the conflict need to occur in certain ways in the overall utterance; the kind of occurrence I call a matter of the "logical form" of the utterance, including semantic presupposition (if any) as one facet thereof. To illustrate, look at the logical form (in this sense) of an utterance of sentence (14); as there glossed, this form needs to be distinguished from that of an utterance involving the same sentence, but, as we may assume has been made clear by a different sort of context, *not* presupposing that the person referred to has a sister. More generally, the logical form of an utterance that is a conjunction or disjunction obviously needs to be distinguished from one that is a conditional or a generalization. As another illustration of how logical form can affect paradoxicality or the lack of it in an utterance, consider disjunctive utterances. The epistemic qualification of the disjuncts in such an utterance will, I believe, often not be epistemically qualified (although the disjunctive content as a whole will) and so a fortiori will not give rise to Moore's paradox in the ways discussed concerning points 1 and 2, whereas of course it was the epistemic qualification of the conjuncts of a conjunctive utterance that gave rise to the original paradigms of Moore paradoxicality.

Thus various restrictions on the form and/or the content of Moore-paradoxical utterances that, from the original paradigms and early exemplars, might have been expected to hold apparently do not do so universally. The following list contains at least some of these restrictions, with some illustrative examples. In such an utterance:

(i) there is no restriction on the propositional content epistemically qualified;

(ii) it is not required that one conjunct be a flat statement and the other be explicitly epistemically qualified; for example, "It is certain that it is raining, but it may not be";

(iii) it is not required that one conjunct be negative and the other affirmative; for example, "It is raining, and/but it may be raining";

(iv) it is not required that one propositional content be logically incompatible with the other—take the last example;

(v) it is not required that both conjuncts be statements, for example, "I realize that it is raining, but may it not be?";

(vi) it is not required that the speaker, in one conjunct, *say* something conflicting with what saying the other only *implies* or *expresses*; compare the example in (iii);

and, in fact:

(vii) neither conjunct need be a statement; for example (assuming a bequest is not a statement), "To my only son I bequeath my gold watch and to my third son, if it turns out that there is such a person, the rest of my estate";

(viii) the utterance need not be conjunctive in form; for example, "If, as is likely, her second child is a boy, she must regret having had only one child";

and of course:

(ix) sincerity conditions of illocutionary acts need not be involved.

V

What if the component parts of an odd utterance are separated, as they might be in a speaker's contributions to a conversation, say, or in a one-speaker discourse? It seems clear from the sorts of example we have been considering that the two components would still be related in the way they were in the paradox. But of course the conflict is not perceived as a single, impossible, paradoxical, odd utterance but rather as a kind of inconsistency in one's remarks, as a situation in which, typically, not both of a certain pair of things can be said, because incoherence in the total discourse would result. Or perhaps the person is not speaking honestly or candidly; or perhaps one has forgotten what one said earlier or has changed one's mind about what one wants to say. There may be many interpretations of the situation. Whatever the cause of the incoherence, the speaker cannot rest with saying both of the things which, placed together, would be Moore paradoxical; the speaker must withdraw at least one of them. The speaker must, or his or her discourse, in this part, will be rendered incoherent; we will not be able to understand it or perhaps the speaker.

But now, despite the apparent fact that the requisite relationships between the components still hold, the present dimension is, for some reason, not one along which Moore paradoxicality is apparently preserved. For some reason utterances of this type are not perceived as odd or paradoxical but rather as rendering the discourse incoherent or inconsistent. Unless it is simply the fact that two bursts of speech are involved, I do not know why this is, but I suspect that it has to do with the fact that there has (typically) been time in the discourse for the speaker to forget or revise what s/he said earlier (as of course we often do without much if any notice).

Also, up to now, it has been a question of epistemic qualifier conflict in just a single speaker's discourse, whether compressed into a Moore paradox or similar odd utterance or (as just discussed) spread out across an inconsistent or incoherent discourse. Allowing more than one speaker to be involved—one making one of the component remarks and one making the other, results in more than just a pair of speakers taking turns giving their opinions to each other. Nor do we get incoherent discourse (necessarily).

What we get is *disagreement*. I believe that the situation is, in fact, that any Moore-paradoxical utterance, including the odd utterances of various sorts considered, will, if one speaker illocutes one component and another speaker illocutes the other, constitute their disagreeing with each other, either of the direct confrontation variety or (for example) of the kind where one disagrees with something the other is assuming, or perhaps some other. Note, for example, that

(16)   I think it is, but/and I think it is not

(not taken in the sense in which it is used to introduce a distinction or a hedge) is a Moore-paradoxical utterance and that in the two-person conversation

(C2)   X: I think it is.
          Y: I think it is not.

the speakers disagree despite the apparent fact that each is referring to himself, to what he himself thinks. Yet in the single utterance

(17)   It may be and it may not be

there is no oddity; nor is there disagreement (but only a reminder) in the conversation

(C3)   X: It may be.
          Y: And it may not be.

Thus there are different sorts of discourse relations, among which are discourse incompatibilities. A particular case of the latter are epistemic qualifier conflicts. When epistemic qualifier conflicts occur at their minimal limits along any of several lines, one reaches hypothetical utterances that resemble the original paradigms of Moore's paradox. Thus what may be (or may be regarded as) linguistic oddity of the same sort they exhibit spreads out over language as a whole, appearing in different guises as it goes: sometimes as Moore paradoxicality, sometimes as self-contradiction, and finally as incoherence or inconsistency in one's discourse and as interpersonal disagreement.

Note

1. Single quotes will be used to form names of what will be called epistemic qualifiers (for example, 'I know'); double quotes, to refer to linguistic expressions (for example, "I know").

References

Alston, W. P. 1964. *Philosophy of Language*. Englewood Cliffs, N.J.: Prentice-Hall.

Austin, J. L. 1962. *How to Do Things with Words*. Cambridge, Mass.: Harvard University Press.

Caton, C. E. 1966. "On the general structure of the epistemic qualification of things said in English." *Foundations of Language* 2: 37–66.

Caton, C. E. 1981. "Stalnaker on pragmatic presupposition," in *Radical Pragmatics*, Peter Cole, ed. New York: Academic Press, 83–100.

Grice, H. P. 1975. "Logic and conversation," in *The Logic of Grammar*, G. Harman and D. Davidson, eds. Encino, Calif.: Dickenson, 64–75. Also in *Syntax and Semantics 3: Speech Acts*, J. L. Morgan and P. Cole, eds. (New York: Academic Press, 1975), 41–58.

Searle, John R. 1969. *Speech Acts*. Cambridge, England: Cambridge University Press.

Searle, John R. 1979. *Expression and Meaning*. Cambridge, England: Cambridge University Press.

Searle, John R. 1983. *Intentionality*. Cambridge, England: Cambridge University Press.

Toulmin, S. E. 1958. *The Uses of Argument*. Cambridge, England: Cambridge University Press.

Matching Illocutionary Act Types

William P. Alston

Several philosophers, including myself, have suggested that sentence meaning consists in usability to perform illocutionary acts.[1] More specifically:

I.   What it is for a sentence to have a certain meaning is for it to be usable to perform illocutionary acts of a certain type.

More crisply, sentence meaning is illocutionary act potential. In this paper I wish to consider a difficulty for this thesis and take steps to remove it. But first I had better give some indication of the notion of *illocutionary act* that is being employed here.

The quickest way of conveying this notion is by reference to our familiar oratio obliqua forms of reporting speech, that is, roughly, for making explicit *what* someone said, rather than what s/he uttered in order to get it said. Such forms typically involve a speech verb followed by what we may call a *content-specifying phrase*. To wit:

A told B that B had left his lights on.
A predicted that the strike would be over soon.
A suggested to B that they go to a movie.
A asked B for a match.
A advised B to sell her utilities stock.
A promised B to read his paper.
A expressed considerable enthusiasm for B's proposal.
A reminded B that it was almost 9:00.
A congratulated B on her performance.
A announced that the meeting had been canceled.

Following Searle[2] I take the main verb of such reports to specify the *illocutionary force* of the speech act reported and the content-specifying phrase to specify the *propositional content*. There are, no doubt, many important and difficult problems concerning the nature and varieties of illocutionary acts, problems that would have to be gone into in a full dress treatment of the subject. But this brief indication will, I hope, suffice for purposes of this paper.

Now for the objection. It looks as if principle I implies that, when a particular sentence is used with a certain meaning, it is thereby usable to perform illocutionary acts of one and only one type; otherwise how could we *identify* its meaning with its usability to perform illocutionary acts of some particular type? But this is clearly not the case. Among the most obvious counterexamples to such a uniqueness thesis are the cases with which John Austin originally introduced the category of illocutionary act in *How to Do Things with Words* (Oxford: Oxford University Press, 1962). There Austin pointed out that one could know just what I meant by "It is going to charge" and still not know whether in uttering the sentence I was *warning* someone or just *stating* a fact (p. 98). Again, he said, the sense and reference with which I uttered "Shoot her" may be clear, and still it may not be clear whether I was ordering, imploring, urging, or advising the auditor to do so (p. 101). In fact, Austin seems to make it part of his concept of an illocutionary act that it is a sort of speech act whose exact character is not determined by the meaning (sense and reference) of the utterance.[3]

The phenomenon to which Austin drew attention in these passages is certainly a common one. For another example, when using "The gate is open" with its most common meaning, I might be warning you, reminding you, conceding to you, agreeing with you, remarking to you, or concluding that the gate is open, as well as just asserting this. Indeed I might be doing two or more of these in the same utterance.

We can see a failure of match in the opposite direction as well. We can have different meanings with the same illocutionary act potential, as well as the converse. If I can concede that the gate is open by uttering "The gate is open" (S_1), I can surely also concede that the gate is open by saying "I concede that the gate is open." This latter sentence clearly does not have the same meaning as S_1; this gives us the converse phenomenon of two distinct sentence meanings that fit their bearers for the same illocutionary act.

One may try to save the illocutionary act potential thesis in the face of these facts by stoutly maintaining that, contrary to our normal intuitions, a sentence has as many different meanings as there are distinguishable illocutionary acts it can be used to perform. According to this position, we would be using S_1 in different senses, depending on whether it is being used to report, to conclude, to agree, or to admit that the gate is open. It could then be claimed that, like many other subtle differences in meaning, these differences are not commonly noted. Now I do not wish to maintain that this move is *obviously* mistaken. I do not take ordinary intuitions as an infallible guide to the way in which meanings should be assigned to expressions; and I would not do so even if these intuitions were considerably more definite and more consistent than is in fact the case. What is crucial for deciding this kind of question is what total semantic description of the language would best do the job; and that determination is a long way off. However, in the present case, ordinary intuition speaks loudly and with considerable unanimity, and I am loath to contravene it just to save a theory. So I will not take this way out.

Nor will I adopt the most obvious way of fitting the thesis to the facts, viz., by supposing each sentence meaning to be identical with a range of illocutionary act potentials. Such a modification would not rob principle I of its distinctive force. Nevertheless, I do not believe that all the illocutionary act potentials associated with a given sentence are associated with it in the same way. And by bringing out the differences, I will show how to single out that illocutionary act potential with which a given sentence meaning may be identified.

I can best approach this by further intensifying the difficulty. Those who stress the fact that illocutionary act potential goes beyond meaning always focus on the illocutionary force aspect of illocutionary acts and fail to note that the same point holds of the propositional content aspect. But the phenomenon is just as unmistakable there. Given appropriate contextual support, I can express any of innumerably many different propositional contents by the sentence, "It will," for example, that a certain bull is going to charge, that the interest rate will go down, that a certain ladder will hold steady. We get an even wider range of propositional content potentials with sentences whose meanings specifically fit them for being used to give answers to yes/no questions, for example, "Yes." In a given context the propositional content expressed by "Yes" will be whatever propositional content was expressed in the question to which it is a response. And because no limit can be put on that, "Yes" can be used to express any propositional content whatever—surely a limiting case of the underdetermination of illocutionary act potential by sentence meaning.

Here too it would be quite inadmissible to respond to the difficulty by distinguishing different senses for each distinguishable propositional content the sentence can be used to express. It would be an insane semantics that would assign a different meaning to "Yes" for each proposition assertible in English.

The underdetermination of propositional content by sentence meaning is even more striking in the referential aspect of propositional content. Let me digress from the main line of the argument long enough to explain how I am thinking of a total propositional content as consisting of different "aspects." When one expresses a proposition that is "about" some particular entities, one will be *referring* to those entities. Thus, if the proposition one is expressing is *one's garden gate's being unlocked*, one is referring to one's garden gate, and if the proposition is *Jim's being married to Sally or Sam's being married to Jane*, one is referring to Jim, Sally, Sam, and Jane. We will say that the proposition involves a *reference* to those entities; this aspect of the proposition will be termed its *"referential aspect."* Thus the identity of a proposition is partly determined by the identity of the entities referred to. All the other contributions to its identity we lump together under the heading of "conceptual content."[4] This includes both the "predication" involved (the gate's being open rather than being closed) and the conceptual content of the referring devices used to pick out the referent(s). Consider utterances of the sentences

(a)   My garden gate is open.
(b)   My garden gate is closed.
(c)   That gate is open.

Sentences (a) and (b) differ in conceptual content by virtue of the different predicates involved; they may or may not differ from (c) in reference (that is, in the identity of the gate referred to), but even if they do not, they differ in conceptual content by virtue of the difference in the concepts expressed by the referring expressions used. To sum up, the referential aspect of a proposition is given solely by the identity of the referent(s). Everything else is assigned to the "conceptual content."

The examples given so far of multiple propositional contents had to do with the predicative aspects. But underdetermination of *reference* by meaning is a much more pervasive phenomenon. It is generally the case that the meaning of one's referring expression does not determine any particular referent. The expressions we most commonly use to refer to particular objects can, each of them, be used without change of meaning to refer to any one of an indefinite plurality of objects. Definite descriptions, such as "this gate" or "the gate," can be used to refer to *any* particular gate; "he" can be used to refer to any male human being, as well as to male dogs and the like; "I" can be used by any speaker to refer to him/herself; a proper name such as "Sam" can be used to refer to anything to which the name has been attached. Thus a sentence containing a referring expression like these is usable to perform any one of an indefinitely large plurality of illocutionary acts that differ in the identity of the referents. I can use "The gate is open" to assert that my garden gate is open, that Sam's front gate is open, that the gate we are now looking at is open, and so on. And where the referring expression is of more general application, the variety of possible illocutionary acts is even greater. "It is very large" can be used to assert of anything of which largeness can be intelligibly predicated that it is very large.

Here again we cannot evade the problem by distinguishing senses. Clearly "he" does not have as many different senses as there are entities to which it can be used to refer. If it did, its meaning would constantly be augmented as new referents come into existence; and speakers of the language would constantly be learning new meanings of the word as they use it to refer to further individuals. But, in fact, there is a constant meaning of the pronoun; once speakers have mastered that, they are thereby in a position to use the pronoun to refer to any of an indefinitely large plurality of objects.

While we are intensifying the difficulty, we may as well also point out that a sentence may be too rich as well as too "poor" for an illocutionary act type, a token of which it has been used to perform. Or, coming at the point from the other end, the illocutionary act the sentence has been used for may be "underdescribed" (relative to that sentence meaning) as well as "overdescribed." The phenomena cited thus far all exhibit the second term of each of these contrasts. "The gate is open" is too poor for *admitting* that *my* garden gate is open and too poor on three counts: The meaning of the sentence does not tie us down to the illocutionary force, the particular referent, or the full conceptual content specified in the illocutionary act description. We overdescribed the illocutionary act performance relative to what is explicitly carried by the meaning of the sentence employed. But we may also truly apply an illocutionary act concept to a speaker without embodying in that concept the full richness of the illocutionary act that is determined by the sentence meaning. Thus, when my sentence was "I admit that my garden gate was unlocked," I may be correctly said to have asserted of a certain gate that it was unlocked; that illocutionary act description leaves out the precise illocutionary force that was carried by the sentence and identifies the referent in even less specific terms than the referring expression used in the sentence. Clearly the illocutionary act performed on a given occasion can be underdescribed in various ways and to various different extents. In this last case I might also be said to have admitted that something is unlocked, to have asserted something about a gate, and so on. Thus a given sentence, by virtue of having a certain meaning, may be used to perform tokens of various too poor illocutionary act types, as well as tokens of various too rich illocutionary act types. This further increases the misfit between sentence meaning and illocutionary act potential.

I have been deliberately intensifying the problem, partly to set it in the truest light possible but also partly because I think that, by seeing the full extent of the difficulty, we will be in a better position to find a solution. For one thing, once we realize how pervasively the misfit affects propositional content as well as illocutionary force, we will be encouraged to think that there must be some solution. Presumably no one doubts that there is some intimate connection between the meaning of a sentence and its capacity to express a certain proposition.[5] Those who are anxious to separate illocutionary force from meaning display no such tendencies with respect to the relation of propositional content and meaning. If Austin had used the propositional content terminology, he would undoubtedly have taken the 'carrying' of such content to be an aspect of the locutionary act (uttering a sentence with a certain sense and reference). Therefore, if the fact that propositional content can vary while meaning remains fixed does not prevent sentence meaning from being intimately related to proposition expression capacities, a like variability in illocutionary force should not prevent sentence meaning from being intimately related to it also and indeed related in the same way.

Furthermore, in extending the difficulty, we have pointed the way to a solution. Think back to the case in which the propositional content of an utterance goes beyond what is embodied in the sentence meaning. What enables us to say more than is contained in the sentence meaning is that we get support from the context. In the cases of additional conceptual content, the relevant propositional content had already been carried by the sentences used in prior utterances—the question being answered or the statement being agreed with. That leaves the speaker free to simply use some device for hooking on to that previous utterance: "Yes" or "That's right." The general point exemplified here is that, where appropriate contextual support is available, one need not use a sentence with a meaning rich enought to determine all the content of one's illocutionary act. There is an inverse correlation between the extent of contextual support and the proportion of one's illocutionary act that one needs to determine by sententce meaning. This general point is equally exemplified by the other cases in which the sentence is too poor. The reason we are able to carry out successful references with expressions whose meanings do not uniquely identify the referent is that we can depend on contextual cues to fill the gap. When we use "the gate" or "it" to refer to some particular gate, we are relying on the previous conversation, the physical context of utterance, or supplementary gestures to make clear to the addressee which gate it is to which we are referring. And why should we not treat variability of illocutionary force in just the same way? Here, too, we are able to say something with a given illocutionary force—admitting, agreeing, or warning—without using a sentence whose meaning restricts us to that, only if the context of utterance in some way makes sufficiently clear how our utterance is to be taken.

Thus we see that the underdetermination of illocutionary act by sentence meaning is by no means restricted to the illocutionary force aspect; nor is it in any way an exceptional or mysterious phenomenon. On the contrary, it is a regular and understandable general feature of speech, an exemplification of the principle of least effort. Where sufficient contextual indications are available, there is no need to use a sentence rich enough to determine the full content of what we say.

But how do these considerations show us how to modify the illocutionary act potential theory of sentence meaning in such a way as to take account of this variability? Here our discussion of overdescription and underdescription is helpful. Underlying that discussion is the general point that an illocutionary act, like anything else, can be conceptualized in many different ways; a particular illocutionary act is a token of many illocutionary act types. One and the same illocutionary performance may be correctly described as asserting that a certain gate is unlocked, admitting that a certain gate is unlocked, admitting that my garden gate is unlocked, admitting that something is unlocked, and so on. And the point about this variability that is of crucial importance here is that an illocutionary act may be described in terms that bring in exactly as much content as is contained in the meaning of the sentence employed, more content, or less content. The illocutionary act may be "exactly described" as well as underdescribed or overdescribed. Thus, if the sentence "The gate is open" is used in a particular instance to admit that my garden gate is open, the illocutionary act will be exactly described as *asserting that a certain gate is open*, whereas it will be overdescribed in its illocutionary force as *admitting that a certain gate is open*. It may be underdescribed in its propositional content as *asserting that something is open* or as *asserting something of a certain gate*.[6] A description may be too rich or too poor in more than one respect simultaneously, as in *admitting that my garden gate is open* (too rich in illocutionary force and propositional content). Indeed, a description may be too rich in one respect and too poor in another, as in *admitting that something is open*.

What we have just been calling a description determines a certain *illocutionary act type*. An illocutionary act type that contains exactly as much content as a certain sentence meaning may be termed the "matching illocutionary act type" for that sentence meaning. Thus, if we restrict ourselves to the most basic meaning for each of the following sentences, the matching illocutionary act type in each case can be specified as follows:

"The gate is unlocked"—asserting that a certain gate is unlocked.
"It is unlocked"—asserting that something is unlocked.
"My gate is unlocked"—asserting that a certain gate belonging to the speaker is unlocked.
"I admit that the gate is unlocked"—admitting that a certain gate is unlocked.
"Start it now"—telling someone to initiate something just after the utterance.
"I order you to start it now"—ordering someone to initiate something just after the utterance.
"Start the engine now"—telling someone to put a certain engine into operation just after the utterance.

We can now see how to modify principle I so as to escape the difficulty of multiple illocutionary act potential. We identify a sentence meaning with its *matching illocutionary potential*, that is, the potential to perform illocutionary acts of the type that matches that meaning. That potential exactly mirrors the meaning; it must, for it was specifically selected to do so. Nor can there be any danger that there is more than one illocutionary act type (potential) that embodies just the same content as that meaning. Hence we may replace principle I with:

> II.   What it is for a sentence to have a certain meaning is for it to be usable to perform illocutionary acts of the matching type (that is, to have the matching illocutionary act potential).

Now let's see if we can be more explicit as to what it takes for a given illocutionary act type to match a given sentence meaning. So far the account has been in terms of the same "content," and it would be desirable to go beyond that metaphor. Here is a first approximation. In seeking a matching illocutionary act type for a given sentence meaning, we are looking for a type such that a sentence is fitted to perform a token of that type just by virtue of having that meaning. Or rather, since this formula would yield many types that are poorer than the meaning, we are looking for the most inclusive illocutionary act type that satisfies this condition. *Asserting that a certain gate is open* is the richest illocutionary act type that "The gate is open" is usable to perform just by virtue of meaning what it does. To be usable to perform acts of any richer type, for example, *admitting that my garden gate is open*, it needs contextual support. These considerations encourage us to adopt the following principle:

> III.   *I* is the matching illocutionary act type for sentence meaning *M* if and only if *I* is the most inclusive type such that a sentence with meaning *M* can be used to perform tokens of *I* just by virtue of having that meaning.

Unfortunately this appealingly simple formula does not work. It founders on the complexities of reference. To demonstrate this, we must first recall the previous point that singular reference is not typically carried out in natural languages by Russellian proper names, the meaning of each name tying it to a particular referent. Rather it is carried out by expressions, each of which is fitted by its meaning to refer to any of an indefinitely large plurality of items, the particular referent on a given occasion being determined, if at all, by contextual features. That is why the matching illocutionary act descriptions in the list specify referents indefinitely: "a certain gate," "something," "a certain garden gate belonging to the speaker," etc., for the meaning of the referring expression ("the gate," "it," or whatever) does not tie us down to any particular referent. The reason why this consideration torpedoes our simple formula, princple III, is as follows. Even when we present the referent in unspecific terms (a certain gate) and thus do as much as we can to match the referential unspecificity of the meaning of the referring expression ("the gate"), we have not succeeded in specifying an illocutionary act that the sentence can be used to perform without any need for contextual support. For a referring expression of the standard type cannot perform its referential function at all without contextual indication of the particular item from the range of possible referents that is being referred to on that occasion. For such referring expressions, unlike Russellian proper names, there is no such thing as context-independent reference. The meaning of a typical referring expression fits it to be used for a certain *kind* of job, where further conditions are required in each case to enable it to actually carry through a job of that kind. The meaning of the expression makes provision, so to say, for its own transcendence. Hence the meaning of "The gate is open" does not *by itself* make it possible to use that sentence to assert of a certain gate that it is open, for unless the context of utterance suffices to pick out some particular gate as the one that is being said to be open, no illocutionary act of that (unspecific) matching type will have been performed.

Another way of making the point is this. Where singular reference is not involved, the matching illocutionary act description can be the fullest description of an illocutionary act actually performed by uttering the sentence. In uttering "All crows are black" (and assuming, contrary to, for example, Putnam, that nothing similar to singular reference is involved in this assertion), I may just be performing an illocutionary act of the matching type—asserting that all crows are black, and that is all (on the illocutionary act level). I may be doing nothing illocutionary that requires a more specific description, for example, agreeing that all crows are black. But, with sentences containing ordinary referring expressions, this is not possible. I cannot *just* perform the matching illocutionary act. The predicate "asserted of a certain gate that it is open" cannot be true of me unless some more specific predicate of the form "asserted of gate G that it is open" is true of me, where "G" picks out some particular gate. Thus, where ordinary referring expressions are involved, the matching illocutionary act can be performed only if an illocutionary act of a referentially specific type can be performed, the latter requiring special contextual support. Hence even the referentially unspecific illocutionary act type does not match the sentence meaning in the way specified by our simple formula.

Nevertheless it is clear that this type comes as close to a match as possible. And so, if we are going to have matching illocutionary act types for sentence meanings that are built up out of, *inter alia*, the meanings of standard referring expressions, we are going to have to rethink what it takes to make an illocutionary act type match a sentence meaning. Let's see if we can find some way in which the usability of "The gate is open" (S) to assert that a certain gate is open is fully determined by its meaning, a way in which its usability to, for example, *admit* that *my garden gate* is open, is not fully determined by its meaning. We will find this way by looking at the matter from the standpoint of the hearer. If I know the meaning with which U is uttering S and know that U intends to be engaging in communication, what does that suffice to tell me about the illocutionary act U is performing? So long as we put the question in that way, in terms of actual illocutionary act performance, we will not get beyond the earlier results. In standard referential cases this will not, for reasons just given, be enough to tell me that U has *succeeded* in performing a token of what we have been calling the matching illocutionary act type. However, even here knowledge of the relevant sentence meaning is sufficient to enable the addressee to know that U *intends* to be performing an illocutionary act of what we have called the matching type.[7] And in this respect the matching type is distinguished from those that are too rich. Just by knowing that U is using S with it normal meaning and that U intends to be communicating, I can know that U *intends* to be saying of some particular gate that it is open; I can know this, whether or not the requisite contextual support is forthcoming to enable U to carry out this intention. But just by knowing the meaning with which U is using S and that U intends to be communicating, I cannot know that U intends to be saying of *my garden gate* that it is open or that U intends to be *admitting* that a certain gate is open.

So, let's modify principle III as follows:

IV. I is the matching illocutionary act type for sentence meaning M if and only if I is the most inclusive type such that an addressee, just by knowing that U is uttering a sentence with meaning M and intends to be communicating, can thereby know that U intends to be performing a token of I.

Having developed a criterion that handles the points brought out thus far, we must next consider whether or not there are other respects in which illocutionary acts that a sentence (when uttered with a given meaning) can be used to perform may fail to match that meaning; and then we can consider whether or not our formula accommodates those dimensions of match and mismatch.

Figurative Speech   In figurative speech a given sentence meaning is exploited not to produce a token of what we would call the matching illocutionary act but rather to say something derived from that by some kind of figurative extension. Thus, when Ross, in Act I, scene ii of *Macbeth*, says "the Norwegian banners . . . fan our people cold," he is not saying, as he would if speaking literally, that some Norwegians are flapping their banners near some Scots so as to reduce their temperature, but rather that the Norwegian army is striking dread in the inhabitants of Scotland.

Parasitic Uses of Sentences   Parasitic uses of sentences include such things as making requests in dramatic productions and speaking ironically. If, in the course of acting in a play, I say, "Would you please look up Susie's telephone number," I am not seriously requesting anyone to look up anyone's telephone number. I am only doing this in the play. But I am making use of the ordinary meaning of the sentence in doing so. Again, if I say, ironically, "What a beautiful day," meaning thereby to remark on the foul weather, I have again exploited the ordinary meaning of the sentence, not to perform the matching illocutionary act but rather to perform a directly contrary illocutionary act.

Indirect Speech Acts   I ask you whether you can reach the salt, thereby (indirectly) requesting you to pass the salt. Or I tell you that you are standing on my foot, thereby (indirectly) requesting you to get off my foot. In these cases the sentence is used with its most ordinary meaning to perform an illocutionary act of a type quite different from the matching type.

In bringing up these cases in this context, I am assuming that in each case the sentence is being used with its most basic meaning, a meaning that is associated with a matching illocutionary type quite different from the act being performed. This assumption may be challenged, particularly in the metaphorical cases. But I need not argue the question. If any of my cases do not involve using a sentence with a meaning that does not match the illocutionary act being performed, they pose no problems for the contentions of this paper. So let's proceed to consider the cases as described.

Actually these cases pose two problems for my account. (1) Are nonmatching illocutionary acts like those in these cases excluded by principle IV? (2) Do cases like these raise any difficulties for the use of principle IV to identify a unique illocutionary act type for a given sentence meaning? Problem 1 can be quickly dispatched. Clearly, just knowing that U is uttering S with some standard meaning does not suffice to assure me that U intends to be making some figurative extension, is speaking ironically, or is generating some indirect speech act. Additional information is needed for these determinations. So there is no danger that these illocutionary act types will be confused with the matching type. But the second problem is a bit stickier. If, when U makes a figurative use of "The Norwegian banners . . . fan our people cold," U is using the sentence in its most basic meaning and intends to be communicating, then clearly an addressee cannot, just by knowing that, know that U intends to be performing the matching illocutionary act, that is, asserting that some Scots are getting their temperature reduced to an unpleasant degree by the waving of some Norwegian banners. Nor just by knowing that U is using "What a beautiful day!" in its most basic meaning and means to be communicating can one tell that U intends to be performing the matching illocutionary act. To tell that in each case, it would seem, one would have to know that the speaker does not intend to be speaking figuratively or ironically.[8]

These considerations indicate that we must add to the information that the addressee *A* needs in order to determine that *U* intends to be performing the matching illocutionary act. We have already parenthetically suggested that *A* needs the information that *U* intended to be communicating; this is needed to rule out cases in which *U* is uttering the sentence with a certain meaning but without performing any communicative act, as when one is rehearsing a speech with one's mind on the meaning of what one is saying. Now we must add further stipulations that will rule out the possibility that *U* intends to be performing some figurative or parasitic illocutionary act instead of the matching illocutionary act. Let's put this in terms of an intention to be making a *straightforward, literal, communicative* use of language. This gives rise to the final revision of the criterion for matching illocutionary act types:

> V. *I* is the matching illocutionary act type for sentence meaning *M* if and only if *I* is the most inclusive type such that an addressee, just by knowing that *U* is uttering a sentence with meaning *M* and intends to be making a literal, straightforward, communicative use of that sentence, can thereby know that *U* intends to be performing a token of *I*.

Let's draw these threads together. It is undoubtedly true that a sentence can be used with one and the same meaning to perform illocutionary acts of many different types. Furthermore, it can be standardly or normally used to do so, apart from any special arrangements. This is possible because the meaning of the sentence used does not suffice to determine all the features of all the illocutionary acts the sentence, uttered with that meaning, can be standardly used to perform. The meaning does make an essential contribution to that determination; we have uncovered no cases in which the content of an illocutionary act is not at least heavily influenced by the sentence meaning. But the conventions and practices of speech are such as to made provision for sentence meaning to interact with contextual indications so as to produce illocutionary acts whose content goes beyond that meaning. That makes it possible for one's utterance to carry illocutionary force or conceptual content or references to particular individuals that are not contained as such in the meaning of the sentence. It also makes possible figurative uses in which one plays (relatively) free variations on the sentence meaning to produce new propositional contents. And it makes possible the lifting of the whole system of illocutionary act types into a new dimension, like drama, in which they have, as a whole, a new sort of force that is systematically related to the original one. But recognizing this diversity, we can still hold on to the crucial identification of sentence meaning with illocutionary act potential by singling out for each sentence meaning a "matching" illocutionary act type, one that determines a particular illocutionary act potential that can be identified with that sentence meaning, because that illocutionary act type has a content that precisely matches the content of that sentence meaning. In this way the illocutionary act potential theory of sentence meaning can be rescued from the difficulties posed by multiple illocutionary act potentials.

Notes

1. An early version of my own view appeared in "Meaning and Use," *Philosophical Quarterly* (1963), 13: 107–124; a more up-to-date version can be found in "Sentence and Meaning and Illocutionary Act Potential," *Philosophical Exchange* (Summer 1977), 2(3): 17–35. For another implementation of essentially the same idea, see John Searle, *Speech Acts* (Cambridge: Cambridge University Press, 1969), especially chs. 2, 3.

2. *Speech Acts*, ch. 2.

3. It might be supposed that the application of Austin's discussion to my theory is complicated by the fact that, whereas my thesis concerns sentence meaning, the kind of meaning a sentence type has by virtue of the semantic structure of the language, Austin is thinking of speaker meaning, what a speaker means by what s/he says. It is true that in these passages Austin talks as if he has speaker meaning in mind. But there are reasons for denying that this is the best interpretation, for presumably if we were to make fully explicit what the speaker meant by what s/he said, that would suffice to resolve the indeterminacies Austin was mentioning. But, on the other side, it may well be that Austin was using a concept of meaning such that illocutionary force cannot be part of the *meaning* of an utterance. In any event I am concerned in this paper with *my* problem, which has to do with the fact that a sentence, when used with one and the same sentence meaning, can be used to perform illocutionary acts of many different types. I mention the celebrated Austin passage only because it is fitted to bring this point to mind.

4. No doubt, much more needs to be done to set out and defend these ideas about propositional identity, but we must pass on.

5. At least no one who makes use of all these concepts.

6. Some of these phrases, particularly "asserting that something is . . ." but also to some extent "asserting that a certain *F* is . . . ," are subject to more than one interpretation. The first one, for example, could be used to mean "asserting that there is something that is . . ." as well as used to mean "asserting with respect to something in particular that it is . . . ." I will always be using such phrases in the second way, using them to report in quite unspecific terms a singular utterance that is about some particular item, not to report an existentially quantified utterance. Sometimes I will convey my intentions less ambiguously by using the *de re* form, for example, "asserting of a certain gate that it is open."

7. This statement is subject to a qualification that will soon be made explicit.

8. Indirect speech acts do not pose the same problem, provided that the speaker in such acts does intend to be performing the matching illocutionary act and to be performing the further act through the former.

PART TWO

Metaphysics

Scattered Objects

Roderick M. Chisholm

I

The classic paper on scattered objects was written by Richard Cartwright.[1] What I present here may be thought of as a commentary on that paper. Like Cartwright, I believe that there are scattered material objects. But my views differ from his in several respects: (1) Where Cartwright makes use of such absolute spatial concepts as *point* and *region*, I make use of the relational concept of *touching* (or *direct spatial contact*). This alternative approach may throw a different light on some of the metaphysical questions that the problem of scattered objects involves. (2) I consider a distinction between two fundamentally different types of scattered object—a distinction that Cartwright does not discuss. (3) I express some doubts about the relevance of "temporal parts" to the metaphysical problems that scattered objects involve.

II

I take the relation of *proper part of* (written henceforth as "part of") as undefined and assume that it is transitive and asymmetric:

(A1)   For every x, y, and z, if x is part of y and if y is part of z, then x is part of z.

(A2)   For every x, if x is part of y, then y is not part of x.

To abbreviate a further principle, I add two further definitions:

(D1) x is discrete from y = Df (a) x is other than y and (b) there is no z such that z is part of x and z is part of y.

(Without the first clause we would have to say of points and monads that they are discrete from themselves.)

(D2) x is composed of y and z = Df (a) y is part of x, (b) z is part of x, (c) y is discrete from z, and (d) no part of x is discrete from both y and z.

(This definition was first proposed by Whitehead.[2]) Consider a table of the following sort: It has a top T; it has four legs, A, B, C, and D; and it has no part that is discrete from each of the parts, A, B, C, D, and T. What is the table composed of? The question has many answers. We may say that it is composed of A and $TBCD$, also that it is composed of B and $TACD$, that it is composed of C and $TABD$, and that it is composed of D and $TABC$. (I use the locution "WX" as short for "that object that is composed of W and X" and "$WXYZ$" as short for "that object that is composed of WX and YZ.") If there are scattered objects, we may also say that the table is composed of T and $ABCD$, that it is composed of TA and BCD, that it is composed of $TABC$ and D, and that it is composed of such entities as the lower half of B and the remainder of the table.

III

We may define the concept of a scattered object if we allow ourselves the additional concept of *touching*, or *direct spatial contact*. (If a book is on the table and the table is on a rug, then, although the book may be said in some sense to be in spatial contact with the rug, it is not in *direct* spatial contact with the rug.)

> (D3) x is a scattered object $=$ Df There is a y and there is a z such that (a) x is composed of y and z and (b) no part of y is in direct spatial contact with any part of z.

The present sense of "scattered," it should be noted, does not preclude the possibility of *order*. "Scattered," therefore, should not be taken to imply "haphazard," "chance," or "random." The essential mark of a scattered object is the absence of a certain type of spatial contact.

IV

"Is there a material object composed of the Eiffel Tower and the Old North Church?"[3] If there is such a material object, then, we may agree, there are scattered material objects.

As Cartwright notes (p. 155), such entities as the following would seem to be quite respectable ontologically: the United States, the solar system, a suite of furniture, a pile of coal, a watch that is spread out on the watch repairer's workbench, printed words, the lowercase letters i and j, the constellation Cassiopeia.

But there are two extreme views about the existence of such objects.

One, which we could call conjunctivism, is the view that for any two individual things there is a third thing that is composed of both.[4] (Or we could qualify the doctrine by saying: "For any two individual things that are discrete from each other, there is a third thing composed of both.")

The other extreme could be put this way: All genuine individuals are *compact*; that is, they are nonscattered.

Sometimes the defender of the second view seems to presuppose the contradictory of that view. S/He may say: "Scattered objects are mere heaps or aggregates; and mere heaps or aggregates are not genuine things." This way of talking seems to imply that there *are* mere heaps or aggregates—and that such things are not "genuine." But if there *are* mere heaps or aggregates and if scattered objects are mere heaps or aggregates, then there are scattered objects.[5]

Consider again the example of Cassiopeia. One might argue as follows: Those particular stars have just been associated by human beings; other creatures might have associated some other group of stars—say, some group of stars that has never in fact been thought of as a constellation—and they might have called that constellation "Alcibiades." Now surely there *is* no constellation Alcibiades. But by similar reasoning there really is no constellation Cassiopeia.

The objection says, correctly, that we focused on Cassiopeia and not on that other group of stars that could have been called "Alcibiades." But the only relevant difference between the two heaps of stars is that we did focus on the former and not on the latter. The heap that might have been called "Alcibiades," unlike Cassiopeia, has no name in our astronomy, and therefore we do not call it a constellation. (If one insists that, although there is a heap, the constituent stars "do not form a constellation," then one is using "constellation" to mean a "heap of stars for which we have a name.").

V

Cartwright makes it abundantly clear that scattered objects play an essential role in the problem of identity through time.

Consider a whole *W* that persists through time—taking on new parts and shedding old ones during the course of its existence: I have depicted "the Ship of Theseus" in the following way:

				W			
Monday:	X	Y	Z	[ABC]			
Tuesday:	X	Y		[ABZ]		C	
Wednesday:	X			[AYZ]	B	C	
Thursday:				[XYZ]	A	B	C

Column *W* depicts some of the parts that constituted Theseus on the four days Monday, Tuesday, Wednesday, and Thursday. The letters immediately to the left of the column depict parts of the flotsam that were later to constitute the ship of Theseus. And the letters to the right depict parts of the jetsam that was composed of the discarded part of Theseus.

The diagram could also be taken to depict a human body. Let us consider it that way and replace W by "Charlie." In doing this, we will be using the name "Charlie" to refer to the type of thing that Cartwright used it for—an individual thing that may lose some of its parts and take on others.

If we look at our diagram, we can find a number of objects that are of a very different nature from Charlie. One of them is that object having parts A, B, and C, which occupied the place of Charlie on Monday. Let us call this object "Harry," thus using a name that Cartwright introduces at a similar point.

Consider the relations between Charlie and Harry. We can say, as Cartwright would, (1) that Harry and Charlie occupy exactly the same place on Monday, (2) that Harry is not identical with Charlie, and (3) that things never "change their identities" (roughly, you cannot be diverse from something today and identical with it tomorrow). Charlie and Harry are intimately related, then, but not identical. What more can we say about the relations between them?

I assume that Cartwright would want to say of *our* Charlie and Harry what he says of *his* Charlie and Harry:

> We have treated Charlie as a continuant, an object that endures for a period of time during which it undergoes change. It would seem only fair to treat Harry in the same way. Like Charlie, Harry underwent a certain change. He occupied a connected receptacle at t [Monday] and a disconnected one at t' [Thursday]. ("Scattered Objects," p. 166)

I believe that, in proposing to treat Harry "as a continuant" like Charlie, Cartwright supposes that, like Charlie, Harry is capable of losing parts—he says that *his* Harry *does* lose certain parts (see p. 169). But is it fair to our Harry to treat him this way? If Harry is that object that has parts A, B, and C and that occupies the place that Charlie occupies on Monday, doesn't Harry exist with precisely the *same* parts on the next three days? He becomes somewhat scattered on Tuesday, more widely scattered on Wednesday, and still more widely scattered on Thursday when he becomes a mass of jetsam.

Charlie—the human body occupying Harry's place on Monday— changed parts several times during the period depicted. But Harry did not change any parts at all. Indeed, Harry's parts would seem to be essential to him. Unless some of his parts cease to be in nihilum, it looks as though Harry will exist forever. What kind of a thing is he, then?

We might define the concept of a *substance* this way:

(D4) x is an individual substance $= \mathrm{Df}$ If x has parts, then for every y, if y is part of x, x is necessarily such that y is part of it.

The definition is put as it is to allow for the possibility that a monad is a substance. It also allows us to say, with Platonists, that abstract objects are substances (but this defect, if it is a defect, is easily remedied).

Those individuals that may survive the loss of their parts may be called *nonsubstantive individuals*. (I hesitate to use "nonsubstantial individuals.") Thus the Ship of Theseus and Charlie are nonsubstantive individuals. The metaphysical problem that Cartwright discusses in terms of what he calls the fusion principle now becomes, What is the relation between nonsubstantive individuals and substances?

By our definition, Harry is a substance and Charlie is not. And so we are left with the metaphysical question, What is the relation between Charlie and Harry?

VI

Cartwright introduces the philosophical concept of a *temporal part* at this point. He suggests that

> although Charlie and Harry are distinct objects, as is revealed by their divergent careers, a certain temporal part of Charlie is identical with a certain temporal part of Harry: Charlie's *t*-stage [Monday-stage], as we might call it, is identical with Harry's *t* stage. ("Scattered Objects," p. 169)

What *are* temporal parts, and what is the reason for thinking that such things as Charlie and Harry *have* temporal parts?

If we take "temporal part" in the technical sense in which, I believe, Cartwright understands it, then it will not do to say merely that a temporal part of a thing is a part that the thing has at a certain time and fails to have at other times, for some parts of the latter sort may be shed and then taken on again ("Let's try it once more with the old carburetor"). A temporal part, however, cannot be taken on again once it has been shed; whatever has it is necessarily such that it has it only once.[6]

There is a reasonably clear sense in which such entities as *states, processes,* or *careers* may be said to have temporal parts—parts that are unique to the times at which they are had and that cannot be taken on and off. Your second year and your twentieth year are different temporal parts of your life history. But our problem has to do with *individual things* and not with processes, states, or careers of individual things.

The question is, Why assume that individual things—such things as people, chairs, and matchboxes—have temporal parts? The assumption does give us a kind of answer to our metaphysical question about Harry and Charlie, but this fact does not seem to me to be by itself a sufficient reason for thinking that the assumption is true. Is there some other reason for thinking that it is true?

Evidently it is useful in theoretical physics to abstract from individual things and to investigate those processes that are the histories of such things. Hence physics may be said to investigate things that *do* have temporal parts. But it hardly follows from this that individual things have temporal parts.

To be sure, there are "process"-philosophers who say that such things as human bodies and matchbooks are really processes. But, so far as I know, no one has ever devoted any philosophical toil to showing how to *reduce* such things to processes. In the absence of such a reduction, I would agree with Broad, whom Cartwright quotes: "It is plainly contrary to common sense to say that the phases in the history of a thing are parts of the thing."[7] Harry is an individual who once had the shape and size of a man, but no process or career can have the shape and size of a man.

Could we modify Cartwright's suggestion, then, and say something similar to "a certain temporal part of Charlie's history is identical with a certain temporal part of Harry's history"? This seems to me to leave us with our problem. How are Charlie and Harry related if *they* are diverse and such that parts of their *histories* overlap?

I feel, therefore, that the appeal to temporal parts will not help.

Harry seems to make out better than he ought to. And, strangely, the one whose status is now unclear is Charlie. I am not really satisfied with any of the proposed solutions to the problem.[8] And so I hope very much that Cartwright will continue to work on it.

Notes

I am indebted to Judith Jarvis Thomson for a number of helpful suggestions.

1. Richard Cartwright, "Scattered Objects," in *Analysis and Metaphysics*, Keith Lehrer, ed. (Dordrecht: Reidel, 1975); reprinted in Richard Cartwright, *Philosophical Essays* (Cambridge, Mass.: MIT Press, 1987). All references to Cartwright are to this paper.

2. A. N. Whitehead, *The Organization of Thought* (London: Williams and Norgate, 1917), 165. Whitehead used "separated from," whereas I have used "discrete from."

3. Cartwright, "Scattered Objects," 155.

4. S. Leśniewski proposed as an axiom of mereology: "For every non-empty class A of individuals there exists exactly one individual x which is a sum of all the members of A." And he said that an individual x is the *sum* of the members of a class A provided only that every member of A is a part of x and that no part of x is discrete from every member of A. See the exposition of Leśniewski's mereology in *Logic, Semantics, Metamathematics*, by A. Tarski (Oxford: Clarendon Press, 1956), 24ff.

5. Compare Cartwright, "Scattered Objects," 158–159.

6. Compare Rudolf Carnap, *Introduction to Logic and Its Applications* (New York: Dover, 1958), 197ff.

7. C. D. Broad, *An Examination of McTaggart's Philosophy*, vol. 1 (Cambridge: The University Press, 1933), 349–350. Quoted by Cartwright in "Scattered Objects," p. 171.

8. My own most recent attempt to deal with the problem may be found in *Profiles: Roderick M. Chisholm*, Radu G. Bogdan, ed. (Dordrecht: Reidel, 1986), 65–77. I suggest there that I may resemble Harry more than I do Charlie.

Parts and Places

Helen Morris Cartwright

Hobbes said, "A body is that, which having no dependence on our thought, is coincident or coextensive with some part of space." Richard Cartwright says, "Bodies in Hobbes' sense are material objects in ours; so at any rate I shall assume."[1] And drawing on the usual topology for three-dimensional Euclidean space, he characterizes a "part of space" or "a receptacle . . . a region of space with which it is possible some material object should be, in Hobbes' sense, coincident or coextended" (p. 153)—with some puzzling consequences for such things as live bodies, automobiles, salami sandwiches, and books of matches, material objects properly put together from a set "consisting of what are in the natural way thought of as parts of the object" (p. 164).

I do not intend to dwell on these consequences or to take a stand on what Cartwright calls the Fusion Principle (p. 161), which would in effect make coincidence with a receptacle both necessary and sufficient for something to count as a single material thing. But I do intend to review the topological notions involved in the characterization of a receptacle and to make a suggestion about "parts." I want to develop the notion of a fusion or mereological sum of parts in a way that is less sensitive to the idiosyncratic makeup of such things as matchbooks, complex machines, and live bodies than Cartwright's treatment demands.

The suggestion I will make rests on a distinction I have discussed before; but here there is a point in tracing it to Aristotle, for although it is not easy to assimilate Aristotle's thoughts on parts and places to contemporary issues about them—nor to say much at all that will go uncontroverted—his views have suggested to me the best strategy I know of for dealing with a consequence of Cartwright's characterization of a receptacle that is at least as puzzling as those he lays to the Fusion Principle. I will first develop the notion of a mereology of certain material things and their topological properties with an eye to setting out this puzzle. An Aristotelian strategy for solving it will call for some further maneuvers.

I

Parts so called in "the natural way" are, I believe, *moria* in Aristotle's Greek; and it is the classification of *moria* that is prominent, for example, in his biological works. But the classification of the parts of living things rests on a wider classification of material things by way of a property for which he coined a term. Things may or may not have "like parts," and here the word is *meros*. There is a long list of *moria* of each sort in *De partibus animalium*;[2] but the theoretical generality of the distinction is perhaps clearest in a passage from the fourth book of the *Meteorologica*.

> I call homoeomeries things such as the metals—bronze, gold, silver, tin, iron, stone and other things like these, . . . and things in animals and plants, such as flesh, bone sinew, skin, intestine, hair, liver, vein, out of which are composed, in turn, the anhomoeomeries, such as face, hand, foot, and other things like these, and in plants, wood, bark, leaf, root and whatever is like these. (IV, 10, 388a13–20)[3]

Hosts of things are to be classified as to whether they are homoeomerous (like bronze or flesh or wood) or anhomoeomerous (like a face or a hand). And without pressing for detail, it is to be noticed that there is another distinction at work here: The relation of a part (*meros*) to that of which it is a part is not to be confused with the relation of a constituent or component to that which is composed of (*ek*) it.

Furthermore, the likeness of parts required of the homoeomeries is of a rather special sort. In something close to a definition, Aristotle says the homoeomeries are "such as, bone, flesh, marrow and the other things of which any part is synonymous [with any other]" (*De generatione et corruptione*, I, 1, 314a19–20). Now things in general are synonymous just in case they have a name in common and meet another condition; the "definition of being" (*logos tēs ousias*) is the same (*Categories*, 1, 6–10).[4] I will shortly suggest that it is possible to glean something of this added condition from the distinction just noticed between the relation of parts to what they are part of and the *ek* relation; but satisfaction of both conditions will simply be called the requirement of synonymous parts.

What does the notion of homoeomeriety come to? Bearing in mind the requirement of synonymous parts, I think this question can be addressed in a preliminary way on home ground. I intend to bank on the fact that examples like those just cited turn up in English marked by the syntax of mass nouns; and I think recent commentators on Aristotle would agree that this is not unreasonable. But I also think there is reason to believe that Aristotle had something like the distinction between mass nouns and count nouns in mind. In *De partibus animalium*, for example, there is an apology for a break in exposition that seems plainly to turn on what amounts to a syntactic ambiguity associated with the names of some parts of living things.[5]

In English we speak of bone and *a* bone, hair and *a* hair, intestine and *an* intestine, and so on. Greek lacks an indefinite article, but when Aristotle calls earth, air, and fire "natural bodies" (*Metaphysics*, Z, 2, for example), the plural is only as confusing as the common presumption that "substances" in English signifies such things as plaster and glue and not Aristotle's paradigmatic *ousiai*—man or horse. "Substances" used with this presumption is like "metals"; metals are *kinds* of metal, specified by listing mass nouns. Bodies, as the word is used in the context just cited, could be metals such as bronze or gold but are in fact elements: earth, air, and fire. For the homoeomeries Aristotle uses only an article with a plural adjective, but his examples of homoeomerous bodies, so I am suggesting, are kinds—specifiable in English, as they are in the passages cited, by listing mass nouns.

But if the homoeomeries are kinds of bodies (or, perhaps, material stuff), it seems that parts of things that are homoeomerous can only be parts of some body *of* a homoeomerous kind, for, to perhaps overstate the point, parts of an abstract kind can only be kinds.[6] The only parts of the kind of thing we call tunafish salad are, for example, tunafish and mayonaise. The only parts of the kind of metal called bronze are metals—copper and tin—and possibly something like carbon. But these things are what bronze is made of; the part relation has been confounded with the *ek* relation; and if the requirement of synonymous parts is so read that the occurrence of *meros* under the quantifier is true of parts of the kind of thing called bone, it appears to make no sense at all.

Respect for the difference between the parts of something and its components also rules out an interpretation of the requirement that seems more promising. The parts of something homoeomerous are to share a name. If it is assumed that such a name is a mass noun or some nominal construction with the syntax of a mass noun, to say that the parts of something of a homoeomerous kind share a name is to say that *its* name is true of all of them. And this just amounts to supposing that such a name is what is called a "dissective" predicate.

Now a predicate F is *dissective* if and only if the first-order schema

(D) $\forall x \forall y (Fy \wedge x$ is part of $y \to Fx)$

comes out true. And if F is the name of one of Aristotle's homoeomeries, then F is true of any part of something of that kind; F is true of some y only if F is true of every x which is part of y. Thus, by the requirement of synonymous parts, F must be dissective—or so it seems.[7]

The trouble is that, as the schema (D) is commonly understood, the names of most of the examples cited fail the test. Quine, for example, tells us by way of illustration that the mass term "water" is dissective "down to single molecules but not to atoms" (1960, p. 98). Parts are commonly taken to include the constituents or components of things; and with this understanding, the only names of homoeomeries that survive are (perhaps) the names of elements, where the difference between the part relation and the *ek* relation may be supposed to lapse.

Aristotle took water to be one of the "simple bodies," an element (*De generatione et corruptione*, II, 3); but it is compounds that he is describing when he says of combining things in a mixture that the result "has to be homoeomerous, and that just as any part of water is water so it is with what has been mingled" (I, 10, 328a10–11). "Water" is to be true of any part of anything that is water, but not because water is an element. The same is to hold for bronze; so "part" in the requirement of synonymous parts cannot be so understood that the parts of something of which "bronze" is true include the copper and tin of (*ek*) which that bronze is composed. If it *is* so understood, counterexamples to the truth of all instances of (D) are counterexamples to it, and no names of nonelementary homoeomeries will be left.

Now it is perhaps tempting to simply relax the requirement. The truth of all instances of (D) is a very near miss; to look for a firmer understanding, so someone might say, is to overburden the text. But it seems to me a mistake to do this if it can be avoided. If the requirement is to be taken seriously, homonymy—the mere sharing of a name—is its simplest demand; surely it is neither unintelligible nor (strictly) false on that score alone. Better to look for some means of amending (D); and I believe such means are available by use of a device that, in English at any rate, can be seen to mark a distinction between parts and components.

Part of something of which "water" is true may only be, after all, *some* of that water. It can be admitted, contrary to Aristotle's chemistry, that part of anything that is water is oxygen and not water—"water" is not dissective. But this is not to say that *some of* something that is water is oxygen and not water. In fact, I think we need only agree that what we have before us is water to see that *none* of it is oxygen; and then perhaps it is also obvious that if some of what we have is oxygen, what we have is neither Aristotle's elemental water nor the familiar compound.

Now the point here can be regarded as ad hominem, directed to anyone who claims to be able to produce counterexamples to the assumption that the names of homoeomeries always provide true instances of (D): Part of *the water here before us* is oxygen and not water; so (D) is false in this instance. But then the point carries quite systematically: Whenever something can be said in English to be the so-and-so and "so-and-so" has the syntax of a mass noun, it is sure to follow that anything that can properly be said to be *some of* the so-and-so is itself so-and-so. And if "part of . . ."

in (D) is taken to have the force of "some of . . . ." one problem about the requirement of synonymous parts will be avoided.

Of course some care is in order, for whereas (D) is at least readable, x and y in "x is some of y" cannot be regarded as replaceable in English by singular terms. "This oxygen atom is part of this bowl of water" may seem straightforward enough; but "This oxygen atom is *some* of this bowl of water" is not straightforward English at all; so in general it will not do to amend (D) by simply putting "some" where "part" occurs in its formulation. "Some of" just does not have the syntax of a two-place predicate.

At the same time it is not unreasonable to suppose that *there is* a two-place predicate true of a pair of things, each of which is water, just in case one is some of the other. Such things are singled out by anyone who claims to have a counterexample to the assumption that "water" is dissective; and the sentence "This water is some of that" is at least as good as the result of putting "part" where "some" occurs here. I mean to assume that there is a class of relations which hold just in case the schema "A is some of B" has a true instance formulated in English. A and B are to designate subjects of singular predication, although they will not themselves be singular terms. They are to be referential phrases like "the water before us," "the so-and-so which . . . ," where "so-and-so which . . ." has the syntax of a mass noun.[8]

Any such relation will be signified by an extensional equivalent of a two-place predicate satisfied by values of the variables x and y designated, respectively, by a pair of terms A and B just in case an instance of the schema "A is some of B," formulated in English, comes out true. In particular, the predicate Some(xy) is satisfied by any pair of things, x and y, designated, respectively, by an appropriate A and B.

Here then is what I will call the Principle of Homonymy for the names of Aristotle's homoeomeries: A predicate F is homoeomerous only if

(H) $\forall x \forall y (Fy \land \text{Some}(xy) \rightarrow Fx)$

comes out true. (H), like (D), is a schema of first-order logic; but I believe it has a true instance for every predicate F which names one of the homoeomeries. It says that, if F is true of anything, it is true of everything properly said to be some of that thing; and it is to convey the relatively unproblematic demand of the requirement of synonymous parts. If F names one of Aristotle's homoeomeries, any part of something of the kind of thing named by F—that is, anything which is *some of* some body of that kind—shares its name.

The Principle of Homonymy is designed to capitalize on counterexamples to the assumption that a predicate F is dissective. And the schema (H) is forthright, as (D) is not, about the fact that, in order to speak of a relation among the parts of something in virtue of which they share a name, one cannot simply translate English into first-order predicate notation. The two-place predicate "Some" does not translate "some of" nor "part of" nor some restricted sense of "part of"—and I am not supposing it translates *meros*. All that is claimed for (H) is that it comes out true when it ought to, and it is in this sense that the Principle of Homonymy is a consequence of the requirement of synonymous parts.

Assume it is given that there are instances of (D) which are false. "Water" is not dissective because, again, the oxygen in the water we have before us is part of that water, and it is not water. "*A* is part of *B*" is true for a pair of terms *A* and *B* which designate a pair of things *x* and *y* which stand in a part relation; they do not satisfy Some(xy) because "*A* is some of *B*" is false in this instance, so I claim; and, in accordance with normal interpretation of a first-order theory, *x* and *y* satisfy $\neg$Some(xy). What needs special emphasis here, however, is a commitment to the existence of values of the variables *x* and *y* of which "oxygen" and "water" are, respectively, true. The existence of counterexamples to the claim that "water" is dissective supports the assumption that *there is* some particular *a* of which "water" is true and the further assumption that there is a set whose elements are all those things which satisfy the predicate Some(xa) and are, by virtue of a true instance of (H), water. One may, if one chooses, speak of the relational *property* had by anything which is some of the water before us. The important point is that "the water before us" in this case designates something which stands in a Some relation to anything having that property.

Where *F* is any predicate which yields a true instance of (H), I will call the set of all those things which bear a Some relation to something of which *F* is true a *Some–F field*. Thus, in the case envisioned, the set of all those things which bear a Some relation to the water before us is a Some–"water" field—the extension of the relational property of being some of the water before us. Now that water, *a*, is in fact the fusion or mereological sum of the elements of the Some–"water" field just specified; and perhaps it is obvious that that field, together with a Some relation in that field, is a mereology. But it is important here to be quite clear as to what this means.

II

By way of preface to what he calls a "small theorem" (p. 162), Cartwright gives a definition of a mereology; here I will make use of another. Let *M* be any nonempty set and *P* any relation which is transitive, antisymmetric, and reflexive in *M*, that is, with the domain of *P* restricted to *M*. Then the pair (*MP*) is a mereology if and only if

1. there is a function f from the set of nonempty subsets of M to M such that, for every nonempty subset A and element x of M,

$$f(A)Px \leftrightarrow \forall y(y \in A \rightarrow yPx);$$

and

2. there is a function c from a subset of the set of pairs of elements of M to M such that, for every x and y belonging to M, if $\neg xPy$, then, for every z belonging to M,

$$zPc(xy) \leftrightarrow zPx \land \neg \exists w(w \in M \land wPz \land wPy).$$

The function f is the *mereological sum* of the elements of the set A, and the function c is the *mereological complement* of y in x.[9]

This definition is equivalent to Cartwright's and applies directly to the mereology exhibited in his small theorem. Mereologies defined in either way are, as he notices, natural models of the Leonard-Goodman calculus of individuals; and they are natural models of the "deductive theory founded by S. Lesniewski and called by him *mereology*,"[10] although according to Tarski, Lesniewski did not think of mereology as a formal theory open to a variety of interpretations.[11]

Assume the resources of a first-order theory with identity and some set theory,[12] and assume that the Principle of Homonymy holds for some predicate F. Then, if S is a Some–F field, the set of all those things which satisfy the predicate Some(xa) for some a of which F is true, and if R is the relation that any element x bears to an element y of S just in case x and y satisfy Some(xy), the pair (SR) is a mereology as I have defined it. The existence of the mereological sum of the set S is a consequence of the assumption that there is some one thing a to which every element of S bears R; for the value of the function f for S as argument is the least upper bound or supremum of S with respect to the relation R, once it is established that R is transitive, antisymmetric, and reflexive in S. Plainly R *is* transitive, antisymmetric, and reflexive in S; and $f(s)$ is then simply a.

The existence of the complement of x in $f(S)$, if $f(S)$ and x satisfy $\neg$Some($f(S)x$), is a consequence of the fact, if it is a fact, that S has more than one member. Closure of S under both the function f and the function c is then a consequence of the assumption that every x and y which satisfy $Fx \land Fy$ and Some(xy) are either distinct or not and, again, the fact that R is transitive, antisymmetric, and reflexive in the set S. Because the relation R is fixed by the specification of any Some–F field S, reference to S can be regarded as implicit reference to the pair (SR); and it is in this sense that every Some–F field—every Some–"water" field, in particular—is a mereology.

Given the existence of Some–F fields, the fact that they are mereologies is neither surprising nor profound, although I think that it has been both. Although it would be beside the point to do so here, one can do without mention of the set S and the relation R, provided that there remains no question about the consequences of assuming that the Principle of Homonymy holds for some predicate F which is true of something.[13] The heart of the matter, once again, lies in someone's claim to have a counterexample to the truth of all instances of (D); once that commitment is made, all that is called for is some reflection on the difference between "part of" and "some of" in English.

I have said that names of Aristotle's homoeomeries provide true instances of the schema (H); and I hope "water" is a sufficiently convincing example. A Some–"water" field is a set, each element of which is some of the water in a particular bowl or a set each element of which is some of the water in this room or (less obviously) some of the water scattered around here. Every Some–"water" field is a mereology, and, I suggest, so is every Some–F field for any predicate F which names one of the homoeomeries.

This is not, however, the end of the story, for if it is agreed that the names of Aristotle's homoeomeries provide true instances of (H), then every predicate F which names one of the *an*homoeomeries *also* provides a true instance of (H). Names of anhomoeomeries—"hand" and "face," and so on—are *obviously* not dissective. A finger and a thumb, things that are in the natural way called parts of a hand, seem not to share *any* interesting predicate short of "part of a hand." "Hand" and every other such predicate can be seen to produce a false instance of (D), and this *is* reason to regard dissectiveness as a (rough) mark of the difference between what is homoeomerous and what is not. And (H) may seem just irrelevant. "My right thumb is some of my right hand" is borderline English at best; if someone means by it that my thumb is part of my hand, then that speaker means something true; but it will not do to say on this account that, because a thumb is not a hand, "hand" provides a false instance of (H).

What this view of the matter overlooks, however, is a nice analogy in English between the syntax of mass nouns and that of count nouns in the *plural*. In fact, it is not altogether implausible to regard dissectiveness as a mark of *an*homoeomerous predicates in the plural—or at any rate once again a near miss. The count noun "marbles" might be said to be dissective down to whole spheres made of agate or glass but not to bits of agate or glass inside those spheres. In fact, "marbles," used in application to microscopic marbles, suggests a naive theory about water. But the point is that the defect in "These bits of marbles are part of the marbles in this bag" and in "These thumbs are part of the hands in this room" *can* be laid once again to confounding parts and components. "Hands" is dissective down to whole hands but not to thumbs and fingers. "Your hands and mine are part of the hands in this room" and "These hands are some of the hands in this room" may well formulate something true. "The thumbs in this room are some of the hands in this room" is straightforward English; and one who says it says something false.

Far from being irrelevant, (H) has a true instance for every anhomoeomerous predicate F. F is to be pluralized; but "hands" is no better than "hand" as a homoeomerous predicate; and, if "hand" is anhomoeomerous, surely "hands" is so as well. The predicate Some(xy) is satisfied by x and y just in case x and y are signified, respectively, by A and B whenever "A is some of B" or "A are some of B" has a true instance formulated in English; and if B is "the so-and-sos" and signifies something of which an anhomoeomerous predicate F is true, anything which can properly be said to be some of the so-and-sos is sure to be something of which F is also true.

The Principle of Homonymy does not, on its own, serve to distinguish names of homoeomeries from names of anhomoeomeries. It can be seen to rule out some adjectives—names of colors, for example; but it does not rule out anhomoeomerous predicates. And the notion of a Some–F field easily extends to the case in which F can be pluralized; in fact, the claim that such a Some–F field is a mereology is here, if anything, on firmer ground.

If S is the set of all those things which are some of the hands in this room and if R is the relation any element of that set bears to any other element just in case the former is some of the latter, the pair (SR) is the analogue of the set of nonempty subsets of S, with R corresponding to class inclusion. But for the empty set, (SR) is isomorphic to a natural model of the calculus of classes. The mereological sum corresponds to set-theoretic union, and the mereological complement to nonempty set-theoretic difference.[14]

But, given that a Some–F field is a mereology whenever F is either homoeomerous or anhomoeomerous, means are at hand for marking the missing distinction. The names of anhomoeomeries will be assumed to satisfy the following *Principle of Atomism*: A predicate F is anhomoeomerous only if

(A) $\forall x(Fx \rightarrow \exists y(\text{Some}(yx) \land \neg \exists z(Fz \land \text{Some}(zy) \land z \neq y)))$

comes out true. A predicate F which provides a true instance of *both* (H) and (A) is *atomistic*: For every x of which F is true, there is a y which bears a Some relation to x and is an *atom* relative to F—something of which F is true and something such that nothing of which F is true bears a Some relation to it other than itself.

"Hands" is an atomistic predicate. Given anything of which "hands" is true, say, the hands in this room, there is something which is (or are) some of it and an atom relative to that predicate. My right hand, for example, happens to be designated by "the hands resting on my desk"; it is (or are) some of the hands in this room, and no other hands can be some of those hands on my desk, that is, as it happens, hands other than my right hand. That hand—or the singleton with which some might say I have identified it—is an atom relative to the predicate "hands."

Now one who agrees to the intelligibility of the schema (H), where F is a predicate with the syntax of either a mass noun or a (plural) count noun, and to the existence of an x and a y which satisfy Some(xy) in either case, may well find the Principle of Atomism obviously true. I am not at all sure that it is so, even in the plural case, but if some predicate F satisfies both the Principle of Atomism and the Principle of Homonymy, every Some–F field will be an *atomistic mereology*, a mereology (MP) which satisfies the added condition

3. for every x in M, $\exists y(yPx \land \neg\exists z(z \in M \land zPy \land z \neq y))$.[15]

Atomistic mereologies are natural models of systems outlined by Goodman.[16] And, given a set X of individuals as Quine has defined an individual,[17] the set of subsets of X minus the empty set, with P taken to be set-theoretic inclusion, is an atomistic mereology.

It would be quite inconsistent with Aristotle's intent to suppose that the names of homoeomeries satisfy the Principle of Atomism; and it seems altogether plausible to say that "water" not only produces false instances of (A) but, along with any other name of one of the homoeomeries, satisfies instead a *Principle of Infinite Divisibility*: A predicate F is homoeomerous only if

(I) $\forall x(Fx \rightarrow \exists y(Fy \land \text{Some}(yz) \land y \neq x))$

comes out true. A predicate F which provides a true instance of both (H) and (I) is *atomless*. Given any x of which F is true, there is something of which F is true which bears a Some relation to x and is *not* identical with x. "Water," so I am suggesting, is an atomless predicate. If something is some water, then for everything which is some of it, there is something which is some of *that* and not the same water; nothing is both some of it and an atom relative to the predicate "water."

If a predicate F satisfies both the Principle of Homonymy and the Principle of Infinite Divisibility, then every Some–F field is an *atomless* mereology—a mereology (MP) satisfying the added condition

4. for every x in M, $\exists y(y \in M \land yPx \land y \neq x)$.

The assumption that a first-order predicate is atomless does not have the widespread intuitive appeal of the assumption that such a predicate is atomistic; and atomless mereologies are not natural models of any formal system that I know of suited to thinking about such things as water and bronze. There *is*, however, an important class of examples of atomless mereologies; and for this reason it will be useful to give somewhat more prominence to Cartwright's small theorem than he does (p. 163).

The theorem can be stated quite simply. It says that, if N is the set of nonempty open domains of a topological space, then $(N \subseteq)$ is a mereology. And it is a direct consequence of a theorem that says that the set of open domains or regular open sets of a topological space, with set-theoretic inclusion restricted to that set, is a complete Boolean algebra,[18] for, as Cartwright observes (p. 162), the set of nonzero elements of any complete Boolean algebra is a mereology,[19] and in the Boolean algebra of regular open sets of a topological space, the zero element is the empty set.

The theorem is easy to state and not hard to prove as a proposition of abstract algebra. Understanding the terms in which it is stated is another matter; and although it holds for the set of nonempty regular open sets of *any* topological space, its present relevance depends on the spatial intuitions from which the topological notions that appear in its statement are derived, for if N is the set of nonempty regular open sets of a Euclidean space, then, since there is no minimal such set other than the empty set, $(N \subseteq)$ is an atomless mereology of regular open sets,[20] and so is every mereology of regular open sets which contains no minimal element with respect to inclusion.

Now I mean to suggest that, if F is the name of one of Aristotle's homoeomeries, every Some–F field is an atomless mereology of three-dimensional elements included in what I will call an Aristotelian space. However, because common contemporary usage would make the elements I am after regions of three-dimensional Euclidean space, I will first make a rather more conservative suggestion: If F is a suitable predicate which satisfies the Principle of Homonymy, then the elements of every Some–F field *coincide* with the elements of a mereology of regular open regions of three-dimensional space—an atomless mereology if F is homoeomerous, an atomistic mereology if F is anhomoeomerous.

The conservative suggestion may look like an equivalent of a thesis of Cartwright, namely, that every material object coincides with a regular open region of space. And showing that this is not quite true will call for some review of his treatment of the notion of a receptacle. I want to derive the puzzle I mentioned at the outset of this paper, for my conservative suggestion represents a partial solution to it and another point in the attempt to understand Aristotle's notion of homoeomeriety.

III

Recall that an *open sphere* about a point p is the set of points less than some fixed distance r from p.[21] Open spheres are receptacles, regions with which some material thing might coincide, although not all receptacles are open spheres; and a region is simply any set of points of three-dimensional Euclidean space.

A point p is a *boundary point* of a region A if and only if every open sphere about p contains both points of A and points of the (set-theoretic) complement of A in the whole of space. An open sphere is open because it contains none of its boundary points; and a region A, spherical or otherwise, is *open* if and only if it contains none of its boundary points and *closed* if and only if it contains all of them.

Every open region is the union of some set of open spheres; and a boundary point of a region A, open or closed, can be redefined by saying that every open region which contains such a point p contains points of A and points of the complement of A, for if p is a boundary point of A as previously defined, and p belongs to an open region—the union of some set of open spheres, an open sphere about p is sure to be included in that union; and since any open sphere about p contains points in A and points in the complement of A, so does the union of open spheres which includes one about p. But, if every open region containing p contains points in A and points in the complement of A, then every open sphere about p, since it is an open region, does so as well; and the two definitions are equivalent.

Now, given that open spheres are receptacles, since every open region is the union of open spheres, it is natural to assume that every receptacle is an open region. The assumption is compatible with the size of a microbe or a galaxy and the shape of a knife or a snowflake just because there is no upper or lower bound on the size of an open sphere and so no maximal or minimal open region. Sets of boundary points of open regions and their subsets, including lines and points, are not open; and no material thing coincides with a line or a point and nothing else, I take it; nor does any material thing coincide with the empty set. So there are fairly obvious reasons for saying that every receptacle is a region which is both open and nonempty. Less obvious considerations lead to the suggestion that receptacles are *regular*.

The union of a region A and the set of boundary points of A is called the *closure* of A; and the *interior* of A is the complement of the set of boundary points of A in A. If A is an open sphere which is the set of all points less than the distance r from a given point p, the closure of A is the set of points at a distance less than or equal to r from p, and the interior of A is simply A. But, if A is any region at all, A is closed if and only if it is identical with its closure and open if and only if it is identical with its interior.

The interior of the closure of a region A is called a regular open region; and A is itself a *regular open* region if and only if A is identical with the interior of the closure of A. If A is an open sphere and B is the closure of

A, the interior of B is A, and A is a regular open region. Again, if B is the closure of an open sphere A, the interior of B is the set of all points of B that are not boundary points of B, that is, A; A is the interior of B; and B is the closure of its own interior. In general, a region B is said to be *regular closed* if and only if B is identical with the closure of the interior of B. Other things equal, one might choose to say that receptacles are regular closed rather than regular open; the notions are dual. What is important just here is that they be regular.

Why say that a receptacle is regular as well as open and nonempty? First it is to be emphasized that an open region is *not* in general regular: The interior of the closure of an open region is not the result of putting all of its boundary points into it and taking them all out again. Consider the region which contains all of the points of an open sphere but one (p. 155). Such a region is open; a region is not closed by removing points one at a time. And, if O is an open sphere and p any point belonging to O, p is a boundary point of $O - \{p\}$, for every open sphere about p contains points of $O - \{p\}$ and at least one point in the complement of $O - \{p\}$, namely, p. So p belongs to the closure of $O - \{p\}$. But p does not belong to the set of boundary points of that closure, for p belongs to the open sphere O and is thus at some distance r from the nearest boundary point of O. This means that there is an open sphere about p which contains only points in the closure of $O - \{p\}$ and none in the complement of that closure—the open sphere containing all points at a distance less than r from p. Since p does not belong to its boundary, p belongs to the interior of the closure of $O - \{p\}$ and not to $O - \{p\}$; $O - \{p\}$ is not identical with the interior of its closure; it is open, but it is not a regular open region.

Any point which belongs to the set of boundary points of a region A and not to the set of boundary points of the closure of A is an *inner boundary point* of A (compare p. 155). Thus p is an inner boundary point of $O - \{p\}$; in general, possession of an inner boundary point by an open region A is both necessary and sufficient to make that region irregular; and surely it would be strange to suppose that such a region is a receptacle. How could a sphere made of glass or stone or rubber coincide with all of the points in an open sphere but one? As Cartwright says, "It is not that objects never have holes; it is rather that holes are never so small" (p. 155).

What is the case for a region missing just one point extends to a region which has in it all of the points of a regular open region but any finite number of points and to one containing all points but those on a line. A line is not a slim cylindrical hole. And, if C is a line on an axis of the open sphere O, then $O - C$ is open and not regular, for every point on C except its endpoints is an inner boundary point of $O - C$, a boundary point of $O - C$ too far from the boundary of O to qualify as a boundary point of the closure of $O - C$. If p is any point on C other than an endpoint, there

is an open sphere about p which contains only points in the closure of
$O - C$ and none in the complement of that closure, namely, the open
sphere containing all points at a distance from p less than its distance from
the nearest endpoint of C. p belongs to the set of boundary points of
$O - C$ but not to the the set of boundary points of the closure of $O - C$;
and $O - C$ is thus irregular.

And the same story can be told for a region that has in it all of the points
of some regular open region but the points on any finite set of lines and
all but the points on a surface. Suppose that $O - S$ is an open sphere cut
by a plane. $O - S$ is open; every point on the plane S is a boundary point
of $O - S$; and every point on S but for those at its circumference is an inner
boundary point—one too far from the surface of O to qualify for membership in the set of boundary points of the closure of $O - S$. And once again
no such region is a receptacle, for no material object could coincide with it.
"This is not to exclude the possibility of cracks; it is simply to insist that
cracks are never so fine" (p. 156). It seems altogether reasonable to assume
with Cartwright that a region of space is a receptacle only if it is regular.
There can be no holes that coincide with a point or a line; and there can
be no two-dimensional cracks, plane or curved.

However, there is a crucial difference in the two-dimensional case. It is
this: Only here is the result of removing boundary points *two* nonempty
regular open regions. The severed sphere $O - S$ is the union of its two
regular open halves, one on either side of the plane S; neither contains any
points of the other or any points on S, where their boundaries intersect.
Because their union, $O - S$, is irregular, no *one* material object—no sphere
made of glass or stone—can coincide with it. This much is a consequence
of the assumption that every receptacle is regular. But the real peculiarity
of the case emerges in the presence of the converse assumption, which
Cartwright also defends, that every nonempty regular open region of
three-dimensional space is a receptacle. Given this assumption, at least *two*
material objects, two half-spheres of glass or rubber, may coincide with the
severed sphere $O - S$.

Regions A and B are said to be *separated* if and only if the intersection
of either with the closure of the other is empty. If A and B are separated,
they are disjoint; neither contains any boundary points of the other; and
the intersection of their closures is the intersection of their sets of boundary
points. A region which is the union of a pair of separated sets which are,
in addition, nonempty is said to be *disconnected*; and a region is *connected* if
and only if it is not disconnected, that is, not the union of any pair of
nonempty separated regions. The severed sphere $O - S$ is *dis*connected;
and here again is the crucial difference in the two dimensional case. Every
open sphere is connected; there is no pair of nonempty separated regions
of which it is the union. So O is connected, and the result of removing a

finite set of points or lines is so as well; such a region is irregular but *not* disconnected. It takes a region of two dimensions to disconnect a region of three; and the result of removing a plane through the diameter of a connected regular open region is *both* irregular *and* disconnected.

Now it is possible, I suppose, that someone will find disconnectedness reason enough for saying that at least two objects, but not one, might coincide with the severed sphere. To do this would be to opt for the absurdity of a two-dimensional crack while accepting the possibility of a two-dimensional divider. Notice, however, that one who comes to this conclusion must do so independently of an issue as to whether there are material objects that are scattered, for a *scattered* object is one which coincides with a *regular* disconnected open region (p. 157).

Now it is interesting and important that the possibility of scattered objects is guaranteed by the fact that disconnected regions need not be irregular. If O and O' are open spheres which are separated, every point in the set of boundary points of the union of O and O' is a boundary point of either O or O'; and since O and O' are regular, every such point is a boundary point of either the closure of O or the closure of O'. But an open sphere about any such point contains points in the closures of neither O nor O', so contains points in the complement of the closure of $O \cup O'$ as well as points in the closure of $O \cup O'$; and every such point will thus belong to the boundary of the closure of $O \cup O'$. No boundary point of $O \cup O'$ is an inner boundary point; and $O \cup O'$, though disconnected, is regular. It is a disconnected regular open region, and any material object which coincides with it is a scattered object.

That there are such things as scattered objects is a consequence of the assumption that every three-dimensional regular open region is a receptacle; but the severed sphere $O - S$ is not among them; and a view that would locate the peculiarity of $O - S$ in its disconnectedness alone can, I think, be dismissed. Two-dimensional dividers are no better than two-dimensional cracks. Moreover, the *possibility* of scattered objects will serve to make the real problem vivid, for the peculiarity of the two-dimensional case can be put another way by thinking about the notion of touch.

It need not be assumed that *every* three-dimensional regular open region is a receptacle, no matter how disconnected it is, or how disparate the objects that happen to coincide with it. On the face of it, *some* material objects really are scattered in the sense defined. My watch lies disassembled on a jeweler's bench; an unsolved jigsaw puzzle is strewn on a table; volume I of Cartwright's copy of McTaggart's *Nature of Existence* is in Cambridge, volume II is in Boston (p. 157). For the moment I will focus on the two-volume book—a single scattered material object made of paper and cloth, printed and bound in two volumes.

An object X *touches* an object Y if and only if the receptacles with which they coincide share at least one boundary point (p. 154). Cartwright's volume I does not touch his volume II; the receptacles with which they coincide share no boundary points. So the union of the regular open regions with those two volumes coincide is, like the union of open spheres $O \cup O'$, a regular open region; and the single scattered object which is his book coincides with a disconnected regular open region. The same will be true of any receptacle with which that object coincides while volume I is in transit to Boston. If B is the regular open region with which volume II coincides while on its shelf in Boston and A is any regular open region with which volume I coincides while in transit, $A \cup B$ is a disconnected regular open region.

And, when volume I has reached Boston and is about to be put in its place on the shelf, the situation remains unchanged if it touches volume II at a single point. If the separated open spheres O and O' share a single boundary point, their union contains no inner boundary points; and the same is true of the receptacles A and B. The situation remains unchanged if volume I touches volume II along an edge. No point on the line in which the boundaries of the receptacles A and B intersect will be an inner boundary point of $A \cup B$, given that A and B are regular open regions, for every point on that line is a boundary point of the closures of both A and B, and every open sphere about such a point contains points belonging to the closure of neither; so it contains points in the complement of the closure as well as points in the closure of $A \cup B$. Every point on the line of intersection belongs to the boundary of the closure of $A \cup B$; none of them is an inner boundary point of $A \cup B$, and since no other boundary point of A and B is an inner boundary point of their union, $A \cup B$ has no inner boundary points.

Just as the loss of a point or a line is not enough to disconnect a three-dimensional region, sharing a single boundary point or boundary points on a line is not enough to make the union of a pair of three-dimensional regions irregular. And given that Cartwright's book is a single scattered object when its two volumes do not touch at all, it retains its unitary status when they touch at a point or a line. If, however, volume I arrives at its place on the shelf beside volume II and their surfaces coincide in a plane, the union of the receptacles A and B is, like the severed sphere, irregular. And then, if all receptacles are regular open sets $A \cup B$ cannot be a receptacle; the book that coincides with it is no longer one material object. Something—a very thin something—has made it (at least) two.

Here, then, is something of a paradox; and it can be formulated generally in a rough way by falling back on the use of "part" set aside in section I. Say that an object X is *in contact* with an object Y just in case X touches Y at all of the points on some two-dimensional surface. What I will call the *Paradox of Contact* may be put: If a pair of objects X and Y are in contact, they cannot be parts of a single material thing—cracks are never so fine. If X and Y *are* parts of a single material thing, they cannot coincide with receptacles separated by a surface—there are no two-dimensional dividers; and then X and Y cannot be in contact.

Note that the paradox arises in just those circumstances in which the existence of a *single* scattered object seems least open to question. If a jigsaw puzzle is put together, it has *just* that sort of unity in *virtue* of which one is willing to call it one and the same when it is broken up again. But, given the reasonable assumption that every receptacle is regular, it is in just these circumstances that it cannot be one material thing at all, for when put together, its pieces (if it is a good one) are in contact and the union of the receptacles with which they coincide will then be irregular.

And my reassembled watch seems not to be an example of a *scattered* object at all; if any one object ever has parts, its parts are parts of one object. But if it can be disassembled, the union of the receptacles of its parts on reassembly will contain as inner boundary points all those points at which its parts are in contact.

IV

My conservative suggestion of section II was in part that if a suitable predicate F satisfies the Principle of Homonymy, the elements of every Some–F field coincide with the elements of a mereology of regular open regions. And I have said in effect that it provides a partial solution to the puzzle I have called the Paradox of Contact. In fact, I think it does resolve the Paradox in the cases just discussed; but this calls for explanation.

Suppose that E is the usual topology for three-dimensional Euclidean space; that is, suppose that E is the set of all open regions of space and that A is any region of space. Then E *relativized to A* is the set of regions which contain points in some open region which also belong to A: X is a region belonging to E relativized to A if and only if X is the intersection of A and some element of E. Any topology relativized to some region of the space for which it is a topology is itself a topology in the usual sense, a set closed under finite intersections of its elements and all unions of its subsets. And, if T is any topology relativized to some region Y included in the space for which T is a topology, an element X of T relativized to Y is said to be *open in* Y, and its complement in Y, Y − X, is said to be *closed in* Y. Such a region Y, together with T relativized to Y, is called a *subspace* of the space that includes Y; and if a topology has been specified in advance, Y is also called a subspace. Thus the pair (AE_A), where E_A is E relativized to A, is a subspace of three-dimensional Euclidean space, and the region A is also called a subspace.

Now a region which is open *in* a subspace need not be open in the whole space of which it is a region, and a region which is closed *in* a subspace need not be closed. If A is a region of Euclidean space which contains a single point p, the intersection of A and any open region containing p is $\{p\}$; so $\{p\}$ belongs to E_A, and $\{p\}$ is open *in* A; but $\{p\}$ is not open. Similarly, if A is the union of a pair of open spheres O and O', the intersection of A and the open region O is O; so O belongs to E_A, O is open in A, and its complement in A, $A - O$, is closed in A. But $A - O$ is the open sphere O'; so O' is closed *in* A, but O' is not closed.

In general, then, the regions of a subspace of a topological space need not in that subspace have the properties they have in the whole space; what is true of a region X absolutely need not be true of X on relativizing E to a region which includes X. But regions of subspaces do inherit some properties which for present purposes, are important. Thus, if a pair of regions X and Y are separated, then X and Y are *separated in A* for any subspace of which they are regions. This is so because the *closure* of a region *in A* is the intersection of A with the closure of that region absolutely. The intersection of X and the closure of Y in A is the intersection of A with the intersection of X and the closure of Y; and that intersection is included in the intersection of X and the closure of Y, which is empty if X and Y are separated. So, if X and Y are separated, the intersection of X and the closure of Y in A is empty, and, by a parallel argument, the intersection of the closure of X in A and Y is empty. The property of being separated is preserved in any subspace that includes a pair of separated regions; and it follows that the property of being disconnected is preserved in any subspace that includes a disconnected region.

The property of being regular is also preserved. If an open region X is regular, it is regular in any region Y which includes it, for if X has no inner boundary points, then, where p is a *boundary point* of X in Y if and only if every region containing p which is open in Y contains both points of X and points of $Y - X$, it is not hard to show that any boundary point of X in Y must be a boundary point of X absolutely; and then such a point cannot fail to belong to the boundary in Y of the closure of X in Y. No such region X can pick up inner boundary points because of relativization.

Suppose now that U is a nonempty set of nonempty regular open regions belonging to E, all of which are included in some regular open region A. Then every element of U is open and regular in the subspace A; and U is *the* set of nonempty regular open regions belonging to E_A. My conservative suggestion can thus be put, in part, by saying that, if F is a suitable predicate which satisfies the Principle of Homonymy, the elements of a Some–F field S coincide with the elements of the mereology of regular open regions belonging to E relativized to A, where A is the receptacle of the mereological sum of S, $f(S)$. But it is possible to be firmer than this.

The region A is an upper bound in U with respect to inclusion. The union of U is also an upper bound with respect to inclusion, but because the union of regular open sets need not be regular, it cannot be assumed that the union of U belongs to U. On the other hand, the interior of the closure of the union of U is not only an upper bound but a least upper bound of the elements of U with respect to inclusion; so A can only be the interior of the closure of the union of the set whose elements it includes. U is just the set of nonempty regular open regions included in the interior of the closure of the union of U.

But given *any* set V of regular open sets of a topological space, the interior of the closure of the union of V is a least upper bound in V with respect to inclusion;[22] and since this is true of every nonempty subset of U in particular, perhaps it is obvious that the interior of the closure of the union of a nonempty subset of U is the function required by condition (1) in the definition of a mereology of section II.

And it is not hard to see what the mereological complementation function required by condition (2) is to be. If X and Y are elements of U and if X is not included in Y, then $X - Y$ is nonempty. It will not do to say on this account that mereological complementation in $(U \subseteq)$ is simply set-theoretic complementation, because $X - Y$ cannot be assumed to be open. However, the complement of the closure of Y in X is a regular open region, and it is not only open but regular open in the interior of the closure of the union of U. Since the interior of the closure of the union of U is A, the complement of the closure in A of Y in X is the interior in A of the closure in A of $X - Y$. That set is nonempty and included in A; so it belongs to U. It has the feature required by condition (2), and the mereological complement in the mereology $(U \subseteq)$ is that function which assigns to each X and Y in U such that Y is not included in X the complement of the closure of Y in X.

So what my conservative suggestion of section II comes to is this: If F is a suitable predicate which satisfies the Principle of Homonymy, the relation which by virtue of coincidence each Some–F field S bears to a mereology of regular open sets is an *isomorphism* between S and the mereology of regular open regions belonging to E relativized to the receptacle with which $f(S)$ coincides. If $(U \subseteq)$ is such a mereology for a Some–F field S, the elements of S correspond to their receptacles in U one to one: x bears the Some relation R to y in S if and only if the receptacle of x is included in the receptacle of y in U. For each nonempty subset S' of S there is exactly one nonempty subset V of U such that $f(S')$ coincides with the interior of the closure of the union of V; and for each pair of elements x and y of S such that $\neg xRy$, there is exactly one pair of elements X and Y of U such that $\neg X \subseteq Y$, and $c(xy)$ coincides with the complement of the closure of Y in X. Moreover, it may now be added that, if a Some–F field S is an atomistic mereology, the mereology of regular open sets with which it is isomorphic in virtue of a coincidence relation is an atomistic mereology in the sense of condition (3), with the relation P as inclusion in that set; if S is atomless, the mereology with which it is isomorphic is atomless in the sense of condition (4).

If F is the name of one of Aristotle's homoeomeries, so I am suggesting, then every Some–F field is isomorphic with the atomless mereology of regular open sets of a certain subspace of three-dimensional Euclidean space. Such mereologies belong to the class of examples of atomless mereologies mentioned in section II, and they are models of the informal but systematic reasons for agreeing to the existence of Some–F fields for a predicate F which is atomless. If F is anhomoeomerous, every Some–F field is isomorphic to the atomistic mereology of a subspace of Euclidean space in which each region includes a region that is minimal with respect to inclusion in that space.

Now again all of this might be seen as no more than an elaboration of Cartwright's assumption that every receptacle is a regular open region of three-dimensional Euclidean space. The elements of Some–F fields, atomistic or atomless, are material objects; the regions with which they coincide are receptacles. And, since every regular open region is regular in any subspace of which it is a region, if the receptacles of elements of a Some–F field are regular open regions, they belong to the set of regular open regions with which I have suggested the elements of that Some–F field coincide. That set of receptacles can be expected to be a mereology; so my conservative suggestion does seem to follow from Cartwright's assumption. But the converse is not true, for although a region cannot pick up inner boundary points on relativization to a region which includes it, it can lose them; in particular, it loses all of them on relativization to itself. If p were a boundary point of a region A in the subspace A, p would belong to a region X, open in A, such that X contains both points in A and points in the complement of A in A; and $A - A$ is empty.

Thus my conservative suggestion furnishes a simple way of salvaging the unity of my reassembled watch without sacrificing the assumption that every receptacle is a regular open region. My watch, like my right hand, is something of an anhomoeomerous kind; at least "watches"—like "hands"—satisfies both the Principle of Homonymy and the Principle of Atomism; and my watch is an atom relative to the predicate "watches." It is the only thing which can properly be said to be some of the watches I am wearing. The set of which it is sole member, together with the relation anything bears to it just in case it is (or are) some of the watches I am wearing, is a mereology; and it coincides with a regular open region, namely, the only member of the mereology of regular open sets in the subspace which is its receptacle. That subspace has no boundary points in itself, and having no boundary points, it has no inner boundary points.

But in fact means are now readily available for salvaging the unity of any number of watches—or books or jigsaw puzzles—without sacrificing the assumption that every receptacle is a regular open region. If S is any Some–F field for an atomistic predicate F, then in accordance with my conservative suggestion S is isomorphic to the atomistic mereology of receptacles of its elements. Now if $(U \subseteq)$ is an atomistic mereology of regular open regions, any element of U—the receptacle of a pair of watches, for example—is the union of atoms of U, elements of U which are minimal with respect to inclusion in U; and the union of U is itself the union of all of the atoms of U. If A is the set of atoms of U, the union of U is the union of A; and it is then not hard to show that E relativized to the union of U is just the set of subsets of the union of A. But, if X is any element of the set of subsets of the union of A, it is included in the union of A; and since in this case its complement is also in the union of A, the complement of X in the union of A is an element of the set of subsets of the union of A. So any such X is both open and closed in the union of U—open because it is an element of E relativized to the union of U and closed because its complement in the union of A is its complement in the union of U and so an element of E relativized to the union of U. Thus every element of E relativized to the union of U, $E_{\cup U}$, is both open and closed in the union of U, $\cup U$. And it follows that every element of $E_{\cup U}$ has no boundary points in $\cup U$. The set of boundary points in $\cup U$ of every such region is empty.

So, if S is the set whose elements are each some of the watches in Boston, then not only the receptacle of its mereological sum $f(S)$ lacks boundary points in itself; the receptacle of every one of its elements—that of my watch, in particular—lacks boundary points in the receptacle of $f(S)$; and, having no boundary points, every such receptacle has no inner boundary points. If the interior of the closure of the union of the region U is the receptacle of $f(S)$, then, since its set of boundary points is empty in itself, the interior of the closure of the union of U is in that region simply the union of U; and the set of nonempty regular open sets of $E_{\cup U}$ is just $E_{\cup U} - \{\emptyset\}$. The isomorphism that, in accordance with my conservative suggestion holds between the mereology of watches in Boston and their receptacles is in fact an instance of the isomorphism mentioned in section II by way of introduction to the Principle of Atomism. Any such atomistic mereology is isomorphic to the set of nonempty subsets of the set of its receptacles, and it is so by virtue of coincidence. The set of nonempty regular open sets of $E_{\cup U}$ is a mereology in which the mereological sum *is* the union of nonempty subsets of the union of U, and mereological complements *are* nonempty set-theoretic complements, for all of its elements are (trivially) regular open regions included in the union of U, the receptacle of $f(S)$.

All receptacles of elements of an atomistic mereology of watches or books lack boundary points in an appropriate subspace. Lacking boundary points in that subspace, they lack inner boundary points; in that subspace they are regular and open, and the assumption that a receptacle is a regular open region is thereby preserved. The Paradox of Contact is resolved just because *in an appropriate subspace* there can be no points of contact by virtue of which my watch or a book fails to be a single material thing. And this way of resolving the Paradox is in these cases not as artificial as it might appear. I have noted that the Paradox arises in just those circumstances in which one is most inclined to say that the parts of something liable to scatter are parts of a single material thing. Well, if liability to scatter is the normal state of affairs—as one would expect of a book in two volumes or a jigsaw puzzle—at least some of those things naturally called parts of such an object ought to occupy receptacles that are separated under *any* circumstances; and if the set of boundary points of disjoint receptacles is empty, this is guaranteed.

Liability to scatter is not quite the normal state of affairs with a single watch; a bad job of disassembling my watch might destroy it, and even with the two-volume book the plausibility of calling it a single scattered object is lost if a volume is torn apart—no book survives. So a natural assumption about liability to scatter is this: that the parts of a scattered object are those only which can be properly reassembled. The parts of my watch—main spring, winding stem, and so on, parts which *are* so called in the natural way—can be supposed to meet this requirement. Moreover the makeup of my watch, like that of a book and a jigsaw puzzle, is a matter of human purposes and ingenuity and not, or not only, the nature of the region of Euclidean space with which it coincides. So one can take the fact that in *its* space—an appropriate subspace including its receptacle—the boundaries of its receptacle are empty and the receptacles of its assembled parts separated, to be a consequence of the fact that my watch *can*, with some skill, be disassembled without loss of unity.

As a way of resolving the Paradox of Contact, my conservative suggestion reflects the systematic exclusion of components as *merē* for which the Principle of Homonymy was designed. Parts of watches surely are components, things which bear an *ek* relation to some material object; and for watches and hosts of other things of which an atomistic predicate is true, the strategy seems to work. It is not very plausible at all, however, in the case of hands. If I lose my right thumb, my attached right hand survives; but modern medicine not withstanding, my hand does not survive as a scattered object, one whose receptacle is the union of that of my thumbless hand and that of my thumb. My thumb is part of a single material thing in a sense firmer than that in which my winding stem is part of my watch; but its receptacle is separated from the receptacle of the rest of my hand by boundary points which, if those two receptacles are regular open regions, are inner boundary points of the receptacle of my hand. And here it just seems wrong to say that in *its* space, the subspace defined by relativizing *E* to, say, the union of the receptacles of hands in this room, the set of boundary points of its receptacle is empty. The boundary points that separate the receptacle of my thumb from that of the rest of my hand are points with which points *in my hand* coincide. My conservative suggestion does not resolve the Paradox in the case of hands nor, I think, in the case of any of the anhomoeomeries cited as examples from Aristotle. It preserves the unity of a *pair* of hands, but only at the expense of making a single hand liable to scatter.

With the names of the homoeomeries, as may well have been noticed long since, liability to scatter may seem to be the rule. Mass nouns are said to be *cumulative*, where, roughly, a predicate *F* is cumulative just in case every sum of parts of which *F* is true is itself something of which *F* is true. And the only real trouble with this as a distinguishing feature of any class of predicates is that it is compatible with the nonexistence of sums. But once it is admitted that there are Some–*F* fields for a given *F*, so mereological sums of the elements of such sets, there are sure to be disconnected receptacles with which they coincide which are regular open regions of space. It is *obviously* possible that a sum of things which are water or glass or bronze is a scattered object.

But here, on the face of it, matters are even worse. Suppose that *O* is an open sphere included in the region of space inside a vessel filled with water; and suppose that no boundary point of *O* is a boundary point of *X*, the whole region with which the water in the vessel coincides. Then the complement of the closure of *O* in *X* is a regular open region; the union of *O* and the complement of its closure in *X* is the union of regular open regions; and it is irregular. Every boundary point of *O* is an inner boundary point of that union, and to see just how implausible it would be to say, in accordance with my conservative suggestion, that the set of boundary points of *O* in *X* is empty, recall that the set of things, each of which is some of the water in that vessel, has no lower bound with respect to inclusion in *X*. The open sphere *O* is one of infinitely many receptacles related to *X* as *O* is, and the water in the vessel coincides with them all. The Paradox of Contact arises all the way down, and relativizing *E* to the union of the receptacles of the water in that vessel offers no plausible resolution.

The strategy might be supposed to work in some cases. If two half-spheres of glass coincide with the severed sphere *O* − *S*, then the union of their receptacles is irregular. So they are no more one material thing than the book whose volumes are now in contact, and it is by no means obvious that Scotch tape or glue will change the situation. Here, as with the book or my watch, there is a pair of things which can be taken apart; and if they are regarded as parts of a single material object—an ornament of some sort, for example—it is once again plausible to say that in the region of space with which they coincide the set of boundary points of their receptacles is empty. The severed sphere $O - S$ *is* regular in itself.

But here also an important contrast begins to emerge between *both* the half-spheres of glass and the water *and* the book in two volumes. For one thing, if it is assumed that in the case just described a half-sphere of glass is just some of the glass which coincides with $O - S$ (see note 8), *no* half-spheres of glass coincide with $O - S$, for each half-sphere included in $O - S$ is a regular open region, and "glass" may well satisfy the Principle of Infinite Divisibility. The case only looks plausible because "half-spheres of glass" has been taken to be an atomistic predicate. Again, assuming that the two half-spheres of glass *are* atoms with respect to "half-spheres of glass," it does not take much imagination to see how, for example, the application of heat might make them coincide with a *connected* regular open region and so a *non*scattered material object made of glass. But most important, it is to be remembered that *two* things may coincide with the union of regular open regions, and if the half-spheres of glass are replaced by half-spheres of ordinary water at room temperature, even the appearance of plausibility disappears.

Perhaps it is conceivable that for a time a pair of raindrops might touch at a point; but I do not see how *two* such things could touch along a line; and to suppose that they touch on all of the points of a plane is surely just to suppose that they have become *one* drop of water. The plane has ceased to be a surface—a set of boundary points—of any receptacle at all; and the irregularity of the receptacle with which that water coincides is due to boundary points of another kind. If A is the receptacle of one drop and B is the receptacle of the other, on contact $A \cup B$ can no longer be either the receptacle of both of two things or of one. The receptacle of those drops of water can only be *connected* by points of contact, and if the only boundary points shared by A and B are points of contact, their receptacle is the interior of the closure of $A \cup B$.

Now it is to be noticed that this way of dealing with the Paradox of Contact is, as a matter of logic, available to one who would salvage the unity of Cartwright's two-volume book or my reassembled watch (compare p. 160). But notice also just how miraculous the possibility becomes if it is taken to be more than logical. Just what is being envisioned by one who assumes that one or the other of those volumes *gains* points on contact, points belonging to neither under other circumstances? It does take something like heat to unite the two halves of the glass sphere; and there is a crucial difference between the relation my watch bears to its winding stem and that which my right hand bears to its thumb—even if my thumb has been lost and somehow successfully reattached.

Very roughly, one might say, the implausibility of supposing that a set of boundary points is an empty set of points of contact rests on the assumption that that boundary is the locus of physical unity, or, more generally, the existence of phenomena falling under some sort of systematic expectation. It takes a good deal of work to bring about the unity of egg yolk, butter, and lemon juice required to produce hollandaise. Whatever the laws are that account for its success, it takes work to prevent the formation of boundaries that give hollandaise the look it has when it has curdled. Nonempty boundaries are the locus of interaction; empty boundaries are the locus of its absence, or at any rate of the absence of interaction of a sort which gives rise to connectedness. And it is here that I want to glean another suggestion from Aristotle.

V

Pretty obviously, bodies in Hobbes's sense are *sōmata* in Aristotle's; and homoeomerous bodies are bodies of some homoeomerous kind—material things which are water or glass or wood. But superficially at least, the characterization of Aristotelian bodies as occupants of space in the terms used so far is simply not available. An Aristotelian body is not something coincident with a receptacle; it occupies a place, and an Aristotelian place is at best the set of boundary points of a receptacle, although even this is misleading on at least two scores. A place is "the limit of the surrounding body, at which it is in contact with that which surrounds" (*Physics*, IV, 4, 212a5–6).[23] "It" here refers to an occupant, and its place is the inner boundary of a body which surrounds it. So a place is not only not a receptacle, it is not, strictly, the boundary of a receptacle, that is, the set of boundary points of a region of space, nor any other set of points.

Receptacles, regions of space with which it is possible some material object coincides, are in fact to be regarded with suspicion. A region of space is, I take it, what Aristotle means by "some extension over and above the body which changes position" (211b16–17). One is tempted to suppose that there are such things just because a place must be something "left behind by each object [when the object moves] and be separable [from it]" (211a2–3); and this is a temptation to be resisted. All that actually happens when, for example, the water in a vessel is poured out of it is that the water is replaced by "whatever body it may chance to be, of those which change position and are such as to be in contact" (211b17–18). And if the temptation *is* resisted, how is a place—a *topos*—to be characterized? Well, I think the problem really is superficial; and in the passage just cited Aristotle suggests part of a general strategy as to its solution.

Suppose that *B* is a ball made of brass, and suppose that *A* is a material object properly described as "that which surrounds" *B*. A *shell* about the point p at the center of B is that object $s(B)$ which is everywhere at a distance from p just the length of the radius r of B. Any point at a distance less than r from p is *interior to* the shell $s(B)$; any point at a distance from p not less than r will be assumed to belong to A, that is, to the complement in A of the set of points interior to $s(B)$. Points interior to $s(B)$ are to be found inside the brass ball B; points in the complement of the set of such points are to be found on $s(B)$ and, for example, in a tank of water in which B is suspended or at the surface of the water or in the air around the tank or at a greater distance from p, perhaps short of the limits of the sublunar world, perhaps not (211a23–25). At any given time, A can be assumed to be a material object including any of these.

Now Aristotle makes it an axiom of any characterization of a place that it be "neither less nor greater" than an occupant of that place (211a1–2, 31–34); it is quite in order to require the usual features of ordinary measurement; and I think the shell $s(B)$ can be seen to be a first approximation to the "proper" place of a brass ball, once it is noticed that the only geometrical feature relevant to the specification of "that which surrounds" is the radius of B. $s(B) = s(A - B)$, where A is any material thing containing points in the complement of the set of points interior to $s(B)$. $s(A - B)$ is "the limit of the surrounding body," whatever that body may be; and $s(B)$ is such that, if X is *any* ball the size of B, and A anything properly described as "that which surrounds" B, then $s(X) = s(A - X)$. s is a function, a *shell* function, with values fixed by the radius of B and a domain containing all those things properly described as "whatever body it may chance to be" of those things which are possible replacements for the brass ball B. But the shell function s can also be specified by saying that its domain contains all those things, $A - X$, such that A is "that which surrounds" any X which is a possible replacement for B and that its values are, again, fixed by the radius of B. A shell is the value of a function characterized in part by way of the usual metric for Euclidean space, and so is every other Aristotelian place, proper or improper.

It is important that Aristotelian places are not eternal. The existence of a place depends on that of a surrounding body and of an occupant for which there are possible replacements. What needs present emphasis, however, is that so long as these things endure, we are in familiar territory. At any given time, that which surrounds an occupant of a place is the formal analogue of the complement of an open sphere in the whole of space; and the difference between them—or between an open sphere or the set of points interior to a shell, and an element of an equivalence class of possible occupants of a place—is not, I think, important. The receptacles of the brass ball B and that of whatever object is taken to be "that which surrounds," that is, the regions of space with which it has been assumed these objects respectively coincide, have been displaced in favor of variable elements of equivalence classes of material things. But I intend to continue to speak of such elements and those things included in them in set-theoretic terms, and that without philosophical prejudice. All that is crucial to characterizing the shell function s as I have is the size and shape, the "extension" of B along with that of a possible replacement X and that of a surrounding body A; and this is just that *property* of material things which permits the application of the usual metric for three-dimensional Euclidean space with the requirement that $s(X) = s(A - X)$.[24]

In fact, I will assume that the shell function s is a function on a certain set of objects *included* in an object A which meets the condition that $s(X) = s(A - X)$ for every X included in A; and s meets this condition, so I mean to assume, because A has the topological properties of E relativized to the receptacle with which A coincides—or rather A. If S is any element of a set of material things equivalent with respect to no more than the region of space with which it is possible they coincide, but now to be regarded as indistinguishable from that common receptacle, I will call S, together with E relativized to S, an *Aristotelian space*. Aristotelian spaces are indistinguishable from *subspaces* of three-dimensional Euclidean space.

Aristotelian places are to be found among the boundaries not of receptacles but of objects in an Aristotelian space. Some places are shells, the two-dimensional boundaries of spherical objects of any size; and shells can be regarded not as sets of points but simply as the values of shell functions. Now boundaries generally have so far been taken to be sets of points; but here, too, mention of *sets* of boundary points can be avoided, for places can be taken to be among the values of a function defined by generalizing on the notion of a shell function.

Begin by supposing that S is any subspace of three-dimensional Euclidean space and that b is a function whose domain is the set of subsets of S. Then b is a *boundary function* if and only if it satisfies the following four conditions:

i. $b(S) = \emptyset$,
ii. $b(X) = b(S - X)$ for every X included in S,
iii. $b(b(X)) \subseteq b(X)$ for every X included in S,
iv. $(X \cup Y) \cup b(X \cup Y) = (X \cup Y) \cup (b(X) \cup b(Y))$ for every X and Y included in S.

All four of these conditions are consequences of the definition of the boundary of a region of S in terms of its set of boundary points as in section IV. Condition (i) simply records the fact that the set of boundary points of a subspace S, that is, $b(S)$, is empty. Condition (ii) is an immediate consequence of the definition of a boundary point in terms of open regions (or open spheres). If X is included in S, then p is a boundary point of X in S if and only if every set which is open in S and contains p contains points of X and points of $S - X$; and, since the complement of $S - X$ in S is X, specification of the set of boundary point of X in S, that is, $b(X)$, just amounts to specification of the set of boundary points of $S - X$ in S, that is, $b(S - X)$.

Condition (iii) registers the fact that any line that bounds a surface is included in that surface, and points that bound a line are included in that line. If p is any boundary point belonging to the set of boundary points of some subset X of S, then every set containing p which is open in S contains points in the set of boundary points of X in S, that is, $b(X)$; but any set which is open in S and contains a point in $b(X)$ contains points in X and points in $S - X$. So every point belonging to the set of boundary points in S of the set of boundary points of X in S, that is, $b(b(X))$, belongs to the set of boundary points of X in S, and condition (iii) follows.

Finally, since the boundary of X in S is included in S whenever X is included in S, the closure of X in S is the union of X and its boundary, the set of boundary points of X in S for every subset X of S. And since the union of X and Y is included in S whenever X and Y are, condition (iv) is a consequence of the fact that the closure of the union of X and Y in S is the union of the closures in S of X and Y. Condition (iv) is equivalent to

$$(X \cup Y) \cup b(X \cup Y) = (X \cup b(X)) \cup (Y \cup b(Y)).$$

Rearranged as it is, it represents a sort of distribution law.[25]

So given the set of boundary points of regions in a subspace of three-dimensional Euclidean space, there is a function whose domain is the set of subsets of that space and which satisfies the conditions (i) through (iv). And if the values of a boundary function b whose domain is the set of regions included in a subspace of three-dimensional Euclidean space, the converse is also true, for the values of b can be seen to be precisely the sets of boundary points in the subspace S as defined by way of open regions. If p is a point in the value of b for some subset X of S, that is, if p belongs to $b(X)$, then by condition (ii) p belongs to $b(S - X)$; so p belongs to the closure of X in S and the closure of $S - X$ in S. p belongs to S intersected with the closure of X intersected with the closure of $S - X$; and that intersection is included in the intersection of the closure of X and the closure of $S - X$; so p belongs to the intersection of the closures of X and $S - X$. Equivalently, every open region to which p belongs contains points of X and points of $S - X$, and, since S is a subspace of three-dimensional Euclidean space, every open sphere to which p belongs has this feature as well. The values of b are the sets of boundary points in the subspace (SE_S); and in fact the topology E_S is fully specified by saying each of its elements is the interior of some region Y included in S: X belongs to E_S if and only if $X = Y - b(Y)$ for some Y included in S.

The relation of a region of a subspace of Euclidean space to the set of its boundary points is a boundary function. But we need not think of the values of a boundary function as sets of points; and if the subspace S is now taken to be an Aristotelian space, the values of the boundary function b provide the required extension of the notion of a shell to boundaries of objects of any shape or size. S is an arbitrary member of an equivalence class of objects having the same extension—and of bodies which are possible occupants of the same place; E relativized to the receptacle with which S coincides is now to be regarded as E relativized to S.

So Aristotelian places need not be regarded as sets of boundary points but with no further commitment as two-dimensional values of a boundary function for the set of objects included in an Aristotelian space. No mention need be made of sets of points at all; all that need be mentioned are sets of objects, their boundaries, and such points as can naturally be assumed to belong to bodies.

Any material object, together with the properties it has solely in virtue of its three-dimensional extension, is the formal analogue of a receptacle together with the properties it has in virtue of being a region of three-dimensional Euclidean space. And given that the whole of space is a subspace of itself, all that has been said about receptacles—regions with which it is possible some material object coincides point by point—carries over almost verbatim to material objects that at a given time are possible occupants of the same Aristotelian place. So I mean to regard it as harmless to replace coincidence with a region by membership in an appropriate equivalence class; arbitrary elements of classes of material objects equivalent in extension will replace receptacles, and boundaries will be included in material objects. The closure and the interior of such an arbitrary object are defined just as they were for receptacles; it is only relativization that calls for some care, and I will now radicalize somewhat my conservative suggestion.

If S is a Some–F field for a suitable F which satisfies the Principle of Homonymy, the elements of S belong to the equivalence classes which define the regular open elements of an Aristotelian space $(S'E_{S'})$. The mereological sum $f(S)$ is in the equivalence class of which S' is an arbitrary member. Indeed, I mean to assume that $f(S)$ is S', the interior of the closure of the union of U, which is the least upper bound of the set U of regular open elements of $(S'E_{S'})$, all of them objects included in S', so included in $f(S)$. The isomorphism that holds in accordance with my conservative suggestion between S and the mereology of regular open regions of a subspace of Euclidean space here rests not on coincidence but on membership in an equivalence class of material things having the same extension. And if, as I am assuming, an element of an equivalence class which is a regular open element of an Aristotelian space happens to be an element of the Some–F field S, the isomorphism is simply identity. In such circumstances S *is* the mereology of regular open elements of an Aristotelian space: Every Some–F field, so I now suggest, can be assumed to have the Euclidean properties of the mereology of regular open elements of an Aristotelian space.

Regularity, connectedness, and separation in such a space are defined just as they were for regions; the assumption that receptacles are regular open regions is now the assumption that an element of an appropriate class of material objects is regular open—the elements of a Some–F field in particular; no such object contains an inner boundary point, one which is not a boundary point of the closure of that object in some Aristotelian space. But the plausibility of this assumption rests on the considerations adduced in section III: Holes and cracks are never so small. This is as obviously true of two-dimensional boundaries as of the objects that they bound; and the fact that it is true of boundaries is a consequence of the definition of a boundary function. Boundaries are closed because by condition (iii) every boundary includes its boundary; and, since a closed set is identical with its closure and boundaries of identical sets are identical, the boundary of the closure of $b(X)$ is the boundary of $b(X)$ for every object X included in an Aristotelian space; and every such boundary contains no inner boundary points.

I think one can fairly assume that an occupant of an Aristotelian place is not only regular but, if the place is "proper," connected as well. Connectedness is again defined as it was for regions: Objects X and Y are separated in a space S' just in case the intersection of either with the closure of the other in S' is empty—no points belong to it. No material object is in this sense empty, but since some boundaries are, the definition is to be so understood that X and Y are any pair of elements included in the space S'. An element is connected in S' just in case it is not the union of elements which are nonempty and separated in S', with this understanding. Places that are disconnected and so "improper" have disconnected occupants; but the union of disconnected occupants may be regular; so the occupant of an improper place may well be a scattered object.

What of the Paradox of Contact? In a sufficiently large Aristotelian space matters can be assumed to remain exactly as before. If Cartwright's copy of McTaggart's *Nature of Existence* happens to occupy a place in such a space, it is as problematic as its receptacle was in the space of regions of points; and my reassembled watch is no better off in such an Aristotelian space than it was as a coincident of an irregular region of points.

Notice, however, that the simple resolution of the Paradox by recourse to subspaces is an immediate consequence of the assumption that the two-volume book is to be located in an Aristotelian space that happens to include nothing but *books*, for in that space the boundaries of that book are empty, and the union of its volumes is on that account regular. And if the place occupied by my watch is to be found in an Aristotelian space that happens to be a Some–"watches" field, it too will be regular, assembled or not. Apparent points of contact between its parts which on assembly would be inner boundary points simply do not exist in any such space. Now I have suggested that this view does amount to a resolution of the Paradox, given a mereology of books or watches. I now mean to argue that Aristotle is committed to such a position for every occupant of a place.

Consider first the requirement on places that was cited as source of the temptation to think that there is "some extension over and above the body which changes position," that a place is "left behind by each object and separable from it." There is, after all, a puzzle here: If things that coincide can cease to coincide, then surely they are not identical. No two things, not even a pair of points can be identical at one time and not at another.[26] Again, assume that Aristotle means by "separable" (chōriston) "separated" as the term has been defined here and that the place occupied by an object X is the boundary of that which surrounds X in some Aristotelian space S'. Then, since $b(S' - X) = b(X)$, the intersection of the closure of X in S' and $b(X)$ is empty, given what we have been told. But $b(X)$ is included in the closure of X in S'; there is a contradiction; and the only means available of avoiding it require that we assume $b(X)$ is itself empty.

But, in fact, I think this is just the situation Aristotle envisions when he calls a place "the limit of the surrounding body," that is, $b(S' - X)$, at which limit an occupant is "in contact with that which surrounds." It is just the situation in which the Paradox of Contact arises, given the assumption that every body is regular and that places are among the values of a boundary function. A place *separates* an occupant X from some body or other, the complement of X in A, whether the Euclidean properties of A are relativized to A or not. And then any points belonging to that place will be inner boundary points of the union of X and $A - X$, that is, A. The apparent inconsistency is not, I think, unintentional; and it appears elsewhere.

The requirement that an occupant and its place be separable is immediately preceded by three others: First, "that place should be the first thing surrounding that of which it is the place"; second, that it should "not be anything pertaining to the thing";[27] and third "that the primary [place] should be neither less nor greater (than the object)" (210b34–11a2). And this much only supports the interpretation I have suggested: A place is the value of a boundary function "the limit of the surrounding body"—in particular, the third requirement, again, supports the use of a metric in defining a shell.

But in the context in which, as I have suggested, receptacles are made objects of suspicion, Aristotle says, in the course of warding off another confusion, that "it is because it surrounds that form is thought to be place, for the extremes of what surrounds and of what is surrounded are in the same [spot]. They are both limits, but not of the same thing: the form is the limit of the object, and the place of the surrounding body" (211b10–14). Form here is *morphē* in its first occurrence, *eidos* in its second, although a natural gloss can be put by saying that the boundary function whose value is the boundary of the extension of an object is not to be confused with the boundary function whose value is the place occupied by that object. And although I am not sure this is all there is to it, an object does take its form with it when it moves and not the place it moves from. If $b'(X)$ is the form of an object X at a time when it occupies the place $b(S - X)$, the functions b and b' are to be distinguished, for if $b'(X) = b(S - X)$ at a time t, we can assume that there is a time t' at which $b'(X) \neq b(S - X)$. And in any case the values of b and b' belong to distinct equivalence classes, given the possibility of local motion; so b and b' are distinct.

At any given time, however, the values of b and b' are "in the same [spot]"—they *coincide*; unless we rely on a distinction that we have been disallowed between points belonging to an object and points belonging to a region with which it coincides, this can only mean that the values of b and b' are *identical*; and then any points belonging to that value will be inner boundary points of the union of X and $S - X$. That union, the body S, will be disconnected by some common value of b' and a place function b as long as S includes X; and S will be irregular whenever it includes any places at all. The possibility of confusing form and place is quite general; any occupant X of a place included in S can be assumed to have a form whether it is a brass ball or a drop of water or a bubble of air or anything else that is a possible occupant of the place $b(S - X)$. *Whenever S includes an Aristotelian place it is irregular*, unless recourse is made to relativization: If at any such time E is relativized to S, then S will be regular just because its boundaries are empty in that subspace.

Now in the hard cases discussed in section IV, my conservative suggestion is no better off for having been radicalized somewhat than it was there, where, faced with the Paradox of Contact, its plausibility lapsed. In particular, the water in a vessel is as hopelessly irregular in an Aristotelian space that includes the vessel as its receptacle was in a space of regions of points. But Aristotle seems to see the case rather differently. In the context of an argument that I will not pursue in detail, he says, "If there were some extension which was naturally [there] and static, then there would be infinitely many places in the same spot" (211b19–21). And if one thinks of the extension of the water in a vessel, this suggests the difficulty detailed in section IV (compare pp. 160–161).

I am not supposing the passage is to be glossed by calling attention to the implausibility of emptying the boundaries of an infinite number of things which are water, nor that Aristotle would describe the position to which I have said he is committed in these terms. On the other hand, the suggestion of section IV—that empty boundaries represent the case in which no radical interaction is going on, that they are the locus of *natural separation*—surely is Aristotelian. And in this passage a difficulty is set up for those who can be supposed to have overlooked something like this possibility in a space that is naturally connected. Aristotle simply draws the distinction needed to repair the apparent inconsistencies I have cited in another way.

We are not to confuse the relation an occupant bears to a body which provides its place with the relation a part (*meros*) bears to something of which it is a part: A thing is in a place "when that which surrounds is divided from and in contact with [the thing surrounded]"; and "when that which surrounds is not divided from, but continuous with [the thing surrounded], the latter is said to be in the former not as in a place but as the part is in the whole" (211a29–30).

Here I think it is clear that given a pair of things X and Y, X is "not divided from, but continuous with" Y just in case X and Y are not separated, and the union of X and Y is connected. The case in which X is "divided from and *in contact with*" Y is that in which X and Y *are* separated, and given that places are closed two-dimensional boundaries, this *is* the case in which the Paradox of Contact arises, unless all such boundaries are empty. Of course, in this case things that occupy distinct places do not touch in the sense of section III; but I am not sure that would have worried Aristotle; and all of this seems right.

If X is a body included in some body S and X is separated from $S - X$, then the relation of X to $S - X$ is the relation of an occupant to a surrounding body which provides its place, and the boundary that separates them is an Aristotelian place as I have suggested it be characterized. If the relation of X to $S - X$ is that of part to the rest of that of which it is part, then the boundary of X does *not* separate X from $S - X$, or at any rate it does not do so in a way that gives rise to paradox.

There are, I suggest, two sorts of Aristotelian space, spaces defined by two sorts of boundary function. One sort simply have as values places defined in accordance with my conservative suggestion radicalized; the other have as values what I will call *mereological* boundaries, and these are designed to accommodate physical possibilities I have so far left out of account. Suppose that S is the Aristotelian space which has the topology of E relativized to the vessel which contains the problematic water. Then the values of the boundary function which defines the topology of S are empty, the place occupied by the water in particular. But it does not follow that the values of that function for all the objects included in S', the object which is nothing but that water, are empty. The intersection of S' and the boundary of S is empty; the water (and its form) are separated from the place provided by the vessel; and if it is assumed that all of the boundaries of objects included in S' are values of a mereological boundary function which defines an Aristotelian space by virtue of satisfying the conditions (i) through (iv), then it does not follow from the fact that the boundary of S' is empty in S', that the boundary of any three-dimensional object properly included in S' is empty.

There are no places occupied by some of the water in a vessel other than the place occupied by all of the water in a vessel, or in two vessels; its place need not be proper. To suppose that there are such places is to mistake the boundary of a part—a mereological boundary—for the boundary of something which is "naturally there and static." A place is the sort of thing that comes into existence with the arrival of a bubble of air or some other material thing which is not water; and such a place will be included in the boundary of the water which surrounds its occupant, a mereological boundary only because it happens to coincide with one. Given the transitory character of places, any description of local motion in that water is apt to be complicated, but that comes as no surprise. The important point is that the possibility of *any* such description depends on the natural difference between water and something for which it provides a place. And if X is an element of the Some-"water" field whose sum $f(S)$ is the water which occupies a place, proper or improper, X is separated from $f(S) - X$ by their common boundary; so their union is irregular if X is not just $f(S)$ itself. But if their common boundary is purely spatial, *that* union is not one anyone would expect to find among the objects included in that water. What one *does* expect to find is the interior of the closure of that union.

My *radical* suggestion of section II is simply this: If F is the name of one of Aristotle's homoeomeries, every Some–F field is an atomless mereology of three-dimensional objects in an atomless mereology of elements of an Aristotelian space in which the only boundaries are mereological boundaries. An X included in such a space S is open in S just in case $X = Y - m(Y)$ for some Y included in S, and m is a mereological boundary function. The set of elements which are open in S is just the set of interiors of subsets of S; and if T_m is that set, then $T_m - \{\emptyset\}$, together with inclusion in $T_m - \{\emptyset\}$, is a mereology in which the sum of elements of a nonempty subset X of $T_m - \{\emptyset\}$, $f(X)$, is the union of X; and given an X and Y in $T_m - \{\emptyset\}$ such that X is not included in Y, the mereological complement of Y in X is the interior of $X - Y$, that is, $(X - Y) - m(X - Y)$.

A mereology of things which are water *would* be isomorphic to the mereology of regular open objects in an Aristotelian space defined by a boundary function whose values are places if there *were* any such space which included nothing but water. There is none; and in a space defined by a mereological boundary function, the Paradox of Contact does not arise.

Mereological boundaries are not cracks; points belonging to them are not holes.

And a mereological boundary does not separate a pair of objects in a way that gives rise to paradox. If it did, that would be because a pair of objects, on contact, remained two; and this is not the normal expectation with a pair of raindrops, for example, which in such circumstances can only be one drop of water. Homoeomeriety is not a (purely) mathematical notion. To say that a space defined by mereological boundaries is isomorphic to a nonexistent space whose two-dimensional boundaries are places only makes contact in that space—separation by the values of a boundary function—a necessary condition for the unity of such things as a drop of water (*De generatione et corruptione*, I, 6). But mereological boundaries are boundaries of objects unified by natural law.

I think my radical suggestion extends to the two half-spheres of glass, now to be identified with the interior of the closure of the severed sphere $O - S$ not because, like raindrops, contact alone makes them one but because of the relative ease with which on contact they can be made one. The plane S scarcely counts, and to say that there is just one occupant of the shell which bounds O is to discount S as a plane of natural separation in favor of a mereological boundary included in a single sphere of glass— and to rely on laws by virtue of which glass is homoeomerous, if it is so. I am supposing that it is in accordance with some comparable story that some of something which is glass or ice or anything else classified as one of the homoeomeries. A *mistake* in classification is a mistake about laws of nature. The notion of homoeomeriety is not, or not only, topological.[28] Mereological boundaries are boundaries of objects unified by natural law; and a mereological boundary function can be supposed to define the structure—the *morphē* or *eidos*—of something of a natural kind in a quite straightforward sense of these terms.

If F is taken to be a homoeomerous predicate, the Principles of Homonymy and of Infinite Divisibility can be seen to register the assumption of natural connectedness and my radical suggestion as an effort to spell this out. As a methodological assumption it raises questions about Aristotle's thoughts on causation far too large to pursue here; but the radicalized version of my conservative suggestion can be taken to reflect Aristotle's distinction between parts and occupants of places in another way. Places are empty boundaries because contact may set up a *barrier* to change. When hollandaise curdles, I take it, bits of egg yolk are surrounded by butter in such a way that mixture cannot go on. A topological boundary has been created for each such bit—empty because it contains no points at which butter and egg yolk can appropriately interact.

And the conservative suggestion radicalized does seem to resolve the Paradox of Contact with some atomistic predicates. Here the Principles of

Homonymy and Atomism represent the assumption that the boundaries of things that are in the natural way called parts of such things as books and watches are as irrelevant to the fact that they are boundaries of components of a single thing as they are to the fact, if it is a fact, that such things are of a single kind. Boundaries in such cases are not mereological; they are not boundaries of parts but mere places.

So also, as I have in effect admitted, the strategy of relativizing E to the union of elements of which an atomistic predicate is true has no plausibility with the names of examples of the anhomoeomeries cited from Aristotle, indeed with the names of any of the anhomoeomerous *moria* that interested him most. The assumption that my attached right hand occupies a place in an Aristotelian space that happens to include nothing but hands would make the relation between my hand and its thumb—where one would expect a mereological boundary—just like the relation between my watch and its winding stem. Modification of this assumption would again raise questions far too large for consideration here; and here I can see no plausible way of extending my radical suggestion either to accommodate both of Aristotle's antithetical pair of terms or to resolve the Paradox of Contact.

The view I have been after has been described as "the separation Aristotle makes between matter as a reservoir of physical possibilities and the framework of locations and places"—to be contrasted in particular with Newton's conception of space, which allows for no such separation.[29] If "matter" is taken to be schematic—short for a list that includes the names of the homoeomeries—this seems right. The trouble is that it is unclear, to me at least, how such a list is to be continued or expanded.

Addendum

Because no closed region of space contains an inner boundary point, it might be supposed that the Paradox of Contact as it is formulated in section III is resolved by simply making receptacles regular closed rather than regular open—that, in fact, there is here excellent reason to opt for closed receptacles rather than open ones. Well, again, the notions involved are dual. The set of regular closed regions of a topological space together with inclusion in that set is a mereology, with the closure of unions of nonempty subsets as mereological sum (compare Kuratowski [1966] p. 74), and the closure of nonempty set-theoretic differences as mereological complement. If K is the set of nonempty regular closed regions of some topological space, then no element of K has an empty interior, and the interiors of elements of K belong to the mereology of regular open regions of the same space. So my conservative suggestion of section II as spelled out in section IV might have made a Some–F field isomorphic to the set of regular closed receptacles of its elements, and, other things equal, the whole of my project might have been carried out on the assumption that receptacles are regular closed.

However, the assumption that receptacles are regular closed cannot be based on having resolved the Paradox of Contact, for that Paradox has a dual. A region is regular closed if and only if its complement is regular open; and it is not hard to show that, if a nonempty region A is properly included in the interior of a region C and $C - A$ is nonempty, then $C - A$ is regular closed if and only if C is regular closed and A is regular open. Suppose the severed sphere $O - S$ is the union of the interiors of the (closed) receptacles of two half-spheres of glass embedded in a block of concrete and that the union of $O - S$ and the receptacle of the concrete is the regular closed region of three-dimensional Euclidean space C. $O - S$ is properly included in the interior of C, so I am supposing, and $C - (O - S)$ is the receptacle of the concrete. Now if X and Y are the two regular open halves of $O - S$, both $C - X$ and $C - Y$ are regular closed; their intersection is closed and *not* regular, for that intersection is $C - X \cup Y$ and $X \cup Y$ is not regular open. But $C - X \cup Y$ is $C - (O - S)$, the supposed receptacle of the concrete. It contains *outer* boundary points, points in its set of boundary points which do not belong to the boundary of its interior. Such points belong to a two-dimensional *membrane* separating the interiors of the receptacles of the two things embedded in the block of concrete. Could a material object coincide with $C - (O - S)$? If a single ornament coincides with the closure of $(O - S)$, why not?

Thanks are due my colleagues at Tufts for making me think harder about the possibility of making receptacles closed.

Notes

1. In Cartwright (1975), p. 153. All unmodified page references are to this article.

2. Book II, See Peck's introduction, especially pp. 28–30, 32–34.

3. Unless there is indication to the contrary, translations are mine. At *Meteorologica*, 385a9–10, wood and bark are listed as homoeomeries; "wood, bark" here in the last clause go with "flesh, bone," and "leaf, root" with "face, hand." Plants parallel animals in having both sorts of parts, although as Lee comments "Aristotle is writing loosely." See Furley (1981) for a penetrating discussion of the whole book.

4. Ackrill translation.

5. Things appropriately discussed as anhomoeomeries have just been discussed along with homoeomerous parts of animals (beginning of Book II, 9, 655b16). "The reason why we have just been taking them with the uniform substances and out of their proper order is that in them the name of the completed structure is the same as that of a portion of it" (Peck translation). He has been talking about bone, though his examples 655b5–7 are "whole hooves" and "whole horns." Compare also *Topics*, V, 5, 135a20–b6.

6. Compare Sharvy (1983), p. 442.

7. Compare Barnes (1982) p. 342; but especially Sharvy (1983), section 2.

8. Such constructions may also be what I called "quantity designating part-whole partitives" in "Parts and Partitives" (1984), section 6.

9. Compare my "Amounts and Measures of Amount" (1975), note 7.

10. Tarski (1983), p. 24.

11. Tarski (1983), p. 334.

12. See, for example, Corcoran's remarks in his introduction to Tarski (1983), p. xviii, and his reference there.

13. What I have in mind is, for example, reflected in the contrast between Tarski's treatment of mereology in the second paper and his treatment of Boolean algebras in the eleventh paper included in Tarski (1983).

14. Compare Tarski (1983), p. 341.

15. An element which is minimal relative to a mereological part relation is an atom, for example, in Goodman's sense. Such an element is also called a Boolean atom; compare Tarski (1983), p. 334.

16. In "A World of Individuals" (1953); see also Goodman (1972) for discussion and further references.

17. Quine (1951), pp. 122–123. An individual is a nonclass.

18. Halmos (1963), p. 25, with Theorem 1, p. 13. Kuratowski (1966, pp. 74–75) calls regular open (or closed) regions open (or closed) domains.

19. See Tarski (1983), pp. 333–334.

20. Compare Tarski (1983), p. 341.

21. r is to be a (nonzero) distance. Cartwright makes it a positive real number; here its significance is geometrical.

22. Compare Halmos (1963), p. 25.

23. All unmodified line references in section V are to Ross's text of Aristotle's *Physics*, Book IV, 4. Translations are Hussey's.

24. I mean to suggest that something like the view Jonathan Lear attributes to Aristotle, especially with respect to geometrical properties such as triangularity, holds for the "extension" of an object and for other properties needed in the (admittedly incomplete) treatment of Aristotle's topology that follows.

25. The definition of the function b is equivalent to the definition of a function β in Dugundji (1966), p. 74, on the set of subsets of the subspace S.

26. Compare Wiggins (1980), p. 33.

27. *Mēden tou pragmatos*, literally "nothing of the thing," as Hussey points out (Aristotle's *Physics*, Books III and IV, p. 211). He also says that " 'X is nothing of Y' allows the inference 'X is separable from Y'." But why not simply gloss "X is nothing of Y" as "X is disjoint from Y," that is, X and Y have no points in common? "X is disjoint from Y" is true if X is the boundary of Y and Y is open; and it does *not* allow the inference "X is *separated* from Y" as the term has been defined here.

28. Compare Furley (1981), who says:

> The doctrine of homoiomeriety, as used by Aristotle, is a biological concept rather than a geometrical one. All biological tissue is, according to him, divisible ad infinitum, but not necessarily into parts always identical to each other in all of their qualities. Aristotle's discussion of blood in [*De partibus animalium*] II 4 shows that in his view a substance may be continuous, and homoiomerous, and yet contain some parts that are solid . . . and some that are liquid. (p. 21)

29. Hussey's introduction to his translation of Aristotle's *Physics*, Books III and IV (p. xxxi), where he makes some interesting remarks about contemporary theories.

Bibliography

Aristotle. 1922. *De generatione et corruptione*, Harold H. Joachim, ed. Oxford: Oxford University Press.

Aristotle. 1936. *Physics*, W. D. Ross, ed. Oxford: Oxford University Press.

Aristotle. 1962. *Categories*, Harold P. Cook, ed. and trans. Cambridge, Mass.: Harvard University Press.

Aristotle. 1963. *Categories and De Interpretatione*, J. L. Ackrill, trans. Oxford: Oxford University Press.

Aristotle. 1966. *Topics*, E. S. Forster, ed. and trans. Cambridge, Mass.: Harvard University Press.

Aristotle. 1968. *De partibus animalium*, A. L. Peck, ed. and trans. Cambridge, Mass.: Harvard University Press.

Aristotle. 1970. *Metaphysics*, W. D. Ross, ed. Oxford: Oxford University Press.

Aristotle. 1978. *Meteorologica*, H. D. P. Lee, ed. and trans. Cambridge, Mass.: Harvard University Press.

Aristotle. 1983. *Physics, Books III and IV*, Edward Hussey, trans. Oxford: Oxford University Press.

Barnes, Jonathan. 1982. *The Presocratic Philosophers*, revised edition. London: Routledge & Kegan Paul.

Cartwright, Helen Morris. 1975. "Amounts and measures of amount." *Noûs* 9: 143–164. Reprinted in *Mass Terms: Some Philosophical Problems*, F. J. Pelletier, ed. (Dordrecht: Reidel, 1979), 179–198.

Cartwright, Helen Morris. 1984. "Parts and partitives: Notes on what things are made of." *Synthese* 58: 251–277.

Cartwright, Richard. 1975. "Scattered objects," in *Analysis and Metaphysics*, Keith Lehrer, ed. (Dordrecht: Reidel), 153–171.

Dugundji, James. 1966. *Topology*. Boston: Allyn & Bacon.

Furley, David J. 1981. "The mechanics of meteorologica IV." *Symposium Aristotelicum*. Typescript.

Goodman, Nelson. 1956. "A world of individuals," in *The Problem of Universals*. Notre Dame, Ind.: University of Notre Dame Press. Reprinted in his *Problems and Projects*. Indianapolis and New York: Bobbs-Merrill, 155–172.

Halmos, Paul R. 1963. *Lectures on Boolean Algebras*. Princeton: Van Nostrand.

Hurewicz, W., and Wallman, H. 1941. *Dimension Theory*. Princeton, N.J.: Princeton University Press.

Kuratowski, K. 1966. *Topology*. New York: Academic Press.

Lear, Jonathan. 1982. "Aristotle's philosophy of mathematics." *Philosophical Review* 91: 161–192.

Quine, W. V. 1951. *Mathematical Logic*. Cambridge, Mass.: Harvard University Press.

Quine, W. V. 1960. *Word and Object*. Cambridge, Mass.: MIT Press.

Sharvy, Richard. 1983. "Aristotle on mixtures." *Journal of Philosophy* 80: 439–457.

Tarski, Alfred. 1983. *Logic, Semantics, Metamathematics*, J. H. Woodger trans. Second edition edited and introduced by John Corcoran. Indianapolis, Ind.: Hackett.

Wiggins, David. 1980. *Sameness and Substance*. Cambridge, Mass.: Harvard University Press.

Ruminations on an Account of Personal Identity

Judith Jarvis Thomson

I

Some philosophers—I will call them Psychological Identifiers—think that X is the same person as Y just in case X and Y meet certain psychological conditions. (I have Locke in mind in particular.) If we wish to make as good a case for them as we can, which psychological conditions should we say they have in mind? Perhaps we can say that their view comes out as follows. Let us pretend that we have in hand a notion 'psychological property'. I say "pretend" because I do not have a satisfactory definition, but here are some sample psychological properties: being in process of thinking about algebra, being in pain, being an entity that wants a new bicycle for Christmas, being an entity that believes it will get a new bicycle for Christmas.[1] Let us supply ourselves with a predicate "X is psychologically the same as Y"—from here on abbreviated "PSYCHOLOGICALLY-SAME-AS (X, Y)"—whose truth conditions are given by the following:

> PSYCHOLOGICALLY-SAME-AS $(X, Y) \leftrightarrow$
> [for all times t and for all psychological properties P, X has P at t if and only if Y has P at t].

If we wish to make as good a case for the Psychological Identifiers as we can, we certainly cannot attribute

> *The Simplest Psychological Criterion:* $X = Y \leftrightarrow$
> PSYCHOLOGICALLY-SAME-AS (X, Y)

to them while allowing the variables X and Y in it to range over whatever there is, for the truth conditions of "PSYCHOLOGICALLY-SAME-AS (X, Y)" being what they are, PSYCHOLOGICALLY-SAME-AS (my left foot, your bicycle). But that difficulty can be easily eliminated in either of two ways: We can continue to allow the variables to range over whatever there is and instead attribute to the Psychological Identifiers

> X is the same person as $Y \leftrightarrow$ [X is a person and Y is a person and PSYCHOLOGICALLY-SAME-AS (X, Y)],

or we can attribute The Simplest Psychological Criterion to them, adding that the variables are to be understood as ranging over, and only over, people. Brevity being a virtue, let us opt for the latter alternative, and take the variables X, Y, and so on, here and throughout this paper, to range over, and only over, people. My left foot and your bicycle, not being people, they are not within the range of the variables and therefore make no trouble for The Simplest Psychological Criterion and therefore make no trouble for an attribution of it to the Psychological Identifiers.

I said about Psychological Identifiers that perhaps we can say their view comes out as follows—and I then offered The Simplest Psychological Criterion as a report of "their view." I do think this is *among* their views; that is, I think they do believe this true. In fact, I think it conduces to clarity in characterizing their views if we see them as, on the one hand, believing that The Simplest Psychological Criterion is true and, on the other hand, believing true a number of interesting further theses about people— further theses which, since they are about people, do have a bearing on personal identity, but which are entirely compatible with The Simplest Psychological Criterion.

That has not been the usual way of characterizing the views of the Psychological Identifiers, perhaps because it has not been noticed that they do accept The Simplest Psychological Criterion, perhaps because The Simplest Psychological Criterion seems to lack the depth that those in search of "identity criteria" for this or that kind of entity are typically in search of. (Deep or not, however, The Simplest Psychological Criterion is not trivial,[2] for it tells us among other things that, if X and Y have all their psychological properties in common, then they have *all* their properties in common.) In any case, what one typically finds is an attempt to incorporate all of, or anyway more of, their views about people that bear on the conditions under which X is identical with Y in a single thesis of the form "X = Y if and only if———" Here, for example, is Derek Parfit's report of what they have in mind:

> The Psychological Criterion: (1) There is *psychological continuity* if and only if there are overlapping chains of strong connectedness. X today is one and the same person as Y at some past time if (2) X is psychologically continuous with Y, (3) this continuity has the right kind of cause, and (4) there does not exist a different person who is also psychologically continuous with Y. (5) Personal identity over time just consists in the holding of facts like (2) to (4).[3]

Parfit himself does not agree. Or at least I think it probable he does not agree. I shall come back to his views later. What we need to do first, however, is to see what exactly this is to be understood to *say*. It is murky; but I think that a number of interesting things come out in the process of trying to understand what Psychological Identifiers may be taken to have in mind by means of trying to understand what Parfit may be taken to be attributing to them in telling us that they accept The Psychological Criterion.

Parifit does not define "strong connectedness" and "overlapping chains of strong connectedness" cleanly, but he gives hints. "Between me now and myself twenty years ago there are many fewer than the number of direct psychological connections that hold over any day in the lives of nearly all adults" (p. 206). That is, Parfit now remembers very few of the experiences had by Parfit twenty years ago, Parfit now believes and wants very few of the things that Parfit twenty years ago believed and wanted, and so on. So Parfit now is not strongly connected with Parfit twenty years ago. But Parfit now is strongly connected with Parfit yesterday, and Parfit yesterday is strongly connected with Parfit the day before, and so on. So, between Parfit now and Parfit twenty years ago, there are overlapping chains of strong connectedness, and Parfit now is therefore psychologically continuous with Parfit twenty years ago.

How are we to understand this? There are two possibilities.

In the first place, we can take the expressions "Parfit now" ("me now"), "Parfit yesterday," "Parfit twenty years ago" ("myself twenty years ago"), and so on, to refer, not to Parfit himself, but to proper temporal parts of Parfit; and we can take the relations 'strong connecteness' and 'psychological continuity' to be two-place relations on temporal parts of a person. Thus we can take my summary of Parfit's hints to say that the proper temporal part of Parfit that exists at and only at now is psychologically continuous with the proper temporal part of Parfit that exists at and only at twenty years ago in that the proper temporal part of Parfit that exists at and only at now is strongly connected with the proper temporal part of Parfit that exists at and only at yesterday, and so on.

Should we read Parfit in this way? I think not. In the first place, the second sentence of The Psychological Criterion begins "X today is one and the same person as Y at some past time if————" If we are to take locutions such as "Parfit now" and "Parfit twenty years ago" to refer to temporal parts of Parfit, the former existing at and only at now and the latter existing at and only at twenty years ago, then we should presumably take "X today" to refer to a temporal part of X existing at and only at today, and "Y at some past time" to refer to a temporal part of Y existing at and only at the relevant past time. But then X today and Y at the relevant past time do not exist at the same times, and a fortiori they are not one and the same person, no matter what follows the "if" in "X today is one and the same person as Y at some past time if————." Parfit, however, plainly thought it an interesting question what should follow that "if".

Here is a second reason for thinking we should not read the expressions

"Parfit now," "Parfit twenty years ago," and the like as referring to proper temporal parts of Parfit: It is (as I think) an extravagant idea that tables and chairs have proper temporal parts,[4] and (as I think) an equally extravagant idea that people do; and I therefore think we should be reluctant to attribute this idea to a philosopher unless s/he explicitly tells us s/he wishes us to. There are passages in Parfit's discussion of personal identity that do seem most easily and naturally understood if we take him to have this idea; but Parfit never explicitly asserts it, and there is anyway another way of interpreting those passages.

This brings me to my third reason for thinking we should not read the expressions "Parfit now," "Parfit twenty years ago," and the like as referring to proper temporal parts of Parfit. What Parfit is doing here is presenting us with an account of what is believed by Psychological Identifiers. Now some Psychological Identifiers do tell us explicitly that they believe people have proper temporal parts: David Lewis is an example.[5] But others do not, and I think we should be as reluctant to attribute that idea to them as we should be to attribute it to Parfit.

So I shall suppose that anyway some Psychological Identifiers do not have the idea that people have proper temporal parts and ask how we are to characterize their views if we do not attribute this idea to them.

II

Here is Parfit again: "Between me now and myself twenty years ago there are many fewer than the number of direct psychological connections that hold over any day in the lives of nearly all adults" (p. 206). I said: So Parfit now is not strongly connected with Parfit twenty years ago. But, I said: Parfit now is strongly connected with Parfit yesterday, and Parfit yesterday is strongly connected with Parfit the day before, and so on. Suppose that we take strong connectedness to be, not a two-place relation, but a four-place relation, which I express as follows:

Strongly-connected-with (X, t, Y, t^*).

What should we take the truth conditions of that predicate to be? Well, the hints we were given suggest this:

Strongly-connected-with $(X, t, Y, t^*) \leftrightarrow$
[X remembers at t many of the experiences had by Y at t^*, and X believes and wants at t many of the things that Y believed and wanted at t^*, and so on].[6]

(Notice that this construal of its truth conditions makes "Strongly-connected-with (X, t, Y, t^*)" true only if $t \neq t^*$ and, indeed, only if t is later than t^*.) In light of what Parfit told us about himself, we can now say that

Strongly-connected-with (Parfit, now, Parfit, yesterday) and Strongly-connected-with (Parfit, yesterday, Parfit, the day before) and so on.

In light of what Parfit told us about himself, we know it would be false to say that Strongly-connected-with (Parfit, now, Parfit, twenty years ago). But he tells us that he now is psychologically continuous with himself twenty years ago. This suggests that we should take psychological continuity also to be, not a two-place relation, but a four-place relation, which might be expressed as follows: Psychologically-continuous-with (X, t, Y, t^*). What should we take the truth conditions of *that* predicate to be? Well, why bother trying to figure this out? Isn't psychological continuity supposed to be a two-place relation? Let us look again at The Psychological Criterion—I reproduce it here for ease of reference.

> *The Psychological Criterion*: (1) There is *psychological continuity* if and only if there are overlapping chains of strong connectedness. X today is one and the same person as Y at some past time if (2) X is psychologically continuous with Y, (3) this continuity has the right kind of cause, and (4) there does not exist a different person who is also psychologically continuous with Y. (5) Personal identity over time just consists in the holding of facts like (2) to (4).

Clause (2) says, "X is psychologically continuous with Y," and that certainly *looks* as if it ascribes a two-place relation to X and Y. Moreover, clause (5) says, "Personal identity over time just consists in the holding of facts like (2) to (4)." Personal identity "over time" must surely just be personal identity.[7] So I take clause (5) to say, among other things, that it is a necessary condition for X to be the same person as Y that X be psychologically continuous with Y; that is, that it is a necessary condition for X to be the same person as Y that X have a certain two-place psychological continuity relation to Y. So we have to see what truth conditions it would be plausible to assign to the predicate

PSYCHOLOGICALLY-CONTINUOUS-WITH (X, Y),

given the purposes to which Parfit wishes to put it.

Well, we already know that psychological continuity is supposed to be a necessary condition for personal identity.

Let us simplify The Psychological Criterion so as to bring out what is really central to the role that psychological continuity is supposed to play in personal identity. First, why the "if" in "X today is one and the same person as Y at some past time if——"; that is, why not "if and only if"? Clause (5), after all, suggests that an "if and only if" would be in place. Second, why the constraint imposed by clause (3)? Parfit himself seems to think any cause would do well enough, and I think that the philosophers whose views he is trying to capture here would agree.[8] (Locke, for example, seemed to have had no interest in the question what might have caused the man who wakes up in the cobbler's bed to think himself a prince.) Third, it would be simpler to eliminate the self-reference introduced by clause (5): We do better to keep in mind that friends of this criterion (as of the others we are and will be looking at) intend to be supplying us, not merely with truth conditions, but with an account of what personal identity in some or other sense 'consists in'. So I suggest we simplify as follows:

The Simplified Psychological Criterion: $X = Y \leftrightarrow$
(2) X is psychologically continuous with Y, and
(4) there does not exist a different person who is also psychologically continuous with Y.

The Simplified Psychological Criterion (like its parent, The Psychological Criterion) makes clear that psychological continuity is not to be understood as sufficient for personal identity. Why not? Consider the following story, which Parfit calls the Branch-Line Case. (I slightly emend the story, for a reason that will come out later.) Alfred got into an otherwise empty Scanner, which beamed information about him to Mars but did not affect Alfred's body while doing so, other than by way of causing him to fall asleep. Martian machinery then constructed an exact replica of Alfred out of new matter. Call it Replica. Replica then woke up, got out of the Martian machinery, and went about his business on Mars. Concurrently, exactly one person woke up, got out of the Earthian Scanner, and went about *his* business on Earth. Replica, says Parfit, is not the same person as the person who got out of the Earthian Scanner. But Replica and the person who got out of the Earthian Scanner are both psychologically continuous with Alfred.

This story suggests that we should take the truth conditions of the new two-place predicate to be given by the following:

PSYCHOLOGICALLY-CONTINUOUS-WITH $(X, Y) \leftrightarrow$
there is a time t in the life of X, and a time t^* in the life of Y, such that either Strongly-connected-with (X, t, Y, t^*) or Strongly-connected-with (Y, t^*, X, t).

For given the way in which Replica was constructed, we may suppose it true that Strongly-connected-with (Replica, wake-up-in-Martian-machinery-time, Alfred, fall-asleep-in-Earthian-Scanner-time) and therefore that

PSYCHOLOGICALLY-CONTINUOUS-WITH (Replica, Alfred);

and given the fact that the Earthian Scanner did not affect Alfred's body while beaming information about him to Mars (other than by causing him to fall asleep), we may suppose it true that Strongly-connected-with (the person who got out of the Earthian Scanner, wake-up-in-Earthian-Scanner-time, Alfred, fall-asleep-in-Earthian-Scanner-time) and therefore that

PSYCHOLOGICALLY-CONTINUOUS-WITH (the person who got out of the Earthian Scanner, Alfred).

But since Replica is not identical with the person who got out of the Earthian Scanner, psychological continuity, so understood, is not sufficient for personal identity.

Is psychological continuity, so understood, necessary for personal identity? The claim that it is, namely,

The Weak Continuity Thesis: $X = Y \to$ PSYCHOLOGICALLY-CONTINUOUS-WITH (X, Y),

is very weak but not trivial. An easy way to see what accepting it would commit us to is to take note of the fact that it is equivalent to: PSYCHOLOGICALLY-CONTINUOUS-WITH (X, X). *That* tells us first that in the life of every person there are two times across which s/he is strongly connected with her/himself, thus (as we might put the point) that no person's life is a series of abrupt, complete psychological changes. And it tells us second that no person lasts only for a point of time. (Both of these are consequences of the fact that, given the truth conditions for "Strongly-connected-with (X, t, Y, t^*)," that expression is not true unless t and t^* are distinct times.) But these are very plausible indeed; and it seems very plausible to think, not merely that The Weak Continuity Thesis is true, but also that Psychological Identifiers believe it true.

So far so good: Let us take the truth conditions of the new two-place predicate to be what I have suggested. We now understand clause (2) of The Simplified Psychological Criterion, which we can rewrite as follows:

$X = Y \leftrightarrow$
  (2)   PSYCHOLOGICALLY-CONTINUOUS-WITH (X, Y), and
  (4)   there does not exist a different person who is also psychologically continuous with Y.

But what are we to do with clause (4)? Its presence in The Simplified Psychological Criterion (as in its parent, The Psychological Criterion) makes that criterion circular.

If we attend to the Branch-Line Case again, we can find a plausible replacement for clause (4) that eliminates that circularity. (I offer one possible replacement for clause (4) here; I draw attention to another possibility in note 10.) The Branch-Line Case was intended to show that psychological continuity is not sufficient for personal identity, and it does show that, but only on the following assumption:

Replica $\neq$ the person who got out of the Earthian Scanner.

Parfit takes that to be obvious, and so, I am sure, would anybody. But what exactly is supposed to make it true? Some philosophers might say: "Well, look, Replica's body is not identical with the body of the person who got out of the Earthian Scanner, as we know from the fact (among other facts) that Replica's body is on Mars and the body of the person who got out of the Earthian Scanner is on Earth and therefore is not on Mars, and *that* is what marks Replica as not the same person as the person who got out of the Earthian Scanner." But I think it plain that Psychological Identifiers would not say this. They would offer us a ground lying in psychological considerations for saying that Replica is not the same person as the person who got out of the Earthian Scanner—indeed, they had better be able to do so or confess they are mistaken about personal identity. But the job is not a hard one. What I am sure they would draw attention to is the following. Replica is now going about his business on Mars; the person who got out of the Earthian Scanner is now going about his business on Earth. There therefore is a time t at which Replica has memories or wants or beliefs or. . . that the person who got out of the Earthian Scanner does not have at t.

We have already met a means by which this point can be put more compactly. Since there is a time t at which Replica has memories or wants or beliefs or. . . that the person who got out of the Earthian Scanner does not have at t, Replica is not 'psychologically the same as' the person who got out of the Earthian Scanner—that is:

> It is not the case that PSYCHOLOGICALLY-SAME-AS (Replica, the person who got out of the Earthian Scanner).

That on any view entails that Replica is not identical with the person who got out of the Earthian Scanner, for on any view psychological sameness is necessary for personal identity.

If, as The Simplest Psychological Criterion says, psychological sameness is also sufficient for personal identity, then it is easy enough to eliminate the circularity, by replacing clause (4) with clause (4'), as follows:

> *The Noncircular Simplified Psychological Criterion*: $X = Y \leftrightarrow$
> (2)   PSYCHOLOGICALLY-CONTINUOUS-WITH (X, Y), and
> (4')   PSYCHOLOGICALLY-SAME-AS (X, Y).

So further, I think, so good. That is, it seems to me plausible to think that Psychological Identifiers accept all the theses we have been looking at. And I would not say that if I did not myself think all these theses plausible, for we are trying to make as good a case for the Psychological Identifiers as we can.

III

Now, alas, things may begin to go downhill, for there is something I have not yet mentioned, something that I think is important to Psychological Identifiers. What I have in mind comes out if we take note of the fact that everything so far said is compatible with my being Napoleon. Not in that I remember Elba and wish I ruled France—I am certain that I have never been to Elba and sure that I have never had a desire to rule anything. Still, what in what has so far been said is supposed to rule out there being a person—call it Napoleon/Thomson—who is Napoleon and also is Thomson? It might be thought this could be ruled out by appeal to psychological continuity, by appeal, in particular, to the fact that

(i)   Strongly-connected-with (Thomson, Thomson-birth-time, Napoleon, Napoleon-death-time)

is false. But it has to be remembered that psychological continuity is a weak relation and that the falsity of (i) is entirely compatible with the truth of

(ii)   PSYCHOLOGICALLY-CONTINUOUS-WITH (Thomson, Napoleon).

In fact, it might be asked why we should not suppose that (ii) *is* true, on the ground that

Strongly-connected-with (Thomson, now, Thomson, yesterday)

is true, and therefore if there is such a person as Napoleon/Thomson was said to be, so also is

Strongly-connected-with (Thomson, now, Napoleon, yesterday),

which entails (ii).

The Weak Continuity Thesis, after all, tells us only that in the life of every person, Napoleon, for example, there are two times across which s/he is strongly connected with her/himself, thus two times across which there is not an abrupt, complete psychological change in her/him. But it allows for any amount of abrupt, complete psychological change elsewhere in her/his life.

Psychological Identifiers are sure to want to rule out *all* abrupt, complete psychological changes. If you think that X is the same person as Y just in case X and Y meet certain psychological conditions, then you are sure to think: wholly different psychology, wholly different person.

I think that the simplest way to capture what Psychological Identifiers have in mind is this. Let us introduce a new one-place predicate, "PSYCHOLOGICALLY-CONTINUOUS (X)," as follows:

PSYCHOLOGICALLY-CONTINUOUS (X) $\leftrightarrow$

[for all times T in the life of X (except the first and last) there is a stretch of time S such that S begins before T and ends after T and such that X exists both when S begins and when S ends and such that for all pairs of times t and t^* in S such that t is later than t^*, Strongly-connected-with (X, t, X, t^*)].

(If X undergoes rapid psychological change during a period of its life, then for times T in that period, there may perhaps be only a small stretch of time S around T within which strong connectedness holds in the way indicated. Still, if there are such stretches around every time T in that period, then X does not undergo an abrupt, complete psychological change in that period.) What Psychological Identifiers believe, then, may be expressed as follows:

Strong Continuity Thesis A: PSYCHOLOGICALLY-CONTINUOUS (X).

That is, whatever person you choose,[9] s/he has the property just pointed to. That being the case (if it is), we are assured of the presence throughout every person's life of those "overlapping chains of strong connectedness" that Parfit spoke of in clause (1) of The Psychological Criterion. Moreover, that being the case (if it is), we are assured that there is no such person as Napoleon/Thomson was said to be. For suppose there were. Then there would be a person in whose life there is an abrupt, complete psychological change (across the pair of times Napoleon-death-time and Thomson-birth-time), and Strong Continuity Thesis A tells us that there is no person of whom this is true.

When Parfit talks about psychological continuity, which does he have in mind?—the two-place relation 'psychological continuity' that I pointed to in the preceding section, or the one-place property 'psychological continuity' that I just pointed to here? Well, both, I suppose. We should probably say that what he has in mind is a two-place relation 'strong psychological continuity,' ascribable by a predicate whose truth conditions are as follows:

STRONGLY-PSYCHOLOGICALLY-CONTINUOUS-WITH $(X, Y) \leftrightarrow$
[PSYCHOLOGICALLY-CONTINUOUS-WITH (X, Y), and
PSYCHOLOGICALLY-CONTINUOUS (X), and
PSYCHOLOGICALLY-CONTINUOUS (Y)].

If PSYCHOLOGICALLY-CONTINUOUS-WITH (X, Y), then Strong Continuity Thesis A guarantees that STRONGLY-PSYCHOLOGICALLY-CONTINUOUS-WITH (X, Y). But I do think that Parfit (like the Psychological Identifiers) accepts Strong Continuity Thesis A and that it was this relation 'strong psychological continuity' that he had in mind in using the words "psychological continuity" in writing The Psychological Criterion.

But is Strong Continuity Thesis A true? At a first glance I think it strikes one as less plausible than anything we looked at in the preceding section.

For example, consider Alzheimer's disease. It does its work slowly, I gather. But couldn't it have done its work quickly?

But *how* quickly? To constitute an objection to Strong Continuity Thesis A, we would have to be able to suppose that Alzheimer's disease could do its work instantaneously. We would have to suppose that the following reports a possible Alzheimer's patient history: Up to and including 4 P.M. precisely, the patient was cheerful, busy, full of thoughts about the past and expectations for the future, etc. At 4:05, and at all times between 4:00 and 4:05, the patient was glum, vacant, lacking in most memories and expectations, etc.

On some views, however, all (macroscopic) change is gradual, and if that is true, then this is not a possible patient history.

I leave this open. The fact that I intended to leave it open explains why I said at the beginning of this section only that now things *may* begin to go downhill.

IV

Now things quite certainly do go downhill.

Let us go back to the Branch-Line Case. I told the story as follows. Alfred got into an Earthian Scanner; Replica was then constructed on Mars; Replica then got out of the Martian machinery, and, concurrently, exactly one person got out of the Earthian Scanner. But to give this report of what happened is not to give the report that Parfit gave: Saying only this is saying less than Parfit said. For what Parfit said was, not merely that exactly one person got out of the Earthian Scanner, but also that *Alfred* got out of the Earthian Scanner. In short, Parfit assumed:

the person who got out of the Earthian Scanner = Alfred.

Parfit seems to have taken that to be obvious, and so, I am sure, would most of us. But would Psychological Identifiers agree? What reason lying in purely psychological considerations could they give for preferring that to

Replica = Alfred?

So far as I can see, the answer has to be none. But I am sure that a Psychological Identifier would say that, if there is no reason lying in *purely* psychological considerations for preferring one to the other, then there is no reason for preferring one to the other.

It may pay to stress that what a Psychological Identifier says here is, not that there is or may be a reason for preferring one of these to the other, although we do not know what it is and therefore do not know which, but rather that there is no reason at all for preferring one to the other.

But then what conclusion would a Psychological Identifier wish us to draw about Alfred?

Since the person who got out of the Earthian Scanner is not identical with Replica, it cannot be the case that *both* are identical with Alfred.

There remain three alternatives. The first might be called The No Scope Position: *Neither* is identical with Alfred. It is worth noticing, I think, that there isn't nothing in this idea—for a Psychological Identifier. Consider a second of Parfit's stories, which he calls Simple Teletransportation. Bert got into an otherwise empty Scanner on Earth, which first caused him to fall asleep, then beamed information about him to Mars, then destroyed his body. Martian machinery then constructed an exact replica of Bert out of new matter. Call it Replacement. Replacement then woke up, got out of the Martian machinery, and went about his business on Mars. Psychological Identifiers would say:

Replacement = Bert.

(Many of us would disagree, I think, but let that pass for the moment.) How so? Why is Replacement Bert, whereas neither Replica nor the person who got out of the Earthian Scanner is Alfred? Well, metaphorically, Bert has only one branch, whereas Alfred has two, and mightn't it seem right to think that that is the crucial point about Replacement? That is, that where, and only where, there is only one branch, that branch is not a mere branch but is the trunk of the tree itself? Dropping the metaphor, mightn't it seem right to think that the crucial point about Replacement is that, not merely is Replacement psychologically continuous with Bert, but more: *Everything* psychologically continuous with Bert is psychologically the same as Replacement? If that is the crucial point about Replacement, then doesn't it seem right to think that Replacement is identical with Bert only because that *is* true of Replacement? And then right, more generally, to adopt

Strong Continuity Thesis B: $X = Y \rightarrow$
$\{$PSYCHOLOGICALLY-CONTINUOUS-WITH (X, Y) and
$(Z)[$PSYCHOLOGICALLY-CONTINUOUS-WITH $(Z, Y) \rightarrow$
PSYCHOLOGICALLY-SAME-AS $(Z, X)]\}$.[10]

But if that is true, then Replica is of course not Alfred, for although Replica is psychologically continuous with Alfred, there is something psychologically continuous with Alfred who is not psychologically the same as Replica, namely, the person who got out of the Earthian Scanner. A similar argument shows that the person who got out of the Earthian Scanner is also not Alfred.

The second of the three remaining alternatives might be called The Narrow Scope Position: Either Replica is Alfred, or the person who got out of the Earthian Scanner is Alfred, but there just is no saying which. Or: It is not determinate which. Or: There is just no answer to the question which. Or: It is just a brute fact that either Replica is Alfred, or the person who got out of the Earthian Scanner is Alfred.[11]

The third of the three remaining alternatives might be called The Wide Scope Position: Either Replica is Alfred, or the person who got out of the Earthian Scanner is Alfred, or neither is Alfred, but there just is no saying which. Or: It is not determinate which. And so on.

But none of these three alternatives is at all plausible. Given the details of the Branch-Line Case, it is surely right to say that Alfred has merely been *copied*, that the person who got out of the Earthian Scanner is Alfred himself, and Replica is merely a copy of Alfred.[12]

Indeed, it is not at all plausible to say what led us to survey these alternatives in the first place, namely, that there is no reason for preferring

the person who got out of the Earthian Scanner = Alfred

to

Replica = Alfred.

So far as I can see, Psychological Identifiers do say exactly that, and the fact that they do counts strongly against them.

It is worth mentioning, however, that none of this counts against either The Noncircular Simplified Psychological Criterion or The Simplest Psychological Criterion. Believing these true is compatible with believing it perfectly plain that the person who got out of the Earthian Scanner is Alfred, for believing them true is compatible with believing that psychological sameness is a function of the physical as well as the psychological— compatible even with believing that physical sameness is a necessary condition for psychological sameness, so that not merely is Replica plainly not Alfred, but so also is Replacement plainly not Bert. In short, it is not the fact the Psychological Identifiers accept *these* two psychological criteria that makes serious trouble for them; it is the fact that they believe, in addition, that personal identity is a function *only* of the psychological— that is, that they accept, in addition, such theses as

It is not a necessary truth that $[X = Y \rightarrow$ the body of $X =$ the body of $Y]$

and

It is not a necessary truth that $[\text{PSYCHOLOGICALLY-SAME-AS } (X, Y) \rightarrow$ the body of $X =$ the body of $Y]$.

V

The objection I drew attention to in the preceding section did not lie in the fact that there are imaginable cases about which Psychological Identifiers are committed to saying: Here there is no more reason for supposing that X is identical with Y than there is for supposing that Z is identical with Y. The objection lay in the fact that a particular imaginable case (namely, the Branch-Line Case) about which Psychological Identifiers are committed to saying this is a case about which it is *very* implausible to say it.

But there are other imaginable cases. Consider the story Parfit calls My Division. All of Charles's body other than his brain is fatally injured; the brains of his two brothers, David and Donald, are fatally injured. Some surgeons transplant the left half of Charles's brain into David; while they are operating, a second lot of surgeons transplant the right half of Charles's brain into Donald. Two people survive these operations; let us call them Lefty and Righty. Lefty has what were David's skull, hands, feet, etc., and Righty has what were Donald's. Each has half of Charles's brain, each is convinced that he is Charles, and each is psychologically just after the operations very very like Charles was just before them. Question: Which is Charles? It really does seem right, on *any* view, to think there is no more reason for supposing one of them is Charles than there is for supposing the other of them is Charles. Not that, although there is, or may be, more reason for preferring one to the other, we do not know what it is; rather that there just is no reason for preferring one to the other.

But then what conclusion are we to draw about Charles?

Let us first ask what conclusion Parfit would have us draw about Charles. Here is Parfit as to what My Division shows: "The main conclusion to be drawn is that *personal identity is not what matters*" (p. 255). What he has in mind is this. Most of us, most of the time, care that we, ourselves, survive. I want, not merely that there will be people in existence tomorrow, I want that I personally be among them. Now consider Charles, and let us suppose that this is true of him too. Let us suppose that no operations have as yet been performed on him: The two lots of surgeons intend to perform the two operations on him, but have done nothing so far. Suppose that if only one operation were performed—if half of Charles's brain were transplanted into David or Donald and the other half destroyed—then Charles would survive, in that he would be Lefty if only the left half-brain were transplanted and Righty if only the right half-brain were transplanted. In short, suppose

(i)   The performing of either operation alone would ensure survival.

(*Should* we suppose that (i) is true? Let that pass. We are here merely summarizing an argument of Parfit's.) But both operations will be performed. Will Charles survive them? Some philosophers believe he will; others believe he won't. Parfit's point is this: Given that (i) is true, it ought not matter to Charles whether he survives the performing of both operations. For suppose he will survive the performing of both; then all is well, Charles gets exactly what he wants, namely survival. But suppose instead he will not survive the performing of both, thus:

(ii)   The performing of both operations will ensure nonsurvival.

But surely the performing of both operations cannot provide less of what matters to a person who wants to survive than the performing of either alone, where the performing of either alone would provide everything that matters. So whether or not (ii) is true, Charles will get no less of what matters than he would if only one operation were performed. It follows that survival itself does not matter.

Suppose that we are moved by this argument and therefore agree with Parfit that it ought not matter to Charles whether he will survive the performing of both operations. We might all the same just be curious. We might wonder, *Will* he survive? (I am tempted to say that, so far as the metaphysics is concerned, *whether personal identity matters is not what matters*. But the current literature on personal identity being what it is, saying that is swimming upstream. See note 15.)

But in any case we may well feel unmoved by the argument. Suppose that we are firmly convinced (as I am sure most people are) that survival itself does matter. Then we might simply prefer rejecting one of Parfit's premises to accepting his conclusion. We might, for example, say that (i) is false. Or we might say that, if (i) is true, then (ii) is false—indeed that, if (i) is true, Charles will survive the performing of both operations, so that he will *of course* get no less of what matters if both operations are preformed, in that he will get survival if both operations are performed. Or, of course, we might say both.

What Parfit draws attention to here *is* of interest. But I think he should have aimed it toward a different conclusion: not toward the conclusion that, given (i), it ought not matter to Charles whether he will survive the performing of both operations, but instead toward the conclusion that one who accepts (i) does best to believe that Charles will survive the performing of both operations. What I have in mind comes out most clearly if we approach it in a roundabout way, as follows.

I had asked: What conclusion are we to draw about Charles? Let us suppose that both operations have now been performed.

Since Lefty is not identical with Righty, it cannot be the case that *both* are identical with Charles.

There remain three alternatives. The first is The No Scope Position: *Neither* is identical with Charles.

The second is The Narrow Scope Position: Either Lefty is Charles, or Righty is Charles, but there just is no saying which. Or: It is not determinate which. And so on.

The third is The Wide Scope Position: Either Lefty is Charles, or Righty is Charles, or neither is Charles, but there just is no saying which. Or: It is not determinate which. And so on.

I think it likely that some Psychological Identifiers would take The No Scope Position, for I think it likely that some accept a thesis we looked at earlier, namely,

> *Strong Continuity Thesis B:* $X = Y \to$
> $\{$PSYCHOLOGICALLY-CONTINUOUS-WITH (X, Y) and
> $(Z)[$PSYCHOLOGICALLY-CONTINUOUS-WITH $(Z, Y) \to$
> PSYCHOLOGICALLY-SAME-AS $(Z, X)]\}$.

If that thesis is true, then Lefty is not identical with Charles, for although Lefty is psychologically continuous with Charles, there is someone psychologically continuous with Charles who is not psychologically the same as Lefty, namely Righty. A similar argument shows that Righty is not identical with Charles. So neither is identical with Charles.

What is of interest is that there are many others who would take The No Scope Position too. As I said at the outset, Psychological Identifiers think that X is the same person as Y just in case X and Y meet certain psychological conditions; let us give the name 'Physical Identifiers' to those philosophers who think that X is the same person as Y just in case X and Y meet certain bodily conditions. But here a difference emerges. Some Physical Identifiers—I will call them Physical Identifiers (Body)—accept

> *The Physical Criterion (Body):* $X = Y \leftrightarrow$
> [the body of X = the body of Y].

A human body B continues to exist through replacement of a 'replaceable' part, that is, a part replaceable compatibly with B's continued existence, such as a finger or kidney or heart. I so use "body" that one's brain is part of one's body; and it seems right to think one's brain not merely a part, but a replaceable part of one's body. If that is right, then David's body continued to exist throughout the brain transplant, and so did Donald's. Physical Identifiers (Body) who think it right—all of them, I should imagine—would therefore conclude that Lefty is David, and Righty is Donald, so neither is Charles.

Parfit takes a dim view of The Physical Criterion (Body), and so do many others who have written about personal identity in recent years. He, and they, think the views of the other Physical Identifiers—whom I will call Physical Identifiers (Brain)—are much more plausible than the views of the Physical Identifiers (Body). Physical Identifiers (Brain) think the brain crucial: They think that, if Y's brain is replaced by enough of X's brain to sustain life, then the resulting person is X. Or anyway, the resulting person is X if it is not also the case that Z's brain is concurrently replaced by a different part of X's brain, a sufficiently large different part as also to sustain life. What do they think if that *is* also the case? What, in particular, do they think about Charles? Well, I think it likely that some of them accept a 'brain analogue' of Strong Continuity Thesis B and would therefore take The No Scope Position too.

Should Psychological Identifiers accept Strong Continuity Thesis B? Should Physical Identifiers (Brain) accept a 'brain analogue' of that thesis? *Here* is the natural home of what Parfit drew our attention to in arguing that personal identity is not what matters. Psychological Identifiers and Physical Identifiers (Brain) think that, if either of the two operations had been performed by itself, then Charles would have survived. How can they also think that, since both operations were performed, Charles did not survive? I am sure there are pairs of operations, each of which would, if performed alone, ensure the survival of a man who is ill (as it might be, one operation implants a soluble capsule of alpha-drug in his heart, the other implants a soluble capsule of beta-drug in his heart), although the joint performing of both operations would kill him, by virtue of the one's interfering physically, chemically, physiologically with the other (perhaps two capsules would take up too much space and cause immediate heart-failure). But the two operations on Charles cannot be thought to have interfered with each other physically, chemically, or physiologically, and it is hard to see, then, how anyone could plausibly suppose that the performing of both of them killed Charles, although the performing of either by itself would have saved him.

Thus Parfit's point can be reput, not as a point about what matters, but as a point about what happened—that is, as an invitation to Psychological Identifiers and to Physical Identifiers (Brain) to reject The No Scope Position in My Division and, a fortiori, to reject Strong Continuity Thesis B and its analogues. And on this matter, we will surely wish to agree: It really does seem as if Psychological Identifiers and Physical Identifiers (Brain) do best to reject The No Scope Position in My Division.

They could instead accept The Wide Scope Position. But why do that? If you think that, if only one operation had been performed, Charles would have survived, then why conclude that the performing of both made it indeterminate whether he survived? To repeat: It cannot be thought that either operation interfered physically, chemically, or physiologically with the other.

There would be no outright inconsistency in Psychological Identifiers or Physical Identifiers (Brain) who accepted The No Scope Position or The Wide Scope Position), but given their views—given, that is, that they believe Charles would have survived the performing of only one of the two operations—they really do seem to do best to say that either Lefty is Charles or Righty is Charles, although with the proviso, as The Narrow Scope Position says, that there just is no saying which.

(Similar arguments suggest that Psychological Identifiers do best to take The Narrow Scope Position in the Branch-Line Case.)

But it pays to stress that if The Narrow Scope Position is true, then Charles survives, for "Either Lefty is Charles, or Righty is Charles" entails that he does. I stress: It is quite determinate that he survives. What is indeterminate is only which of the survivors (Lefty or Righty) he is.

As I said, Parfit thinks that it ought not matter to Charles whether he will survive the two operations. But as I also said, even if we agreed with him, we might well wonder, out of mere curiosity, whether he will. What does Parfit think? What does Parfit think *has* happened once both operations have been performed? Oddly enough, he takes The No Scope Position[13] (see pp. 259–264). I do find that odd. Physical Identifiers (Body) take The No Scope Position, but Parfit is plainly not among them: He throughout has little to say to friends of The Physical Criterion (Body). For example, his argument to the effect that it ought not matter to Charles whether he survives both operations can certainly not be thought to have been addressed to Physical Identifiers (Body), since they would reject (i), which is its main premise. So is Parfit a Psychological Identifier who accepts Strong Continuity Thesis B or a Physical Identifier (Brain) who accepts a 'brain analogue' of that thesis? But how odd that would be, given the consideration he wished us to attend to. Why, then, didn't he accept The Narrow Scope Position or even The Wide Scope Position? Perhaps he just did not notice the availability of The Narrow Scope Position. (Although he tells us again and again that such statements as "Lefty is Charles" and "Righty is Charles" are neither true nor false, I have been unable to find a passage in which he declares himself on disjunctions of them.) Perhaps he would say that The Narrow Scope Position is internally inconsistent. Perhaps, that is, he thinks that its being indeterminate which of Lefty or Righty is Charles entails that "Lefty is Charles" and "Righty is Charles" are neither true nor false (perhaps, in fact, that is *why* he thinks they are neither true nor false), and perhaps he thinks that *that* entails that "Either Lefty is Charles, or Righty is Charles" is neither true nor false and a fortiori is not true. But he gives no argument for this (possible) objection to The Narrow Scope Position, and I take the liberty of ignoring it.[14]

What view should *we* take about what happens to Charles in My Division? Well, if we are Psychological Identifiers, or Physical identifiers (Brain), I think we do best to take The Narrow Scope Position. For my own part, I think we ought not be either. My own view is that people just are their bodies, and The Physical Criterion (Body) strikes me as at least plausible as any of the criteria that turn up in the literature on this issue. I therefore think The No Scope Position best and thus that what happens to Charles in My Division is that the poor man dies. But I shall not argue for The Physical Criterion (Body);[15] what I am concerned with throughout is Parfit's account of personal identity.

But what exactly *is* it? Is he a Psychological Identifier? Is he a Physical Identifier (Brain)? (It is clear enough that nobody can opt for both sets of views, since they yield incompatible results in the case Parfit called Simple Teletransportation.) I shall come back to these questions in the following section.

VI

My Division is not a story with respect to which Physical Identifiers (Body) do best to say that it is indeterminate which of two people some given person is. I think it is thought to be easy to construct a story with respect to which they do best to say this, but that seems to me to be a mistake. One suggestion, often made, is that the following story will do: Edward's body splits into two equal parts, like an amoeba, there being two people who survive, one of which we may call Left-Side, and the other Right-Side. But that surely will not do. A sensible Physical Identifier (Body) replies that neither Left-Side nor Right-Side is Edward. After all, if an amoeba splits into two equal parts, neither of the two resulting amoeba is the original one.

I do not say it is impossible to construct a story with respect to which a Physical Identifier (Body) does best to say, "Here it is indeterminate which of two people some given person is," just that it is not obvious how.

What can easily be done, however, is to construct a story with respect to which a Physical Identifier (Body) does best to acknowledge indeterminacy of a different kind. Here is the story Parfit calls the Physical Spectrum. Scientists told Frank that either they would do nothing to him or they would perform one or another of a series of operations on him. The operations would all involve the destruction of one or more of the cells of his body, followed by immediate quick replacement of them by one or more new cells. In the first operation only one cell would be destroyed and one replaced for it; in the second, two cells would be destroyed and two replaced for them; and so on until in the last operation, all his cells would be destroyed and replaced by the same number of new cells. In each of the operations the replacements would be made in such a way that exactly one person results, a person who is just after the operation very like Frank was just before it.

Let us suppose that they in fact performed an operation on Frank that is somewhere roughly in the middle of the series, replacing enough of the appropriate cells to make it indeterminate whether the resulting body is Frank's body. And let us call the resulting person Resulting Person. Is Resulting Person Frank? Since it is indeterminate whether the resulting body is Frank's body, Physical Identifiers (Body) must say it is indeterminate whether or not Resulting Person is Frank.

Saying this is not saying it is indeterminate which of two survivors is Frank. There is, by hypothesis, only one survivor. The indeterminacy Physical Identifiers (Body) are committed to here is only as to whether that survivor is Frank and thus as to whether Frank survives at all.

Their view here can be reput as follows: Either Frank survived, or it is not the case that Frank survived, but there just is no saying which. Or: It is not determinate which. And so on. This view is in one way similar to the view I earlier called The Narrow Scope Position and in another way similar to the view I earlier called The Wide Scope Position; we might as well call it The Narrow Scope Position for One Survivor.

If the cells replaced in Frank included an appropriate number of brain cells, then Physical Identifiers (Brain) are also committed to saying it is indeterminate whether or not Frank survived, and thus also committed to The Narrow Scope Position for One Survivor.

But why shouldn't Physical Identifiers take this position? Some of Parfit's remarks suggest he believes that Physical Identifiers should all quail before the imaginability of the Physical Spectrum. I cannot think why. After all, indeterminacy of this kind is exactly what one would expect if a person is a physical object, since it is so familiar a fact that there are imaginable cases in which it is indeterminate whether or not a physical object (such as a ship or a shoe or a sock) has survived.

Some of Parfit's remarks suggest he believes that Psychological Identifiers should all quail before the imaginability of a similar story, which he calls the Psychological Spectrum. Here too a series of operations, but this time they involve not replacing cells but tinkering with them, so that in each succeeding operation in the series a greater psychological change is produced. What of the middle of the series? Psychological Identifiers must surely take The Narrow Scope Position for One Survivor in the case of operations in the middle of the Psychological Spectrum, just as Physical Identifiers must in the case of operations in the middle of the Physical Spectrum. Should that outcome be expected to shock or startle a Psychological Identifier? I hardly think so, strong connectedness itself being so obviously a vague relation.

The presence in Parfit's text of those two sets of remarks gives a reader reason to think he believes that the imaginability of the Physical and Psychological Spectra shows that Physical and Psychological Identifiers are all mistaken. If Parfit does believe this, however, *he* is mistaken.

On the other hand, Parfit does not explicitly claim to have shown them to be mistaken. Moreover, there are still other passages that suggest he believes the stories would be welcomed by Physical and Psychological Identifiers.

I think it really is not clear what answers we should give to the questions I asked at the end of section V: Is Parfit a Psychological Identifier? Is he a Physical Identifier (Brain)? There are reasons to think he thinks the views of the Psychological Identifiers preferable to the views of the Physical Identifiers (Brain);[16] but I do not think them strong enough to conclude from them that he is a Psychological Identifier.

What does come out clearly is only that Parfit thinks there can be indeterminacy as to whether a person will survive. (I do not say it comes out clearly that he thinks there can also be indeterminacy as to which of two persons some given person is, for it should be remembered that Parfit took The No Scope Position in My Division. Still, perhaps he would have taken The Narrow Scope Position in My Division if he had noticed its availability.) But that there can be indeterminacy as to whether a person will survive is something that all Physical and Psychological Identifiers are committed to, and it is therefore open to Parfit to become either.

VII

Some people would object to what came out in sections V and VI. The people I have in mind think it a strong, perhaps even a conclusive, argument against an account of personal identity—whether that of the Physical Identifiers or that of the Psychological Identifiers—precisely that it does allow for indeterminacy of one or the other or both of the kinds we have looked at, that is, indeterminacy as to who a person will be or indeterminacy as to whether a person will survive. Parfit has two connected arguments against those people. First, he says personal identity is everywhere determinate only if a person is a "separately existing entity" (such as a "Cartesian Ego"), and there is no good reason to think this true (although he says there might have been).[17] Second, he invites them to locate a point on the Physical and Psychological Spectra at which one person (for example, one Cartesian Ego) is replaced by another and to provide a reason for thinking that it really is Lefty (or Righty) who is Charles in My Division.

These responses seem to me unsatisfactory. Here, for example, is a passage that Parfit quotes from Chisholm:

> When I contemplate these questions, I see the following things clearly and distinctly to be true. . . . The questions 'Will I be Lefty?' and 'Will I be Righty?' have entirely definite answers. The answers will be simply 'Yes' or 'No'. (p. 309)[18]

Chisholm thinks: I will be looking at the world from Lefty's eyes, or I will be looking at the world from Righty's eyes, and it cannot be indeterminate which. For my own part, I feel a strong inclination to agree. Again, suppose that the scientists tell me they plan to perform a middle-of-the-series operation on me. Will I survive it or won't I? Well, either I will or I won't; either I will lose consciousness permanently or I won't; and I feel a strong inclination to think it cannot be indeterminate which. I think we all feel those things. Parfit tells us that even he feels them, although he says he is making a strenuous effort to overcome the tendency.

Parfit does not help us when he says we feel those things because we think a person is a separately existing entity. It is (to put the point mildly) unclear what it comes to to think a person is a "separately existing entity," so it is unclear what Parfit is accusing us of.

Nor does he help when he goes on the offensive, as he does when he asks where the line is to be drawn and whether it wouldn't be arbitrary to draw it at this place rather than that.

The fact is that we are perfectly content to allow for the possibility of indeterminacy when people are not involved. Is this the ship you built? Is the wave that swamped your sand castle the very same wave as the wave that swamped mine? Is this paint chip red or is it orange? We are not at all troubled by the possibility that there may just be no answers to these questions. No account of personal identity is going to leave us fully satisfied unless it brings out *why* we feel this kind of thing will not do when it comes to people. I am sure we must be wrong to feel it. (As I said, I am myself a friend of the Physical Identifiers (Body), but all Physical and Psychological Identifiers do best to think we are wrong to feel it.) But what its sources are remains an open question. I have only a few comments.

We can all imagine a paint chip whose color is indeterminate as between red and orange. We can all imagine a situation in which it is indeterminate whether or not the wave that swamped your sand castle is the wave that swamped mine. When I imagine some surgeons and scientists operating on Charles or Frank I can imagine, as it were 'from outside,' what it would be like for there to be indeterminacy with respect to personal identity. But how am I to imagine this 'from inside'? Suppose some surgeons tell me they are going to divide my brain tonight and give half to each of two brain-damaged people. Suppose I am also told that The Narrow Scope Position is true, so that tomorrow it will be indeterminate whether I am Lefty or Righty. I am told that Lefty and Righty will be brought from the operating room to the Statue of Liberty, Lefty to the the front of it, Righty to the back of it. Now I imagine they both open their eyes. What do I imagine that *I* see? Not a blur (like the superimposition of a picture of the front of the statue on a picture of the back of the statue), for I do not imagine that Lefty or Righty sees a blur. And not a flickering either, for I do not imagine that either of them sees a flickering.

Again, I am told that scientists will perform a middle-of-the-series operation on me tonight and that it will therefore be indeterminate tomorrow whether or not I have survived. What am I to imagine for myself if I am to expect it to be indeterminate whether or not I have survived? If anything at all, I seem to be imagining surviving, but if nothing, I seem to be imagining not surviving.

These questions could be asked about Charles or Frank: What am I to imagine *for him*?

There seem to be no answers to these questions; and that seems to make imagining indeterminacy 'from inside' impossible; and perhaps it is that which makes us feel there cannot be indeterminacy with respect to personal identity.

But I fancy that these difficulties (although perhaps not others) issue from a misconstrual of what is involved in imagining *determinacy* 'from inside.' Suppose I really will be in front of the Statue of Liberty tomorrow—it will quite determinately be me who will be looking at the front of it. What do I do when I imagine its being quite determinately me who sees the front of the statue? Perhaps I form a mental image of the front of the statue. (Or I draw a picture of the front of the statue.)

If we notice only that, then it is no wonder imagining indeterminacy 'from inside' seems impossible. For there is no image (or picture) that is indeterminate as between being of the front of the statue and being of the back of the statue—unless it is blurry or flickers.

But it is a mistake to notice only that.[19] For if I merely form an image (or draw a picture) of the front of the statue, then I have not imagined *my* seeing the front of the statue—for that is how the statue will look to anybody who is looking at it from in front of it. (It obviously will not do for me to insert into the lower left of the image (or picture) a short round creature in a dirty raincoat. That is how I expect to look tomorrow, but is no part of what I expect to see.)

But if imagining my seeing the front of the statue requires adding, in imagination, with respect to the image (or picture), "and it will quite determinately be *me* who sees that tomorrow," then perhaps it should be easy enough to imagine indeterminacy 'from inside': Perhaps I should merely form two images (or draw two pictures) and add, in imagination, with respect to them, "It will quite determinately be Lefty who sees one, and Righty who sees the other, but it will not be determinate which *I* see." Or, in the case of indeterminacy as to whether I survive: one image (or picture), with respect to which I add, in imagination, "And it will not be determinate whether *I* see that."

Of course the question what I am referring to when I say to myself, with respect to a mental picture I have formed, "It will quite determinately be *me* who sees that tomorrow" remains a good one. But if this is all there is to imagining my seeing, tomorrow, what the picture is a picture of, then perhaps we ought to feel less uncomfortable with the straightforward answer: just a thing made of flesh and blood.

Notes

I am grateful to Jonathan Bennett, George Boolos, Paul Horwich, and Derek Parfit for helpful comments and criticism of assorted drafts of this paper. I am grateful also to the National Endowment for the Humanities, which provided support during the time in which this paper was completed.

1. I hope the reader will be so far indulgent as to allow me to be *very* relaxed about what counts as a psychological property. One point is worth stressing here perhaps: I mean to include properties that a person may have at times at which s/he is unconscious. (For example, you might be speaking truly if you said of a certain small boy, "He wants a new bicycle for Christmas," even though he is asleep at the time of your saying it.) But see also the concluding paragraph of note 15.

2. Or at least it *may* be nontrivial. See the concluding paragraph of note 15.

3. Derek Parfit, *Reasons and Persons* (Clarendon Press: Oxford, 1984), p. 207. Page numbers in parentheses throughout this paper refer to pages in *Reasons and Persons*.

4. See Judith Jarvis Thomson, "Parthood and Identity Across Time," *Journal of Philosophy* 1983, 80(4): 201–220.

5. See David Lewis, "Survival and Identity," in *The Identities of Persons*, Amelie Oksenberg Rorty, ed. (Los Angeles: University of California Press, 1976), 17–40.

6. Or anyway: ... $\leftrightarrow$ X has at t sufficiently many "direct psychological connections" of sufficiently many of these kinds with Y at t^*. Let us leave this as vague as Parfit does. (See pp. 205–206.)

7. Parfit is not among those philosophers who think it can be the case that X is the same person as Y at one time but not the same person as Y at another.

8. If reference to causality is omitted here, and I think it should be, then reference to memory shoud be omitted in the account I gave of strong connectedness. What should replace memory there is Parfit's notion 'quasi-memory'. See p. 220ff.

9. Could there be a temporally discontinuous person? I think, actually, that Psychological Identifiers do want to allow for the possibility of temporally discontinuous people, thus that they would say that, although *Thomson* is not Napoleon, that is not because Napoleon could not have 'died' and then come back into existence at some later time. The trouble with Thomson, I think they would say, is merely that she has the wrong psychology. To accommodate temporally discontinuous people, we have to add a clause to the truth conditions of "PSYCHOLOGICALLY-CONTINUOUS (X)," as follows:

PSYCHOLOGICALLY-CONTINUOUS (X) $\leftrightarrow$

[for all times T in the life of X (except the first and last) there is a stretch of time S such that S begins before T and ends after T and such that X exists both when S begins and when S ends and such that for all pairs of times t and t^* in S such that t is later than t^* *and such that* X *exists at* t *and* t^*, Strongly-connected-with (X, t, X, t^*)].

10. This is a strong thesis, and there is good reason (which will come out in the following

section) to think that Psychological Identifiers do well to reject it. But those who accept it might think we would have done better to replace clause (4) in The Simplified Psychological Criterion not, as I did in section II, with clause (4′) but with

(4″)   (Z)[PSYCHOLOGICALLY-CONTINUOUS-WITH (Z, Y) →
        PSYCHOLOGICALLY-SAME-AS (Z, X)] ∧
        PSYCHOLOGICALLY-SAME-AS (X, Y)

in that we would thereby have been displaying more of what they believe.

11. I am grateful to George Boolos for allowing me to be the first to publish his collection of such expressions used by philosophers. It also includes "there is no (objective) fact of the matter as to which," "it is not definite which," "no one is in a position to say which," "there is no correct answer to the question which," "nothing counts as a right or wrong answer to the question which," and "nothing shows, decides, settles, determines, fixes which."

12. Mark Johnston's happy analogue for the Earthian Scanner is the Xerox machine. See his "Reasons and Reductionism" (forthcoming). We may bring it to bear here as follows: When you make a Xerox copy of a letter, it is not the case that the outcome is two copies and no original (The No Scope Position), and it is not the case that one or the other is the original but it is indeterminate which (The Narrow Scope Position), and it is not the case that one or the other or neither is the original but it is indeterminate which (The Wide Scope Position).

13. Parfit does not explicitly assert The No Scope Position in My Division. What he says is only: "I claim that there is a best description of the case where [Charles] divide[s]. The best description is that neither of the resulting people will be [Charles]" (p. 260). But I should think that, if the best description of what happens is "Neither is Charles," then neither is Charles.

14. The literature on vagueness contains a variety of different views on the questions pointed to here. See, for example, the articles in *Synthese* 30 (1975) and the articles commenting on them in later issues of the same journal.

15. But I cannot resist a few remarks.
    Physical Identifiers (Brain) think 'brain continuity' necessary and sufficient for personal identity. Why? I do not think I have your car in my garage when I transplant the steering mechanism of your car into the car in my garage. I do not think I have your computer on my desk when I transplant the CPU chip of your computer into the computer on my desk.
    Parfit asks "Why should the brain be singled out in this way?" and he says, rightly, I am sure: "The answer must be: 'Because the brain is the carrier of psychological continuity' " (p. 284). But then (he asks) isn't the carrier of interest because the carried is of interest? So isn't it psychological continuity itself which the Physical Identifier (Brain)—like the Psychological Identifier—thinks metaphysically crucial to personal identity?
    But *why* take psychological continuity to be metaphysically crucial to personal identity? It is plausible that there are two things at work in the many people who think it is. (A) They think that what *matters* matters. And (B) they think that what *matters* is psychological continuity. David Lewis, for example, is among the 'they' that (A) refers to: The article by him, to which I have referred, opens with the question, "What is it that matters in survival?" But oughtn't we wonder if it isn't wishful thinking to try to find out what it is for people to survive by focusing our attention on what they hope survival will provide for them? And I think (B) should strike us as equally puzzling. Yes, I do greatly hope that there will be in existence tomorrow a person who will then be strongly connected with me today, thus who will, tomorrow, have many of the following psychological properties: remembers my father, believes it never rains but it pours, prefers chocolate to vanilla, and so on. But that is largely

because I want *me* to be in existence tomorrow and think it likely I won't be unless there is such a person. (I do hope there will be in existence tomorrow a person who will, tomorrow, have *some* of the psychological properties I have today, whether or not that person will be me, for example, the property 'wants the hungry to be fed'. That is because I want the hungry to be fed and do not care that it be me who feeds them. But it could easily be the case that there is in existence tomorrow a person who has, tomorrow, *those* among the psychological properties I have today, without there being in existence tomorrow anyone who is, tomorrow, strongly connected with me today.) Indeed, if offered a choice between, on the one hand, my not existing tomorrow and there being someone other than me in existence tomorrow who is, tomorrow, strongly connected with me today and, on the other hand, my existing tomorrow but not being, tomorrow, strongly connected with myself today, then it seems to me obvious that I would choose the latter.

Since I have confessed to thinking The Physical Criterion (Body) at least as plausible as any of the criteria that turn up in the literature on this issue, it might well be asked why I said, earlier, that I think The Simplest Psychological Criterion a plausible thesis. Couldn't there be two animated human bodies, thus two people, who are psychologically the same throughout their lives? For example, on different but similar planets? The short answer is: I have been relying on the reader's allowing me to be very relaxed about what counts as a psychological property. The long answer tries to supply an account under which The Simplest Psychological Criterion is both true and nontrivial. I grant, however, that this *may* be impossible.

16. See, for example, the argument on p. 284 to the effect that we should be more interested in psychological similarity than in bodily continuity.

17. Sidney Shoemaker criticizes this idea in his review of *Reasons and Persons* in *Mind* (July 1985) 94 (375): 443–453.

18. Parfit (p. 309) is here quoting from R. M. Chisholm's "Reply to Strawson's Comments," in *Language, Belief, and Metaphysics*, Howard E. Kiefer and Milton K. Munitz, eds. (Albany: State University of New York Press, 1970). Chisholm's Lefty and Righty are people whom this paper would call Left-Side and Right-Side; that is, they are products of fission.

19. I *think* the point I make here is first cousin to some of the points made by Bernard Williams in "Imagination and the Self," in his *Problems of the Self* (Cambridge: Cambridge University Press, 1973).

Gödel's Ontological Proof
Jordan Howard Sobel

Photocopies of three handwritten pages, titled "Godel's Ontological Proof," have recently begun to circulate. The handwriting is Dana Scott's. The ideas are Kurt Gödel's; they agree substantially with ideas conveyed in two pages of notes in Gödel's own hand dated 10 February 1970 and titled "Ontologischer Beweis."[1] These three pages contain a sketch of a theory of positive properties, individual essences, and necessary existence that culminates in a theorem that says that it is necessary that there is a being that has every positive property. The system is Leibnizian in spirit and Spinozistic in axiomatic form.[2]

In what follows parts of the theory are set out. Then comments are made concerning its underlying logic. Next a reconstruction is provided of the proof in it that it is necessary that there is a being that has all positive properties, the God of the theory. I then maintain that, given the terms and conditions of the system, no being that possessed all positive properties could reasonably be maintained to be God. Next it is demonstrated that there is a collapse of modalities in the system—that in it everything that is actual or true is so of logical necessity. One reaction to these difficulties of the system would be to relinquish the axiom that makes necessary existence a positive property and, consequently, a part of the essence of God-likeness. In conclusion, brief comments are made on this possible reaction and on the related ideas that one should simply give up on the ontological argument and that one *can* do this without giving up on God.

I

"Positive property" is a primitive of the theory. The intended sense of this primitive—the idea that motivates the theory—can be gathered from explanatory sentences in Gödel's own hand. He writes in "Ontologischer Beweis":

> Positive means positive in the moral aesthetic [this word is not en-
> tirely legible] sense (independently of the accidental structure of the
> world). Only then [is/are?] the ax. [axiom/axioms?—the reference

may be specifically to something equivalent to Axiom 2, given later, or to all the axioms] true. It may also mean pure 'attribution'* as opposed to 'privation' (or *containing* privation). This interpret. [supports a] simpler proof. . . .
*i.e., the 'disj' normal form in terms of elem. prop. contains [only? all?—I cannot decipher the mark here] member without negation.

(Both "pure" and "disj." are above-the-line insertions.) Gödel was inclined to endorse a Platonic equation of goodness with "positive being" (although it is not clear that an unreserved endorsement can be read from the words quoted, for there is a question whether in the phrase "may also" the emphasis intended was on "may" or on "also"). As will be evident and as Gödel seems to have realized, his theory would be served by and may indeed depend on some such equation. It may need a moral aesthetic interpretation of "positive" for theological and religious relevance; and, for the prima facie truth of at least some of its axioms ("simpler proof," Gödel writes), it may sometimes need or be better served by a logical/ontological interpretation of this primitive.

We are told that of every property and its negation exactly one is positive (although it is at best unclear why on either an axiological or logical interpretation of "positive" this should be so):

Axiom 1 $P(\neg \varphi) \leftrightarrow \neg P(\varphi)$.

And it is stipulated that every property that is contained in a positive property is itself a positive property:

Axiom 2 $P(\varphi) \wedge \Box \forall x[\varphi(x) \rightarrow \psi(x)] \rightarrow P(\psi)$.

(The gloss given for Axiom 2—"A property is positive if it necessarily contains a positive property"—says something different but plays no role in the theory.) It is then proved that every positive property is possibly instantiated:

Theorem 1 $P(\varphi) \rightarrow \Diamond \exists x \varphi(x)$.

The proof given for this theorem assumes $P(\varphi)$ and $\neg \Diamond \exists \varphi(x); \Box \forall \neg \varphi(x)$ is derived, then $\Box \forall x[\varphi(x) \rightarrow x \neq x]$, and, using Axiom 2, then $P(\hat{x}[x \neq x])$; it is next observed that $\Box \forall x[\varphi(x) \rightarrow x = x]$ and that therefore, by Axiom 2 again, $P(\hat{x}[x = x])$. It is then stated that "$\hat{x}[x \neq x] = \neg \hat{x}[x = x]$" which contradicts (half of) Axiom 1" (p. 1). The idea, evidently, is that, given this identity (which is a case of a general convention concerning negations of properties), it follows from $P(\hat{x}[x \neq x])$ that $P(\neg \hat{x}[x = x])$ and that the pair $P(\neg \hat{x}[x = x])$ and $P(\hat{x}[x = x])$ is incompatible with Axiom 1. It is noteworthy that Theorem 1—"that every positive property is possible"—follows from Axioms 1 and 2 alone, together with a natural convention for negations of properties, and a generous interpretation of "property," according to which interpretaton, being self-identical and being non-self-identical are both properties.

It is next stipulated that "x is God-like if it possesses all positive properties" (p. 1).

Def G. $G(x) \leftrightarrow \forall \varphi [P(\varphi) \rightarrow \varphi(x)]$,

that is, "G is defined logically as an intersection of positive properties. Any such property ought also be positive" (p. 2).

Axiom 3 $P(G)$.

Given Gödel's generous interpretation of "property," the intersection of all positive properties is itself a *property*, and by Axiom 1 either it or its negation is a positive property. Furthermore, although the Leibniz-Moore doctrine of the organic unity of values may give pause here when one is concentrating on the value-guise of "positive," when one concentrates on its logical/ontological guise, that the intersection of all positive properties should itself be positive, seems hardly remarkable. Axiom 3 is one point at which the logical/ontological interpretation of "positive" seems to lead to a simpler proof. Axiom 2 is for similar reasons another such point. But then these axioms are *also* points at which one may wonder whether one can have it both ways—points at which Platonic equations of (quantities of) goodness with (quantities of) being or essence are, by unintended implication, challenged.

It is observed immediately after the inscription of Axiom 3 that

$\Diamond \exists x G x$,

"the possibility of a God-like being," holds as a corollary; it is an obvious entailment of Axiom 3 and Theorem 1. Leibniz, we recall, wrote that the argument that

> M. Descartes borrowed from Anselm . . . is not fallacious, but it is an incomplete demonstration which assumes something which should also be proved. . . . it is tacitly assumed that this idea of a wholly great or wholly perfect being is possible and does not imply a contradiction. . . . it is desirable that able people should fill the demonstration out.[3]

Gödel can be read as undertaking this task, as Leibniz himself did. It is noteworthy, however, that the efforts of these two able men were very different. *Gödel* reaches the possibility of the intersection of all positive properties by way of the *positiveness* (Axiom 3) of this intersection, whereas Leibniz in his best attempt argues *directly* for the compatibility of all perfections.[4] Leibniz is in fact in no position to argue indirectly for it in

Gödel's manner, for Leibniz based his argument on the supposed *simplicity* of each perfection:

> By a *perfection* I mean every simple quality which is positive and absolute or which expresses whatever it expresses without any limits.
> But, because a quality of this kind is simple, it is unanalyzable and indefinable. . . .
> From this it is not difficult to show that *all perfections are compatible with each other* or can be in the same subject.[5]

Assuming that there are several perfections, *Leibniz* held, by implication, that their intersection is *not* a perfection.

"Being a positive property," Scott writes, "is logical, hence, necessary" (p. 2).

Axiom 4 $P(\varphi) \rightarrow \Box P(\varphi)$.

Gödel, in his own hand, justifies Axiom 4 in these terms: "because it follows from the nature of the property" ("Ontologischer Beweis," p. 1; the axiom is there numbered "2"). Axiom 4 may be another point at which the logical/ontological interpretation of "positive" was supposed to help underpin the system's axioms, although Gödel viewed the moral aesthetic positiveness of properties somewhat in the way Moore and Leibniz viewed "intrinsic good-makingness," explicitly, as attaching to properties "independent of the accidental structure of the world." Their views, extended to moral aesthetic positiveness, would not so much "underpin" as *include* Axiom 4.

In Gödel's theory an *essence* of an individual is a *comprehensive* property, a property of this individual that entails each of its properties.

Def Ess $\varphi \, \text{Ess} \, x \leftrightarrow \varphi(x) \wedge \forall \psi [\psi(x) \rightarrow \Box \forall y [\varphi(y) \rightarrow \psi(y)]]$.

Given this definition of an essence, it is shown that, if an individual is God-like, then not only does it have every positive property, but it has only positive properties, so that God-likeness is its essence.

Theorem 2 $G(x) \rightarrow G \, \text{Ess} \, x$.

Suppose for conditional argument that $G(x)$. Then, for any ψ, if $\psi(x)$: (i), $P(\psi)$. (This is by Axiom 1 and Def G.); and so, (ii), $\Box \forall x [G(x) \rightarrow \psi(x)]$. (This by Axiom 4, given that $\Box(G(x) \leftrightarrow \forall \varphi [P(\varphi) \rightarrow \varphi(x)])$, as an immediate consequence of Def G; thus $\Box(P(\psi) \rightarrow \forall x [G(x) \rightarrow \psi(x)])$; and thus $\Box P(\psi) \rightarrow \Box \forall x [G(x) \rightarrow \psi(x)]$, by modal distribution.) Thus by Def Ess $G(x) \rightarrow G \, \text{Ess} \, x$, which is Theorem 2.

Necessary existence is defined in the system in terms of essences. It is stipulated that:

Def NE $NE(x) \leftrightarrow \forall \varphi [\varphi \, \text{Ess} \, x \rightarrow \Box \exists x \varphi(x)]$.

According to Def NE, a thing has necessary existence if, for each essence of it, it is necessary that something has this essence. I note that in the system things have *unique* essences—"φ Ess $x \wedge \psi$ Ess $x \rightarrow \Box\, \varphi = \psi$" (p. 3)—and one can say that a thing has necessary existence if it is necessary that something has its essence. I note further that in the system things cannot *share* essences: "φ Ess $x \rightarrow \Box\, \forall y[\varphi(y) \rightarrow y = x]$" (p. 3).[6] This means that in the system a thing has necessary existence by Def NE if and only if it is necessary that there is exactly one thing that has its essence. Furthermore, if the generous interpretation of "property" in force has as a consequence that, for each thing, there is a property of being identical with it, this property will be a part of a thing's essence; and if it has necessary existence, then by Def NE it will be necessary that it *itself* have its essence and exist with this essence in every world. If by the generous interpretation of "property" there is for each thing a property of being identical with it, one can say with Scott that in the context of the system "NE(x) means that x necessarily exists if it has an essential property" (p. 3).

"Being logically defined in this way necessary existence is a positive property" (p. 3).

    Axiom 5 $P(\text{NE})$.

This seems another point at which the logical/ontological interpretation of "positive" helps to underpin axioms and make for a "simpler proof." Even if, as I suppose, it is not clear that NE is "positive" in any "moral aesthetic" sense, there does seem to be "nothing negative" about it. Also, of course, intuitive motivation aside, there can be no objection to *defining P* in part by Axiom 5, and the same goes for the system's other axioms. No real harm, as distinct from confusion and inconvenience, can possibly come from definitions. We can, in particular, either by more or less subtle implication or quite directly, include existence and necessary existence in definitions of kinds of things (for example, deities), for it is not as if we can thereby define things of any kinds of things we *please* into existence. (See my "Names and Indefinite Descriptions in Ontological Arguments," *Dialogue* (1983) 195–201, especially pages 196–197.)

    The proof that it is necessary that there is a God-like being is written down immediately after Axiom 5. In the system, letting NE be a positive property is tantamount to letting it be necessary that there is a being that has every positive property. The strategy for the proof is that an argument for the *possibility* that there is a God-like being and an argument for the *disjunction* that it is *either necessary or impossible* that there is such a being should combine to make an argument for the *necessity* of such a being. This strategy can be discerned in the proofs of Theorem 3 presented in section III.

II

The underlying logic of the system is modal, second order, and includes identity. In this logic property symbols are allowed to occupy both term and predicate positions. Indeed this can happen in a single formula. Consider, for example, Def G:

$$G(x) \leftrightarrow \forall \varphi [P(\varphi) \rightarrow \varphi(x)],$$

in which the property variable φ stands in both term positions and a predicate position.

The system's logic includes a property abstraction operator and property symbols based on it: Both $\hat{x}[x = x]$ and $\hat{x}[x \neq x]$ occur in the notes under discussion. The schema $\neg \varphi = \hat{x}[\neg \varphi(x)]$ is given without comment, evidently as an explanation of notation for "negative properties" (p. 1). It is likely that the convention intended is better conveyed by the schema $\neg \hat{x}[\varphi] = \hat{x}[\neg \varphi]$, as, for example, in $\neg \hat{x}[x = x] = \hat{x}[x \neq x]$, which property identity plays a role in the proof of Theorem 1 (p. 1). Similar conventions could be established for "conjunctive properties," etc. Only one property of properties occurs in the notes, namely, P, the property of being a positive property. The property abstraction operator is not used in the notes to make symbols for properties of *properties*.

Quantification into modal contexts is countenanced in the system, but, with one exception,[7] every case of such quantification is one of *property* quantification. Presumably, every "closed" property symbol of the system has the same extension at every world, namely, some function from worlds to subsets of individuals (intuitively, a function whose value for a world is the set of individuals of this world that have the property signified by the symbol). If this is right, then *property* quantification into modal contexts is unproblematic in the logic of the system.

The modal logic of the system is evidently S5. The proof of Theorem 3 involves an S5 modal reduction.

The logic of the system is not elementary, and if pressed, *might* prove problematic. But at least with respect to the conservative demands made on it in the notes under discussion and in the demonstrations that follow, the system's logic is, I think, sound.

III

Here are Theorem 3 and a proof, more or less as they stand in the notes under discussion. As has been indicated, the proof unites a proof (the proof of Theorem 1) that it is possible that there is a God-like being, $\Diamond \exists x Gx$, with a proof that either it is not possible or it is necessary that there is such a being: $\neg \Diamond \exists x Gx \lor \Box \exists x Gx$, or, equivalently, $\Diamond \exists x Gx \rightarrow \Box \exists x Gx$.

Theorem 3 $\Box \exists x G(x)$.

Proof $G(x) \to NE(x) \land G \text{ Ess } x \to \Box \exists x G(x)$
$\exists x G(x) \to \Box \exists x G(x)$
$\Diamond \exists x G(x) \to \Diamond \Box \exists x G(x) \to \Box \exists x G(x)$
But $\Diamond \exists x G(x)$ by Theorem 1
$\Box \exists x G(x)$ QED.

Here is a reconstruction of this proof.

1.	~~Show~~ $\Box \exists x G(x)$	Direct Derivation
2.	~~Show~~ $\Box \forall x[G(x) \to \Box \exists x G(x)]$	Necessity Derivation
3.	~~Show~~ $\forall x[G(x) \to \Box \exists x G(x)]$	Universal Derivation
4.	~~Show~~ $G(x) \to NE(x) \land G \text{ Ess } x$	Conditional Derivation
5.	$G(x)$	
6.	$P(NE)$	Axiom 5
7.	$P(NE) \to NE(x)$	Def G, BC, 5, MP, UI
8.	$NE(x) \land G \text{ Ess } x$	6, 7, MP, 5, Theorem 2, MP, Adj
9.	~~Show~~ $NE(x) \land G \text{ Ess } x \to \Box \exists x G(x)$	Conditional Derivation
10.	$NE(x) \land G \text{ Ess } x$	
11.	$G \text{ Ess } x \to \Box \exists x G(x)$	10, S, Def NE, BC, MP, UI
12.	$\Box \exists x G(x)$	10, S, 11, MP
13.	$G(x) \to \Box \exists x G(x)$	4, 9, HS
14.	$\Box[\exists x G(x) \to \Box \exists x G(x)]$	2, IE(Q-conf)
15.	~~Show~~ $\Diamond \exists x G(x) \to \Diamond \Box \exists x G(x)$	Conditional Derivation
16.	$\Diamond \exists x G x$	
17.	~~Show~~ $\Diamond \Box \exists x G(x)$	Indirect Derivation
18.	$\neg \Diamond \Box \exists x G(x)$	
19.	~~Show~~ $\Box \neg \exists x G(x)$	Necessity Derivation
20.	$\Box[\exists x G(x) \to \Box \exists x G(x)]$	14, Repetition
21.	$\Box \neg \Box \exists x G(x)$	18, Modal Negation
22.	$\neg \exists x G(x)$	20, Necessity, 21, Necessity, MT
23.	$\neg \Diamond \exists x G(x)$	19, Modal Negation
24.	$\Diamond \exists x G(x)$	16, Repetition
25.	$\Diamond \Box \exists x G(x) \to \Box \exists x G(x)$	Modal Reduction Theorem S5
26.	$\Diamond \exists x G(x) \to \Box \exists x G(x)$	15, 25, HS
27.	$\Diamond \exists x G(x)$	Axiom 3, Theorem 1, MP
28.	$\Box \exists x G(x)$	26, 27, MP

In a Necessity Derivation (see lines 2 and 19), that a formula is itself necessary is established by deriving it from necessities, that is, from axioms, definitions, theorems, and necessity formulas. Necessity Derivations are subject to two restrictions: (1) Only necessities can be "entered from without"; and (2) every "entry from without" must be "entirely from without" and not in part from a line below the Show-line for the derivation.

But for the first restriction, $(p \rightarrow \Box p)$ would be derivable; and but for the the second, $(p \rightarrow \Box Q)$ would be derivable from $\Box(p \rightarrow q)$. The somewhat involuted form of the derivation seems required in order to honor these restrictions. To shorten the above derivation, Def G, Theorem 2, and Def NE are not entered on separate lines in the Necessity Derivation for line 2, and so this derivation is in technical (but obviously only technical) violation of "entry from without" restriction (i) (see lines 7, 8, and 11). One might prefer not to count Theorem 2,

$G(x) \rightarrow G$ Ess x,

itself as a necessity formula but to take it as it stands as short for the necessity sentence

$\Box \forall x[G(x) \rightarrow G$ Ess $x]$

and to count the annotation "Theorem 2" on line 8 as short for "Theorem 2, Necessity, UI." Similarly for all theorems and for all definitions and axioms.[8]

IV

There is a proof in the system that there is a "God-like" being, a being that has every positive property. Before rejoicing, however, we should ask what such a being would be like, what properties, designated in ordinary terms, it would have and not have. It is obvious that, although we *can* by various devices include existence in definitions of kinds of things, we cannot thereby define into existence things of any kinds we *please*. Partial answers to questions concerning the properties, designated in ordinary terms, of God-like beings, that is, of "G-beings," can be gathered from the fact that a God-like being would have by Def G not only *all* positive properties but *only* positive properties (from Axiom 1 and Def G by a small argument); and from the fact that in the system *every positive property is necessarily instantiated*:

Theorem 4 $P(\varphi) \rightarrow \Box \exists x \varphi(x)$.

This theorem, which is not set out by Scott or Gödel in the notes under discussion, wherein development of the system stops with Theorem 3, is an easy corollary of Theorem 3, given that G contains every positive property.

1.	~~Show~~ $P(\varphi) \to \Box\exists x\varphi(x)$	Conditional Derivation
2.	$P(\varphi)$	
3.	$\Box P(\varphi)$,	2, Axiom 4, MP
4.	~~Show~~ $\Box\exists x\varphi(x)$	Necessity Derivation
5.	$\Box P(\varphi)$	3, Repetition
6.	~~Show~~ $\forall x(G(x) \leftrightarrow \forall\varphi[P(\varphi) \to \varphi(x)])$	Univ Derivation
7.	$G(x) \leftrightarrow \forall\varphi[P(\varphi) \to \varphi(x)]$	Def G
8.	$\Box\exists xG(x)$	Theorem 3
9.	$G(a)$	8, Necessity, EI
10.	$\exists x\varphi(x)$	6, UI, BC, 9, MP, UI, 5, Necessity, MP, EG

More briefly, and in somewhat inexact words, by Def G the property G contains every positive property, and, by Theorem 3, G is necessarily instantiated. So every positive property is necessarily instantiated.

Given Theorem 4, it should be obvious and beyond reasonable question that any *real* being, as distinct from an abstract or only notional one such as "the stoplight" or "Santa Claus's suit," that possessed all and only *positive* properties and thus only *necessarily instantiated* properties, would not be red, blue, or, indeed, any color at all. It should be obvious that it is not *logically* necessary that there is a thing that has the property of being both real and red, that there *could* have been no real red things; that it is not the case that there is in *every* possible world a real red thing or a real colored thing. So no God-like real being would be red, for by Theorem 4 a God-like being would have only necessarily instantiated properties.[9]

It is not disturbing that no God-like real being would be red. But it should be nearly as obvious, and may *be* somewhat disturbing, that no God-like real being would be *sentient* or *cognizant* either. It is at least a firm modal intuition of *mine* that there are possible worlds in which there are not only no real *red* things but no *sentient* or *cognizant* ones either.

There *could*, I am convinced, have been nothing other than earth, air, fire (without red embers), and water. At least that seems to me to be a *logical* possibility. Such a world, one devoid of all consciousness, seems to me *perfectly* conceivable, Bishop Berkeley's "master argument" to the contrary notwithstanding.

> *Phil.* How say you, Hylas, can you see a thing which is at the same time unseen? *Hyl.* No, that were a contradiction. *Phil.* Is it not as great a contradiction to talk of *conceiving* a thing which is unconceived? ("Three Dialogues between Hylas and Philonous," in *Berkeley's Philosophical Writings*, D. M. Armstrong, ed. (New York: Collier-Macmillan, 1965), p. 162)

To which question *I* answer no, it is *not* impossible to conceive of things in this world that never have been and never will be thought about or even conceived of by anyone, although I of course can give as *examples* only things that *might* never have been thought about or conceived of by anyone. More pertinently to our present subject, one can conceive of a world in which *nothing* is thought about or conceived and in which there is in fact no conscious being to do any thinking or conceiving. Or at least so it *seems*, and Berkeley has not given, nor can one find suggested in his writings, a good argument for doubting this seeming. (I have, of course, not tried here to do full justice to the many subtle and interwoven equivocations at work in Berkeley's argument.)

It at least *seems* plain that it is no more necessary, *logically* necessary, that there is a sentient or cognizant real being than that there is a red one. And on modal issues, as on all issues, we have at least initially only intuitions to go by. Intuitions are not arguments, but they give rise to presumptions and establish *burdens* of argument. For example, the burden of argument would plainly be on one who claimed that it is logically necessary that there is a *red* being, whereas no argument seems called for in defense of this claim's negation. I think that, similarly, the burden would *no less* be on one who claimed that it is logically necessary that there is a sentient or cognizant being or indeed a being of *any* mode of consciousness, for it certainly *seems* that there could have been nothing but quite unconscious things, and this seems so just as clearly as it seems that there could have been nothing but nonred things or indeed quite colorless things.

A God-like being, indeed every being, has for every property either it or its negation. But, subject to arguments sufficiently powerful to reverse firm intuitions, we now see that a being that was *God-like* in the sense of the system would, in connection with many religiously important properties, have not them but their negations. It is now evident, subject to the availability of good counterintuitive arguments which we have no reason to believe exist, that the God of the *system*, if real, would *not* be omniscient, omnipotent, just, or benevolent, and would indeed lack every "attribute of God" that might recommend it as an object of worship; and that the God of the system—its God-like being—could not, by anyone who would speak in ordinary terms, be called "God."

V

If clear and firm modal intuitions are to be trusted, a "God-like" real being would *lack* many religiously important properties. That is the conclusion of the previous section. We now add that it is demonstrable in the system (or in the system slightly augmented) that such a being would *have* properties, the having of which would be embarrassing—*logically* embarrassing even if not religiously so. Given the generous interpretation of "property" that is in force for the system, a God-like being would have properties that entailed the existence of every existent and the truth of every truth. Since a God-like being would have only necessarily instantiated properties (see Theorem 4), it follows in the system that whatever is true is so necessarily and that whatever exists does so necessarily.

To show that every existent is a necessary existent, I use the principle that every individual has an essence.

Essences. $\forall x \exists \varphi \ \varphi \ \text{Ess} \ x$

This principle, if not, as I think it is, already implicit in the system, is only a slight amplification of it. A reason for thinking that *Essences* is implicit in the system is that, although certain *contingent* beings (for example, people such as Adam) would be prime candidates for being things that lacked essences and "complete concepts," in the system any being that lacked an essence would be a *necessary* being. This is by Def NE. (Suppose that x lacks an essence so that $\forall \varphi \neg \varphi \ \text{Ess} \ x$. Then $\forall \varphi [\varphi \ \text{Ess} \ x \rightarrow \Box \exists x \varphi(x)]$, and so by Def NE, NE($x$).) I note that one reason for resisting *Essences*—namely, that its imposition would leave no room for free agents—is not available to one who accepts the system under discussion. We return briefly to this point at the end of this section.

Also used in demonstration is the following *abstraction principle for properties of individuals*:

Properties $\hat{\beta}[\varphi](\alpha) \leftrightarrow \varphi'$,

where β is an individual variable, α is a term, φ is a formula, and φ' is a formula that comes from φ by proper substitution of α for β.[10] The principle, *Properties*, which in its scope is the key to the demonstrations of this section, gives formal expression to the very generous interpretation of "properties" that is in evidence in the notes under discussion. Principal applications of *Properties* are flagged by "NB," and verbal expressions of crucial properties are emphasized. Parts of two cases of *Properties*, specifically,

$$x \neq x \rightarrow \hat{x}[x \neq x](x)$$

and

$$x = x \rightarrow \hat{x}[x = x](x),$$

are implicit in the notes under discussion (p. 1).

Another principle employed below is *the principle that things have unique essences*:

Uniqueness of Essences $\forall \varphi \forall \psi \forall x (\varphi \ \text{Ess} \ x \wedge \psi \ \text{Ess} \ x \rightarrow$
   $\Box \forall y [\varphi(y) \leftrightarrow \psi(y)]),$

which principle is presumably equivalent to $\varphi \ \text{Ess} \ x \wedge \psi \ \text{Ess} \ x \rightarrow$

$\Box\varphi = \psi$, a principle endorsed in the notes under discussion (p. 3). We proceed to demonstrate that in the system (or in the system as augmented by *Essences*) every existent has necessary existence.

Theorem 5 $\forall y\ NE(y)$.

1.	~~Show~~ $\forall y\ NE(y)$	Universal Derivation
2.	$\Box\exists x G(x)$	Theorem 3
3.	$G(a)$	2, Necessity, EI
4.	~~Show~~ $y \neq a \to NE(y)$	Conditional Derivation
5.	$y \neq a$	
6.	$\psi\ \text{Ess}\ y$	*Essences*, UI, EI
7.	$\exists y(y \neq a \land \psi\ \text{Ess}\ y)$	5, 6, Adj, EG
NB8.	$\hat{a}[\exists y(y \neq a \land \psi\ \text{Ess}\ y)](a)$	*Properties*, BC, 7, MP
9.	$\Box\forall z[G(z) \to \hat{a}[\exists y(y \neq a \land \psi\ \text{Ess}\ y)](z)]$	3, Theorem 2, MP, Def Ess, AV, BC, MP, S, UI, 8, MP
10.	$P(\hat{a}[\exists y(y \neq a \land \psi\ \text{Ess}\ y)])$	Axiom 3, 9, Adj, Axiom 2, MP
11.	~~Show~~ $\Box\exists y\psi(y)$	Necessity Derivation
12.	$\Box\exists x(\hat{a}[\exists y(y \neq a \land \psi\ \text{Ess}\ y)])(x)$	10, Theorem 4, MP
13.	$\exists y(y \neq b \land \psi\ \text{Ess}\ y)$	12, Necessity, EI, *Properties*, BC, MP
14.	$\psi\ \text{Ess}\ c$	13, EI, S
*15.	$\exists y\psi(y)$	Def Ess, BC, 14, MP, S, EG
16.	~~Show~~ $\forall\varphi[\varphi\ \text{Ess}\ y \to \Box\exists x\varphi(x)]$	Universal Derivation
17.	~~Show~~ $\varphi\ \text{Ess}\ y \to \Box\exists x\varphi(x)$	Conditional Derivation
18.	$\varphi\ \text{Ess}\ y$	
19.	~~Show~~ $\Box\exists x\varphi(x)$	Necessity Derivation
20.	$\Box\exists y\psi(y)$	11, Repetition
21.	$\Box\forall y[\varphi(y) \leftrightarrow \psi(y)]$	6, 18, Adj, *Uni-Essences*, UI, UI, UI, MP
22.	$\exists x\varphi(x)$	20, Necessity, 21, Necessity Q-dist, BC, MP, AV
23.	$NE(y)$	Def NE, BC, 16, MP
24.	~~Show~~ $y = a \to NE(y)$	Conditional Derivation
25.	$y = a$	
26.	$NE(y)$	Def G, BC, 3, MP, Axiom 5, UI, MP, 25, LL
27.	$NE(y)$	4, 24, SC

(*For brevity, I have not first derived a universal generalization of Def Ess, and then instantiated it it *c*. These steps are to be understood as intended. Such steps are displayed in the shorter demonstration of Theorem 6.) Again in somewhat inexact words, although this time not much more briefly: Any God-like being has necessary existence since by Axiom 5 necessary existence is a positive property. By *Essences* any being *different* from a God-like being has an essence, *and*, by *Properties*, a God-like being has *the property that something different from it has that essence*. From this it follows that that essence is necessarily instantiated, for every property of a God-like being is necessarily instantiated. But, by *Uniqueness of Essences*, that essence is the essence of the (arbitrarily selected and representative) "different being" under consideration. By Def NE, that being has necessary existence, and so (because that being was an arbitrarily selected and representative "different being") every being that is *not* God-like has necessary existence. So *every* existent being has necessary existence.

We now proceed to demonstrate that in the system whatever is true is necessarily true.

Theorem 6 $Q \to \Box Q$

1.	~~Show~~ $Q \to \Box Q$	Conditional Derivation
2.	Q	
3.	$G(a)$	Theorem 3, Necessity, EI
4.	$a = a \land Q$	Identity, 2, Adj
NB 5.	$\hat{a}[a = a \land Q](a)$	4, *Properties*, BC, MP
6.	~~Show~~ $\forall x[G(x) \to G \text{ Ess } x]$	Universal Derivation
7.	$G(x) \to G \text{ Ess } x$	Theorem 2
8.	$G \text{ Ess } a$	6, UI, 3, MP
9.	~~Show~~ $\forall x(G \text{ Ess } x \leftrightarrow G(x) \land \forall \psi(\psi(x) \to$ $\Box \forall y[(G(y) \to \psi(y)])$	Universal Derivation
10.	$G \text{ Ess } x \leftrightarrow G(x) \land \forall \psi[\psi(x) \to$ $\Box \forall y(G(y) \to \psi(y)]$	Def Ess
11.	~~Show~~ $\Box[\exists y G(y) \to \exists y(\hat{a}[a = a \land Q](y)]$	Necessity Derivation
12.	$\Box \forall y(G(y) \to \hat{a}[a = a \land Q](y)]$	9, UI, BC, 8, MP, S, UI, 5, MP
13.	$\exists y G(y) \to \exists y \hat{a}[a = a \land Q](y)$	12, Necessity, Q-dist
14.	~~Show~~ $\Box Q$	Necessity Derivation
15.	$\Box \exists y(\hat{a}[a = a \land Q])(y)$	11, Modal Distribution, Theorem 3, AV, MP
16.	$\hat{a}[a = a \land Q](b)$	15, Necessity, EI
17.	Q	16, *Properties*, S

(This derivation could be simplified. Lines 4 and 5 could be replaced by a line containing $\hat{a}[Q](a)$ inferred by *Properties* from line 2. Carrying this simplification through, line 16 would be line 15 and have on it $\hat{a}[Q](b)$.) Again in somewhat inexact words, if something is true, then by *Properties* a God-like being has *the property of being in the presence of this truth*. But every property of a God-like being is necessarily instantiated, from which it follows that this truth is a necessary truth.

I note that *Essences* is not used in the derivation of Theorem 6. This means that a reason for resisting *Essences*—namely, that omitting it would make room for freedom in the world and for free individuals—is not available to one who accepts the rest of the system. The necessity that Leibniz was so concerned to avoid *obtains* in Gödel's system. In it everything that is true is necessarily true: in the system, of everything that is true, that it is true is necessary. And this necessity obtains whether or *not* it is stipulated that every individual has an essence in the Leibnizian sense, a complete individual concept.

VI

The solution to the difficulties of the last two sections—the best and smallest even if not inconsequential change that would obviate them—can seem obvious: Stop counting necessary existence as a positive property. Do not claim that a God-like being would have necessary existence. Give up on the ontological argument.[11] And this can seem a small price. From a certain point of view it can seem obvious that no being which had properties that made it an object worthy of worship *could* also have necessary existence. But then, on reflection, it can also seem obvious that no being that *lacked* necessary existence could be a proper object of worship. These two perspectives taken together and refined can be made to yield a kind of ontological argument for the *impossibility* of a God—an argument like one that J. N. Findlay presented in 1948. He summed up his case against the possibility of a God in these words:

> The religious frame of mind . . . desires the Divine . . . both to have an inescapable character . . . and also the character of 'making a real difference'. . . . [I]f God is to satisfy religious claims and needs, he must be a being in every way inescapable, One whose existence and whose possession of certain excellences we cannot possibly conceive away. . . . It was indeed an ill day for Anselm when he hit upon his famous proof. For on that day he not only laid bare something that is of the essence of an adequate religious object, but also something that entails its necessary non-existence.[12]

It is true that Findlay, by 1970, had changed his mind about his 1948 disproof of the existence of God. "I have moved," he wrote in 1970, "to a position where, by a change of attitude to a single premiss, the disproof has swung over into something that may, if it betrays no inward, logical flaw, converge towards a proof."[13] Findlay was still convinced that an Absolute would be a necessary existent (p. 39), which while having a "contingent side" (p. 40) would have a necessary nature: "If there is an Absolute of a certain essential sort, then there cannot *not* be an Absolute of that essential sort" (p. 24). But he was in 1970 no longer prepared to say that nothing that was by its nature worthy of the name "Absolute"—or, presumably, worthy by its nature (as distinct from its possibly "contingent side") of *worship*—could have a nature that was in all ways necessary. I confess, however, that the 1948 proposition on this point still seems right to me and that I am in fact confirmed in my conviction by the *last* things set down in Findlay's 1970 book. A necessary being would I think need to be of the nature of a Form, or of an abstract entity such as a number. Findlay seems to agree.[14] In any case he holds that God, *that* would-be necessary being, would have to be of the nature of a Form, because, according to Findlay, only a Form can be truly worthy of worship.

> I give it as the verdict of my feeling that only a Form, something basically universal, can be truly adorable, can in any way deserve the name of 'God'. One cannot rationally worship this or that excellent thing or person, however eminent and august: only Goodness Itself, Beauty Itself, Truth Itself, and so on are rationally venerable, and to bow one's knee to an instance is to commit idolatry.[15]

There is I think nothing irrational about liking a Form or abstract entity, having a favorite Form or abstract entity (my favorite number is 105), being thrilled by the prospect of some Form or abstract entity, or even *adoring* such a thing. Nonetheless I submit that to *worship* a Form or abstract entity would be like declaring one's love and devotion to a recorded announcement and similarly *absurd*.[16]

Given its presumed religious objectives, the solution to the system's difficulties, especially to those of section IV, is *not* obvious. It is not obvious that, given these objectives, these difficulties of the system have a solution, for it may be that, as Findlay suggests, the "religious frame of mind" does demand that its object be both worthy of worship, and necessary and inescapable in all ways. Certainly Gödel's system is inspired by and in the service of the demand that God be necessary, as are so many other philosophical/theological systems. And it seems—it does at least seem—that no thoroughly and exclusively necessary being *could* be a *proper* object of worship.

Appendix 1. Axioms and Definitions

Axiom 1	$P(\neg\varphi) \leftrightarrow \neg P(\varphi)$
Axiom 2	$P(\varphi) \wedge \Box\forall x[\varphi(x) \to \psi(x)] \to P(\psi)$
Theorem 1	$P(\varphi) \to \Diamond\exists x\varphi(x)$
Def G	$G(x) \leftrightarrow \forall\varphi[P(\varphi) \to \varphi(x)]$
Axiom 3	$P(G)$
Axiom 4	$P(\varphi) \to \Box P(\varphi)$

Def Ess. φ Ess $x \leftrightarrow \varphi(x) \wedge \forall\psi[\psi(x) \rightarrow \Box\forall y[\varphi(y)$
                       $\rightarrow \psi(y)]]$
Theorem 2 $G(x) \rightarrow G$ Ess x
Def NE $NE(x) \leftrightarrow \forall\varphi[\varphi$ Ess $x \rightarrow \Box\exists x\varphi(x)]$
Axiom 5 $P(NE)$
Theorem 3 $\Box\exists xG(x)$
Theorem 4 $P(\varphi) \rightarrow \Box\exists x\varphi(x)$
Essences $\forall x\exists\varphi\ \varphi$ Ess x
Properties $\hat{\beta}[\varphi](\alpha) \leftrightarrow \varphi$
Uniqueness of Essences $\forall\varphi\forall\psi\forall x(\varphi$ Ess $x \wedge \psi$ Ess x
                       $\rightarrow \Box\forall y[\varphi(y) \leftrightarrow \psi(y)])$
Theorem 5 $\forall y NE(y)$
Theorem 6 $Q \rightarrow \Box Q$

Appendix 2. Notes in Kurt Gödel's Hand

[Very rough notes, transcribed by J. H. Sobel with the permission of John Milnor on behalf of the custodians of Kurt Gödel's *Nachlass*. The lettered footnotes are Gödel's, although he uses not letters but the marks φ, $\times$, and $\cdot$.]

Feb 10, 1970

Ontologischer Beweis

$P(\varphi)$ φ is positive $(e \quad \varphi \in P)$
Ax 1 $P(\varphi)\cdot P(\psi) \supset P(\varphi\cdot\psi)$[a]   Ax 2 $P(\varphi) \vee^{\,b} P(\sim\varphi)$
Df 1 $G(x) \equiv (\varphi)[P(\varphi) \supset \varphi(x)]$ (God)
Df 2 φ Ess. $x \equiv (\psi)[\psi(x) \supset N(y)[\varphi(y) \supset \psi(y)]]$
         (Essence of x)[c]
         $P \supset_N q = N(p \supset q)$ Necessity
Ax 2 $P(\varphi) \supset NP(\varphi)$ $\Big\}$ because it follows from
         $\sim P(\varphi) \supset N \sim P(\varphi)$ the nature of the property
Th. $G(x) \supset G$ Ess. x
Df $E(x) \equiv (\varphi)[\varphi$ Ess. $x \supset N\exists x\varphi(x)]$ necessary Existence
Ax 3 $P(E)$
Th $G(x) \supset N(\exists y)G)(y)$
         hence $(\exists x)G(x) \supset N(\exists yG(y)$
         " $M(\exists x)G(x) \supset MN(\exists y)G(y)$ M = possibility
         " $\supset N(\exists y(G(y)$

---

[a]and for any number of summand
[b]exclusive or
[c]any two essences of x are *nec. equivalent* [It is not clear from my copy exactly where this footnote belongs.—J. H. S.]

[page two of Gödel's notes]

$M(\exists x)G(x)$ means the system of all pos. props. is compatible. This is true because of:

Ax 4: $P(\varphi)$. $\varphi \supset_N \psi : \supset P(\psi)$ which implies

$$\begin{cases} x = x & \text{is positive} \\ x \neq x & \text{is negative} \end{cases}$$

But if a system, S of pos. props. were incompatible, it would mean that the sum prop. s (which is positive) would be $x \neq x$.

Positive means positive in the moral aesthetic sense (independently of the accidental structure of the world). Only then the ax. true. It may also mean pure "attribution"[d] as opposed to "privation" (or *containing* privation). This interpret. simpler proof.

. . . .

If φ pos. then *not*: $(X)N \sim \varphi(x)$. Otherwise: $\varphi(x) \supset_N x \neq x$
hence $x \neq x$ positive so $x = x$ neg contrary Ax 4 on the exist. of pos. prop.

---

[d]i.e., the 'disj' normal form in terms of elem. prop. contains [only? every? I cannot decipher the mark here.—J. H. S.] member without negation

---

Appendix 3. Notes in Dana Scott's Hand

[Transcribed by J. H. Sobel with the permission of Dana Scott, and John Milnor on behalf of the custodians of Kurt Gödel's *Nachlass*.]

GÖDEL'S ONTOLOGICAL PROOF

$P(\varphi)$ means φ is a *positive* property
$\neg \varphi = \hat{x}[\neg \varphi(x)]$

AXIOM 1. $P(\neg \varphi) \leftrightarrow \neg P(\varphi)$
That is, either the property or its negation is positive, but not both.

AXIOM 2. $P(\varphi) \wedge \Box \forall x[\varphi(x) \to \psi(x)] \to P(\psi)$
A property is positive if it necessarily contains a positive property.

THEOREM 1. $P(\varphi) \to \Diamond \exists x \varphi(x)$

Proof.   Suppose $P(\varphi)$ and $\neg \Diamond \exists x \varphi(x)$
$\therefore \Box \forall x \neg \varphi(x)$ $\therefore \Box \forall x[\varphi(x) \to x \neq x]$
By Axiom 2, $P(\hat{x}[x \neq x])$
But $\Box \forall x[\varphi(x) \to x = x]$
By Axiom 2, $P(\hat{x}[x = x])$
But $\hat{x}[x \neq x] = \neg \hat{x}[x = x]$
which contradicts (half of) Axiom 1.

[page two of notes]

DEF. $G(x) \leftrightarrow \forall\varphi[P(\varphi) \rightarrow \varphi(x)]$

      x is God-like if it possesses all positive properties.

AXIOM 3. $P(G)$

           Indeed, $P(\varphi)$ is a logical property and G is defined logically as an intersection of positive properties. Any such property ought also to be positive.

CORO. $\Diamond\exists x G(x)$

AXIOM 4. $P(\varphi) \rightarrow \Box P(\varphi)$

           Being a positive property is logical, hence, necessary.

DEF. φ Ess. $x \leftrightarrow \varphi(x) \wedge \forall x[\psi(x) \rightarrow \Box\forall y[\varphi(y) \rightarrow \psi(y)]]$

      φ is the *essence* of a if x has φ and this property is necessarily minimal.

THEOREM 2. $G(x) \rightarrow G$ Ess. x

    Proof. Suppose $G(x)$. $\therefore G(x)$

    Suppose $\psi(x)$. If $\neg P(\psi)$, then $P(\neg\psi)$; then

    $\neg\psi(x)$. $\therefore P(\psi)$

    But $P(\psi) \rightarrow \forall x[G(x) \rightarrow \psi(x)]$ logically, by def.

[page three of notes]

    $\therefore \Box P(x) \rightarrow \Box\forall x[G(x) \rightarrow \psi(x)]$ by Modal logic.

    But $\Box P(\psi)$ by Axiom 4.

    Hence $\Box\forall x[G(x) \rightarrow \psi(x)]$

    Thus G Ess. x.

NOTE. φ Ess. $x \wedge \psi$ Ess. $x \rightarrow \Box\varphi = \psi$

        φ Ess. $x \rightarrow \Box\forall y[\varphi(y) \rightarrow y = x]$

DEF.   NE $(x) \leftrightarrow \forall\varphi[\varphi$ Ess. $x \rightarrow \Box\exists x\varphi(x)]$

      NE(x) means that x necessarily exists if it has an essential property.

AXIOM 5. $P(\text{NE})$

           Being logically defined in this way, necessary existence is a positive property.

THEOREM 3. $\Box\exists x G(x)$

    Proof. $G(x) \rightarrow \text{NE}(x) \wedge G$ Ess. $x \rightarrow \Box\exists x G(x)$

    $\therefore \exists x G(x) \rightarrow \Box\exists x G(x)$

    $\therefore \Diamond\exists x G(x) \rightarrow \Diamond\Box\exists x G(x) \rightarrow \Box\exists x G(x)$

    but $\Diamond\exists x G(x)$ by Theorem 1.

    $\therefore \Box\exists x G(x)$.   QED

Notes

I am indebted to Willa Fowler Freeman-Sobel for her comments on many drafts of this paper, to members of Zepot Metodologiczny Polskiego Towarystwa Filozoficzego, Oddziat w Krakowie (The Methodological Section of the Polish Philosophical Association, Krakow Branch), to whom an early version of this paper was presented on 21 March 1985, and to Judith Jarvis Thomson and George Boolos.

1. Both the three pages that are in Scott's hand and the notes that are in Gödel's are included in Gödel's *Nachlass*, held by the Institute for Advanced Study, Princeton, New Jersey. Gödel discussed his proof with Scott in February 1970. Scott presented his own notes to a seminar of his on entailment sometime during the following academic year. Transcriptions of both sets of notes are presented in appendixes 2 and 3.

All page references, unless otherwise indicated, are to the pages in Scott's hand. Appendix 1 contains all formal definitions, axioms, and theorems that appear in the present paper, some of which are due to the present author.

2. The ontological *argument* of the system is, however, very different from the arguments that can be found in works of Leibniz and Spinoza. Leibniz's argument is similar to Descartes's and is spoiled, I think, in the same way. I discuss the flaw that I claim spoils Descartes's Fifth Meditation proof in "Names and Indefinite Descriptions in Ontological Arguments," *Dialogue* (1983), 22: 195–201.

3. G. W. Leibniz, *New Essays on Human Understanding*, P. Remnant and J. Bennett, eds. and trans. Cambridge: Cambridge University Press, 437–438.

4. Gottfried Wilhelm Leibniz, "That a Most Perfect Being Exists: November 1676," *Philosophical Papers and Letters*, Leroy E. Loemker, trans. and ed. (Dordrecht: Reidel, 1969), second edition, 167–168. I do not know that this was Leibniz's best attempt to prove the compossibility of all perfections, but, since Leroy E. Loemker said so, I believe that it was.

> How [to] establish the possibility of a most perfect being? The closest Leibniz comes to an answer is his demonstration, to Spinoza in 1676 . . . a demonstration which he achieves only by defining perfections from the start as simple notions. . . . A more successful proof [Loemker was not persuaded by Leibniz's argument.] is never reached . . . though Leibniz later repeats his criticism of Descartes and restates the argument. (p. 52)

5. "That a Most Perfect Being Exists: November 1676," p. 167.

6. Gödel's essences are like Leibniz's complete individual concepts. However, it seems that for Gödel that no two individuals have the same essences or are alike in all their properties, is unproblematic and hardly remarkable. Probably, given his generous interpretation of "property", he viewed it as a trivial consequence of the fact that everything is identical with itself and not with any other thing.

7. I note that Def φ Ess $x \to \Box \forall y[\varphi(y) \to y = x]$, which is either short for or immediately implies $\forall \varphi \forall x(\varphi$ Ess $x \to \Box \forall y[\varphi(y) \to y = x])$. However, this principle plays no role in proofs, and its importance to the appropriateness of Def NE could be neutralized by revising that definition to

Def NE*   NE(x) $\leftrightarrow$ $\forall \varphi[\varphi$ Ess $x \to \Box \exists x \forall y(\varphi(y) \leftrightarrow y = x)]$.

8. Rules and procedures for my derivations are basically those of the identity calculus of Donald Kalish, Richard Montague, and Gary Mar, *Logic: Techniques of Formal Reasoning*, second edition (New York: Harcourt Brace Jovanovich, 1980). In this calculus existential

instantiation must be to a variable novel to the derivation, and the variable of generalization in a universal derivation cannot be free in a line antecedent to this derivation. For my extension of this calculus to S5, see "Names and Indefinite Descriptions in Ontological Arguments," *Dialogue* (1983), 22: 195–201. If unrestricted quantification into modal contexts in countenanced in the extended calculus, then $\Diamond \forall x F(x) \rightarrow \forall x \Diamond F(x)$ is a theorem. This is an unwanted result: As Buridan argued, from "It could be that everything is God" (which would be true if there were nothing other than God), "Everything could be God" (everything distributively, you, me, indeed, everything) does not follow. Unrestricted quantification into modal contexts would also lead to the possibly unwanted theorems $\Diamond \exists x F(x) \rightarrow \exists x \Diamond F(x)$ and $\Box \forall x F(x) \leftrightarrow \forall x \Box F(x)$. Such results can be avoided by imposing restrictions. Present purposes, however, allow decisions regarding such restrictions to be postponed. For the record, however, adjustments to the calculus that I am now inclined to favor include these: First, restrict Necessity Derivation to necessity formulas in which no individual variable is free. Stipulate that only such formulas can be derived in this way and that only such formulas can be "entered from without" into derivations. Second, add inference rules: for variable α and formula φ, from $\exists \alpha \, \Box \, \varphi$ to infer $\Box \exists \alpha \varphi$, and from $\exists \alpha \, \Diamond \, \varphi$ to infer $\Diamond \exists \alpha \varphi$. Third, restrict to nonmodal contexts applications of Leibniz's Law. These adjustments would, I think, serve a semantics that allowed domains of worlds to overlap, to be identical, and to be entirely different.

9. Would a God-like being have *every* necessarily instantiated property? Presumably not, for it seems that there are properties such that both they and their negations are necessarily instantiated. For example, it seems that *being an even number* is necessarily instantiated: It seems that it is true in every world that the number two is even. And for similar reasons it seems that *not being an even number* is necessarily instantiated: It seems that it is true in every world that the number three is not an even number.

10. Depending on policies relating to identity and modal contexts, one might choose to require that β not be free in φ within the scope of a modal operator.

11. A less radical solution that is specific to the difficulties of section V would consist in confining the essence of a thing to its "intrinsic" properties. To implement this solution, one might take "intrinsicness," construed either as a property of individual properties or as a property-to-individuals relation, as a further primitive, and set axioms appropriate to it and suited to the ends of the system. It would, it seems, need to be a consequence of the axioms that, although a thing's essence would include each of its positive properties, it would not include such properties as 'being in the presence of the truth that Q' or 'being different from something that has the essence ψ'. Elaborating such a theory of "intrinsicness" would not be a trivial task.

12. J. N. Findlay, "Can God's Existence Be Disproved?" *Mind* (1948), 57: 182.

13. J. N. Findlay, *Ascent to the Absolute* (London: Allen & Unwin, 1970), 13.

14. Not everyone agrees. Thus, according to Peter van Inwagen, "anyone who thinks he knows, or has good reason to believe, that there is *no* necessary concrete being is mistaken" ("Ontological Arguments," *Noûs* (1977), 11: 386). He rests this stern conclusion in part on the following contention: The argument *from* "all the (relatively) uncontroversial examples of necessary objects are abstract" and "all the uncontroversial examples of concrete objects are material, or, at least, depend for their existence on material objects" and are thus not necessary, *to* the conclusion that no being is both concrete and necessary, is a "remarkably weak" quasi-inductive argument (pp. 383–384). It is clear that I think this argument from properties of uncontroversial examples is a good argument, as well as the best one the case permits, given that no precise analysis of concreteness is in hand (compare p. 380), even if

such an analysis is possible. We have, I think, no better reason for thinking that no red being or sentient being is also necessary.

15. J. N. Findlay, "Towards a Neo-neo-Plantonism," in *Ascent to the Absolute*, 267 (the last paragraph of the book).

16. The "recorded announcement" illustration of absurdity is given by Thomas Nagel in "The Absurd," *Journal of Philosophy* (1971), 17: 716–727.

"The Concept of the Subject Contains the Concept of the Predicate"
David Wiggins

When a philosopher's published work is almost entirely made up of discreet masterpieces that make no reference to the craftsman himself, his fame will carry some sense of mystery, and mystery will attract rumor. What rumor suggests in the present case is that among Richard Cartwright's unpublicized interests and expertises is an extensive understanding of Leibniz. If only the deficiencies of what follows were to demonstrate to Cartwright the need for Cartwright's own intervention in this field, I should have made a signal contribution to Leibniz studies.

I

In the *Discourse of Metaphysics*, in the correspondence with Arnauld, and in numerous other works dating from the same period, Leibniz says that a proposition is true if and only if the concept of the subject contains the concept of the predicate. For instance:

> In every true proposition, necessary or contingent, universal or particular, the concept of the predicate is in a sense included in that of the subject, *praedicatum inest subjecto*, or I know not what truth is. (Letter to Arnauld, 14 July; L. E. Loemker, trans., *Philosophical Papers and Letters*, second edition (Dordrecht: Reidel, 1969) p. 377).

In Leibniz's later philosophy the containment principle disappears altogether. But, as in the quotation just given, wherever Leibniz states the doctrine, he applies it to necessary and contingent propositions equally.

Philosophers have found difficulty in understanding how Leibniz can have supposed that this was a good principle of truth for the case of contingent propositions. Less excusably, they have even questioned Leibniz's sincerity when he insisted that his recognition of contingency was one of the points that distinguished his philosophy from Spinoza's.

The first aim of this essay is to explain what commended the principle to Leibniz and how it leaves room for contingency. I claim that the problem that some modern scholars have found with the principle can be solved quietly and simply by reference to suggestions that Leibniz himself makes in the *Discourse of Metaphysics*. This will come with a suggestion about why nevertheless, in the decade after the *Discourse of Metaphysics*, Leibniz's containment principle simply dropped out of Leibniz's logic and metaphysics. I hold that this abandonment need have nothing to do with any problem about contingency.

The second aim is to say something about a distinct problem that Leibniz himself thought he saw in the accommodation of contingency. This problem has at best an indirect connection with anything that might motivate the claim that, by virtue of containment's being a necessary relation, the containment principle must render contingent true propositions "analytic" (in Kant's sense). What I think is happening is that a doctrine of possible worlds devised for the understanding of God's choice and creation of the actual world proves to be mismatched with questions about what this or that individual might or might not have done. At this point, where the question at issue relates to the identification de re of particulars, I think Leibniz is less sure footed than I give him credit for being in his treatment of containment and necessity. In fact, I think he ignores at least one point that he has himself quite clearly perceived in another connection. The oversight that I attribute to him is underdetermined, however, by Leibniz's rationalist starting point in the theory of truth. It is also instructive metaphysically.

II

What commended the containment principle to Leibniz? Suppose one thinks, as Leibniz does—this is his principle of sufficient reason—that nothing holds true, obtains, happens, or exists without a reason and that there must always be a reason why this rather than that holds true, obtains, happens, or exists.[1] And suppose that, to avoid an infinite regress of causal explanatory reasons,[2] one gives a teleological construal to 'reason', insisting with Leibniz—this is the effect of his principle of the best—that any finally adequate explanation of anything must locate the thing to be explained within a total state of affairs that would commend itself as the transparently, self-evidently best to a rational omniscient mind that singled out from all others as the most perfect the world that is "simplest in hypotheses, and richest in phenomena."[3] Then a proposition will hold true if and only if it holds in the world that has the simplest laws but is richest in essence, or richest in the variety of real substances that it furnishes.

What then is a world? And more to the point, what sort of thing is a world that is even a candidate to be chosen by the rational omniscient mind as fit to be made real? Well, at least this much is clear from the numerous Leibnizian texts that bear on this matter: No world that is a serious candidate to be chosen by God could contain more substances than it does.[4]

Each of the worlds that God chooses between is as rich in quantity/variety of essence as it can be given the set of laws that regulates it.[5] In the second place, once the substances are specified for some world, there is no simplifying the laws of that world. For the specification of the substances (even the specification of their kinds) fixes the laws.[6] So looking at the matter as if from the point of view of God and as if from a moment 'before' there are any created substances—hence from a moment at which there *are* no actual substances to 'pick' (or 'select' or 'recruit') for the best world, and at which all choice has to be purely on the basis of description—one can say that the choice God makes is between rival specifications. And since it is the substances in a world that furnish both its variety/quantity of essence and realize or embody its laws, these specifications must be rival specifications of *substances* or, in more Leibnizian language, rival sets of individual concepts. God's choice qua specificatory is the choice of a set of substances: The set will be maximal (that is, a set that cannot consistently contain more substances); and the members of the set will jointly embody the simplest set of laws there can be for any world that furnishes so much richness or variety as this one does.[7]

A point we must notice here, though its importance will not be clear until later, is that where the issue is one of the relative merits or titles to be realized of the worlds projected in different world specifications, the question of whether this individual concept and that individual concept belonging to different maximal sets are or are not concepts of the same substance simply does not arise. God has no need either to ask or to answer this question. And if it were asked, well, no basis has been provided on which to answer it. (Contrast "If I had made a table yesterday, would that have been the very same table as I shall actually make tomorrow?" which is an inherently silly question at least in most contexts, with the question "Could the table I made yesterday have been made two days later?" which might reasonably collect the answer yes.)

Suppose now, naturally enough, that everything that is real in a world is either a substance or some sort of a dependency of substances. Then everything that is actually true will either be a truth about the substances of the actual world or stand in some relation of dependency to such truths. But what then are substances? Leibniz's idea of substance is neither that of a qualityless substrate nor that of a shifting crowd of concepts or universals struggling to be seated on one another's laps. Indeed his concept of a substance is more or less the same as Aristotle's, even if, as his system develops, his idea of the extension of the concept diverges more and more strikingly from Aristotle's. Pace what is suggested or assumed in many comments and criticisms that distinguish insufficiently between the individual concept and what the concept is of, a Leibnizian substance is a real thing, not a congeries of characters, or a concept. What is true, however, and may have given rise to such misconceptions is that, in the Leibnizian framework within which we have to speak of God's choice, each and every substance will indeed *answer* to a complete concept or divine specification. This complete concept fixes everything bearing on the question of the eligibility of the whole world that contains the substance. A fortiori it fixes thereby everything that there is to know or understand about the substance itself.

> All true predication has some foundation in the nature of things, and when a proposition is not identical, that is to say when the predicate is not expressly comprised in the subject, it must be comprised in it virtually and that is what the Philosophers call *in-esse* when they say that the predicate is in the subject. Thus the term of the subject must always include that of the predicate, so that whoever understood perfectly the notion of the subject would also judge that the predicate belongs to it.
>
> This being so, we can say that the nature of an individual substance or of a complete being is to have a notion so complete that it is sufficient to comprise and to allow the deduction from it of all the predicates of the subject to which this notion is attributed. Whereas an accident is a being the notion of which does not include all that can be attributed to the subject to which this notion is attributed. Thus, the quality of King which belongs to Alexander the Great, in abstraction from the subject, is not sufficiently determined for an individual, and does not include all that the notion of this Prince comprises; whereas God seeing the individual notion of *haecceity* of Alexander sees in it at the same time the foundation and reason of all the predicates that can be truly said of him, as for example that he would conquer Darius and Porus, even to the point of knowing it *a priori*.[8]

III

Given Leibniz's starting point, the containment principle is an entirely natural principle for him to have adopted.[9] It is not the love of necessity nor any essentialist passion that suggests the principle. Nor is it Leibniz's enslavement to the Aristotelian logic of subject and predicate that underlies Leibniz's metaphysics. It is the principle of sufficient reason, working in concert with philosophical ideas that are really quite ordinary and are neither silly nor readily replaceable. These are ideas about what a world is and what there is to talk about in one (namely, substances and their dependencies). Nevertheless, this conjunction of the ordinary with the peculiarly rationalist or Leibnizian comes with implications that we might not have expected.

Finite beings such as we are can learn that a substance has property F only in isolation, through our senses or a posteriori, and without seeing this truth's connection with other truths. But for God 'Fa' is one part of the specification of the world whose title to be realized is rationally and morally self-evident and quite independent of the sense perception of anything. The a priori determination of the truth that the substance a has the property F cannot, however, be a determination of this truth taken by itself. The determination must arise from the identification of the most perfect world, and this identification will have depended on the comparison of all the members of an infinite or indefinite series of complete specifications of infinitely or indefinitely many worlds, specifications that fix simultaneously both the laws and the set of substances in each of them.

The world that defeats all rivals defeats each one overall with respect to simplicity and diversity taken together. So the rationale of any *actual* substance's being as it is will depend on everything in virtue of which the world that contains it, namely the actual world, defeated all rivals. But then it follows that under the a priori aspect of things—or under their praedicatum inest subjecto aspect—every contingent truth about the actual world presupposes every other contingent truth about it.

> [E]very substance is like a whole world, and like a mirror of God or of all the universe which each expresses after its own fashion, much as the same town is variously represented according to the different situations of the man who is looking at it. Thus the universe is multiplied as many times as there are substances, and the glory of God is also redoubled by the same number of wholly different representations of his work. One can even say that every substance bears in some sort the character of God's infinite wisdom and omnipotence, and imitates him as far as it is capable. For it expresses, albeit confusedly, all that happens in the universe past, present, or future, and this has some resemblance to an infinite perception or knowledge; and as all other substances express this one in their turn and accommodate themselves to it, one can say that it extends its power over all the others in imitation of the omnipotence of the creator.[10]

The a priori proof that the substance a if F is something we can describe, but it is not something we can imagine (or even imagine ourselves imagining) ourselves giving. But for Leibniz it is enough that there must be such a proof or determination. And so long as there must be, the next step is natural enough. Since the divine notion of each substance involves the notion of each and every other substance that belongs in the same world, Leibniz draws the conclusion not only that all the truths about the other substances in a world can be read off the complete concept of any one of them but also that each substance is self-sufficient and autonomous, that each substance is *itself* a world apart, as if nothing else existed besides God and it; that substances are windowless, do not causally interact, and are adjusted to one another by a divinely conceived pre-established harmony.[11] And then yet other things are supposed to follow.

IV

Some links are stronger than others in this marvelous and questionable sequence of deductions, all resting or purporting to rest on the idea of sufficient reason as teleologically interpreted.[12] I shall not pause to assess any of these further deductions here, because that system of metaphysical ideas is simply the backdrop for the claim I do wish to defend. Not only, my claim goes, is praedicatum inest subjecto a natural principle for Leibniz to have chosen to try to spell out his "goodlike" conception of truth,[13] but also the principle itself is modally innocent. To try to show this, I need to make three preliminary points, however.

First, an a priori proof is a proof that does not rest on materials provided by sense perception. Formally, Leibniz's use conforms to the definitions of "a priori" and "a posteriori," which Kant was destined to propose in the preface of the *Critique of Pure Reason*. This is to say that, since God's criterion of perfection is not dependent on experience or a posteriori, God's determination of '*Fa*' is a priori in Kant's sense. But this sort of determination, being in part axiological, is unlike anything that the expression "a priori" would lead anyone to expect nowadays, unless his thinking were insulated from all Kantian, post-Kantian, and positivist influences. What we, who are subject to these influences, should expect an a priori proof or determination of $F(a)$ to have to rest upon is considerations that are purely logical or mathematical, not axiological considerations. But Leibniz was not to know what a strange note his use of the term "a priori" was destined to sound in our ears.[14] And as things are, the only way to understand fully what Leibniz meant by an a priori proof of a proposition that is a posteriori for us is to understand the elements of the rest of his theory of truth. The reader has my own interpretation of this in section II.

In the second place, Leibniz never calls a proposition in which the concept of the predicate is contained in the concept of the subject *analytic*. So nor should we—if Leibniz is the philosopher we want to discuss—even if many Leibniz scholars do talk like this. It is simply not Leibniz's fault that Kant defined an analytic judgment as one in which the predicate was contained in the subject and that, in doing so, he created the expectation that all analytic judgments would be necessary. Had Leibniz been available to comment on Kant's proposals then, at a cost I shall compute in due course (section IX), he could have made two points: (1) Unless it is given a special nonexistential interpretation, "the F and G thing is F," which

Russell would have rendered "there is just one F and G thing and it is F," is not a necessary judgment at all. Surely the unique F and G thing, that thing itself, even though it is F and G, might not have been F or G. I shall return in due course to this point, and to the complex question of Leibniz's right to insist upon it.[15] (2) Given his intention that all analytic judgments should be necessary, Kant could have had an in every way better definition of "analytic": A judgment is analytic if and only if it can be reduced to a truth of logic (whatever logic may turn out to be) using only logic and noncreative, a priori for us definitions.[16]

The third preliminary must be to furnish some semantical explanation of the praedicatum inest subjecto rule that will show how Leibniz could have supposed it would apply equally and indifferently both to quantified, as we should say, and to singular sentences, or apply equally, as Leibniz would say, to the case in which A stands for an individual concept and the case in which A stands for a general concept.

The background to the rule is of course Aristotelian syllogistic in the various modifications and extensions that Leibniz proposed to it. A typical Aristotelian syllogism is expressed in the form

If A belongs ($\dot{υ}π\acuteαρχει$) to all B, and B belongs to all C, then A belongs to all C.[17]

Here "A," "B," "C" typically hold places for substantives or adjectives, rather than for singular terms like "Caesar." So, far from fitting smoothly into the theory, those always gave trouble to its traditional exponents, because the way in which "Caesar" is a subject of "Caesar crossed the Rubicon" is really quite different from the way in which "broad-leaved plants" is the subject of "All broad-leaved plants are deciduous." We shall come in due course to Leibniz's method of aligning these two kinds of subject. But concentrating first on the case where the theory of the syllogism is at its best, one surmises that the modern preference will probably be to follow the view that Frege would have taken of "A," "B," "C" as they occur in sentences that are typical of syllogistic and to say that these letters hold places for expressions that stand for concepts. Understood so, "All broad-leaved plants are deciduous" asserts that a certain subsumptive relation holds between the concepts *deciduous* and *broad-leaved plant*, or that whatever falls under the concept *broad-leaved plant* falls under the concept *deciduous*. Most modern views descend from this idea. It is very different from the idea that has prevailed in most traditional expositions of syllogistic. But oddly enough, this is really the view that Leibniz wants to take too.[18]

There are all sorts of important differences of terminology and of detail between Leibniz and Frege or Russell. Following Aristotle, who paraphrases "All broad-leaved plants are deciduous" as *"deciduous* belongs to (ὑπάρχει) every broad-leaved plant" Leibniz would prefer to say that *deciduous* is contained in (inest or continetur) all of the subject, viz. broad-leaved plants. But there is at least one similarity that we must carefully remark—namely, that Leibniz is in a position to be party to the thought that the terms of Aristotle's proposition are the concepts *deciduous* and *broad-leaved plants* and not these terms taken together with their sign of quantity. If so, the "all" has really to be syncategorematic in function. Insofar as it is expressed, it must be seen as going with the "belongs" or "contains."[19] In the "universal calculus" it is *absorbed* into the sense of "contains."

Two questions remain. The first, which I can postpone to the end of section VIII, is how to preserve the containment rule for other kinds of quantified sentence. The other is the Leibnizian treatment of expressions such as "Caesar." We can say, if we like, that the concept *broad-leaved plant* contains or comprises the concept *deciduous* if and only if broad-leaved plants are a subset of deciduous plants, or the concept *deciduous* applies to everything that falls under the concept *broad-leaved plants*. But Julius Caesar is not a set or subset of anything. Nor is he a concept that can contain another concept. This, however, is not necessary to solve Leibniz's semantical problem, if we will transpose that to the Leibnizian metaphysical context of God's choice and "the objective foundation" of the contingent truths about substances that determine the whole actual world.

It is unnecessary because, for purposes of the divine calculations that fix these truths, a truth such as "Julius Caesar crossed the Rubicon" is arrived at not through the identification of Julius Caesar himself or any actual stream but through concepts that are divine *specifications* of things that are to answer to certain descriptions. These specifications or concepts will comprise one small part of the larger specification of the complete world whose complete specification will commend that world to God over all others as the most perfect world. And, unlike the name "Caesar" or the demonstrative "this man," these substance-specifications themselves, being purely general, *can* be conveyed by complex concept expressions that will fit smoothly into Aristotelian syllogistic.[20]

V

With these preliminaries completed, I quote the *Discourse of Metaphysics* statement of the difference between necessity and contingency:

> All contingent propositions have reasons for being so rather than otherwise, or (which is the same thing) . . . they have proofs a priori of their truth which make them certain, and which show that the connection of the subject and the predicate of these propositions has its foundation in the nature of the one and the other; but they do not

have demonstrations of necessity, since . . . these reasons are only founded on the principle of contingency or of the existence of things, that is to say on what is or appears the best among several equally possible things; whereas necessary truths are founded on the principle of contradiction and on the possibility or impossibility of essence themselves, without regard in this to the free Will of God or of creatures.[21]

The task will now be to put this together with the containment doctrine and to show how the principle of the best really does distinguish the necessary from the contingent.

Let us write

$$(Ax)[. . .x, \text{_____} x]$$

to state that the concept designated by ". . .x" contains the concept that is designated by "_____ x" or that whatever satisfies the condition ". . .x" satisfies the condition "_____ x."[22] Then Aristotle's sentence "all broad-leaved plants are deciduous" will be rendered as

$$(Ax)[\text{Broad-leaved plant } x, \text{ Deciduous } x].$$

And "Caesar crossed the Rubicon" will be rephrased to make it formally suitable for the neosyllogistic framework as (in the first instance)

$$(\text{The } x)[\text{Caesar} = x, \text{ Crossed Rubicon } x].$$

This last sentence will be true (Leibniz could stipulate) just if all things that uniquely fall under the individual concept *identical with Caesar* fall under the concept *crossed the Rubicon*[23] or (as Russell could stipulate) just if one and only thing falls under the concept *identical with Caesar* and the concept *crossed the Rubicon* belongs to this concept. Recall how it is to be told whether or not it is so included. Ordinary human beings look in history books. But someone who came to understand God's purpose could proceed as follows: "Caesar" being the name of an actual substance to be encountered in the world and the actual world being the world that combines the greatest variety of forms ordered by the simplest and most beautiful laws, what s/he has to do is to ascertain which concept the concept *identical with Caesar* is, that is, identify the concept through some other specification also true of Caesar but more illuminating of the ground's for God's choice of the world he has chosen containing Caesar. "Embracing the infinite in one intuition," s/he has to recapitulate God's grounds for his choice of the actual world, discover the identity of the concept *identical with Caesar* with the concept designated by the choice-relevant specification of Caesar, and show that this concept comprises the concept of crossing the Rubicon.[24] Starting out with the substance Caesar himself, picking him out as that very individual,[25] someone with this insight is already assured by the principle of sufficient reason and the best that there is *some* choice-relevant specification Caesar answered to. So, understanding the interconnection of all these things with all things, s/he must find a way to replace the courtesy concept expression "identical with Caesar" by some more complex expression comprised in the overall world specification by reference to which it can be shown that the corresponding world combines the greatest variety of forms with the simplest laws. This new complex expression would stand for the same concept. So the new sentence would be bound to have the same truth value as "Caesar crossed the Rubicon." The truth value would be the truth if and only if *crossed the Rubicon* were one constituent (or Fregean mark) of the concept that the new specification stood for.

VI

It may be suggested that this is already enough to make "Julius Caesar crossed the Rubicon" necessary. For it is surely necessary, indeed analytic, someone may say, that anything that uniquely satisfies the condition "(_____ and crossed the Rubicon)," where "_____" holds a place for the rest of the specification of Caesar's individual concept, crossed the Rubicon.

To this there are two replies, however. First, a necessity of this sort, attaching as it does to the new sentence, is highly sensitive to sense as well as to reference. Even if the new sentence is necessary, it does not follow that the sentence that it replaces was necessary. What binds together the truth values of the old and the new sentence is not logical necessity but only "the principle of contingency or of the existence of things" (that is, the principles of sufficient reason and the best). Surely the sense of the name "Julius Caesar," which we all understand passably well, cannot be the same as that of a vast conjunction, still less that of a conjunction accessible only to God. So the intersubstitution is not salvo sensu but at best salva veritate. It may be said that for God the sense of the name "Caesar" would correspond to that omniscient or omnipotent way of thinking of Caesar. But if that is said, then the objector has lost sight of the question of the modality of *our* sentence, which employs the name "Caesar" in *our* sense, a sense that we explain in a way that has at some point to be entity invoking.[26] It is Leibniz's right to insist on this.

In the second place, even the analyticity of the new sentence, if it were analytic, could show nothing about Caesar himself, no more than the analyticity of the sentence "All who sit and smoke in the corner smoke in the corner" shows that anyone who sits in the corner and smokes *must* smoke there.

At this point, those who are determined to find necessity in the containment relation may try another tack. Surely the concept that the predicate "_____ and crossed the Rubicon" stands for is the same as the concept that "identical with Caesar" stands for, but the concept that "_____ and crossed the Rubicon" stands for necessarily contains the concept *crossed the Rubicon*; so, the concept *identical with Caesar*, since this is the same concept, necessarily contains *crossed the Rubicon*.

If this were not only a good route but also the only route to the objector's desired conclusion, it would be fair to point out that, by virtue of its reification of concepts, it disregards Leibniz's professed nominalism.[27] But that is a last ditch defense (and no more secure than Leibniz's claim that it is always possible to see general terms as compendia loquendi, or as a handy way of speaking of substances). And in any case, I do not think we should make the concession that the objector has even a good route here to his conclusion.

Is everything that a concept contains (every mark of the concept) essential to it? It may be said that there can be nothing more to the identity of a concept in Leibniz's scheme than the set of its Fregean marks (and that the identity of the object itself that falls under the concept is not a distinguishable or individuating element in Leibniz's scheme). But that is questionable. Maybe Leibniz inadvertently discourages us from questioning it in the *Discourse of Metaphysics*, where he seems to be prepared to equate the individual concept of x with the nature or essence of x. (Perhaps everything in an essence is essential to that essence itself? Perhaps that is something special about essences. Though even this claim might merit a little argument.) But later this point about concept and essence was sorted out clearly and definitively:

> of the essence of a thing is what belongs to it necessarily and perpetually; of the concept of a singular thing, however, is also what belongs to it contingently or by accident, or what God sees in it when he has perfectly understood it.[28]

And once we respect Leibniz's distinction between concept and essence, the whole objection begins to wilt. Suppose that concept A = concept B if and only if everything that belongs to concept A belongs to concept B, and vice versa; and suppose that identity itself is a necessary relation. It *still* does not follow that whatever A contains it necessarily contains.[29]

VII

At least two distinctions are relevant here. First, there is the distinction Leibniz might have wanted between the essential and the non-essential. Thinking about that in terms of worlds, one may reflect that what is essential to *worlds* in Leibniz's scheme is the range and variety of substances that they contain and the laws that these substances exemplify. No world is better than any other, for instance, simply by containing a certain particular individual as such (as opposed to another one like it). If so, and if a set of substances constitutes the form and matter of a world, then it may seem—this is speculation—that what is essential to a Leibnizian substance is *at most* something non-individuating, either something that is essential to substance as such or something that is essential to a substance's exemplifying a certain general form or conforming to some general law.[30] But, as I say, this is speculation. There is very little in Leibniz about this question, and it seems to me that no one who examined the texts with an innocent eye could attribute to Leibniz any strong interest at all in the issues that we debate nowadays under the label of "essentialism."

The second distinction to be borne constantly in mind is the distinction between concepts and the objects that fall under them. So far, the objector has failed signally to offer even the appearance of getting beyond divine specifications, or individual concepts, and engaging individual substances themselves in his necessitarian argument.

VIII

In a last effort to engage individuals themselves, someone may ask us to consider the sentence

The man sitting in the corner smoking is smoking.

Obviously, the objector may say, the man sitting in the corner does not have to smoke. This (it is now evident) is not a necessary truth but a contingent one. But the trouble for Leibniz, the objector will now say, is that the sentence already has an a priori proof. We do not need to appeal to the principles of sufficient reason and the best or to embark on any reduction of the proposition to prove it. For it is already in the form

The F G is F,

which is the terminus of reduction; so ex hypothesi nothing more than we already have is required to prove it. All we need is what Leibniz calls the principle of contradiction. Therefore, by Leibniz's doctrine, the sentence must be necessary.

But this objection is mistaken. We cannot get a proof for a proposition by hiding one part of it away in a presupposition. (Compare standard criticisms of certain traditional arguments for the existence of God.) Putting that presupposition back into the judgment itself, we should get

(The x)(x is a man sitting smoking in the corner, x is smoking),

which, for Aristotle, Russell and Leibniz alike (although for different reasons) will both have existential import and be contingent. What is more, the a priori proof of the existential part of the judgment would have to proceed, as the *Discourse of Metaphysics* has it, through "the principle of contingency or the principle of the existence of things, that is to say [through] what appears best among several equally possible things." It would need to be shown, but it *could not* be shown using only the principles of identity and contradiction, that the man in question enters into "the most perfect series" or the series that pleases God or that he was "compossible with more things than anything incompossible with him."[31]

This account of the matter suggested by what Leibniz wrote in 1686 is so straightforward that it may seem it must be inadequate. For if it is right, then why did Leibniz eventually give up the containment doctrine of truth? And why did he take such pains to develop an analogy (seen by many commentators as a new answer, not as a further elaboration of a *Discourse of Metaphysics* answer) between the specification of substances or the identification of their concepts on the one hand, a task that Leibniz comes to see as entailing infinitary analysis (because the specification of every substance involves the specification of all the others), and the computation of surds, irrationals, asymptotes, etc. on the other? (See *Generales Inquisitiones*, dated later in the same year as the *Discourse*, namely 1686, §130–§137.)

My brief answer to these questions would be to suggest first that Leibniz's giving up the containment principle of truth had nothing at all to do with necessity and contingency but arose from his perception of the complexity of achieving in terms of relations of containment any general statement of the truth conditions of *all* true sentences and from the enhancement of his awareness of the complex rôle played by negation in what we should call quantified sentences. "All A's are B's" and "All A's are non-B's" conform well enough to Leibniz's rule, but what about their contradictories? Already in 1679, we see him hard at work on this problem. "The concept of the subject either in itself or with some addition involves the concept of the predicate." (See Couturat, p. 51.) He distinguishes "direct" from "indirect" connections of subject and predicate. In due course, Leibniz enters a qualification—"the concept of the predicate is *contained in some way* in the concept of the subject." (This occurs in 'On Freedom', cited later (section IX).) The final blow to the containment formula, I surmise, was Leibniz's long-delayed but finally clear perception, in the decade after the *Discourse*, of the general character of the interaction that we describe as the interaction between quantification and negation.[32] In a pure calculus of containment, it is only where A is an individual concept that "A non continet B" will be equivalent to "A continet non-B." ("A does not contain B" may be true because some A's are non-B's. "A contains non-B" will be true, where it is, only if every A is a non-B.) Even after seeing this clearly, Leibniz could have gone on saying that a proposition in whose truth conditions the concepts A and B occur essentially will be true only if the A stands in *some* relation one could specify in terms of containment between concepts to B. But this is so vague as to be almost vacuous. It is not what Leibniz first had in mind when he wanted to state a simple rule of truth.[33] I surmise also that Leibniz noticed that the abandonment of the general containment doctrine did not undermine his doctrine of the individual concept of an individual substance and its determination of what is true of that substance.

So much for the first of the two questions that I announced in the paragraph before last. About the other, I should say that the analogy with infinitary analysis seems not to have been introduced as a *substitute* for the containment rule. In the paper *Generales Inquisitiones* it stands side by side with it in a complementary relation. Surely the analogy starts out as a striking dramatization of the mind-boggling complexity of the interconnection of things and of all the considerations that would be involved in showing that any particular series of things would be the most perfect.[34]

IX

When Leibniz eventually saw the inadequacy in detail of the containment principle to his doctrine of truth, this did not need to disturb the metaphysical principles that had suggested the principle to him in the first place. As always, these principles were in a state of development, but there were other reasons for that. Nor did his doctrine of contingency in the *Discourse* become superfluous in the absence of the doctrine of truth. For the doctrine of the individual concept and the idea that all truths ultimately repose upon the title of some set of these to be realized remained. That doctrine and the Leibnizian account of the simple subject-predicate (unquantified) case still stood in need of the *Discourse* defense. (Indeed the same defense is surely both presupposed and required by the doctrine of infinitary analysis.) It is true that Leibniz continued to speculate actively about problems of necessity and contingency. But it is hard to believe that this was because Leibniz did not recognize what had been achieved in §XIII of the *Discourse*. Surely, it was because there were *other* modal worries in the offing, most of them perfectly visible in some shape or form to Leibniz himself, worries that had little to do with the individual concept's containment of all the truths about the object that fell under it. These were worries about the modal status of statements of God's nature and existence, of the principle of sufficient reason, of the principle of the best, of the claim that God chooses the best, and of the fact that this or that is the best or most perfect.[35] Because my concern here is with the principle of containment, I do not need to address any of these other difficulties or try to relate any of them to Leibniz's conception of the problem of freedom. There is, however, one problem that persists beyond the *Discourse* and that may still appear, contrary to everything I have been claiming, to rest on the idea that the relation between a a concept and its marks ought for Leibniz to have been a necessary one.

In an essay entitled "On Freedom" (1689), Leibniz begins by saying that at one time he used to consider that

> fortune, as distinct from fate is an empty word, and that nothing exists unless certain conditions are fulfilled, from all of which together its existence at once follows. I found myself very close to the opinions of those who hold everything to be absolutely necessary.[36]

But Leibniz had been pulled back from this precipice, he says, by considering possibles that are not actual. Then, he continues:

> Having recognized the contingency of things, I raised the further question of a clear concept of truth, for I had a reasonable hope of throwing some light from this upon the problem of distinguishing necessary from contingent truths. For I saw that in every true affirmative proposition, whether universal or singular, necessary or contingent, the predicate inheres in the subject or that the concept of the predicate is in some way involved in the concept of the subject. I saw too that this is the principle of infallibility for him who knows everything a priori. But this very fact seemed to increase the difficulty, for, if at any particular time the concept of the predicate inheres in the concept of the subject, *how can the predicate ever be denied of the subject without contradiction and impossibility or without destroying the subject concept?*

It ought not to be assumed that the problem being mentioned in the words I have italicized is that Leibniz thinks that every sentence in which the concept of the subject has a constituent the concept of the predicate somehow *ought* to have expressed a necessary truth. For we know that he did not think that. Perhaps the problem is that, not having the sense/reference distinction, he cannot see quite how the sentence reduced can fail to have the same modal status as the sentence it is reduced to. But, even though the sense/reference distinction would have clarified and assisted here, Leibniz surely solves that problem well enough in the *Discourse* by making it clear that, wherever a proposition is contingent, the process of reduction will itself rest on something non-logical and non-necessary. It seems then that the problem that worries him is rather that we still need to know how the predicate can be denied of the subject, as Leibniz indeed puts it, *without destroying the subject concept.*

This supposed problem, which I declare to be different from the supposed problem of the necessity of containment, surfaces in one of the initial misunderstandings on the part of Arnauld that got the Leibniz-Arnauld correspondence off to such a bad start.[37] Over and over again, among the many good points Leibniz makes, he rashly concedes to Arnauld that, if he himself, that is, the actual Leibniz, who went of his own free will upon a certain journey, had not gone upon that journey, then

> there would be a falsity which would *destroy my individual or complete notion*, or that which God *conceives of me*, or did conceive even before he decided to create me. For this notion involves *sub ratione possibili-tatis*[38] existences or truths of fact, or decisions of God, on which facts depend. (Letter of 14 July 1686)

Suppose that it is contingent that Leibniz went on a certain journey. Then it might seem that nothing prevents us from making sense of his not doing so. But then either we *can* make sense of Leibniz's "destroying" Leibniz's individual notion—which sounds totally unintelligible—or better, Leibniz thinks, the man who refrained from the journey would not have been Leibniz (the Leibniz of whose refraining from the journey we supposed that sense could be made). Surely Leibniz ought to have looked again at the first horn of this dilemma. Instead, he builds the difficulty into his presentation of his system by his seeming to rule positively, in *Theodicy* and other writings, that no particular individual—no actual Adam or Tarquinius Superbus or Leibniz or whoever—can figure in each of two possible worlds that differ in any respect at all; so that, if a necessary truth is one that holds in all possible worlds, then it will be necessary that Adam—if one means literally Adam—should have had the posterity he did have and necessary that Leibniz—if one means *literally* Leibniz—should have gone on the journey he went on. "Leibniz could have refrained from making the journey he made" is then saved by a system of reinterpretation.

What is it that prevents Leibniz from reexamining the first horn of the dilemma? Putting the question it raises more literally, What incoherence is there in the idea that the very person who went on a certain journey, the person whom it so happens we can identify in that particular way, might not have gone on that journey—in which case he would have had to be identified in some other way? Well, given his doctrine of the individual concept as determinant of the whole being of a thing, Leibniz attaches no sense to the idea of the very same individual's figuring in a different Leibnizian world from the one it actually figures in. Yes. But why is this? Why insist, in the face of the question of the contingency of the journey (a contingency Leibniz does not doubt), on that particular form of the doctrine of the individual concept?

The answer to these questions is speculative; but the question itself is nothing short of compulsory. And my own provisional suggestion would be this: Leibniz's system of possible worlds starts out as a device for the comparison of possible worlds in respect of ontological richness and nomological simplicity; and within that framework (or so I have claimed) questions of identity and difference across possible worlds are simply not provided for. At the 'moment' of God's choice that the system is intended to illuminate, *there is* nothing except God and the ideas in the mind of God. There can be no question therefore of the criterion of identity for individual concepts being given in the form that concept C_1 = concept C_2 if and only if C_1 is of the same individual substance as C_2 is of. Rather, the model must supply in advance all the marks of every individual concept for every Leibnizian possible world, and then $C_1 = C_2$ if and only if every mark of C_1 is a mark of C_2 and vice versa.

Where the question of creation is under consideration, this is fair enough; and the framework that delivers this result really does not enable us to pick out one and the same individual in two different possible worlds (two Leibnizian ones, I mean). But this finding should not distract attention from the fact that the question of the different titles to realization of different possible worlds is an utterly different question from the question of whether or not an identified individual, a given particular encountered in the world or thought of de re, might have refrained from a journey that he actually made. With Saul Kripe's semantics for modal logic laid out in front of us, it is not hard for us to conclude that the question of the alternatives for such an individual needs to be explored in a different framework. This framework will require possible world specifications to include explicit information, quite inappropriate for Leibnizian specifications, about the identities of the individuals that figure within some world. And then, once we have actual individuals to talk about, there will be no difficulty in imagining circumstances under which individuals fail to conform to their actually given individual concepts. What is more, nothing will prevent us from adopting the Leibnizian framework for one sort of question and the Kripkean for the other.

If we decide to look at things in this way, there is scarcely any temptation to slide from the claim that no sense attaches within the Leibnizian framework to cross-world identity to the claim that different Leibnizian worlds must contain *different* individuals. Indeed Leibniz too would have seen this as a lapse, as so described. ("It is one thing not to understand a thing, and another for us to understand its contradictory," he says.) Nevertheless I yield to the temptation to think that it is something like this slide that, without benefit of the Kripke semantics, Leibniz was himself involved in.

As always with Leibniz, however, there is more than one thing at stake here, philosophically speaking. Had he warmed to the proposal just made and come to regard both conceptions of possible worlds as available to him, then he would have been faced with the need to allow that, strictly speaking, God's deliberative thoughts of substance are not properly referential at all. He would have been forced into allowing a bifurcation between properly referential thinking ("hic homo quem designo etc") and completely determinate specification effected by complete individual concepts which, being still general in character, fix every last detail of Adam's or Julius Caesar's life without ever reaching down to these substances themselves in the manner that referential thinking does. Such a bifurcation, once admitted, would have had the effect of reopening the question of the principle on which Leibniz had so often depended (for instance in his theory of God's choice, where it enabled him to equate the variety of forms with the quantity of created substances), namely, the identity of indiscernibles. And it would have signaled a real gap between something's being a member of "the most perfect series" or being "compossible with more substances than any substance incompossible with it"[39] and its being something actual or real. These definitions suggest that creation is a metaphor for something outside time. Once such a gap looms, however, it is hard to avoid interpreting the idea of God's act of creation much more literally than is suggested by the Leibnizian definition of existence. And then we have to wonder how God's creating some substance can come within a time series *after* his conceiving of the maximal set of concepts that contains it as a member but *before* the beginning of a time series that stretches, according to Leibniz, infinitely[40] back into the past.

X

There is no question, on the general interpretation I offer, of Leibniz's having confused an object with its complete concept. What is at issue is not a mistaken identification of these. Nor is there any doubt that Leibniz recognized that there was thought such as demonstrative thought that essentially concerned individuals. After all, his whole account of human a posteriori knowledge of the world and its substances depended on this. What he failed to appreciate was rather the sharpness of the divide between the thinking that goes into such a choice as God makes and properly referential thinking. Once we recognize what is so special in the latter, however, then we must recognize the possibility of singling out Caesar or Leibniz, the man himself, a sort of singling out that Leibniz does recognize, and saying of that person within whose specification it is written that he will choose to go on a journey but *choose freely* to do so, that he (literally, he, that very man) *might* have refrained from making the journey.[41] And we must recognize the possibility of imagining the possible world in which that very individual does not make the journey, albeit a possible world that does not belong in the set of possible worlds between which God has to choose. Leibniz too could have recognized all this, consistently with the principles of sufficient reason and of the Best—if not consistently with absolutely everything else that he seems to have wanted to say.

Notes

This paper was written while I was a Fellow at the Center for Advanced Study in the Behavioral Sciences, Stanford University, in the 1985–86 academic year. I am grateful for the financial support provided there by the Andrew W. Mellon Foundation and for the additional support of a grant in the Humanities from the British Academy.

I have been greatly influenced in my thoughts about the topic of this paper by Hidé Ishiguro, both by conversation with her and by her writings on Leibniz. It is to her reading of Leibniz that I owe the thought that it is even possible for contingency to be saved in Leibniz's system. In this connection, see especially her "Contingent Truths and Possible Worlds," in *Leibniz: Metaphysics and Philosophy of Science*, R. Woolhouse, ed. (Oxford: Oxford University Press, 1981); *Leibniz's Philosophy of Logic and Language* (London: Duckworth, 1972).

1. Compare, for example, *Die philosophischen Schriften von G. W. Leibniz*, C. I. Gerhardt (G.), ed. (Berlin, 1875–90), vol. VII, p. 289, translated in *Philosophical Writings*, H. Parkinson, ed. (London: Dent, 1973), 145.

2. Gerhardt, VII, 302, Parkinson translation, p. 136.

3. *Discourse of Metaphysics*, §VI. In connection with Leibniz's confusion in this sentence between laws in rerum natura and hypotheses, which are *judgments* about the world, compare the general tenor of the criticisms I urge in section IX. For the *Discourse* I have used the translation of P. G. Lucas and L. Grint (Manchester: Manchester University Press, 1953).

4. No doubt other worlds are possible worlds, but what I am concerned with here is that they are not, as I shall say, *Leibnizian* possible worlds.

5. Compare Bertrand Russell, *A Critical Exposition of the Philosophy of Leibniz* (Cambridge: The University Press, 1900), 67. Disagreeing so much as I do with some of Russell's interpretations, I seize the opportunity to salute the sharp insight and strong sympathetic grasp that inform his exposition here of Leibniz's theory of the compossibility and incompossibility of individual substances.

6. Compare Couturat, ed., *Opuscules et fragments inedits de Leibniz* (Paris, 1903), pp. 16–24:

> I think that in this series of things there are certain propositions that are most universally true, and which not even a miracle could violate. This is not to say they have any necessity for God but rather that when [God] chose the particular series of things he did choose, he decided by that very act to observe these principles as giving the specific properties of *just this* particular series of things.

7. Here and elsewhere one struggles with the fact that Leibniz's criterion of excellence is a two-factor criterion.

8. *Discourse of Metaphysics*, §VIII.

9. Nevertheless the astute and the logically minded will wonder whether, in addition to making the containment principle seem natural, we have *derived* the containment principle from sufficient reason. In section VIII we shall find such doubts confirmed.

10. *Discourse of Metaphysics*, §IX.

11. See, for example, "A Specimen of Discoveries about Marvellous Secrets," Parkinson, p. 79. If Leibniz had distinguished carefully, as I have tried (wherever something depends on it) to distinguish, the specification of a set of substances from the set of substances themselves that *answer* to that specification (instead of employing the language of concepts or notions, which permits interpretation in *either way* and then both at once), maybe this

conclusion would not have appeared quite so obvious. There is no absurdity in the idea that there should be causal relations between entities e_1, e_2, e_3, even though there is no possibility, within the not necessarily yet actualized specification itself, of saying which entities each of e_1, e_2, and e_3 are without mentioning all the others.

On the other hand, maybe Leibniz's argument was not an argument from the supposed need for it to be possible to specify the individuals in a world independently of their causal relations. Perhaps the point was that, when the world is put together so that it will run as God wills but without God's intervention and adjustment, each substance must be "wound up" exactly, in the light of how all other substances will act, so that substances will *combine* to produce the outcome that is good. So each substance must be wound up to have precisely its own positive active force. Compare again, "A Specimen," Parkinson, 84–85.

12. Elsewhere, I have traced the continuity (and the differences) between Leibniz's teleological conception of explanation and the teleological conception that Plato puts into Socrates' mouth in the passage of Plato's *Phaedo* that Leibniz quotes so often (96c following). See my "Teleology and the Good in Plato's *Phaedo*," *Oxford Studies in Ancient Philosophy* (December 1986), 4: 1–18.

13. For the expression "goodlike," see Plato, *Republic*, 509^{b}14.

14. Nor was he to know that the time would come, after Kant, when it would be expected, however lazily or naively, that all a priori proof would be "analytic."

15. See Sections VI through VIII.

16. See G. Frege, *Foundations of Arithmetic*, §3 (Breslau: Koebner, 1884).

17. Compare *Generales Inquisitiones*, §16 (Couturat, p. 366) and §132 (Couturat, p. 388).

18. Had Russell studied Leibniz a few years later, at the point when his own view of generality had advanced to the same stage as Frege's, he would not have failed to notice Leibniz's anticipation:

> When in a universal affirmative proposition I say 'every man is an animal' I wish to say that the concept of animal is involved with the concept of man. (For the concept *man* is the concept *rational animal*.) And when I say 'every pious person is happy', I mean that anyone who understands what it is to be pious will understand that in this concept true happiness is included. (Couturat, p. 85)

> When I say that every man is an animal I mean that men are to be sought among the animals, or that whatsoever be not animal is not man either. (Couturat, p. 235)

Furthermore, what Leibniz meant by a notion or concept coincides quite well enough for the purposes of the analysis of generality with what Russell and Frege meant. Note for instance the following formulation of Frege's:

> The word 'some' states a relation that holds in our example [viz. 'some numbers are primes'] between the concepts of number and of prime. Similarly 'all' [in 'all bodies are heavy'] states a relation between the concepts *body* and *heavy*. (Review of Schroeder, in Gottlob Frege, *Philosophical Writings*, P. T. Geach and M. Black, eds. (Oxford: Basil Blackwell, 1952), p. 93n

In case we doubt that this is essentially the same account as Leibniz's, we should note that Leibniz gives no signs of wanting to suggest a different account of the logical form that is involved in necessary truths and the logical form present in contingent generalizations such as "all gold coins are circular."

19. See especially, Couturat, pp. 49, 85, 243.

20. For evidence of Leibniz's actual awareness of the detailed intricacies of characterizing all this in terms of containment, see Couturat, p. 51. Also see section VIII.

21. *Discourse of Metaphysics*, §XIII.

22. For these "binary quantifiers," see my " 'Most' and 'All'," in *Truth, Reference, and Reality: Essays on a Philosophy of Language*, M. Platts, ed. (London: Routledge & Kegan Paul, 1973), 318–346.

23. So long as we see ourselves as making extensions of Aristotelian syllogistic, then we must attend here to the question, much worried over by Leibniz, of existential import. If we were to take "all" as having existential import, as Aristotle does, then the upshot would be that the "all" conditions for a 'The' quantifier would coincide exactly with Russell's truth condition for the upside-down iota quantifier, a sign normally of course explained with the use of an existential quantifier.

24. For "embracing the infinite is one intuition," see Gerhardt, VII, 309 ("A specimen," Parkinson's translation, p. 80). For the account that Leibniz would have needed of the sense and reference of predicates and of concept-identity, see Frege's letter to Husserl dated 24 May 1891 and my commentary on this in "The Sense and Reference of Predicates," *Philosophical Quarterly* (1984), 34: 311–328.

25. For Leibniz's recognition of his right to such direct or demonstrative reference, see, for example, *Generales Inquisitiones*, Couturat, p. 360, especially

> At certum individuum est Hic, quem designo vel monstrando vel addendo notas distinguentes.

26. Compare again the account of direct and demonstrative identification cited from *Generales Inquisitiones* in note 25. Note that this is the counterpart for singular terms of the extension-involving account of general terms that I attribute to Leibniz in *Sameness and Substance* (Oxford: Blackwell, 1980), pp. 10–11, 76–86.

27. See, for example, "Preface to Nizolius," Gerhardt, IV, 138–76.

28. *Textes Inedits*, G. Grua, ed. (Paris, 1948), 383. This important passage was first brought to my attention by a discussion of it on page 263 of Robert Merrihew Adams's "Leibniz's Theories of Contingency," in *Leibniz: Critical and Interpretive Essays*, Michael Hooker, ed. (Manchester: Manchester University Press, 1982).

29. One might as convincingly argue that, because substance $A =$ substance B if and only if A and B occupy all and only the same places and because identity between substances is a necessary relation, any place that A or B occupies it necessarily occupies!

30. Compare the conclusion I reach in another way in *Sameness and Substance* (Oxford: Blackwell, 1980), 120.

31. Compare Couturat, pp. 9, 360 (sub 'existens'), 405.

32. Compare Wolfgang Lenzen, " 'Non est' non est 'est non'," forthcoming in *Studia Leibnitiana*.

33. Compare the way in which some modern philosophers have started out wanting to characterize truth in terms of the predicate of a sentence applying to its subject—and then found in due course that that special case will not generalize. Either they have then fallen silent, or they have been forced into an account of "application" or "truth of," which is (1) at least as language relative, and (2) at least as complex, as Tarski's definition of satisfaction.

34. Note also the calm with which Leibniz registers the manifest imperfection of the analogy at *Generales Inquisitiones*, §136. Such calm would be harder to understand if the infinitary analysis analogy were intended to be a self-sufficient solution to some problem seen as otherwise insoluble.

35. See again Robert Merrihew Adams, "Leibniz's Theories of Contingency."

36. Parkinson, p. 106; Loemker, p. 263. I have followed Parkinson's dating.

37. These misunderstandings were not really Arnauld's fault—or even the fault of the text of the *Discourse*. Arnauld was working from an abstract conveyed to him, at Leibniz's request, through the Duke of Hessen-Rheinfells.

38. "In general terms" (Parkinson).

39. Compare Couturat, p. 360 (sub *existens*).

40. See Gerhardt, VII, 302 (Parkinson, p. 136).

41. The other thing that must be noted, at least where Leibniz's difficulty with Leibniz destroying his own individual concept is concerned, is that a concept is not in itself such as to determine anything at all, whether fatalistically or causally. It is not the concept but the actual nature of each individual and the individuals that are coexistent with it in the same world that fixes or determines the history of the world. And note how badly Leibniz *himself* will need to say this when he engages with the problem of human freedom.

Index